COMPLETE GUIDE TO

GAME CARE & COOKERY

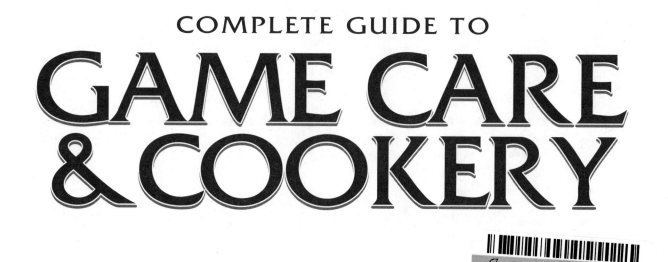

P9-DNW-441

SAM FADALA

©2003 Sam Fadala

Published by

krause publications
An F&W Publications Company

700 East State Street • Iola, WI 54990-0001
715-445-2214 • 888-457-2873
www.krause.com

Our toll-free number to place an order or obtain a free catalog is 800-258-0929.

Library of Congress Catalog Number: 2003108885

ISBN: 0-87349-539-X

Cover designed by Al West

Interior designed by Sandy Kent

Edited by Kevin Michalowski

Copyright-Free Illustrations from *Animals*, Dover Publications, Inc.

Printed in the United States

Acknowledgment

Special thanks to Judy for her diligent effort
in working with various recipes
that appear in this book.

Dedication

For my partner, Judy,
with thanks for all the hard work
to make this a better book.

About The Author

Sam Fadala has been a full-time outdoor writer for the past quarter century. His work has appeared in nearly every major outdoor publication and he has authored more than two dozen books. He has lived in Wyoming for the past 27 years, with travels to Canada, Finland, Mexico, and Africa in pursuit of wild game and adventure. Currently, he lives in southern Wyoming with his wife, Judy.

About The Cover

Ducks Unlimited®, working in conjunction with Lawry's®, has unveiled a new line of seasonings created specifically for wild game. From fish to venison to game birds and small game, these new marinades, seasonings and spice blends take all the guesswork out of creating great-tasting meals with wild game.

These easy-to-use products can make any dish a gourmet treat in just minutes thanks to Lawry's long history of creating new flavor secrets. Combine that with Ducks Unlimited's dedication to conservation and you've got the perfect combination for great-tasting meal ideas from a healthy natural resource.

For a free recipe booklet featuring 20 deliciously different wild game and fish recipes with Ducks Unlimited® products, call 1-800-248-9687 or write to Ducks Unlimited Recipe Booklet, c/o The Walker Agency, P.O. Box 14390, Scottsdale, AZ 85267-4390. All of the featured seasonings are packaged under license from Ducks Unlimited, and a portion of every purchase of Ducks Unlimited Seasonings & Rubs, Marinades and Seasoning Blends will be donated to Ducks Unlimited's ongoing conservation efforts in North America.

Preface

There is no finer food than that which you have worked hard to obtain and prepare. Not only is game meat lean, healthy and succulent, but the manner in which it is acquired adds greatly to the enjoyment of the meal. As you prepare your dish you can't help but relive the thrill of the hunt, the beauty and solitude of the camp and pride of your accomplishments.

Cooking your wild game is just one more element — an extension really — of the hunting experience. Preparing and eating a meal of wild game completes the circle.

This is the fourth edition of Sam Fadala's *Complete Guide to Game Care and Cookery*. The recipes are all new and the information has been updated to reflect new trends and technologies, but the spirit remains. Hunting is the culmination of all that is great and wondrous about being human, it connects us to our past, brings our families closer together and brings us back to the natural cathedral that inspires us all. To do it well is to honor all that makes us whole.

Kevin Michalowski, Editor

June 2003

Table of Contents

Getting Started

I learned respect for game from a man who never hunted, my maternal grandfather and namesake, Sam Manetta. Sam landed on Ellis Island, New York, in 1912. He couldn't read, so when he saw a sign in a restaurant window that said "No Italians Need Apply" he walked right in. With his steel-gray eyes, milk-white skin and light-colored hair, the proprietors of the restaurant had no clue that they had hired a man from the Tyrolean country of the Italian Alps. Until one day when co-owner Jimmy O'Connor innocently asked, "Anyway, Sam, where did you come from?" The answer brought a roar. "Mike, come in here. We've hired a ..." And indeed the brothers had! The three men enjoyed a good laugh over it and my grandfather was not fired. Dishwasher, pantry boy, short order cook, Sam eventually earned the status of master chef with all the accompanying recognition and honors. He had his own 15-minute TV show when that medium was in its infancy. His reputation prompted the mayor of a major city to ask Sam to take charge of a resort he and his sister owned in Canada. The food was sending guests away by the numbers. Flown by helicopter to Phoenix, jetted to Montana, driven by limousine to the resort, Chef Sam fixed the food problem. No more guests went AWOL.

Hunting for Food

Trophy hunting is challenging and exciting. Seeking out that special buck or bull is

Below right: Game meat can be made not only palatable, but gourmet all the way. This moose roast meal is basic, but also tender and tasty.

Below: No matter how grand the animal, such as this magnificent bighorn ram photographed in Wyoming, the food value of wild game remains important.

a worthy endeavor. Contrary to my own past beliefs, I now know that most large-racked, big-tusked, or wide-skulled big game animals are mature and entirely harvestable. But the food aspect is always my number one reason for filling game tags. I recall an evening meal prepared by my grandfather. It was javelina, not the easiest game to fix. My father, a non-hunter, was raised on "store-bought vittles." He prized only those game dishes that were especially palatable. "This is delicious," he praised, and it was. I enjoyed hunting for that "wild pig," but sitting around the dinner table watching everyone relish the meal that my shot provided was the greater reward.

Why We Hunt

Why do we hunt? A seminar on that topic found the instructor asking that question. "I was born to hunt," I blurted out. No high-tossed philosophy. No justification. The professional running the seminar smiled and said that was the right answer. Hunting is multi-faceted. Non-hunters find it difficult to understand why we take to the field when plenty of meat is available at the supermarket. Some of our big game ventures require hard trekking over tough terrain, backpack camps on high mountains and hauling carcasses to camp in cold or heat.

Why do we bother when all we have to do is jump in a vehicle and drive to a meat counter down the road? We hunt because it's a way of life. We take home only a tiny percent of what we see. Our greatest joy is just being in the great outdoors viewing wildlife. But we are hunters. We carry bows and guns. We have licenses. We know that game departments issue tags to be filled and we intend to fill ours. It's the right thing to do; a realistic part of game management. We do not apologize for it. But when the food aspect is left out, the silver memory of taking a game animal or bird loses some of its luster.

One of the greatest joys of hunting is just being there in an outdoor environment like this one.

Game cannot be stockpiled. This high
desert mule deer buck may live six or
seven years, but will more likely succumb
to winter or a lion before that span.

Game cannot be stockpiled. This high desert mule deer buck may live six or seven years, but will more likely succumb to winter or a lion before that span.

Hunting Licenses and Tags

Buying a hunting license or tag purchases an opportunity, not game. We become part of the management plan harvesting a renewable resource. Some people don't like the word harvesting. They consider it a euphemism, such as "passed away" instead of "died." Hunters kill game. There is no catch-and-release after a bullet, shotgun pellets, or an arrow has fulfilled its mission. However, those who believe that game can be stockpiled are naïve. Wildlife comes and wildlife goes, cycling all the time. One bad winter can destroy entire herds, as can disease and drought. Hunters following the rules do not wipe out game populations. In fact, hunter's dollars protect habitat from total development.

The True Hunter

Of course it is opinion; however, I consider the true hunter a person who enjoys the entire experience. The true hunter is capable of reasonable woodsmanship along with the ability to cleanly take game from dove to moose. He or she is also capable of proper field dressing, transportation, storage, and turning that game into a palatable meal. The hunter who has a wall full of wonderful trophies, but does not know how to skin a rabbit is a shooter/collector. Some of these men (and women) work hard following the guide into all manner of difficult circumstances. But a Nessmuk they are not. Nessmuk—George W. Sears— was an old-time woodsman, camper, and game chef. He was a real hunter in my book. He could do it all.

The full hunting experience includes the challenge of those steep hills in the background which soon will be climbed by the author in search of mule deer.

Some of the finest game meals are prepared to gourmet quality without the fuss. A good game meal was served from this Kentucky hunting lodge kitchen in no time.

Food Prejudice

No person is without food prejudice. My friend, the late Ted Walter, pulled off a good joke in a Tombstone, Arizona food market one evening. We stood at the meat counter talking to the butcher. What's good? We wanted to know. He suggested fresh beef tongue. We had him wrap one up. Meanwhile, a lady standing by couldn't take it any longer. "How could you stand to eat something that came out of an animal's mouth?" she asked with disgust. My friend pointed to a carton of eggs in her basket. Message delivered. I have eaten caterpillars in Africa and grasshoppers stirred into refried beans in Mexico. These were, to me foreign, but when we had a young man in Sonora try peanut butter he later confessed that he thought we were trying to poison him.

Goals of the Fourth Edition

This edition is all new. While many topics from the first three editions are retained by virtue of their relevance, every chapter has been rewritten. All recipes are either entirely new or refurbished by the author with help from various sources. Recipes are not copyrightable. The reader is invited to take at will from those presented here. Pass them around. Modify them. But most of all enjoy each one. The new recipes, while retaining the original goal of gourmet cooking without the fuss, are a somewhat elevated. "You must have slaved all day to prepare this meal." That's what we want to hear, knowing all the while that the well-prepared game meat and side dishes went together with minimal effort and time. There are a few exceptions, such as lasagna, which require patience. But ours is a busy world. Therefore, while it may be interesting to learn how to make homemade bologna or pepperoni, these recipes have been left out this time because they are impractical. Game processing centers all over North America do a fine job of making summer sausage, salami, and similar cold cuts. Hunters are invited take their game to these establishments for these special treats.

Fishing for hunters is part of the fourth edition of *Sam Fadala's Complete Guide to Game Care & Cookery.*

Bonus Chapters

Three bonus chapters are presented in the Fourth Edition. Chapter 27 deals with fishing for the pan. Even blue ribbon trout streams dedicated to catch-and-release trophy fishing allow some fish to be kept for cooking. High mountain lakes, ponds, and streams everywhere provide good food. Catching fish for the eating is the thrust of this chapter, especially with regard to hunters who often find themselves camped near a good supply of fresh fish. Chapter 28 follows the goal of the book—caring for the catch, faithfully preserving what has been caught so that it cooks up into a fine dining experience, especially in camp. Chapter 29 contains tried and true fish recipes, including smoking methods and turning leftover fish into a tasty salad.

Safety First and Always

Guns are tools. They are entirely inanimate and possess no ability to get up and harm anything or anyone. Accidents happen, of course, but they are often the result of negligence. We must always follow the rules, especially the Ten Commandments of Arms Safety as laid down by the National Rifle Association. These rules are available at most gun shops and will not be reprinted here. They're mostly common sense—such as not pointing a muzzle at anything you don't intend to shoot. There is no excuse in for a gun "going off" when dropped; however, there is also no excuse for carelessness.

Longbows and recurves are back in force. Safety with these older style bows hinges mainly on stringing. The rule is: use a stringer. I visited a highly experienced archer one afternoon. One lens of his eyeglasses was shattered. While stringing a bow without a stringer, it slipped. The tip came back with terrific force. Had he not been wearing eyeglasses, he could have been blinded. Compound bows are under terrific pressure. They must be handled with respect. Then there are broadheads. One evening I was sharpening a Bear Razorhead while talking. I looked up to emphasize a point and wham! The result of my negligence was a slice in my right leg.

Just like broadheads, knives and other cooking implements can inflict damage. A guide lost his life when a knife slipped as he field dressed a big game animal. The blade cut his femoral artery and the bleeding could not be stopped. All sharp instruments from field knives to cleavers in the kitchen must be treated as dangerous and used with respect.

Archery means dealing with sharp things, especially broadheads like this one which is keen enough to shave hair.

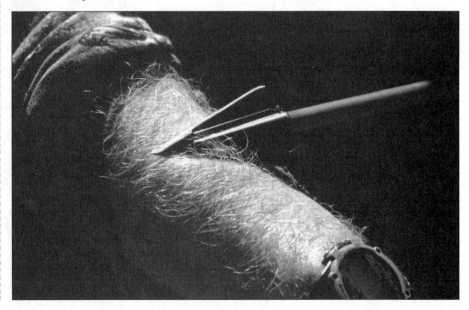

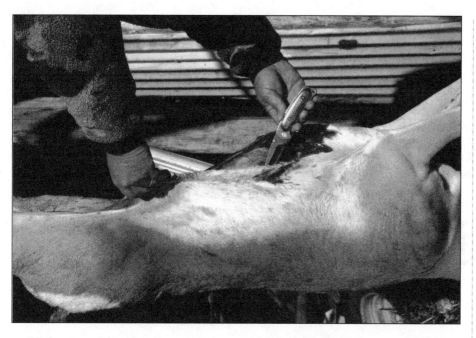

Obviously the whole "point" of a knife like this Buck is cutting and if it can slice into this antelope buck, it can do likewise on the hunter. Be careful with knives.

High country hunting or any outing requiring physical exertion can result in a health hazard. A physical checkup for older hunters is strongly advised, especially for desk-bound workers heading for the Rocky Mountains. Going with a partner is smart for obvious reasons. Survival tools are essential on some hunts. A GPS, for example, can prevent getting lost. A compact first aid kit is advisable in daypack or fanny pack. There are also good survival kits to be had. Something as simple as a walking staff can prevent twisted ankles or worse. Finally, for hunting remote areas a packframe with tent and sleeping bag aboard can save the day in a storm.

Using the Book

This book is actually two in one as the title promises: game care and cookery. While there are hundreds of cookbooks available, many dealing with game and fish, few go into taking care of the food before it reaches the table.

"Oooh, wild meat is gamey." We've all heard that lament and it can be true. Imagine a pork roast that was ill-dressed, dragged through the dirt a half mile, left in camp to bake in the sun, put on top of a vehicle and hauled 1,000 miles, then "aged" in a garage for another week before it became a pork roast. It would be "gamey" too.

Natural meat is tasty and nutritious, when handled and prepared the right way. And that's what this book is all about.

A physical checkup for any hunter is important, especially when hiking high country like this.

Hunting For All The Right Reasons

I had never taken the right fork of that lonesome high country road; that day I would. After parking the blue Chevy I slipped on the packframe, grabbed my walking stick, laced the sling of the 100-year old Savage Model 1899 30-30 on a frame hook and paced away.

The area was packed with wild horses; most of the antelope had moved on. Where I had once seen two dozen bucks, I ran across only three. The first was mature but short-horned. The second, a yearling. I passed up both. The third was a wide-horned prize. Stalk, aim, fire—it was over. Was I trophy hunting? Had I no interest in tagging a special buck I would have dropped the first pronghorn I saw.

There is nothing wrong with trophy hunting. There is something wrong—in my opinion—when "sport" is the *only* reason for collecting an animal or bird. Sport, as applied to baseball, billiards, or rock climbing is honorable. Sport *hunting* has taken on a darker side, although it is just as honorable as hitting a baseball, sinking the eight ball in a side pocket, or toe-nailing up a rock wall. When the *only* reason for

There is nothing wrong with trophy hunting, but going only for the trophy is leaving out the basic reason for taking game—the food value.

hunting is putting a head on the wall or a stuffed quail under glass on a coffee table, a phantom creeps in, painting an otherwise bright scene with murky brushstrokes. This is considered shooting an animal or bird for the heck of it.

Hunting is a Harvest

Wild game is a renewable resource. The grim die-off of Arizona's Kaibab before our time proved that herds can destroy themselves. I personally witnessed a white-tailed deer explosion that ended in general starvation and disease. These are not excuses created to justify sport hunting; they are reality. Take some, leave some. That's why it's called a harvest.

Bag limits for birds and tag numbers for big game are predicated on wildlife management principles. A healthy deer herd, for example, can increase its numbers by about one-third annually. Taking part of that increase is called management. Logically, where game numbers are smaller permits are equally limited by a lottery system. Obtaining a hunting permit for some species is extremely difficult.

Wildlife is a renewable resource. This fine Kentucky whitetail taken at Deer Creek Outfitters in Sebree is beautiful, but it also provided prime meat.

The Permit System and Hunting License

Although I live in Wyoming where some fine opportunities come during the whiter months, I head for Arizona in the winter. To escape the cold? Not really. I'm used to it. I go to Arizona to hunt quail, dove, javelina, and my favorite game animal—the remarkably elusive Coues whitetail. But there's a problem: drawing a tag. My success rate is 33 $1/3$ percent, one tag for every three applications.

The tag system limits the number of hunters in a given area for a specific species. Furthermore, not all tags are filled. A 20 percent to 30 percent success rate on Arizona's Coues, for example, is considered higher than normal. Lawful hunting under the guidelines of a game department will not deplete wildlife.

Market Hunting

It happened; there is no denying it. Market hunting in the 1900s cut into game numbers, especially waterfowl, but also deer.

Will you get to hunt? You may have to enter a drawing where luck will play a huge roll in whether or not a tag is secured. Nick Fadala got this buck in Wyoming following a game department drawing.

On the other hand, we have come to believe stories that are absolutely preposterous. These foolish tales have been retold so many times that we—even hunters—believe them. I got a call from a friend who recited the report of a single afternoon of passenger pigeon shooting by a New York club. Six shotguns cleared the sky of 30,000 passenger pigeons in only one afternoon.

"Kenn," I said, "that's terrible. Those blankety-blank game hogs!" Then I put the brakes on. Wait a minute. Let's do the math. If an afternoon is comprised of six hours, that's 5,000 birds an hour. Never happened! You'd need a machine gun.

Equally ridiculous is the story of the American bison massacre. It could not happen—and it did not happen—the way we believe. There were 60 million free-roaming bison in America during the 1800s. That's the agreed-upon figure that anti-hunters love to use. In only a few short years, hunters' deadly bullets killed almost all of the animals. The U.S. Government wanted bison wiped out, all right, to control the Plains Indian, whose guerilla warfare practices were deadly. Free ammo was given out. A salted bison tongue sold for a Yankee dollar when an accomplished carpenter might earn three bucks a day.

The myth of hunters "shooting off" the American bison has lived on for over 100 years, but it was and is a mathematical impossibility.

Above right: No way could hunters with single-shot blackpowder cartridge rifles like the Sharps shown here, wipe out 60 million bison over millions of acres. But there is no denying that they did try to do just that.

The slaughter was terrible, unconscionable, lamentable and downright wrong, especially the shooting for sheer fun as Sir Gore (appropriate name) did on his American hunting safari. Professional buffalo runners, as they preferred being called, shot thousands of shaggies.

Hold on a minute, let logic seep in. Bison lived on millions of acres. Think of the magnitude. Arizona, New Mexico, Texas, South Dakota, North Dakota, Wyoming, Nebraska, Kansas, Montana, Oregon, Washington—forget the plains provinces of Canada. You'd need an airplane to cover it all. No way could hunters, most of them carrying single-shot blackpowder cartridge rifles and traveling on horseback, by mule drawn wagon or on foot, wipe out 60 million bison.

But something else did. Something much smaller than a bullet. Disease brought in by domestic cattle. Anyone who thinks disease cannot take such tolls should study the results of the black plague or for that matter Spanish Influenza, which after World War I killed more people than all the bombs and bullets fired in that debacle.

Anti-Hunting

Because movie actors, teachers, politicians and other highly visible individuals and groups with loud voices say hunting is wrong, thousands of people have joined the ranks of anti-hunters. Anti-hunting organizations comprise the spearhead aimed at those of us who take part in what we know is an honorable annual harvest.

Following the disastrous September 11, 2001, terrorist attack on the World Trade Center one of these groups came out in defense of chickens. A spokesperson exclaimed we should all understand what multitudes of chickens suffer every day.

Ranking chickens and humans in the same pod is typical of anti-hunting sentiment. When I talk with anti-hunters, especially vegetarians, I tell them that I protest eating any food from a crop. After all, potatoes were grown where elk used to

This barren looking terrain is home to antelope. When land just like this was cleared for raising wheat and potatoes, the antelope lost their home.

winter. Apple orchards used to be deer habitat. And the vast wheat fields, such as those of Nebraska, once comprised home to all manner of wild animals. Nebraska, by the way, was called "The Antelope State" in the 1900s. The name had to be changed. "It's like coming home from the movies some night and finding your home and food gone forever," I complain. It's nonsense, of course. I eat vegetables and fruit.

What We Hunt

The categories for this book include rabbits, squirrels, other small game, upland birds, waterfowl, exotics and big game.

Rabbits

A rabbit is a rabbit and a hare is a hare, but we'll lump them together. The ubiquitous (darn near everywhere) cottontail rabbit is the number one small game animal in North America if not the world. He's a real rabbit, *altricial* by nature, meaning born blind and helpless in a fur-lined den. Nobody knows how many rabbits live in North America but all 50 states have them, including Georgia which has the *pontoon* or marsh rabbit, an Olympic champion swimmer.

All cottontails are of the genus *Sylvilagus* with eight major species. My home state has four: nuttals, small, thriving in aspens, junipers and foothill shrub communities at higher elevations; the eastern cottontail; the pygmy, smallest of the four; and the desert cottontail, most numerous. Not all rabbits are legal game; check local regulations.

I call rabbits replacement animals; they come and go quickly. While a single pair can conceivably turn into thousands in only a few seasons, few survive beyond a year.

Hares on the other hand are *precocial*, born with fur often in a form instead of a den, eyes open and ready to run in no time. Jackrabbits, which are hares not rabbits, are usually classified as non-game, and while my grandfather was able to turn

Rabbits remain the number one small game in North America. They're abundant and their meat represents high protein.

Left: The author prefers hunting cottontails with a bow, small-bore muzzleloader, pistol, or 22 rimfire rifle, but a shotgun like this Ruger 28-gauge is very effective when the shots are fast in heavy cover.

jackrabbit boned meat into a rich red spaghetti sauce, few jacks are taken to the kitchen. Where I live they are classified as varmints because of the damage they cause crops and ranchlands.

The snowshoe rabbit isn't a rabbit either. He's really the varying hare, varying in color from gray/brown to white with the seasons. He has the typical hare lip, meaning split longitudinally, and he's not a rodent. Rodents have two incisor teeth; hares have four. Snowshoes, by my experience, are almost as difficult to prepare as jackrabbits, but they are edible fare.

Squirrels

We're interested in tree squirrels as opposed to ground squirrels, the latter being non-game animals. The tree squirrel ranks behind only the rabbit in popularity as a small game animal. There are six different types, including the little red squirrel of coniferous forests, the smallest and most difficult to prepare for the table.

Chickarees or Douglas squirrels dwell in pine and spruce trees of the Northwest Coastland.

Then comes the gray squirrel, definitely table-worthy. The western gray is bigger than his eastern cousin. Otherwise, they're of the same clan.

Tassel-eared or Abert's squirrel is—in my judgment—the most beautiful of the family, larger than the gray with striking color and of course the tufts at the ears that give its name.

The eastern American fox squirrel is the sumo wrestler of the group growing to a length, including tail, of two feet.

Finally there are flying squirrels, which don't have wings but glide from tree to tree almost as if they did.

Other Small Game

Rabbit and squirrel are king and queen of small game, but not the only edibles. Raccoons have been cooked in Ozark kitchens for decades and possum is certainly fit for the table. Muskrats may not be on the usual list, but trappers in the Far North were known to live on this meat for weeks at a time when other game was not available.

We usually think of birds like this quail as upland game, although cottontail rabbits fit the niche, too.

Exotics

The only reason these are called exotics is because they don't fit our everyday food list. Plump grub worms are candy to certain children of Africa, but not proper food for us. I wonder what those same children would think of some of the things we call good eatin?

Rattlesnake is the first exotic on my list. When we don't know how to explain the taste of an offbeat food we say it's like chicken. Rattler really does taste like chicken, only milder.

Bullfrogs cross over. Many consider frog's legs perfectly normal, but most people have never tasted them. Sea turtles turn into the finest soup I've ever slurped, but once again, few have enjoyed this treat. Landlocked turtles are also good food.

Woodchucks, rockchucks and prairie dogs are food. So is beaver. Mountain lion is wonderful. I once cooked up mountain lion loin that my guests praised as "The best white pork meat I've ever eaten."

Porcupine is edible, but my attempts to make this meat palatable ended in coyote bait. I tried bobcat; it attacked my taste buds and is off my edible list.

Upland Game

All the game birds that aren't connected to water are upland from the smallest dove to the largest wild turkey. Where I hunt, sage grouse and mountain grouse have open seasons. The first is harder to fix but when done right can be mistaken for strips of venison. The second is simply delicious in camp. Quail are supremely good, especially the large Mearns of the Southwest, the best quail I've ever eaten. Partridges are also fit for a king's table. And by the way, it's said that kings paid their chefs more than their generals. Why not? Woodcocks are good. Pheasant is excellent. Ptarmigan is another fine upland bird, as are wild pigeons and rails. And don't forget wild turkeys, sometimes classified as big game—what a feast they create.

Waterfowl

Ducks and geese are on the edible list. Ducks are making a comeback thanks to wetland rehabilitation, while geese are doing great everywhere. In some areas golfers—many of them non-hunters if not anti-hunters—consider the goose a real pest. Hundreds have found the golf course a fine place to live, eat, and—well, the other part of eating. Many don't even bother to migrate. Golfers have learned to watch where they step. Sandhill cranes are also huntable, but not on a wide scale.

Big Game

King of all big game in North America is the white-tailed deer or simply whitetail. A whitetail can live in your pocket and you won't feel the lump. He's at home in the garden, on the lawn, raiding the flowers in the backyard, sharing the salt lick with domestic stock, climbing on top of haystacks in winter to partake of the bounty, uncovering corn meant for the hogs and helping himself to all special feeds and vitamins put out for cattle and horses.

In some areas the whitetail herd is so successful that residents who used to blast

The snake crawling up this tree is not considered food by most of us, and yet in some cultures it would be relished. Rattler, however, is another story. It "eats fine" breaded after a time in universal marinade.

Turtles are a lot better eating than they look, although very few cultures use them for food.

The whitetail deer is to big game in North America what the cottontail is to small game. This deer can live in your back pocket and you won't feel the lump.

hunters are now praying for them. As one put it, "Deer are just rats with horns." She had suffered two car collisions with whitetails and had long given up on a garden.

On the other hand, we hunters love our whitetails. They're distributed over most of North America and their meat is prime. One of my favorite dishes of all time is marinated whitetail ribs prepared over hot coals, but they must be from a mature buck in good condition.

Mule deer and blacktails head up the rest of the big game spectrum. Mule deer are widespread over the West, while blacktails are limited to parts of California, Oregon, Washington and of course the Sitka of the Alaskan coast.

Elk are also high on the big game list. Many hunters consider elk the best of all wild meat. That's personal, of course. I love elk but would trade all mine for moose meat and those whitetail ribs.

Wild boar is another edible big game animal. The Rocky Mountain goat is also on the list, but its meat is not ranked with the bighorn sheep, which one writer said was simply the best in the world, wild or tame.

Antelope can be outrageously good but requires special care in the field and zero aging. It's delicate meat. Give me a marinated antelope haunch over coals and I'll promise an experience in tender and tasty gourmet dining with no fuss at all.

Grizzly is not considered fine food, while black bear can be, but it's another meat that demands special attention in the kitchen. Javelina, the little wild pig of the Southwest, falls into the same category, demanding both special field care and culinary artfulness. There's musk ox, which few of us will ever taste, and bison, which can be wonderful. Today, there are restaurants that serve buffalo burgers and other treats from the shaggy beasts. Caribou have constituted good food for thousands. A complete big game list would include everything from seal and walrus to the wild goats of Hawaii and California.

The Right Reasons

Hunting is not for food alone. It is a king among sports requiring skill and knowledge, sometimes endurance and resolve. But hunting also represents literally tons of good meat harvested annually.

The trophy animal is three things: genetically strong, well-fed and mature—especially mature. There are exceptions. Super feeding programs can produce big bucks, bulls and boars in short order. But in the main the record head is mature.

Taking a big buck does not drain the genetic pool. Do we think the big guy never left his seed for posterity? I tagged a Boone & Crockett pronghorn in 1989. A biologist aged that buck at seven and a half years. He had but a season or two left in him. Winter is tough on bucks because rut precedes the cold weather.

So the theme is written again in bold letters— **trophy hunting is OK.**

It's also wonderful to bag rabbits, squirrels, dove, pheasants—all game—for the pure joy of being in the field. Regardless of what game we hunt, the food aspect must never be ignored. Admire the rack of the big buck. Praise the colors of the cock pheasant. Then apply the principles of game care and cookery to complete the hunt.

2

Game Meat is Nutritious

Controversy remains over game meat and cholesterol. One faction says game meat, such as venison, is actually higher in cholesterol than beef. Another group claims that the *type* of cholesterol makes all the difference. "Game meat," these people say, "is not high in *bad* cholesterol."

I cannot prove or disprove either claim. I can, however, show anyone that game meat is less fatty than beef and many other domestic meats because it is not marbled. Deer, elk, bison—any big game—may have plenty of fat on the carcass. However, while choice beef is marbled—that is it has fat running throughout the muscle—wild game does not.

When we slap a prime steak on the gas grill it smokes up to sizzling goodness. Lay a piece of boned game meat on the same grill and it may turn into a slab of shoe leather. Worry not. There is a way to grill game meat to lip smacking perfection. (The Leg O' Lope recipe is an example.)

This is not an anti-beef book. I like beef. It's good meat. But, across the board—and this is simply a catchall figure—wild meat is seven times less fatty than a big juicy USDA Choice beefsteak.

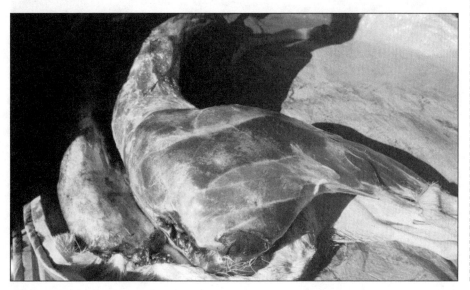

Game meat is not marbled. It is very low in fat and high in "good" cholesterol, according to studies.

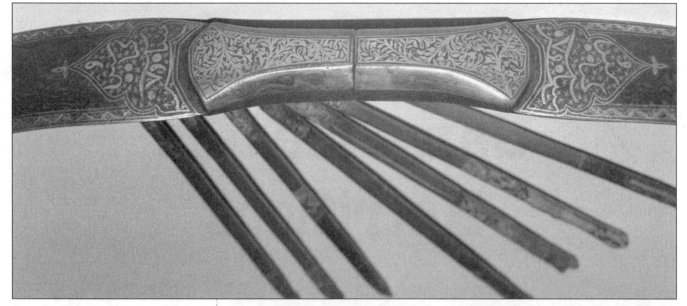

An ancient bow like this was used for hunting where it gathered in game meat to be consumed by the entire tribe.

Right: The American Plains Indian was good enough with his bow to procure meat for himself, his family, and his tribe.

What did ancient man eat? In September 1991 two German hikers in the Italian Alps made a fantastic find. A frozen body came into view on the trail. Since many mountaineers have been lost in the Alps, authorities considered the corpse just one more victim of the mountain.

Not so. Here was the complete mummy of a 5,000-year-old man preserved in a glacier. The Iceman, as some called him, would never have been uncovered except for a non-typical warming trend. He was born 3,000 years before Christ preached his Sermon on the Mount. He trod his mountain home prior to the time Plato or Socrates taught in Greece, and long before Columbus landed in the Americas.

Some tried to make him a goat herder or shaman to avoid his true place. But the Iceman

The author credits hunting with his "tolerable decent health," as he puts it. It's the walking that does it.

was a hunter. His bow and arrows lay with him, along with knife and axe. I found it fascinating that his gear was much like my own when I bowhunt with traditional tackle.

His stomach contents contained a variety of foods, including meat. The Iceman was omnivorous, dining from both the animal and vegetable kingdoms. I suspect he was typical of his time.

I believe meat has always been part of the human diet and always good for us in spite of opposition from vegetarians and super vegetarians who call themselves *vegans*, consuming nothing that was "killed" when picked. An apple is OK because the tree did not die when that apple was taken. But a carrot? No, no. It dies when pulled from the earth. As the kids say, "Give me a break!"

As a culture, our ancestors worked harder physically than we do. Perhaps they could ingest more fat that we can get away with and remain healthy. My oft-mentioned maternal grandfather routinely consumed a half dozen eggs every morning. He theorized that those eggs were good for him. It was the sulfur, he claimed, that kept his body healthy.

I doubted it then. I doubt it now. But what I cannot deny are the facts of his life. He retired at 65 because someone told him it was the thing to do. Bored, he returned to work as a master chef full-time for 10 years. He retired again at 75. Again bored, he worked part-time for the next several years. If the cholesterol in those eggs got him, it sure took its time. Grandpa thrived into his 90th year, lucid and mobile to the end.

So let's all slurp down those six eggs every morning, right? Not at all. Heredity plays a role. So does lifestyle. I suspect, without proof, that considerable exercise burns up at least some of the fat we consume. I believe, on evidence, that red meat is good for us in moderation.

I also know of no information that has shot down the data provided by Professor Marty Marchello working from North Dakota State University. An expert in range and animal sciences, Marchello studied the nutritional values of various meat sources, especially antelope and deer, diligently, carefully, scientifically investigating wild meat with regard to human consumption and health. He concluded that red meat in general is good food.

Hunting is healthy exercise (but have a physical examination before hiking in altitudes like this—over 10,000 elevation).

Eat well, be well—this game supper is well-rounded with meat and vegetables, the diet of the ancient Ice Man over 5,000 years ago.

Walk here and calories are bound to be "burned." Our busy lifestyle in the early 21st century makes it difficult to get to places like this very often, but we can ride bicycles and use the gym to get in, and remain in condition. Meanwhile, a diet of meat, vegetables, and fruit can't hurt, especially low fat game meat.

Fat, however, remains suspect, especially in large quantities. Game meat is lean. A fall buck or bull may pack a lot of fat, but it is not marbled into the muscle. I have discarded literally pounds of fat from beneath the hide of many wild animals. Since this fat was not integral to other edible tissue it could be stripped away.

We know the Iceman ate red meat. We also know from studies of ancient human bones that red meat has always been part of our diet along with grains and other foods. The old story about the well-balanced diet is not a leaky bucket.

Unfortunately, our modern diet is often a teeter-totter forced down on one end by a multitude of fat and sugar—fast food and fun food. Fat and sugar make for tasty fare and so we gaily consume as much of both as possible every day.

Being healthy is obviously a wonderful goal. And what we eat has much to do with how we feel and age. Lean red meat in sensible amounts, along with bicycle riding, hiking, walking, playing tennis, home exercise and doing the gym routine regularly—especially with a trainer who knows the best methods to accomplish specific goals—are keys to feeling good.

Modern lifestyle often throws obstacles in the way of these goals and genetics also play a role. I've a friend who at age 65 is the oldest living male in the history of his family. The rest of the male clan crossed the river in their 50s. Milton took another path. He lives a healthy life, including eating wild game and exercising. He has beaten the odds.

The American Heart Association stepped forward to say that wild game is an acceptable part of a healthy diet. But there are people who don't buy it because they do not want to give hunting, even for food, a good name.

I wrote an article on the nutrition of wild meat for a Pennsylvania magazine. The erudite readership went up in smoke. They had read that wild meat contained more cholesterol than domestic.

They were right—and wrong. In his studies Marchello pointed out that all meat is composed of white and red muscle fiber. Wild animal red muscle fibers are dense. Cholesterol is found more in red than white muscle fiber so it follows that game meat is high in cholesterol. But grip the reins. There's a little thing called EPA, turned into letters because it's actually eicosapentaenoic acid. EPA acts to lower blood cholesterol and wild meat has more EPA than domestic.

Polyunsaturated fatty acids are also known to lower blood cholesterol. Cottontail rabbit meat contains 25.4 percent polyunsaturated fatty acids by laboratory test. Antelope meat runs about 31.6 percent. Squirrel goes 37.6 percent. Moose, which we think of as an animal with heavy concentration of fatty tissue to withstand frigid winters—which they do remarkably well, shows a surprising 39.1 percent polyunsaturated fatty acids. Rabbit meat is especially interesting because it runs so high in protein that a straight diet of it is not wise.

This brings us to the story of early explorers of the Far North. Many fell ill, especially during winter, some of them dying. Suspicion of poisoning grew. But did the Eskimo poison his caucasian visitor? Of course not. The white men ate only the lean, shunning the rest, while the Eskimo consumed even some of the first stomach contents of caribou, sort of an acidy salad. The natives remained healthy because of their more complete diet.

As for calories, game meats are generally lower than domestic. The numbers are significant. But comparisons to current beef are unfair because today's ranchers are feed experts raising an entirely different animal. Regardless, one study showed whitetail deer meat at 149 calories per 100 grams weight with USDA Choice beef running 180 calories for the same amount.

Americans spend millions on diet books and foods. Most of this is lighting dollar bills on fire to watch them burn. We lose weight. We gain it back. The yo-yo effect. Only a change in lifestyle, including what and how much we eat, plus exercise, will keep us fit. Taking in fewer calories can help. Game meat has fewer calories.

On the other hand, running scared of store bought meat is groundless. The United States and Canada have good standards in place. Sometimes the watchdogs go to sleep on the job and bad meat slips by them. But considering the millions of pounds consumed annually in North America, coming across bad meat is rare. Tests show more saturated pesticide and herbicide in beef than in game, but I have no information classifying domestic meat as harmful because of these chemicals. Furthermore, the American and Canadian people have demanded a reduction in growth hormone treatment, which has been heeded. Suppliers are listening.

The old cliché "We are what we eat" runs true, as all clichés do. That's how they got to be clichés. Consider starting from camp in early morning with nothing for fuel but a hot cup of coffee. Midday comes around. What's in the daypack? Not much. Crackers and a big candy bar. These whack the hunger pangs. The body feels good

This kind of exercise—getting a game animal from field to camp on your back—is not recommended without a physical checkup.

Cottontail rabbit meat, like the fine dish shown here, is rated at 25.4 percent polyunsaturated fatty acids according to laboratory reports.

What's in a daypack? Not a lot of food. The wise hunter thinks about collecting good protein on the trail—maybe a few fish for the pan as well.

This shows the daypack slung on the author's special packframe. It also shows how the frame is modified with aluminum struts to make the shelf rigid for carrying game out. Included in this shot is a view of the rifle slung on the special strut the author built into his Freighter packframe.

for a little while, then a half hour later weakness sets in. The body has rebelled. Taking in sugar may hit the spot, even promote a surge of energy, but soon that sugar tells the system to stimulate the pancreas, resulting in a little flood of insulin.

The wise hunter carries good grub with him because the hunter is an athlete. He may sit in a ground blind or perch high in a tree stand all day, but not always. Thousands, especially those going for big game in the West, hike for miles carrying packs on their backs. And after taking game, the meat is carried from the field. ATVs, vehicles and beasts of burden are right for getting game out. But sometimes we are the beasts of burden.

I packed a buck antelope taken by my brother. The haul was short, less than a mile and mostly downhill; total weight was around 90 pounds. Such activity requires a bit of endurance, meaning the machine must be fed the three basic food groups: protein, fat and carbohydrates.

One thing is certain—on a tough hunt, eat right. This means a little starch in camp, a little sugar, too, and for me, wild meat taken on the trail, mainly in the form of cottontail rabbits and mountain birds. And yes, fish, too, as discussed in Chapter 27. Fishing for hunters is more than fun. It's a good source of fine camp food.

Some time ago a catch phrase was born: "The process is the product." This little quip fits hunting perfectly. The process of hunting any game that requires getting out and moving around promotes health by itself. So while hunters are in the field looking for big game, small game or birds, just being there is promoting good health. The meat we take—followed by proper care in the field and good processing, stored wisely and prepared into tasty dishes—is an adjunct of the hunt itself.

There can also be an economic string attached to hunting—or not. Game taken close to home is economical. Trips down the road are not. So we don't hunt just for the meat. We hunt because we were born to. But the meat is a terrific bonus. So let's talk next about how to hunt for food.

Atkins

All of the above information on the nutrition of wild meat and the "balanced diet" was intended for the average consumer. But there is another healthy way to eat. It is the Atkins diet, which works on the basis of body chemistry. The anti-Atkins studies I have seen all failed to discredit the plan, which is heavy on protein, very light on carbohydrates (but Atkins does *not* exclude carbohydrates). Game meats work fine on the Atkins plan, although fat can be added to lean meats.

Nutrient Content: Tale of the Tape

Species	Protein %	Fat %	Cholesterol (mg/100g*)	Calories (Kcal/100g*)
Beef (USDA Choice)	22.0	6.5	72	180
Beef (USDA Standard)	22.7	2.0	69	152
Lamb	20.8	5.7	66	167
Pork	22.3	4.9	71	165
Wild Boar**	28.3	4.38	109	160
Buffalo	21.7	1.9	62	138
Whitetail Deer	23.6	1.4	116	149
Mule Deer	23.7	1.3	107	145
Elk	22.8	.9	67	137
Moose	22.1	.5	71	130
Antelope	22.5	.9	112	144
Squirrel	21.4	3.2	83	149
Cottontail	21.8	2.4	77	144
Jackrabbit	21.9	2.4	131	153
Chicken	23.6	.7	62	135
Turkey (Domestic)	23.5	1.5	60	146
Wild Turkey	25.7	1.1	55	163
Pheasant (Domestic)	23.9	.8	71	144
Wild Pheasant	25.7	.6	52	148
Gray Partridge	25.6	.7	85	151
Sharptail Grouse	23.8	.7	105	142
Sage Grouse	23.7	1.1	101	140
Dove	22.9	1.8	94	145
Sandhill Crane	21.7	2.4	123	153
Snow Goose	22.7	3.6	142	121
Duck (Domestic)**	19.9	4.25	89	180
Mallard	23.1	2.0	140	152
Widgeon	22.6	2.1	131	153

*100 grams equals about 3 1/2 ounces.

**Not trimmed of fat before analysis. In the above chart, all visible fat was trimmed before analysis. However surveys show that carcasses of domesticated animals have 25 to 30 percent fat while the average fat content of wild game animals is only 4.3 percent. Not only is the quantity of fat lower in game, but the quality is also healthier. Fat from wild game contains a much higher proportion of polyunsaturated fatty acits — good fat — and is lower in saturated fat — bad fat.

SOURCE: NORTH DAKOTA STATE UNIVERSITY

Good Fat, Bad Fat

Species	— % Fatty Acids —		
	Saturated	Monosaturated	Polyunsaturated
Beef	46.3	45.5	8.2
Buffalo	43.2	45.0	11.8
Mule Deer	45.6	30.6	23.9
Whitetail Deer	48.0	31.8	20.2
Elk	48.4	26.6	24.9
Antelope	41.2	27.1	31.6
Moose	36.6	24.3	39.1
Boar	35.7	47.0	17.3
Caribou	46.6	36.4	17.0
Rabbit	39.0	35.6	25.4
Squirrel	15.2	47.2	37.6

Some game meat is higher in dietary cholesterol than domestic meats, but the combination of more lean body tissue, generally fewer calories, less saturated fat and a significantly higher percentage of cholesterol-reducing polyunsaturated fatty acids makes game a heart-healthy choice. Game meat also has a significantly higher content of EPA than domestic meat. EPA is thought to reduce the risk of developing altherosclerosis, one of the major causes of heart attack and stroke.

SOURCE: NORTH DAKOTA STATE UNIVERSITY AND U.S. DEPARTMENT OF AGRICULTURE

3

Hunting For Food

Dispersing hunters is important in game management. In spite of population growth and urban sprawl, there remain millions of lonesome acres in North America for hunters to roam.

Right: The author hunting a high mountain range in Wyoming. Hunters here are widely dispersed. Knowing the habitat is vital to success.

So if hunting is good for us and the resulting meat is healthful, that means we have to get out there and harvest game. Small game, upland birds and waterfowl require licenses, plus a stamp for migratory avians. Sometimes these hunts are also limited by drawings. I'm thinking of sandhill cranes. There simply aren't enough cranes to allow open seasons. On the other end of the continuum dozens of species are huntable with the simple purchase of a license.

Big game hunting out West is generally by permit. As a resident of my home state I can get a general elk or deer tag. But I cannot buy a sheep, moose, mountain goat, buffalo or antelope tag over the counter. I must apply for these in a drawing, which makes sense. The drawings limit the number of hunters. They also disperse hunters into special game management units. For example, this coming season I'm in for an archery-only elk hunt in Wyoming's northern mountains. My second choice is a general elk tag in case I don't draw the special hunt.

Obtaining a permit is a simple matter of contacting the game and fish department of a particular state and either applying for a license and/or tag via the Internet

or obtaining and returning the necessary forms by mail. Now that we have the proper permits in hand, let's go hunting.

Knowing the Territory

Small game, large game, waterfowl, upland birds, it doesn't matter. A hunter has to know his territory. This is a matter of scouting, which is a tree with several branches. Information from game departments, the Bureau of Land Management, U.S. Forest Service, along with maps, plus rancher/farmer help, are all scouting methods. It's important to know the general hunting arena. However, game lives in the niche, that ideal spot within the larger habitat. Finding that focus point leads to real success.

Tree Stands and Windmills

Tree stands have gained immense popularity, especially east of the Mississippi River. My first thought on tree stands was—not for me. I'm a pursuit hunter. Sitting up in the air waiting for game to come to me, rather than going forth to find buck, bull or boar appeared boring. I was wrong. A windmill taught me better.

Kelly Glause of Evansville, Wyo., took over as master guide of a ranch. One of his first efforts was building safe platforms in windmills, a natural spot to see game. I decided to try a windmill. I loved it. One day I had a front row seat as a golden eagle killed a mature mule deer doe. I did not enjoy watching the deer die that way, but it was an intriguing part of nature.

I can't say that windmills or tree stands have replaced my penchant for hiking. However, I have witnessed hundreds of interesting events from on high.

I'm also glad I was aloft when a big black bear came by in Maine. He just happened to insist on taking a trail near my perch. I lost the first two opportunities as he balked and fled. But when he appeared for the third time my Remington Model 700 ML 50-caliber muzzleloader placed one 385-grain lead bullet driven by 110-

Above left: Hunting from tree stands is nothing new. This old ladder led a hunter aloft at some time in the past.

Above: Safety is the most important aspect of tree stand hunting, followed by the right location for the stand. Here a rifle is attached to a pull-up rope rather than carried aloft by the hunter.

Still-hunting is not staying still. It's covering the niche with intent purpose ending with a stalk.

Spot and stalk is one more successful method of taking big game. Here, Nick Fadala searches for deer with binoculars rested on the Moses Stick for a steady game-finding view.

grains volume Pyrodex RS spot on. The bruin ranked number one for Maine muzzleloader at the time, dropping to fourth place last I heard.

The only negative on tree stands is taking a nosedive out of one. This is not the forum for lessons on tree-stand safety; however, climbing carefully up or down and retaining that safety belt are basic. Windmills are, on the other hand, no problem. An ordinary ladder leads up and down and a platform with rails provides an ideal seat.

Like a hovering hawk, there is much to be seen from tree stands and windmills and I hope to do more of both. It's also comforting to know that as age seeps in, which happens to us all, I'll still be able to go up and sit, when the mountain trails become a little too steep. Furthermore, there is nothing dishonorable about stands, no more than it's wrong to wait under a white sheet in the snow for geese to fly in.

Still-Hunting

Still-hunting is not standing or sitting still. It means moving stealthily through the habitat with an eye out for game. The successful still-hunter knows game habits and the lay of the land. Some hunters call it field position. That's a good term. Being in the right place means not only spotting game, but also getting a shot if a buck, bull or boar spooks. If you jump game and cannot get a shot, you are out of field position, which often cannot be helped.

An interesting book on the subject is Theodore Strong Van Dyke's 1882 *The Still-Hunter*, out of print but still available through searches.

Still-hunting is an exercise in frustration when game spooks ahead by detecting a hunter's scent. Two aids are wind detectors and cover scent mist. Powders and other media show the exact behavior of the wind far better than wetting a finger or dropping a leaf. And a little puff now and again from a spray bottle of water/cover scent mix works in fooling sharp noses.

Spot and Stalk

I view this method as a less sophisticated brand of still-hunting. It works especially well in open country. I use my Moses Stick. It's a walking/shooting/binocular rest staff made from the balsa-light, oak-strong *agave* cactus stalk. Mine have rubber crutch bumpers and tanned leather handles a third of the way down from the top. The top is padded to firmly hold binoculars for a steady view, which is paramount to finding game as opposed to glancing at something already spotted with the naked eye.

Ideally, the hunter finds game before it sees him or her. Then the stalk begins, keeping the wind right and using available natural concealment to get close for one perfect shot. I've had good luck on western wild turkeys with this approach, locating them from high ground and then sneaking down to position myself for an ambush. Wild turkeys often take a trail, and though they are wary, it is possible to take a position (especially if camouflaged) and wait for the clan stroll by.

Sleeping Over

One of the most successful hunting methods is backpacking into a territory and staying put rather than heading to camp at the close of the day. There are wonderful packframes, mountain tents, and lightweight sleeping bags these days. My packframe is a modified Camp Trails Freighter with hooks for rifle slings and a metal shelf. It has carried in quite a bit of gear and packed out considerable game. For shelter a Coleman Exponent™ Inyo™ 2 backpack tent offers shelter against any storm, along with a Coleman Exponent™ Summit(tm) 0 sleeping bag.

The wilderness hunter should never set foot afield without provisions for a storm, including food and shelter. Also a GPS. I use a Magellan Color. It lends a lot of confidence. I know that I can go in that extra mile and still find may way back to camp.

The Ground Blind

Pits dug directly into the earth are ground blinds. So are other methods of concealment that are not related to tree stands or windmills. Little wooden houses are perfect examples of ground blinds. Deer, antelope and other wildlife soon get used to these structures set up near waterholes or trails.

Turn Yourself Into a Ground Blind

This is a new hunting method for me. On an antelope hunt I located a few scattered watering sites nowhere near roads. Setting up a real ground blind meant packing one a long distance. However, I found that a hunter can turn himself into a ground blind. I have a little Quick-Set Blind from The Game Tracker Company that weighs next

Sleeping over is a great way to "live with the game." If that special spot is not too far from a road, a lot of gear, including a warm sleeping bag, can be packed in with multiple trips.

A hunter can turn himself into a ground blind, as shown here using a Woolrich Camouflage blanket and a face mask.

A mini-drive can be accomplished by as few as two hunters, one walking with the wind at his back; the other posted along a game trail or path.

to nothing. It comes in a carrying case and flips open into three walls. The blind sets up against a tree or brush, hunter fully concealed within.

Another way to turn yourself into a ground blind is full camouflage, including face mask and gloves, then backing into brush or relying on a screen of foliage for concealment. The beauty of either method is finding a well-used trail or waterhole and being able to become invisible in mere minutes.

The Drive

The mini-drive is one hunter taking cover while his partner attempts to push game to him. A full-fledged drive is the same thing with more hunters.

Drives can work amazingly well, providing the setup is smart. That means deciding correctly where the waiter waits and the pusher pushes. For example, my partners and I managed to fill deer tags on a depredation hunt by having one rifleman wait along a well-used trail while two zig-zagged through the thicket in his direction. The pusher need not make a lot of noise. I've found that allowing game to purposely catch my scent moves them. The stump-sitter takes a position where he can see incoming animals, while the pusher meanders quietly toward him, allowing human scent to carry on the breeze. It works.

Walking in the Stream

Another method—new to me—is walking in the stream. I got the idea from a pair of high-top waterproof RedHead boots from the BassPro Shop. In one special whitetail thicket I was frustrated by bucks jumping ahead of me and disappearing. I had the scent problem under control with detection powder plus a spray bottle. But there was no way to be quiet on that floor of woody debris.

However, if I walked right down the center of the stream that divided the thicket, there was no way deer could hear me coming. I'd pace a bit, look into the growth ahead with binoculars, move a little more, glass again. Several times I came upon feeding whitetails that had no idea I was on the planet, let alone 50 yards away.

Snowtracking

Common sense says that if we find fresh tracks in the snow (or on any ground that will hold them) all we have to do is follow and buck, bull or boar will be waiting at the other end. But most of the time this is not what happens.

Why not? Because game animals are aware of their back trails. Deer and other game are sensitive to being followed. The only good luck I've had snowtracking is locating the trail, staying directly on it for a little while, then taking off at an angle, the idea being to get ahead of the game. More than once I've moved ahead and looked back to find the animal or herd looking directly back on its trail.

Scents and Lures

Many wild animals live by their noses. Even desert, High Plains and Badlands mule deer, which use eyes first to detect an intruder, count on their noses when bedded down in cool draws and pockets. Scents can be used to create an artificial trail from feeding ground to tree stand or ground blind. The hunter must know the general movement of game in the area before this will work.

Cover scents are another story. I was concealed one time in a ground blind. Twice a herd of deer came in, two mature bucks with does. While neither buck was a heart-stopping trophy, one was better than average for that area and I wanted to take him home.

Introducing a new line of seasonings from Ducks Unlimited.

Enhance the flavor of meat, game and fish with our new Spices, Rubs & Marinades featuring Lawry's® Seasonings. You'll also be supporting wildlife habitat conservation through Ducks Unlimited. For a retailer, visit ducks.org.

Smokey Sweet Game Jerky

Any waterfowl or antlered game makes this a delicious and handy snack that can be enjoyed anytime.

1/2 cup Ducks Unlimited® Seasoned Hickory Marinade
1/2 cup Ducks Unlimited® Honey Teriyaki Marinade
1 quart game meat (12 oz.), thinly sliced
1 teaspoon Ducks Unlimited® Steak & Chop Seasoning & Rub

In large resealable plastic bag, combine the first three ingredients and mix well. Seal bag and refrigerate for at least 2 hours. Remove game and pat with paper towel to remove excess marinade. Place strips flat on a baking sheet and sprinkle Steak & Chop Seasoning & Rub over strips. Place in oven set at low temperature (below 180°F). Prop open oven door about 1-inch. Drying time varies from 4 to 6 hours. When done, jerky should bend but not break. Store in a tight-sealing container in a cool, dry place.

Makes 6 to 8 snack servings.   Prep. Time: 10 minutes
Marinate Time: at least 2 hours   Cook Time: 4 to 6 hours

Grilled Pepper Duck

The bold flavor of this hickory smoked duck is perfect for warm weather grilling.

1 1/2 cups Ducks Unlimited® Seasoned Hickory Marinade
3 tablespoons Ducks Unlimited® Steak & Chop
    Seasoning & Rub
2 large ducks, split in half along the backbone
2 green bell peppers, seeded and halved
1 large yellow onion, quartered

In extra large resealable plastic bag, combine Seasoned Hickory Marinade and Steak & Chop Seasoning & Rub. Place duck, peppers and onion in bag; seal. Marinate in refrigerator for 1 to 12 hours. Remove duck, peppers and onion from bag, discarding used marinade. Grill duck over medium-high heat for 8 to 10 minutes per side. Grill vegetables over medium-high heat until tender and slightly charred; then slice. Top duck with grilled peppers and onion.

Makes 4 servings.   Prep. Time: 15 minutes
Marinate time: 1 to 12 hours   Cook Time: 16 to 20 minutes

Citrus Baked Trout

Nothing beats the flavor of freshly caught trout and this delicious dish can be prepared streamside or in your oven.

2 tablespoons Ducks Unlimited® Lemon & Lime Pepper
   Seasoning & Rub
1 teaspoon Lawry's® Garlic Powder With Parsley
4 whole trout, cleaned and dressed (12 to 16 oz. each)
1/2 red onion, sliced into 8 thin slices and separated into rings
2 medium oranges, sliced into 6 slices each
4 tablespoons butter
4 pieces butcher string (3 feet long each)

Sprinkle Lemon & Lime Pepper Seasoning & Rub and Garlic Powder With Parsley on inside and outside of each fish. Place 3 onion rings, 3 orange slices and 1 tablespoon butter inside each fish. Tie string snugly around each fish to secure stuffing and tie off string at ends. Place fish in shallow baking dish and bake in a preheated 400°F oven until fish is lightly browned, about 15 to 18 minutes. Remove string and serve.

Makes 4 servings.   Prep. Time: 10 minutes
Cook Time: 15 to 18 minutes

But before I could draw my Pronghorn Ferret recurve bow, the herd stopped, turned and headed back the way it had come. I was absolutely hidden. The blind had been set up for days and tracks around it proved that the deer were not afraid of it. Those animals scented my presence. I applied cover scent. Next time, the same herd strolled right in. I had a shot at 30 paces. What happened? I missed. The limb of my bow caught one wall of the blind as I drew. Anyway, that's my excuse for the errant arrow.

Calling Game

On a turkey hunt in Kentucky I witnessed the calling skills of dedicated gobbler hunters. Everyone knows that calls are ideal for these big birds, and of course for elk. But what remains unpopular is calling antelope. I don't know why. I have a Lohman antelope call that has Pied Pipered a number of bucks in close. The call works best during the rut, which is OK because many antelope seasons occur at that time.

Calls run from rattling antlers to grunt tubes to birch bark moose megaphones. It's easy to get an entire calling education with videos and recording tapes as well as the good instructions that come with the calls themselves.

I have a raft of calls and use them often. I've had deer walk up within bow range, elk come in to investigate, and wild turkeys either answer to let me know where they were or come in.

Moose, elk or javelina calls can work even for quail and dove or pronghorn antelope. My daughter Nicole was in her teen years when she headed into the Wyoming high rolling sagebrush hills to gather a buck and two doe antelope. Her tags were filled in one day, partly due to a Lohman Antelope Challenge call.

I learned to use the call not only from an audiotape and written instructions provided by the company, but also from listening to rutting bucks bark and chatter. Interestingly, part one of the call is the alarm cry—Wow! If that, and only that, is sounded, Mr. Pronghorn skips away with raised rump hairs to show his disdain. However, add part two, a Chuck! Chuck! Chuck! Chuck! and a rutting buck may come right in, as one did for Nicole. Interestingly, two does were drawn in as well. She had her three tags filled from one location. All because of a call.

Decoys

There are endless decoys that work. Goose and duck decoys are among the most obvious. However, as a bowhunter I've even had luck with a dove decoy. Wild turkeys often investigate a decoy when they will not come any closer to a call. Decoys work for deer and antelope, too. I've pulled antelope in by calling first then holding up a set of fake horns.

One of the most amazing exhibitions of decoying I've witnessed, and only on the TV screen, was decoying moose with pretend antlers. The biologist explained that moose rely heavily on identification through antler observation. Her words were proved on camera.

Going Guided

A true hunter learns his territory and knows how to find game in it. But there is nothing wrong with going guided and I have. For example, Tenderfoot Outfitters in Gunnison, Co., puts on a fine elk and mule deer hunt, along with a little fishing on the side. The guides running this show are extremely aware of taking care of the meat. All guides I know are.

Calling game is an ancient practice. Today's commercial calls produce the right sound every time.

Decoys are another age-old hunting tool. These turkey decoys often serve to bring a gobbler in close.

Going guided means putting an expert's knowledge to use, such as Tim Stull, manager of Deer Creek Outfitters in Kentucky.

Hunting for Economy

When my family was young and growing we hunted big game for economy as well as good meat. Wyoming offered several tags per hunter and we had five in the family. Filling a freezer was a reality, especially when a couple elk were added to the collection.

However, most of the time hunting for big game meat is not a bargain. "Wild meat can cost a hundred dollars a pound!" We've heard that lament. And it can be true. No one who goes out of state, for example, purchasing an expensive non-resident big game license/tag can even entertain thoughts of the meat paying for the trip. We hunt for food. You bet.

But food is only part of the adventure. This is less true for small game, even fish. When the trip is close to home, either can pay off economically.

I've bagged my limit of ten cottontail rabbits a half-hour from the door. I had some of the best protein available for the cost of a little gasoline, a dozen or so 22 Long Rifle rounds, and a very reasonable small game license.

Near camp, I've caught a limit of trout that fed the whole crew with some left over for neighbors. If anyone has checked the cost per pound of fish in the supermarket these days they know it's easy to prove that the expense of light fishing tackle is overweighed by a good catch.

The food we hunt for is a bonus. It's not meant to be a mainstay. Most hunters get their supply of meat from the grocery store. But that does not take away from putting deer, elk, boar, antelope and other wild meat in the freezer. And if the carcass is large enough, it can provide meals for a good part of the year. We hunt because we love it. But the meat must always be a prime consideration. And it is.

Sam Fadala's Ten Tips for Bowhunters

1. Do not shoot at a game that is looking directly at you. It's too easy for the animal to "jump the string," which translates into dodging the arrow.

2. Never shoot at rapidly moving game. Great archers like Howard Hill could get away with this, judging the proper lead, but the rest of us are better off waiting for a slower moving or standing target.

3. Carry brightly colored ribbon to mark the trail after taking a shot. This way it's easy to go back to the last place that spoor was spotted. Pick the ribbon up afterwards rather than littering the landscape.

4. Of course use only sharp broadheads on big game.

5. Wait at least 30 minutes before trailing game after a shot. Very often a buck, bull, or boar will simply lie down and go to sleep if not pressured.

6. Use brightly colored fletching. It's much easier to locate the arrow for signs of a hit after a shot. Bright fletching also makes following the flight of the arrow much easier.

7. Don't follow directly on the trail of a big game animal after a shot. Walk to the side instead of obliterating sign that may be useful to double check later.

8. Remember that a well-hit buck, bull, or boar may move downhill. So if the trail is unclear, check for fresh tracks moving downcountry. But never forget to inspect the full circle where the animal stood at the shot.

9. Aim low on whitetails. They're notorious for crouching at the hiss of a shaft or slightest sound from the bow. By aiming a little low on the chest area, when the deer ducks it will drop down into the path of the arrow.

10. Carry a few extras in the field — glove, tab, release, especially a string. And don't forget any necessary tools to install a new string.

4

Ammo and Arrows for Meat Hunters

My brother got it right. He said that if a big game hunter, whether looking for deer in the rolling hills of Kentucky or elk at the timberline in Wyoming, wanted an insurance policy slung on his shoulder, he'd carry a scope-sighted high-power rifle. On the other hand, he confessed, if the same hunter desired a lifelong memory painted in colors of challenge with historical tinges and a true sense of accomplishment, that rifle would be a classic.

Most of the time I choose the classic. Over the years that has been a longbow, recurve, muzzleloader, 30-30, or most recently a Marlin 336 CB Cowboy chambered for the 38-55 Winchester cartridge.

Tools of the Harvest

Just as farmers must have implements to harvest crops, hunters must have tools to bring home the bacon, or in this case the venison. These tools range from primitive type bows to the most advanced long-range rifles of the new century.

But more to the point: It is the bullets, shot and arrows that fly from these tools that put game meat on the table. And so this chapter follows that trail…the ammunition and arrows that do the work, beginning with that tiny piece of shaped lead called an airgun pellet and ending with state of the craft bullets.

A lot will be left out—on purpose. Telling the whole story would require a book of its own. There have been literally hundreds of different projectiles all the way from stone arrowheads to bullets with holes running through them length-wise. An example of the latter being the Krnka, which has been brought back in modern form for muzzleloading and is known simply as "The Bullet."

One of the author's all-time favorite rifles is his Marlin 336 CB Cowboy in 38-55. Handloads out of this well-made rifle register just over 2,000 feet per second muzzle velocity with a 255-grain soft-point bullet.

Left: Another photo of the author's Marlin 336 CB Cowboy lever-action rifle chambered for the 38-55 Winchester cartridge.

Literally hundreds of different bullet designs have leaped from blueprint to reality. The Barnes XLC is one of the newer inventions.

Barren (without fawn) mule deer was taken on an antlerless-only deer tag in Wyoming. The author's Marlin 38-55 wasted no edible meat.

Airgun Pellets

When an uncle returned from Germany after World War II, he brought with him a Diana pellet rifle. I acquired that rifle as a young boy since the uncle was not a sport shooter. Too young to appreciate the fine workmanship and figured walnut stock, I ran the rifle through its paces, even loading that precision bore with steel BBs, sometimes three or four topped off with a small piece of toilet paper to hold them downbore—the shotgun effect, you might say. I learned to hunt with that pellet rifle.

Today, there are many sophisticated pellet rifles and pistols on the market. They can be extremely accurate. They are also deadly and must be handled with the same respect accorded any gun. Pellets in 17, 20, 22, and 25 caliber are readily available. All will put small game in the bag with headshots. Pellets are limited to close range, which can be a disadvantage. On the other hand silence and short-range allows pellet gun use where powder-driven bullets might prove either an annoyance, a hazard or both.

The 22 Short

I called Mr. Mullens the Louisiana Man. He, his wife and son KD had moved from the South to Yuma, Az., where I attended high school for four years. When KD and I met, the topic immediately turned to hunting. Since my father did not hunt, KD, his dad, and I became a threesome. If you couldn't eat it, you didn't shoot it. That's not necessarily the best policy with regard to rodents and varmints, but it was Mr. Mullens' rule and we followed it.

There was only one small game cartridge for the Louisiana Man—the 22 Short. Be it cottontail or bullfrog, one 29-grain 22 Short bullet from the man's ancient Remington Model 7 rolling block rifle did the job.

Later, I hunted with the 22 Short in hollow-point for small game. I still do sometimes, although 22 Long Rifle match ammo is my first choice. Under certain closer-range circumstances, however, the 22 Short, especially in the hollow-point version, is ideal for rabbits, squirrels and other small game.

The 22 rimfire cartridge remains one of the best meatmakers of all time, not only for small game, but also mountain grouse and partridge where allowed by law.

22 Long, Long Rifle

Today, my favorite small game rifle is the 22 rimfire regardless of form, single-shot to semi-auto. My favorite ammo is match grade. Yes, it costs more, but I like the extra accuracy. On cottontails, for example, it's usually a 10- to 12-shot expenditure for the 10 rabbit limit where I live. On the other hand, I've found no 22 Long Rifle ammo inaccurate or useless. So let the hunter choose and fire away. The 22 Long is also viable for small game with its 22 Short bullet in a 22 Long Rifle case.

I have found hyper-velocity 22 Long Rifle ammo unnecessary for small game, albeit excellent on varmints.

22 Magnum

The newest 17-caliber Hornady rimfire is interesting, accurate and varmint-worthy, although not ideal for collecting small game. A good marksman, however, will find it useful on wild turkeys up to javelina, where it is legal.

The 22 WMR—Winchester Magnum Rimfire—drifts on the same tide. It is more powerful than required for squirrels and rabbits, but fine for wild turkeys up to javelina.

German RWS 22 WMR ammo, while expensive, offers a little extra power. Its 40-grain bullet takes off at 2,150 feet per second muzzle velocity (fps mv) by my tests, where most American fodder runs closer to 1,900 fps mv.

There are many 22 WMR chambered rifles such as the returned Savage Favorite single-shot.

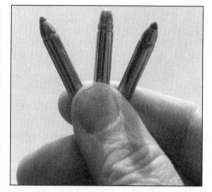

The 22 WMR (Winchester Magnum Rimfire) is absolutely unique in the 22 rimfire world. Today, it comes in various loads for specific functions, including wild turkey and javelina (where legal).

Larger Rimfires

There were dozens of larger-caliber rimfire cartridges in the 19th century. This is not so remarkable. After all, the 44 Flat was a milestone in cartridge development and it was a rimfire.

These larger-caliber rimfire rounds were useful for turkeys and similar game at close range in the hands of a good marksman, but their demise is understandable. The garden-variety 22 rimfire cartridge is sufficient.

Today, the cupboard is bare. I see no sign of change on the horizon. But the few who own an old rifle firing 32 rimfire can still find ammo to burn. I purchased a small cache from the Navy Arms Company some time ago and more recently from Old Western Scrounger.

Although the 22-250 was created for long-range varmint shooting, which is happening here with a Savage Model 12 rifle, it is legal for deer in some areas, as are other "hot" 22 centerfire cartridges.

The 25-20 and 32-20

It was wrong, in my opinion, but the 32-20 was once considered a deer cartridge. The 25-20 was more sensibly plied against smaller game. Today, the 32-20 is back, especially in the Thompson/Center single-shot pistol. It's a good turkey cartridge and can handle up to javelina with proper bullet placement.

The 25-20 is still around in Model 1892 Winchesters and a few other rifles. It's also a decent wild turkey/javelina round for hunters who stalk for close shots.

The 17 Remington

A Montana hunter that I know has taken several antelope and deer with one shot each using the 17 Remington with its tiny 25-grain bullet at more than 4,000 fps mv. The 17 Remington is legal in Montana for big game, illegal elsewhere. It's not a recommended meat hunter's cartridge, but obviously works in the hands of one careful hunter.

While hot 17s explode prairie dog size targets, very little meat loss is experienced in chest shots on larger animals. The 17 Remington is a varmint cartridge and best left as one, but it did require this mention.

Hot 22 Centerfires

A game warden told me that when called out to dispatch deer injured by vehicles on the highway he relied on a 220 Swift. "I never needed a second shot," he said.

I know hunters who use the 22-250 on deer regularly, even the smaller 222 Remington and 223. Admittedly, hot 22 centerfires can work on big game, but I cannot recommend them across the board for gathering a supply of winter protein.

The 6mm Clan

A friend's dad hunts only with the 243 Winchester for big game, including elk. Mr. Nelson's constant motto is "Get close or don't shoot at all." And so for him this little 6mm is a giant killer.

Smaller yet, the 6mm/222, a wildcat built by necking up the 222 Remington case to handle 24-caliber bullets, put many pounds of venison on the table for my family.

The 6mm Remington is in the same league as the 243 Winchester, with the 240 Weatherby a magnum of the clan capable of pushing a 100-grain bullet at 3,350 fps mv. A well-placed 24-caliber missile is a good meat projectile for deer-size game. Many hunters like its modest recoil.

The 25s

The 25s, from 250 Savage to 257 Weatherby, are all good big game rounds, especially for deer-sized animals. Good shots have taken elk and moose with 25s, too, but that does not make them ideal for that application.

I have a 25-284, which is ballistically a 25-06 that I trust on deer and antelope. With a 120-grain bullet at 3,000 fps mv, it's elk worthy, but only with perfect bullet placement.

On the other hand, the 257 Weatherby with a 120-grain bullet at up to 3,400 fps mv, achievable with IMR-4831 or IMR-7828 powders in a 26-inch barrel, will drop an elk on the spot—with the boiler room chest cavity strike.

The 6.5mm Family

The 6.5mm clan has always done well in the field. Norma tamed this size in the 6.5mm/284 wildcat into a factory number. On the other hand, I find the 260 Remington nothing more than a stepsister to the original 7mm-08 Remington. I cannot think of one thing that it can do that the larger-caliber 7mm-08 cannot do as well or better. Of course it works on big game with a 120-grain bullet at 3,000 fps mv. But I've loaded the 140-grain bullet in the 7mm-08 to the same velocity. To each his own. Anyone choosing the 260 Remington will probably be happy with it as long as the barrel is at least 22-inches long. Velocity in shorter barrels, by my own chronographing, is weak.

One of the big boys on the 6.5mm circuit is the 264 Winchester. My own tests with a 24-inch barrel achieved 3,100 fps mv with a 140-grain bullet—deadly, but not as impressive as the large case would suggest.

The author's 25-284 wildcat is a special rifle with Morrison Precision barrel and high-resolution Bausch & Lomb scope. It's put into service when "the chips are down."

The 270s

Out West the 270 Winchester ranks close to the famous 30-'06 in popularity. It is a true 7mm, whereas most 7mms are actually 7.2mm. With a 130-grain bullet at 3,100 fps mv, the 270 Winchester has done it all from whitetails to polar bears.

The 270 Weatherby Magnum is the 270 Winchester on steroids. It fires the same 130-grain bullet at 3,450-fps mv from a 26-inch barrel.

And now we have the 270 WSM—Winchester Short Magnum—which scoots the 130-grain pill away at 3,300 fps mv from a 24-inch barrel.

A new breed of big game cartridge was born with the short magnum clan. This is a 270 Winchester Short Magnum cartridge.

The 7mms

Little need be said about this bullet diameter because the facts have already been stated in countless success stories. The 7x57mm Mauser can drive a 140-grain bullet at 2,900 fps mv all the way to a 175-grain bullet at 2,550 fps mv. I've gotten such figures from a handy 22-inch barrel. One personal load with a 7mm-08 found the 175-grain bullet flying at a flat 2,700 fps mv, but the average is closer to 2,600 fps mv, which makes it an elk cartridge.

The ahead-of-its-time 284 Winchester remains a good big game cartridge in spite of lacking popularity.

The 280 Remington, essentially a 7mm/06, is another fine round.

Any of the 7mm magnums make ideal all-around cartridges for North America from whitetails to moose with 160-grain bullet leaving the launching pad at more than 3,100 fps mv.

The 30s

There are so many 30-caliber cartridges that a listing is impractical. The 300 Savage and 308 Winchester have proved capable for all big game, for example, while the 30-caliber magnums, such as the famous Weatherby, have dropped all manner of ponderous beasts worldwide. Personally, I remain a fan of the oh-so-common 30-30. I find it to be an excellent meat cartridge, taking deer-sized game cleanly without the fuss. My shots, however, are normally less than 150 yards.

Ron Cox fires a Savage Striker pistol chambered for the 300 Winchester Short Magnum cartridge, a powerful 30-caliber.

The 30-'06

The 30-'06 Springfield remains a premier all-around cartridge. Ballistically, it's superior to the 270 Winchester. This is not sentiment for the old gal, but rather entirely provable with a chronograph. A meat hunter carrying a 30-'06 with 150-grain or 180-grain ammo is never making a mistake. I've pushed 150-grain bullets at 3,000 fps mv in the old '06 and 220-grain bullets at 2,600 fps mv in the same rifle. That's quite a spread.

Over 30-Caliber

Elmer Keith ranked with Jack O'Connor in popularity among American gun writers for many years. He was a big bullet man. Keith was right about projectile diameter increasing delivered energy to the target, all other aspects being equal. For example, I once took on an involved project—testing various calibers all built on the 30-'06 case from 6mm to 375. The 375/06 produced the highest power in my testing, although due to its high ballistic coefficient, the 338/06 had higher remaining energy at 300 yards.

From 8mms to 45s and larger, the bigger bores do the job, but the average meat hunter gets by with 30s and smaller. Regardless, larger-bore rifles are game meat getters.

This coming hunting season my major rifle will be a Marlin 336 CB Cowboy chambered for the 1884-designed 38-55 cartridge. I have total confidence in the cartridge firing handloaded 255-grain bullets at 2,020 fps mv against all the big game on my list from javelina to elk.

The Handguns

Most hunters will use rifles to collect wild meat. That is why this chapter was dedicated to long guns. However, there is no doubt that good hunters everywhere have taken all manner of game—even elephants—with handguns. Handgun cartridges range widely, right up to the 45-70.

Muzzleloaders

Muzzleloaders for big game blazed their own clear trail marked with the modern in-line rifle, mostly 50-caliber, plus shotguns capable of heavy shot and powder charges. The original idea of following the tracks of Dan'l Boone and Davy Crockett has long been abandoned for guns that closely resemble modern firearms.

The trend began when hunters discovered the many special blackpowder-only opportunities available. The majority of these sportsmen were not interested in carrying long-barreled original-like firearms. Several companies answered their requests for more practical rifles and shotguns.

Caliber 50 is a wise choice for big game, although 54 is better for round ball shooting. The round ball gains mass out of proportion with caliber. So while a 50-caliber ball runs around 180-grains weight, a 54 can go 230 grains.

The sootburning shotgun is capable of delivering a terrific wallop. Knight's 12-gauge, for example, is allowed as high as two ounces of shot behind a strong powder charge. Today's choked muzzleloading shotguns produce dense patterns.

Shotguns

Rifles are for small game and big game, but most birds are put in the pot with the scattergun. Exceptions are mountain grouse and, in some locations, the wild turkey.

Waterfowl must be hunted with the shotgun, with the rare exception of archers like the late Ben Pearson who took ducks out of the air with arrows.

The upshot of shotguns is shot. Factories are producing the best shotgun shells with the most authority in the history of the industry. I recently took possession of Federal's Premium Tungsten-Iron High Velocity load. Muzzle velocity is 1,400 feet per second. My samples were in 12 gauge, 3-inch, Nos. 4 and BB shot sizes. Tungsten-Iron shot is 94 percent as dense as lead. It is also hard so pellets do not mash down in the choke. Therefore, there are no little discs winging away like flying saucers. Patterns of 90 percent at 40 yards are realized from proper chokes. These loads have 6-petal protective shot cups but remain intended for barrels designed for steel shot. It's possible to score (damage) other barrels. **A special warning:** Check your birds for shot content. You don't want to crunch down on a Tungsten-Iron pellet!

As with all modern ammo, today's shotgun shells are the best the world has ever seen—and in a huge variety of loads.

On a Kentucky wild turkey hunt, my shotshells were 12-gauge, 3-inch containing two ounces of shot, absolutely unheard of in times past when the 1¹⁄₄-ounce 12-gauge shotshell load was considered heavy. Hunters are learning to manage steel shot better, too, with chokes that produce good patterns.

Other shot materials have also come along. Bismuth, for example, is legal for waterfowl because it's non-toxic, but shoots like lead. Meat hunters going with shotguns today have nothing more to worry about than choosing the load best suited to the quarry. Today's shotgun slugs are better than ever with guns made to fire them accurately.

As for buckshot, I tested various types in the past without much success on targets. Too few pellets struck the mark. There is, however, a buckshot load from Polywad, Inc. (800-998-0669) that is showing great promise. The largest buckshot has no more punch per pellet than a muzzleloading squirrel rifle and would be illegal for big game hunting in most places. Multiple hits are required for lethality, and that is what the Polywad buckshot load promises.

Bows and Arrows

Bowhunting has claimed a giant share of the field for several decades. Interestingly, the longbow and recurve have returned in surprising numbers. My informal survey at a Colorado state gathering showed the split to be close to 50/50. Likewise at similar state meets in Arizona and Wyoming. Of course the compound remains king across the board. The compound bow is to archery what the modern muzzleloader is to blackpowder shooting.

Regardless, I turned back to traditional tackle. My bow that will see the most action is from master bowyer Herb Meland of Casper, Wyo.—his Ferret IV with all-glass laminated limbs. It's smooth-drawing, silent-shooting, no stack, and I feel zero handicap with it.

While the compound is without doubt high-tech with sights, mechanical release and high let-off, a practiced longbow or recurve hunter can put his arrow right where

The bow and arrow has always been a siginificant game harvesting tool and it still is.

he wants it, fluidly, quickly, every time. Besides—and this is a personal observation—shooting traditional is a lot more fun. Those dedicated to practice will do well with a stick. Hunters who don't have the inclination or time should stay with the modern mechanical bow.

Arrows

Many different arrow types are good for hunting. The aluminum shaft with the famous Easton name is extremely accurate and reliable. Today we have carbon arrows that fly fast and true.

And there are still excellent shafts made of wood. I have used them all. In longbows and recurves, wood seems appropriate. The two types I prefer are Port 0rford cedar and Sitka spruce. I find no difference in how either flies or penetrates.

After a long stalk, I fired a wooden arrow at an antelope buck. The shaft sailed off toward the horizon. I thought I had missed, the arrow passed through so cleanly.

Arrowheads

Personal, perhaps, but I find no reason for the open-up mechanical broadhead to exist. The idea is shooting a target point that opens up into a head on contact with the game.

While great success has been amassed with open-up mechanical heads, there have been massive failures as well. I consider any of the good fixed-blade heads superior.

I can prove that the non-mechanical arrowheads I shoot are extremely accurate. A couple seasons ago I let loose an arrow at a mule deer buck. The deer turned at the same instant. That buck might have gotten away, but instead it traveled only 50 yards before piling up. I credit the four-blade Coyote II broadhead for a happy ending.

Bullet Construction

In a perfec.t world, bullet construction would have little to do with hunting for meat. Fast-opening projectiles would prevail always. There would be no concern for penetration or bone-breaking ability, the so-called mushroom effect working in the chest cavity to put game down pronto.

Not all bullets end up in the boiler room. That's why every bullet-making company in the world has its own design with special construction. Choice is based on which bullet shoots best in a specific rifle.

The Meat Hunter's Goal

A fine-line balance is ideal—the game, from squirrel to moose—goes down quickly with one bullet or one arrow. At the same time, the meat is saved. The cliché about no free lunch rings true, however.

Just as you can't make an omelet without breaking eggs, you can't drop game without displacing tissue. That's why placement is always paramount. Even a 22 rimfire bullet can spoil a lot of meat when plunked into the plump hindquarters of rabbit or squirrel. Likewise a broadhead arrow.

Match the projectile to the game. That's the best motto. It works from airgun pellets to shotgun shells, to big game bullets of all calibers as well as broadheads.

5

Field and Camp Cutlery

A knife is just a knife? No way. Knives are much more than tools, although of course cutting is their major function. These knives are customs, second from the bottom one of the author's built by Herb Meland of Casper, Wyoming.

This chapter is divided into two distinct parts, field cutlery and camp cutlery because the two are different, yet closely related. But first, a few general comments on the most important piece of equipment in field or camp—the knife.

Knives—General Comments

A knife is a knife is a knife. No way! A friend's wife called for a little assistance. "You won't believe this, but Joe wants another knife for his birthday. He has a dozen already. What would he do with another? And by the way, where do I find a custom knife?"

Of course Joe wanted another cutting edge. Sportspeople and cooks can never have too many knives. That's because they vary tremendously, not only in quality and design, but also materials and especially *function*.

Joe's small request cost his wife $200. And worth it—a lifetime investment he'll pass on to one of his sons. His handmade knife was personally designed for fieldwork by an expert bladesmith. Fortunately, however, hardworking first-class knives are available for a lot less *dinero*.

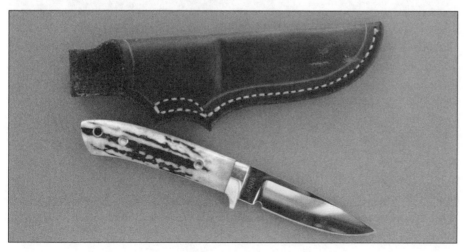

Another custom knife owned by the author is a Wayne Depperschmidt creation. There is nothing ordinary about a knife like this one.

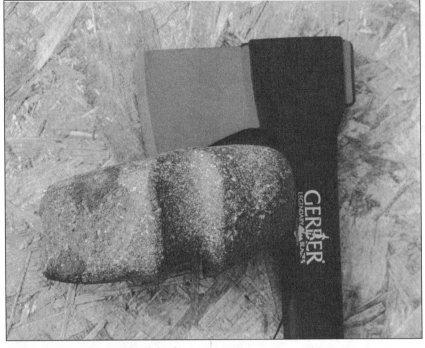

Be it a knife or a hatchet, its major function is serving as a wedge parting a medium. The ancient axe head on the left and the high-grade modern hand axe on the right share this common function.

What a Knife Does

The knife blade is a wedge designed to divide whatever it cuts into. Even the thinnest knife blade works this way. Function is the reason there are so many different knife styles. One type cannot do it all, or at least not well.

Imagine preparing a quail with a large fixed blade hunting knife, or trying to skin a big game animal with a filet knife. Both jobs may be accomplished, but not easily, not well, and in fact not even safely with the wrong knives.

Design Equals Function

The most important aspect of a knife, aside from quality, is design. However, this can sometimes be overemphasized. A friend insists, "I can only work with a drop point knife." If I handed him a knife with blade and tang on the same plane—no drop in the point at all—my amigo would carry on just fine. On the other hand, a skinning knife is one thing, a field dressing hunting knife another and a filet knife entirely different from the first two.

Knife designs vary in accord with the work they were intended to perform. There are literally a few hundred designs. Only three receive attention here: fixed blade, folders and jackknifes, with mention of customs. Each has its own strong points and specific uses.

Design equals function, but sometimes a knife can accomplish multiple tasks. This well-designed Benchmade folding knife can field dress a rabbit in the morning and an elk in the afternoon.

Design equals function. This excellent Cold Steel knife is made for heavy-duty work. It was used here to cut kindling for a campfire.

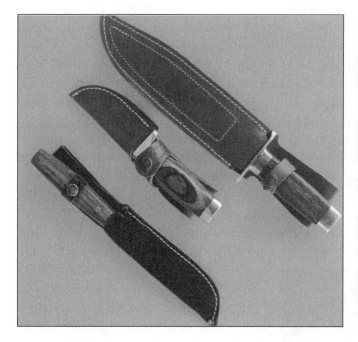

Field Cutlery

The Hunting Knife (Fixed Blade) | For our purposes the hunting knife is fixed blade of medium to large size. It has long been known as a sheath knife because it demands a sheath or scabbard to prevent the owner from cutting himself or his gear.

The design goes back to the Stone Age. The 5,300-year-old Iceman had a fixed blade flint knife in a protective sheath. Mountain men heading west to collect fame (few did) and fortune (forget it) found adventure (only a handful lived to return home). But sure as rain falls in Juneau, these trappers relied on the fixed blade knife every day, even making the name Green River, a type of blade, famous in history.

While some tales of defending against bears and two-legged attackers with a blade are fanciful, there is no doubt that one extra large knife was considered a deadly weapon. It was the Bowie, outlawed in some places as a dangerous implement of death and destruction.

Butcher knives were also popular during westward expansion. These were cheap blades with riveted-on wooden handles. Crude, yes, but they served many purposes, including heavy trade with Indians of the Far West.

Hunting Knife Uses | Size is both an advantage and disadvantage in a medium to large fixed blade hunting knife. It's too big to put in a pocket, which may be negative, but on the other hand it's large enough to work hard, surviving considerable application of force. Fixed-blade hunting knives are also long enough to core out a big game animal by reaching far enough into the canal to loosen entrails from their hold.

And nothing can happen to a quality hunting knife with the exceptions of losing or breaking it. Admittedly, I've yet to see my first folder or jack-knife come apart either, but there's no doubt that the hunting knife is more rugged. And it can be used more widely than smaller knives, performing chores other than field dressing game.

Size often dictates function. While this large Bowie from the Traditions Company is hardly ideal for field dressing game it does a lot of work in both the home and camp kitchen serving as a stout chef's knife.

Above left: Fixed blade knife simply means that the blade does not fold into the handle. These three are from the Traditions Company.

A small folding knife like this is excellent for upland game birds as well as small game animals.

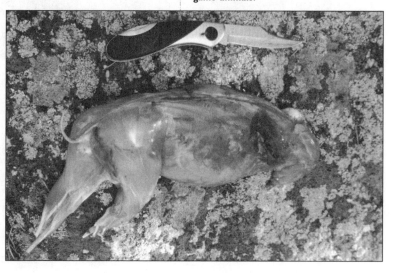

The Custom Hunting Knife | Some custom hunting knives are intended for collection only. They are costly and decorative. Other custom knives are the opposite. They're meant to do all kinds of hard work. I own two rugged custom knives. Herb Meland, better known for his superb longbows and all-glass limb recurves from Pronghorn Custom Bows shop in Casper, Wyo., crafted one. The other came from the capable hands of Wayne Depperschmidt, a Colorado knifemaker.

Meland's knife was designed for very heavy use on big game of the elk and moose class. I once field dressed a moose with this big knife, including reducing the carcass to quarters for packing to camp without once touching up the blade.

Wayne's knife was meant for all-around field dressing of big game. It resides in my pack ready for action on all kinds of game.

The Folder | While compact pocketknives and jackknives are superb for small game in the field, larger folders are better for big game. These knives generally have

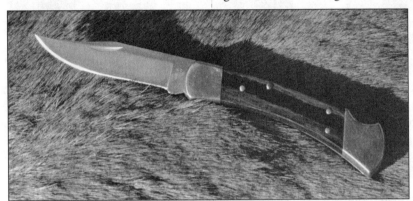

The famous Buck Model 110 is a rugged folding knife that has been used by many hunters for decades.

single strong blades capable of dressing all big game. They normally do not take the place of fixed blade knives. However, there are many hunters who rely solely on larger folders for all fieldwork. It's true that a good folder can do it all, but I still like the added potential of a fixed blade knife plus folder.

The Jackknife | The jackknife—also known as the pocketknife—for our purposes is small enough to fit neatly in a pocket or zipper pouch of a fanny pack or daypack. It usually incorporates two or more blades. Folders, on the other hand, and again for our specific purposes only, are larger and usually have only one blade. They serve both in the field and in camp. More on the jackknife in the camp blades section that follows.

The Pack or Field Saw | This is not the meat saw of Chapter 10 that is intended for processing. The pack saw is portable and designed for cutting through bone. It also works on meat in the field, although in no way replaces a knife. It cuts the

This high-grade field cutlery kit includes a pack saw for sectioning big game to manageable proportions.

sternum right down the center to separate front quarters. It's good also for sawing away rib cages that do not have enough meat to be worth carrying to camp. Saws are not wedges. Saw blades rasp media apart with teeth like a shark.

The major emphasis of the field or pack saw is size. It must be compact for carrying, especially in a fanny pack or daypack. Sometimes the field saw has two sets of teeth, one on each side of the blade, coarse for cutting wood and other camp chores, finer for meat and bone.

Small Game, Birds and Field Cutlery | I have found no need for anything other than a jackknife (pocketknife) or small folder for field dressing rabbits, squirrels and birds of all descriptions and size, including the wild turkey.

Chapter 8 on field dressing these edibles reveals why the little blade works so well.

The most important criterion is medium blade thickness—neither thick nor thin—and a sharp point. Portability is also important. It's nice to simply reach into a pocket to retrieve a little knife for the job at hand. Today, there are many single-blade compact folders that are smaller than some jackknives, so specific type is not important.

Blade configuration, however, is important, especially that sharp point for working in the vent area of birds or small game. The blade also needs modest rigidity. A knife with flexible blade is wrong for this work—and easy to get cut with.

Big Game Field Cutlery in General | "I can do an elk with a pocketknife." Good brag and often true. There are some hunters who are willing to field dress a big game animal with a knife better suited to paring fingernails. But not me and hopefully not you. Using such knives is a stunt. Medium to large folders and fixed blades big-game knives are practical for field dressing deer, elk and other big game.

Two seasons before writing these words I had the privilege of living in the mountains for a full month of hunting. My backpack on this long hunt had three knives:

One is a Benchmark folder with high-tech synthetic panels and blade with very sharp point. This lightweight, thin knife fit into the zipper pocket on the back of my pack, easy to get to, a feather to carry. It worked for small camp edibles such as cottontails and mountain grouse as well as antelope and deer.

The other two knives were fixed blades. One was a lightweight space age Gerber Gator with blade shape conducive to skinning since some of the meat processing was to take place in camp. The other was the custom Wayne Depperschmidt knife noted earlier.

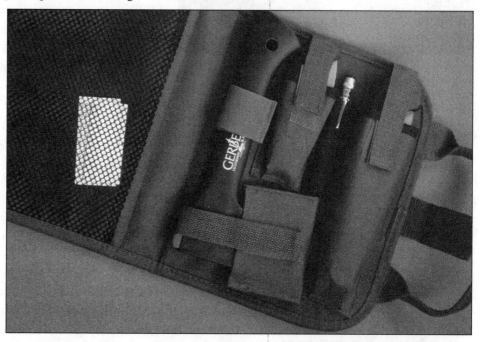

A full-fledged field big game dressing kit such as this one from Gerber can reduce a bull elk to packing size in relatively short order.

While the folder was ideal for camp game, antelope and deer, the fixed blades did most of the work on elk.

Specifics on these three knives are not important because the individual will elect styles that suit his or her own desires and needs.

The Field Big Game Dressing Kit | My full-fledged big game field dressing kit is from Gerber. It has a knife, small axe, game saw and sharpener. The knife is a skinner because the kit is intended to reduce the carcass to carrying dimensions, which means removing the hide. The small axe is for whacking through large bone. The saw is for cutting smaller bone. Meanwhile, the combination of skinning knife, meat saw, and axe works to separate edible meat from leave-behind scraps.

An axe, like a knife, is a wedge. It's made to part media with shattering blows. Consider rib cages. The rib cage of a fat mature whitetail buck is a delicacy for others and me. I have enjoyed these tasty spiced ribs cooked over hot coals. But the rib cage of the antelope is almost meatless. It's best left behind as food for coyotes and other animals.

The Caping Knife | This is a very small knife designed for one specific function: removing the cape from a big game animal headed for the taxidermy shop. The cape is that portion of the hide that includes the head and neck of the animal down to the mid-shoulder. It's a good idea to go longer than necessary when caping a trophy. All the way to mid-section is not too long.

Camp Cutlery

Sometimes a knife intended for one purpose is great for another. This Mini-Tac from Cold Steel is a tactical knife, but the author found it ideal in both camp and home kitchen.

As with field cutlery, state of the art camp cutlery is the best ever, partly due to improved metals, but also enhanced designs. Anyone doubting these words is invited to compare the typical hunting knife, game saw or hand axe of yesteryear with what we have now.

The Jackknife | Not to tell the tale twice, but the jackknife serves as well in camp as it does in the field on small game. It comes in so many styles that whole books are devoted to it. For us, however, the jackknife is pocket-ready, usually with multiple blades.

Invented, some say, by Jacques De Liege in the 17th century, hence *Jacque knife*, there is no end to its use. Jackknives were even carried to the moon. They're good for many camp chores: work on a piece of leather, open a food can, pick out a wood sliver in a finger, cut food on the dinner plate, whittle wood into kindling, repair a hangnail, trim a piece of canvas for a tent patch, clean a fish—let your imagination run wild. The list goes on and on.

What it's not good for, but is often used as, is a screwdriver, especially on bolts and screws that have loosened on everything from rifle to camp cot.

The Swiss Knife | Everyone has seen a Swiss Army Knife. This knife style has been around for decades. The theme is a knife that fits into a pocket but has more than just blades. It has can openers, screwdrivers and other small but useful implements. I don't believe I've walked into a cutlery shop that didn't have a Swiss model for sale.

The downside of the Swiss Knife is size and bulk. I've encountered some that would be an unhandy lump in a pocket. However, in camp this historic knife is very much at home. It prevents the misuse of a jackknife. No sense in bending a jackknife blade trying to make a screwdriver out of it when the Swiss Knife sports one or more.

The Multi-Tool | On the same general theme as the Swiss Knife, the multi-tool also incorporates many different implements in one unit. These are seen in holsters riding about the waistband of various workers. But they're also good tools for camp, although I would not carry one on the trail except for extended camps in the outback.

Along with a cutting edge, the multi-tool may have scissors, screwdrivers, saws, pliers, can openers and other implements. Various companies offer multi-tools, which may be found not only in knife shops but also sporting good stores as well as Wal-Mart and similar outlets.

Many Blades, One Knife | Over the years there have been a number of knives with multiple blades sharing a common handle. The current Bear Cutlery model comes to mind. The blades attach for work in various ways. In camp, these can come in handy with blades for different jobs from peeling an onion to cutting bread to slicing off a few elk medallions for supper.

The Hand Axe | No camp of any duration should be without a hand axe. The models I happen to use are both from Gerber, one in cruiser length, the other shorter. The hand axe is useful not only for whittling down a bit of wood for the evening fire, but also for making things such as tent pegs.

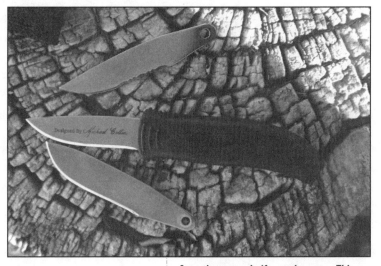

Sometimes one knife can be many. This one from Bear Cutlery is such a knife—one handle, three blades.

Hand axes go back eons, often found in the hands of soldiers. The Lewis & Clark Expedition of the 19th century found many hand axes on that long trail of discovery. The Iceman had a hand axe with a copper blade.

One Man's Camp Knife | By chance I had a Mini-Tac from Special Projects around my neck in camp. It became a favored camp knife. Compact, it slides out of its high-impact scabbard holster in a flash. Moreover, its thin blade is ideal for many camp chores. While the tanto shape blade spells tactical, the Mini-Tac is ideal for peeling potatoes, slicing fruit, preparing fish and meat for cooking and other chores. I recommend one for camp.

Go For Quality | I've seen them. You've seen them. Knives for a dollar or so, especially little folders on the checkout counter at hardware stores. Buy these for rough work. Put one or more in your toolbox. But go for quality when choosing a knife for field and camp duty.

One good reason to buy quality is longevity. One time I forgot my Buck 110 folder on a bush after field dressing an antelope buck. I didn't notice the loss until I was home putting my gear away. I intended to go back, but soon winter set in. That knife rested on a bush, covered with snow, until spring when a son went back after it. He found the knife right where I'd left it. I still have that knife and it's as good as new.

Additionally, the better blade does a better job. It may not always sharpen as easily as some, but it will stay sharper longer and cut keener. In the long run, the quality knife is the better buy. A good knife is a lifetime-plus investment.

Keeping them Sharp with the Right Tools

There are two broad categories of knife sharpening tools—compact and full-size. My long-range camps have one full-size unit, but it's impractical to carry a full-fledged knife-sharpening instrument into the field.

There are various ways to maintain a sharp knife-edge. This Buck unit is one of the best. Three stones rotate into position, including fine for the final touch.

The latest Buck Knives catalog reveals a multitude of handy knife sharpeners for the field. They all work well.

After the hunt, it's time to use one of the larger tools that holds the blade at the correct angle while stones of various grades grind on the edge.

Angle is vital to sharpening a knife. This Catco sharpener is designed to maintain the edge of the knife at a precise angle.

A Multi-Method for Knife Sharpening | I use more than one tool to sharpen my knives. Realtors say that the three most important aspects in selling a piece of property are location, location and location. The three most important points in sharpening a knife blade are angle, angle and angle.

Some people are good at sharpening knives by eye. I'd like to be, too, but I am not. That's why I use a device that constantly maintains the angle of the edge with relation to the sharpening stone.

Now that we have good field and camp cutlery tools, let's apply them in the next chapters on dressing big game, small game and birds.

Mini-Glossary of Knife Terms

Back of Blade | Opposite side of the cutting edge of a knife blade.

Bolster | The metal end of the folding knife.

Boning Knife | Knife with thin, narrow blade for removing meat from bones.

Camp Knife | Large hunting knife, capable fo choping as well as cutting.

Clip-Point | Blade shape where top front of point is a concave cutout, making a very sharp point.

Drop-Point | Forward part of blade falls below the level of the handle.

False Edge | Back of blade is sharpened part-way.

Fixed Blade | Blade doesn't fold into handle, but always remains rigid.

Folding Knife | Generally with one blade that folds into handle.

Gut Hook | There are at least two kinds of gut hooks incorporated into knives. One is shaped like a wire with a sharply and tightly curved end. The hooked end is used on small game and birds to withdraw viscera. The other type of gut hook is integral to a knife blade. It is used mainly to cut the incision on the underside of big game for the evacuation of viscera.

Guard of Knife | A projection that stops the hand from going forward of the handle.

Handle Scales | The side panels ona jackknife or pocketknife.

Lockback Knife | A folding knife whose blade locks in place.

Pommel | A metal (usually) protective cover ont heend of a knife handle.

Sheepsfoot Blade | Short blade with a straight edge and a rounded blade back.

Spear-Point | Both top and bottom of the blade are rounded to the point.

Spey Blade | Thin, sharp blade with rounded point.

Tang | The portion of the knife blade that runs back through the handle, all or part-way.

Tanto | Short Japanese sword, but now a popular knife blade style with a squared front portion of the blade.

6

Field Dressing Big Game

Alabama was the scene, whitetail hunting the game. The lodge where I hunted reminded me of Africa in one way: No game was dressed in the field. I understood the logic in Zimbabwe. Remains left over from field dressing drew hyenas from miles away. But why follow the same practice in Alabama?

The reason, I learned, was the specific method of processing preferred by the professional butcher. His way included hanging the carcass intact with a few swift knife movements to expel the offal into a container for disposal.

I regard the aftermath of field dressing biodegradable material. It is not litter. Litter is beverage cans, plastic shopping bags, bottles, jars and other junk that Mother Earth will not take back. Wild animals use what remains after preparing a big game animal in the field. Anything not eaten by skunks, coyotes, badgers, buzzards, vultures, crows, ravens or other scavengers returns to the soil.

And so my method of field dressing big game happens where the name promises—in the field. The importance of proper field dressing cannot be overemphasized. Lousy care after the animal is tagged ensures lousy table fare. As with computers, it's garbage in, garbage out. Start with bad meat and odds are you'll end up with a bad meal.

A hunter inept in the art of field dressing his own game is incomplete in his skills. But the step-by-step process discussed in this chapter is not the only right way. The goal is simple: The properly field dressed carcass will be free of intestines, bladder, heart, liver, lungs and reproductive organs—the works. There will no digestive materials or dirt within the cavity. Major bloodshot tissue will be cut away.

But before we get to field dressing, a few other tips are in order.

Look Before You Leave

It's the right thing to do. The hunter shoots. He misses clean. He walks away. Wrong.

I was in the process of filling additional deer tags one season when I came upon a lone mule deer doe perfect for harvesting. The deer had no idea that I was on the same mountainside. A spot and stalk had worked: locating with binoculars, closing in for a good shot. Because of open ground, the opportunity would come from about 200 yards. I cranked the scope of the 308 up to full power, took careful aim, squeezed the trigger and. . . nothing.

The deer looked my way, then walked off. I watched through binoculars as she strolled leisurely toward a patch of forest. After covering a few hundred yards she toppled over. The 180-grain bullet fired that day was wrong for the 308, too hard. It passed through without much tissue disruption.

Had I not stayed with the animal visually, I may have lost a fine supply of prime venison. Always look after a shot. Walk to the last spot where the game stood. Check for body fluids, hair, anything that may indicate a hit. Move on only when certain that the miss really was a miss.

The Approach

At the shot a whitetail buck dropped so fast I thought I heard the thump when it hit the ground. There was no doubt that the buck was mine. As I approached, fired case remaining in the chamber, up jumped the deer. I worked the lever of the rifle, took aim and luckily put a second bullet where head and neck join—no lost meat.

How that buck got up and ran I cannot say. The bullet had expanded correctly, creating a wound channel completely through the chest cavity. If a well-hit animal can take off, imagine what one marginally hit can do.

The other reason for the cautious approach is the fact that a big game animal can kick a hunter into next Sunday. Walk up from the offside of downed game, not in front of it. I carry a walking stick. A few prods with the stick tell me if the animal is dispatched or not.

While a bird's eyes close when it's defunct, a mammal's eyes are open. Closed eyes on a mammal indicate that it could get up and take off. I check the eyes of a downed big game animal with binoculars from a little distance. Up closer, a long twig is useful in touching the open eye. If the eye twitches, the animal is not entirely finished.

The Meat-Saving Bullet

Saving meat is important. However, using a bullet that is too hard, thereby failing to expand, can mean lost game. As part of field care, an expanding bullet or very sharp broadhead is correct. Better to lose 10 pounds of meat than the whole carcass. And frangible bullets passing through the chest cavity don't harm edible meat.

Shoot Again

If after that first hit the animal remains on its feet for any length of time, put another bullet or arrow into the rib cage. Same story—better to take a chance on losing a few pounds of meat than watching the whole entrée flee over the hill.

Buried Arrowheads

Any arrow can break off in a carcass leaving the broadhead in the body somewhere. Care must be taken to find that head before it slices into a probing hand.

Darkness Falling

Should a game animal require following after a shot, which is normal for the usual arrow strike, the hunter must be careful. Leaning over a bowshot animal with a protruding broadhead has the potential of devastation.

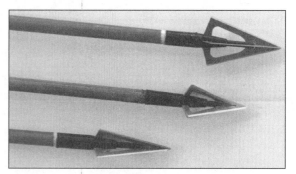

Be careful, especially when field dressing a game animal after dark. You don't want a tine in the eye and you don't want to find one of these Coyote broadheads with your hand.

Field Dressing Steps

1. Unload firearm. Set it aside where it will not be in the way. Likewise bows and arrows.

Set unloaded rifle aside before doing anything else. Wipe away any fluids from cape before taking photos of your prize.

2. Work game animal into position for field dressing: back to ground, belly up. Have game in position before removing any cutting instruments from pocket or pack.
3. Set up for safety. Position body directly over carcass with back legs facing behind to left and right. A helper must stand at the side so a slip of the knife can never touch him or her.
4. Lay out the compact first aid kit from fanny pack or daypack. Careful work prevents cuts, but just in case, there should be bandages and disinfectant handy. Wash a cut with soap and water first. Dry with sterile gauze. Apply disinfectant. Bandage to keep foreign matter out.
5. Eye protection—few of us think about placing lenses in front of our eyes while working on a carcass. After years of not doing so, I now have clear-lens safety glasses with me at all times in the field. My plan is getting into the habit of

Work from a safe position, not off balance. The knife that field dresses any game can also cut you. Here the first cut is being made on a mule deer buck to remove the reproductive organ.

using them not only when dressing game, but especially in night camp gathering wood where a twig can stab an eye.

6. I never used latex gloves. One of my hunting partners insisted on placing a few in my daypack. I use them now.

7. Bleeding the carcass comes next, but is it necessary? We know that a broadhead causes evacuation of body fluids. Likewise high-speed bullets, even those of the 30-30 class. Also, cutting the neck can spoil the cape if a mount is desired. Bleeding the carcass can't hurt, but in most cases, it won't do any good either.

8. Musk glands are best left alone. Metatarsals are far from the meat and will be discarded intact with the inedible lower legs. A special note on javelina: Hunters have been instructed for ages to remove the musk sac on the back of this animal. I did so until my partner John Doyle asked why I wanted to ruin the meat. He was right. By leaving the musk sac intact the tubules are not cut. Musk does not drain into the meat nor get on the knife blade. The sac comes away intact when the little hog is skinned. Musk glands may be removed later for use as lure, but not in field dressing.

Freeing the reproductive organ by cutting all along its full length close to the body.

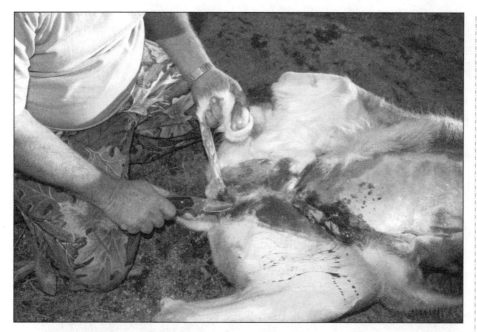

The entire reproductive organ is free now, as can be seen in this illustration.

9. The carcass is properly positioned and it's time to cut along the reproductive organ of the male animal. Do not cut deeply. Do not allow the point of the knife to slice into the abdominal cavity. Cut around the reproductive organ to separate it from the carcass. The organ is cut entirely free, but the tubes running from it remain intact. Female reproductive organs are removed automatically in the next step.

10. Free the lower intestine by circumventing the entire bung area with the knife blade. This is a coring-out process. Done correctly, the male reproductive organ remains with the lower intestine. The lower intestine is now free of the pelvic canal and female organs.

11. Next, insert the sharp point of the knife just under the skin and in front of the cored-out anal canal. The objective is to cut on the centerline from anal region all the way to the sternum (breastbone). *The blade does not penetrate the viscera!*

12. The belly *hide* is now skinned back out of the way until much of the abdominal cavity *skin* is exposed. The actual skin that retains the entrails is *not* cut.

13. Now it's time to make a centerline cut from the anal area to the sternum *just under the skin*. This cut exposes the entrails, but does not pierce them. After this long cut is made, the viscera are visible.

14. Remove much of the skin that once covered the viscera. This is inedible tissue. It's sliced away on both sides of the centerline cut, which now leaves the entrails easy to remove.

15. Gently pull the male reproductive organ through the anal canal. Care must be taken not to break the bladder. The organ remains intact with the viscera. When the viscera are removed, the organ, along with the urinary bladder, will come out intact.

The reproductive organ is free here but not removed. It will be removed with the coring out process. It's a good idea to skin the hide back fully from the abdomen (belly) of the animal to prevent cutting hair and also to allow a clear view of the tissue that has to be cut into or removed.

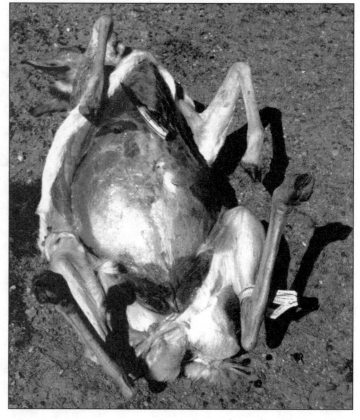

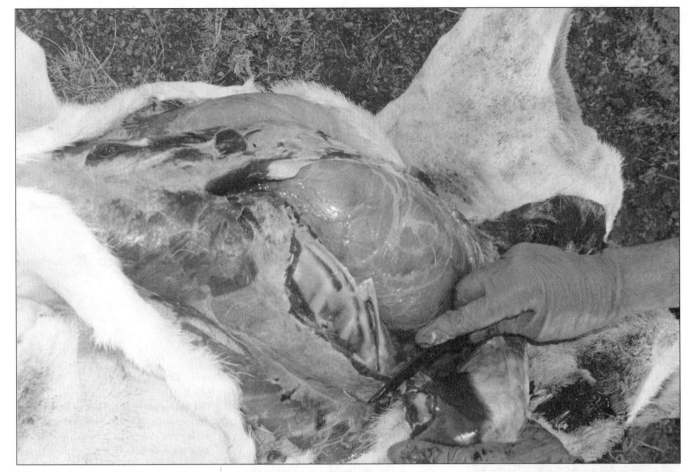

This shows how the skin that covered the belly is entirely removed with the knife blade. (Step 12)

Right: This is the coring out process where the intestine that runs through the pelvic canal is cut free from its walls. The reproductive organ will come out with the lower intestine. (Step 15)

Far right: Here the reproductive organ has been pulled, along with the lower intestine, intact, back through the pelvic canal. The organ and intestine are intact and uncut. Both will be discarded with the offal. (Step 16)

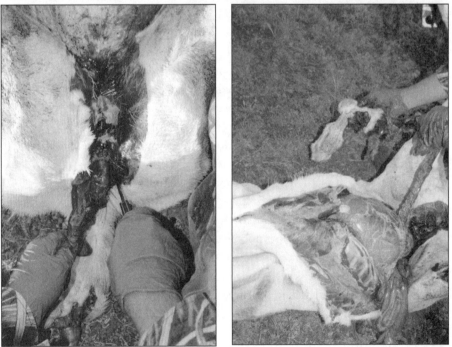

16. Turn the carcass sideways and spill viscera onto the ground. This step unloads the intestines and other offal.

17. The heart and lungs remain within the carcass separated by the diaphragm. If the hunter is going to get cut, it'll probably happen now because this step is blind; the cut is made by feel alone. With knife inside the carcass a cut is made

around the entire outer edge of the diaphragm. Now the heart and lung area is exposed. Reaching up fully into the chest cavity all the way to the throat area, the windpipe and esophagus are cut free so that heart, lungs and all can be pulled out. At this point lying on the ground next to the carcass is a complete visceral bundle—upper and lower intestine, stomach(s), gall bladder, urinary bladder, heart, liver, lungs, most of the windpipe—the works, intact. The liver is cut free from the offal. The gall bladder, looking like a tiny attached balloon, is carefully removed and discarded. The heart is cut free with pericardium (covering tissue) intact to protect it from dirt.

18. An optional step is sawing completely through the sternum instead of cutting through the diaphragm, dead center, thereby exposing heart, lungs, windpipe and esophagus. If the animal is not taxidermist bound, this option is acceptable.

19. Another option is splitting the pelvic bone, also called the aitch or cinch bone. This exposes the tissue that is attached to the reproductive organ and urinary bladder as well as lower (small) intestine, which are now carefully cut free. The aitchbone can be divided with a heavy knife blade or game saw. Beating the knife with a rock is common practice, but not necessarily good for the knife.

20. If extra water (or snow) is handy, rinsing out the entire body cavity is never a mistake at this point.

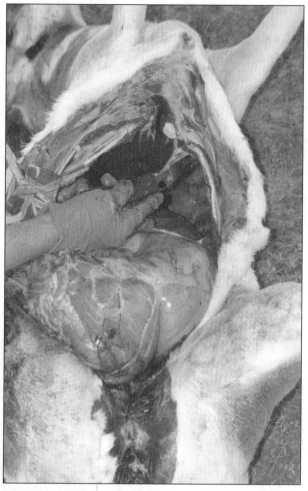

Now the diaphragm is cut free where it joins the walls of the body cavity. The diaphragm is the wall of tissue separating the heart/lung section from the abdominal cavity. It must be removed to get to the heart and lungs. (Step 17)

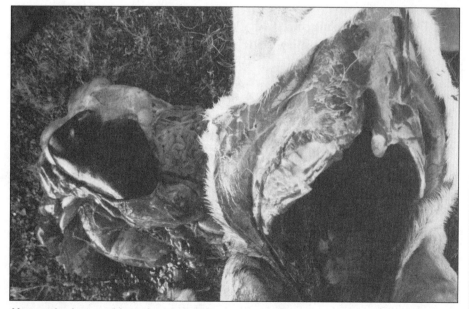

After cutting heart and lungs free the entire body cavity is emptied onto the ground. (Step 17)

If the liver is to be saved, be sure to carefully cut around the gall bladder and discard it.

If there's water available, wash out the body cavity and let the field dressed carcass drain for a while before attempting to pack it out.

21. Draining and cooling come next. Deer-sized animals can be easily turned over belly down, or with helping hands lifted up into a tree. Don't let dirt enter the cleaned-out cavity.

22. Cleaning up is next. This involves primarily the hunter. The area will be messy, but everything on the ground is biodegradable. Come back in a few days and this point will be proved.

23. Boning a carcass is ideal for the backpack hunter. Unfortunately, in some cases the law interferes with this process where evidence of sex must be maintained. Not using horses or ATVs, hunting on foot the old way, plus being willing to pack the meat out on your own back can bring the punishment of a fine. Where legal, however, boning, especially elk, moose, or any larger animal, saves the meat, leaving behind bones and hide. The animal is placed belly down, back up. A cut is made straight down the back from head to tail. The hide is then removed to either side of the carcass. From this point, the loins can be cut free, front shoulders removed, meat sliced from haunches, and so forth until nothing remains but a skeleton with viscera in it.

24. Quartering presents a similar legal problem. It's not easy to maintain evidence of sex on all four quarters plus head/hide. Quartering takes place after eviscerating the carcass. The carcass can be cut in half at the end of the loins. Then the two hindquarters are separated with a saw or hatchet right down the spine. With head/neck cut off, the two front quarters, with or without the rib cage, can also be divided with hatchet or saw.

24. Take care of the carcass by hanging in the shade, preferably in porous game bags to prevent attack by blowflies. It's sad to pass by hunting camps with game hanging in the sun, a practice indicating lack of knowledge or no respect for the meat. In warmer areas the carcass is hung by night, taken down by day and insulated with old sleeping bags.

25. In that aforementioned perfect world, all bullets and arrows would find their perfect mark. But sometimes it happens—the bad shot. As much of the affected area as possible, hide and tissue, should be cut off and discarded during field dressing. Trying to save damaged meat may end up spoiling the entire animal. Bad stuff simply has to be cut away and cast off. Ideally, the carcass will be washed thoroughly with water as soon as possible.

Conditions Vary

Antelope hunting is often done in warm weather. The carcass should be processed and packaged into the freezer as soon as possible. Likewise any other game hunted in warm weather.

On the other hand, it may be freezing. My sons and I went on a winter depredation hunt in Wyoming one year. With chill factor, it was 52 degrees below zero. Our three deer took a week to thaw out back home hanging in the garage before we could process them. The meat did not spoil.

Take Pride

Take pride in being a complete hunter, knowing not only how to find, stalk and tag game, but also how to field dress the big game carcass.

The buck has been field dressed with body cavity rinsed out and drained. Now it's time to tie it aboard the packframe for the trip to the vehicle.

7

Field Dressing Littler Edibles

We begin our hunting careers on small game and we end them with small game. As long as a hunter remains even mildly mobile he can harvest the smaller edibles. Brave physically challenged people do so very well, many of them also going after larger animals. Recall that small game means cottontails and squirrels—numbers one and two in popularity.

There are multitudes of other small edibles. But if a hunter can adequately manage to field dress these two gems he can handle the rest. Turtles, muskrats, bullfrogs, woodchucks, rockchucks, prairie dogs and similar critters are touched on in Chapter 15 on exotics.

Turtles fall out of the group for field dressing. After all, they're not mammals. Neither are bullfrogs, but they're easy to prepare in the field. We're only after the legs, leaving the rest for the midnight cleanup crew of skunks, raccoons, coyotes and other scavengers. Nothing biodegradable goes to waste in Mother Nature's outdoor kitchen.

A tree squirrel in early morning light has been carefully approached for a perfect meat-saving shot.

Above left: Author hunting cottontails with 28-gauge shotgun.

Above: One of author's favorite small game guns, a Smith & Wesson Model 41 shown with a brace of cottontails.

First the Right Tools

From Chapter 4, we know that 22 rimfires and shotguns are most-used and probably most appropriate for small game. Muzzleloading squirrel rifles are also ideal, especially caliber 32. (See Krause's *The Complete Blackpowder Handbook*.) Air rifles are also legal in some areas.

The bow is equally valuable for harvesting any small game animal (or for that matter, any exotic). In the winter I enjoy still-hunting snowfields for cottontails with longbow or recurve. I've also bowhunted tree squirrels.

A bow is perfect around ranch houses and other property being devastated by the sharp teeth of the rabbit. Broadheads are a good choice. I use older heads as well as those retired and exchanged for more effective models.

The 22 rimfire pistol makes a fine cottontail taker. Last season my Smith & Wesson Model 41 filled the frying pan with white meat on long big game hunts. I had just finished lessons with a former SWAT Team sniper who turned me into a fair handgun marksman, good enough for meat-saving bullet placement.

Shotguns require no special treatment here. All gauges work. I like No. 5 shot. Other hunters prefer No. 6 for small game.

Rabbits, Hares and Squirrels | Rabbits and hares are simple to field dress because they skin easily. Squirrels are a little more challenging. With either, the only thing to watch out for is hair. The fine hair floats around and can land on and attach to the carcass. A few hairs here and there cause no problem, however, because they're dismissed during the field cleaning process explained below.

Field Dressing Steps

1. Slip on those surgical gloves and roll up your sleeves. Domestic as well as big game animals are prone to fleas. Rabbits, hares, squirrels and other small game are no exception. Fleas are less of a problem in winter, though, because fleas abandon the defunct carcass when it's laid in the snow. With sleeves rolled up, gloves on, the hunter is ready to go to work. Use a small knife, preferably one with a narrow blade. It must have a sharp point. The knife blade has to be sufficiently thick and strong to break through the lower leg bones, which are actually quite fragile.

2. Grab a handful of loose skin/fur either on the back or stomach of the rabbit/hare mid-center. Run the point of your knife through this spot to make a cut. Now pull the skin in opposite directions—half toward the head, half toward the tail. If you tug hard enough, you can pull most of the hide free in

Here is a field dressed rabbit ready to bag. It has been totally cleared of offal, washed, allowed to cool and dry a little, and can now be placed in a plastic bag.

Here is a tree squirrel taken with bow and arrow.

two parts that are discarded. The fur will end up lining small dens and other nests. Squirrels get the same treatment; only the hide is tougher, requiring harder pulling and sometimes a little knife work to free it.

3. The rabbit or squirrel is now skinned except for pieces of hide attached around head and legs. This hide is removed intact with head and legs. The head is severed and discarded, likewise the *lower* leg joints. Neither neck nor lower legs are difficult to cut through with a decent knife. A little twisting finishes the removal job.

4. What we have now is a naked carcass devoid of any hide. It's time to remove the entrails. Rabbits are easiest to clean out. Using the sharp point of the knife, a cut is made front vent all the way forward through the rib cage. Remember that head and neck are gone. Be certain that the slice has been made *through* the pelvic bone. Think of this bone as the aitchbone on the big game carcass, which can be severed down the center to expose intestines at that point. Cutting through the pelvic bone of small game exposes the intestines running through to the anal passage. Be certain that the intestines in the canal are entirely loose so they can be expelled.

5. With the viscera totally exposed the easy way to evacuate the contents is with a swift snap or swing of the carcass, sort of like cracking a whip. This puts centrifugal force to work, expelling the entire innards. Squirrel offal is not always as easy to evacuate as rabbit or hare. A little coaxing with gloved fingers, along with minor knife work may be necessary.

Nick Fadala hunting cottontails with old Winchester 22 pump action rifle.

6. The tailbone area of rabbit, hare or squirrel is removed by making a notch-shaped cut on each side of the tail with the blade of the knife working toward the body. This sections the tailbone free. At this time, some of the loose skin that once made up the abdominal walls can be cut free and tossed out. It is not worth retaining. Don't worry about the skin that covers the loins. This will be removed during processing for cooking or freezing.

7. Rabbits, hares and squirrels clean and cool quickly. Each should be cleaned and cooled, however, before bagging for transportation from the field. Cleaning requires only a little water (carry a canteen) or snow. The goal is removing any hair or other undesirable matter from the carcass. Snow is a perfect coolant, but exposure to the air also works.

8. Dry it and bag it next. Plastic food bags from the grocery store work well. But the meat must be dry. If not, water will collect in the bag. It may even cause souring of the meat. The carcass is dried with a clean cloth carried in the game vest or pack. After the washed, cooled and dried edible is bagged, it's ready to carry from the field.

A Job Well Done

The job is well done when the carcass is free of hide, furred tail, tailbone, as well as lower limbs, head; is entirely clean of any loose hair or any other negative substance; cooled and bagged. The job is done entirely in the field so that the meat goes home ready for processing.

The sooner these smaller game animals are cared for in the field after taking them, the easier it is to do a good job, especially squirrels, which can set up when cool, making them difficult to skin. Remember also that the more time between the shot and field dressing, the greater the opportunity for gastric juices to act upon the meat.

The Pelt

In some cases pelts are worth saving. Squirrels, especially, can have extremely beautiful hides. Rabbit fur was once quite marketable, but not so much today, at least not on the small scale a hunter would deal in. The fur can be used as insulating stuffing, but it's unlikely that any of us will save it. The goal of this book is practical game care and cookery, and the fact is few of us will retain a rabbit hide for use or sale. Squirrels do make fine mounts, however, but the wise hunter takes the entire animal to the taxidermist so he or she can make the proper cuts.

Author recommends gloves for field dressing game, though he admits, "sometimes I just forget."

Field Dressing Upland Birds and Waterfowl

The author learned a lesson the hard way by almost losing 15 quail as a young hunter. This grouse will soon be field dressed to preserve its edibility.

Sometimes lessons come hard. I was a young hunter who just found the gemstone of Gamble's quail habitat. Like a hound dog with a broken leash, I dashed about the habitat, jumping covey after covey. My shooting was sharp. Before long I had the full compliment of 15 birds in my game vest, the limit at the time.

The day was typically Southern Arizona warm and as I half-trotted from one opportunity to the next I did not take time to take care of my birds. I was too intent on filling out. Proudly, I brought the bagful of epicurean delights to the doorstep of my grandfather, who delighted in handling each one, poking a finger at its breastbone to determine age.

I dutifully de-feathered and dressed each topknot delight until all 15 lay before me, plump ransoms for a king. But something was wrong. I picked one up. The aroma emanating from the cavity was not friendly. My grandfather came out to the back yard to see how I was doing. Almost tearfully I said, "Nano, I think the birds are spoiled."

He picked one up, sniffed, shook his head, and said something about souring, but he'd do his best with them. After a bath in ice cold water liberally laced with salt and baking soda, with white vinegar added for the last half hour of treatment, grandfather marinated the quail, I know not in what.

They were saved, but no longer among the finest delicacies in the land. We ate them. They were all right. But even after my grandfather's expertise and effort, the birds were just edible.

No quail that came into my possession, nor any other upland bird, duck or goose, ever went sour on me again. The lesson was learned. Field care for birds means getting the innards out. Birds' digestive tracts are loaded with

Above left: The tools of the harvest are important in procuring edible upland birds. This wild turkey is a prime example. A load of shot from a 3-inch 12 gauge shell landed in the head/neck region, not into the breast meat.

Above: Snow is perfect for cooling a newly taken bird, such as this grouse.

powerful fluids that break down tough foods. Shot going through can turn loose these agents to wreak havoc on the edible meat.

Today I might shoot three quail before field dressing the birds in the field, but no more. I also take care of all upland birds in the field. Likewise ducks. And if I lose the opportunity to fill a limit because I was doing my birds, that's fine. At least what I take home will be the best food available, not tainted.

Tools of the Harvest

As with small game, the tools of the harvest make a big difference in the product. The goal is quickly dispatching the quarry without damaging the meat. We hunt small game with 22 rimfire rifles and pistols, bows and arrows, along with shotguns firing modest charges of No. 5 or No. 6 shot (most of the time). Upland birds are hunted with shotgun or bow and arrow. Rifles are illegal with the exception of mountain grouse in the West. Local regulations, as always, must be carefully checked to find out what is, and is not, legal. Wild turkeys, depending upon the area, may also be hunted with rifles. It is legal to use air rifles for birds in some areas.

I have had good luck on mountain grouse and wild turkeys with blackpowder squirrel rifles, calibers 32 and 36, shooting a patched round ball. The little lead pill at modest velocity drops birds without overly attacking the meat. Waterfowl are hunted with non-toxic shot by law, primarily steel shot. But Bismuth and other non-toxic metals are also allowed.

Ammo manufacturers currently offer more viable loads than ever for upland birds and waterfowl. It's a rather simple matter of matching the load to the game. Most of the time, within normal range, pellets pass through ducks. And from pits where shots are close, delivering the pattern to the head/neck region of geese takes no special talent.

Field Dressing Kit

In the last chapter, the small game hunter carried a compact knife with a modestly strong blade and a sharp point. The same knife is ideal for field dressing upland birds and waterfowl. The small game hunter also had a canteen of water for clearing the cavity and meat of hair or other negative products. The upland bird hunter should also carry water. While there is normally a supply of water in duck hunting, sometimes geese are taken in dry fields, so a little water comes in handy. It's also advisable to carry a clean rag, plastic bags and latex gloves.

Field Dressing Steps

1. Drawing birds is not difficult, and as noted above field dressing can be imperative for good eating. In anything resembling warm weather, the sooner the bird is field dressed, the better. Quail are not the only birds that can go sour in the field. A new hunter brought by a brace of pheasants for a little help in processing for the freezer. They were taken on a warm Nebraska day and within four hours had begun to sour. So let's get to it. The same general steps attend all birds. They go like this: Clear all feathers from the vent area up to the breastbone. Make an incision from the vent to the base of the breastbone. Now come two more cuts. These begin in between the vent and breastbone, each cut running from center out. The result of the three cuts—one longitudinal from vent to breastbone, two going out from that incision, is a cross that looks like this: +. The cross allows access to the entrails of the bird. Gloved fingers are the best tools for drawing the bird, which requires reaching in and simply pulling out everything in the cavity: heart, lungs, liver, gizzard, stomach, the works. Heart, gizzard and liver can be used in making stock. The rest of the viscera are returned to nature.

2. Bleeding the big game animal that's been stopped with a high-speed bullet is usually unnecessary. However, bleeding some of the larger birds is not a bad idea. It's simply a matter of slicing through the neck to sever the main vessels there. Or the head can be removed entirely, if lawful. Remember that in some areas the head may be required for identifying some birds—especially ducks.

3. The front end of the bird requires another step, which is to remove the craw. This sac is located between the neck and breastbone. It contains the food ingested by the bird along with acidy fluids. Because of its contents, the craw may sour rapidly. To get rid of it, find it first with probing fingers. Then simply cut it out with the sharp, pointed knife. Study the contents of the craw to learn what foods the bird was eating. This is an especially good idea for wild turkeys. The craw, for example, may be full of grasshoppers, revealing that the bird was working a field somewhere. Find the field; find more wild turkeys next season. The two operations discussed so far, drawing and removing the craw, only take a few minutes.

4. Cut away all loose skin around the cavity. This tissue, which may be tainted with visceral juices, is of little food value and is best discarded. The entire tail section may also be removed at this time. This eliminates the entire vent area.

A cleaning party goes to work on freshly taken dove. Here, the birds will be "breasted" only because the rest of the bird offers nothing worthwhile for the pan.

5. At this juncture the bird is free of all internal organs, along with the craw. But feathers remain intact, so the only washing that can be accomplished is within the body cavity along with that slightly exposed area where the craw was removed. Gloved fingers and a little water do the job of clearing out gastric juices. Gizzard, liver and heart, if kept, also get a water rinse.

6. A baking soda treatment is optional. A little baking soda dropped into the viscera-free cavity, followed by water, can neutralize remaining acids. In fact, the baking soda can be introduced in Step 5 during the water washout of the cavity.

7. A little drying with that clean rag is in order. A wet cavity promotes spoilage. The bird is now ready for cooling out.

8. Cooling a drawn bird requires nothing more than allowing air to get to it. Hang a wild turkey for a little while to allow air to circulate from all sides. Smaller birds can be set on a bush.

9. Being careful to obey the letter of the law, a bird may be skinned or plucked in the field. This is legal where I hunt for dove, for example. Dove field dressing differs from quail and other larger birds. At first it may seem wasteful; however, only the breast is useful. There isn't a quarter teaspoon of meat on both legs combined. The hunter pushes a thumb under the breastbone and simply divides the dove in two parts, breast away from the rest of the body. Since the entire body cavity with entrails is discarded, a touch of water on the

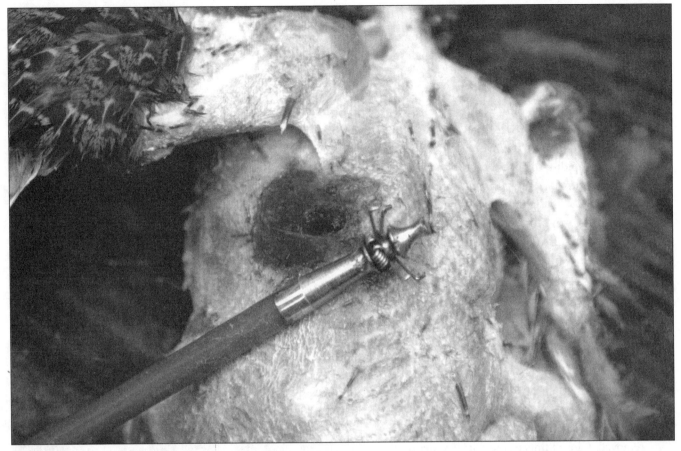

Here is a bird that's been plucked. The Zwickey JUDO point made a significant, but shallow entrance and no meat was lost.

underside of the breast is sufficient to clear away gastric juices that may have been released by pass-through shotgun pellets. One wing is left intact on the dove for identification—mourning dove or whitewing. The other wing can be cut off with a knife. The breast can be left feathered or plucked on the spot in a few seconds. A game ranger may demand identification of pheasants, grouse of all kinds—all of these birds, but drawing, skinning and plucking are OK as long as a wing or wing and head are left intact. Skinning may make more sense than plucking. A simple slit with knifepoint under the breast skin provides a starting point. The skin, feathers intact, is pulled free and left in the field. Wild turkeys are best plucked instead of skinned because we like to see that browned breast fresh from the oven. The skin also prevents the breast meat from drying out when deep-fried.

10. Breasting doves, as explained above, makes sense. Larger birds can also be breasted for frying purposes. On a bowhunt in the high mountains I came onto a covey of blue grouse, taking two. These big birds are delicious in camp, requiring nothing more than frying the breast meat and thighs. I decided to breast both birds in camp and cook them up right away since it was supper-time when I reached my tent. There was enough meat for my two partners and myself. However, rather than going into the vent area, here is how I breasted the birds. The breast is exposed completely by skinning it, thereby removing all feathers. The naked breast meat is now removed intact by making a long slice right along the keel that divides the two halves. By cutting very close to the bone, the breast meat is filleted away in two big pieces, one for each side. This also works on pheasants and other birds. On birds the size of mountain grouse and larger, the filleted breast meat is cut into steaks, for lack of a better term.

Sage grouse, which may weigh five pounds, turn into at least six steaks, sometimes eight. The slices are not overly thick, which helps in effective marination. The legs can be defeathered and cut free on blue grouse. They're not very meaty, but can provide a mouthful. Chapter 13 contains details on processing game birds.

Hanging

Larger birds, generally grouse on up, and especially wild turkeys, can be hung in camp pending the trip home. It's wise to use a protective covering. Cheesecloth, which is what game bags are made of, is ideal because it allows air passage while keeping out flies. Tape up any openings.

Where legal, it is all right to bone a bird in the field, securing the meat in a plastic container. However, be certain to leave one wing attached when the law calls for that measure.

Gizzards

The gizzard, if kept, must be worked on in the field. Make a cut about a quarter-inch deep crosswise on the gizzard. Turn the gizzard inside out along this slice. Dump the interior contents of the gizzard out. Study the contents for future reference. Next, remove the wrinkled skin. This peels off like the skin on a peach, only easier. Throw the tough skin away. Wash the gizzard. Dry it. Place in a plastic bag to keep clean.

Super Fast and Easy

Saved for last, here is a super fast and easy method of field dressing upland birds. It works well up to blue grouse size. At first, this process seems wasteful. But it is not. Even on large blue grouse, the legs carry very little meat. So leaving them behind in the woods is not wasteful. Furthermore, the earth takes back everything left behind. These particulars may pass through the digestive system of a coyote first, but Mother Earth will claim all in the end.

To field dress an upland bird super fast and easy place it between your feet with one boot firmly on each wing close to the body. Bend down and grasp both legs close to the body of the bird. Now stand up pulling hard on the legs. The complete body cavity with innards, plus legs, pulls away from the edible breast meat, leaving the breast and wings intact. For identification purposes, at least one wing should be left on until the bird is processed.

Mounts and Memories

A turkey bound for the taxidermist must be handled differently. It can be drawn, but not by the usual method of pulling away a multitude of feathers. Rather, no feathers are removed. Clean small cuts are made through the skin. The entrails are pulled free, the cavity rinsed, and the bird transported to the artist as soon as possible. If transporting is delayed, the bird can be hung for awhile.

It should be carried in a cornucopia, which is simply a large wrapping of newspaper or other paper shaped like a cone. The head of the turkey is pushed down into the cone. This keeps all of the feathers going in the right direction. Quail and any other bird bound for the taxidermist can also be placed in the cornucopia.

A hunter may wish to save some feathers from various birds for different reasons. A turkey fan, as well as one from grouse and partridge, makes a nice display. The base meat holding the fan together is dried with salt for preservation.

The Value

The value of upland birds and waterfowl is difficult to measure. The meat alone carries a high ticket price; however, the activity of hunting itself is difficult to assess. A lot of people pay a lot of money for less exercise and have nothing to take home for the table.

Know One, Know All

Knowing how to field dress one bird—be it goose, duck, prairie chicken or quail—is knowing how to do all game birds. The dove is an exception because it is breasted and not drawn. But most birds under most hunting situations are drawn, meaning the entrails are removed.

9

From Field to Camp and Home

Sometimes the most expedient way to pack game out is simply toting it over a shoulder. Of course, safety is always the byword. A hunter never wants to appear as game!

There are a number of methods for getting game from field to camp and camp to home. Incorrect ways promise spoilage. Here are a few proper methods to consider. But first, the wrong way.

The Wrong Way | Small game and birds carried from field to camp warm are prone to spoilage. Likewise allowing these smaller edibles to heat up either from field to camp/vehicle, or vehicle to home promotes ruination.

Big game packed on the hoods of cars or trucks sends the wrong message to other hunters and non-hunters, let alone anti-hunters. It's obvious that big game suffering the direct rays of the sun will spoil on longer trips. Pride in taking a big game animal in fair chase is deserved. However, showing the carcass in transit can tarnish the hunter's image as well as promoting the growth of bacteria in the meat.

Small Game

Small game can be packed out of the field by hand, with string-tied legs, with a small game tote, in a sturdy plastic garbage bag, in a cotton sack, or game vest, to note a few acceptable methods. Carrying any game bird from goose to quail in hand is OK. Tying the legs together makes an even handier carry.

There are also small game/bird totes in various styles. One is a leather strap, fairly wide, with slits in it. Legs are secured in the slits and the strap is slipped over a shoulder. Other totes include a number of homemade models. Totes allow open-air carrying to promote cooling, especially for game that has not been plucked or skinned. Black garbage bags are strong enough to contain field dressed small game and birds without breaking out. A clean cotton sack is also useful.

Game vests are among the better means of carrying birds and small game—with one major drawback. Heat from the hunter's body can invade the vest, warming up the contents.

There are many different types of ATVs on the market, each one suited to its own specific function. Here is one that works well in hauling game in from the field.

Here is an ATV in action taking a deer from woods to lodge in Kentucky.

The author likes to hunt with a packframe. Here his Camp Trails Freighter is shown with modifications, including a strut to carry the rifle via its sling. The daypack is slipped off of the frame and the frame then becomes available for carrying game.

Big Game

There are many means of getting big game from field to camp or vehicle and then home for processing or to a plant, the following included.

The ATV | The ATV—All Terrain Vehicle—is both a curse and a blessing.

Curse: After two days trying to catch up to a particularly large Wyoming antelope, the moment of truth arrived. The stalk went well. However before I could squeeze off the shot, *Zoom!* Here it came. A four-wheeler ripping across open ground in a cloud of dust and raspy roar of its engine. The buck bolted in his own cloud of dust. A day later I found him again and this time there was no ATV to drive him off. ATVs were not invented for hunters to scare game away or tear up the terrain.

Blessing: Meanwhile, there is nothing wrong with riding on established routes to good drop-off hunting spots. The ATV is even more appreciated for getting downed big game from field to camp. One of my partners hunting with Deer Creek Outfitters in Sebree, Ky., took a fine whitetail buck. A guide buzzed in on his ATV, collected the prize, and handily ushered it to the cleaning station intact. The carcass was dressed at the station, not in the field as a deterrent to coyotes, which were prevalent in the area.

ATVs are everywhere and their numbers are growing. The ATV provides a prime means of getting into backcountry on hundreds of established routes such as logging roads as well as two-trackers everywhere. The ATV is also an excellent means of reaching downed game and carrying it from field to camp.

Backpacking | By far the majority of my own big game, including moose, travel from field to camp via packframe. There is great freedom in backpack hunting. It's wonderful to find an exciting spot and stay there for a day or two with mountain tent and sleeping bag.

My special frame, a modified Freighter from Camp Trails, has a reinforced shelf to prevent a carcass from slipping down. I use quarter-inch, not eighth-inch, nylon cord to secure the animal or quarter in place. After field dressing, daypack, tent and sleeping bag leave the frame and the animal is tied in place. Then daypack and other gear slip onto the top struts and away we go. I use a walking stick for balance plus arm power aiding leg power.

Small deer and antelope can be carried whole. Larger deer are cut in half at the last rib just behind the loins. The front half will weigh a bit more than the back half. A 160-pound deer, for example, goes 85 pounds for the front half, 75 for the back half—approximately.

The Backpack | There are large packs that can be used to transport game, rather than tying a carcass onto a packframe. Where the law allows, the big game animal can be boned, the meat cooled and placed in plastic garbage bags and then loaded into the pack itself.

Boning | Boning a carcass in the field makes sense for backpacking big game to camp. Boned meat is placed in strong plastic garbage bags and either tied directly onto the packframe or slipped into a large pack.

Unfortunately, boning big game can invite a violation where the law requires evidence of sex attached to a carcass. In other words a hardworking hunter, taking game out on his own back, may be ticketed by a game warden.

Meanwhile, leaving behind antlers or hides (if unwanted) plus all other inedible portions of a carcass is good management. Every scrap will return to nature.

Hopefully, a game warden checking a carcass will use his biological knowledge to determine sex rather than handing out a citation to an honorable hunter carrying boned meat out on his own back. Antlers and reproductive organs are not the only means of identifying sex of a big game animal. For example, the pelvis tells a great deal about the sex of an animal.

Boning and Jointing Process | By noting how an animal is put together, we know how to take it apart. Lower legs—essentially inedible—are freed at the joint and discarded. (Cut a little above the joint itself.) Front shoulders are literally sliced free with a knife. Loins are removed intact with long clean knife cuts close to the spine. Hams are cut away from bones along lines on the meat denoting different muscles. This leaves a skeleton with offal and other non-edible parts in the field.

On the Shoulder | In the past, all my Coues whitetails, a deer that seldom breaks 100 pounds field dressed, where packed out whole over my shoulders, the way a wounded soldier is carried from the field, especially in the movies. But no longer. Now I either attach the entire carcass to my packframe, or if way back in the hills, the meat is boned away, skeleton and hide left behind, head/antlers with cape carried to camp.

I've watched my friend John Kane, a professional government hunter these past 20-plus years, pick up and pack away a full quarter of elk. But that's him, not me.

It's a long way to camp, but at least it's all downhill—this time, so the deer won't be boned, but it will be field dressed and then packed out.

Far left: Here's a buck all tied on and ready for transportation to the vehicle. Legs were left intact on this buck. Sometimes they're shortened at the first joint to compact the load.

Left: Before striking out, test your balance. Falling is no fun. Falling with a load on your back is even less enjoyable.

The author uses two walking stick, his own and his brother's, for arm powder aiding leg power, and for balance. Knees are wrapped with Ace bandages as a precaution against strain. Forelegs removed for this time for compactness of the package.

Nor are most of us that powerful. My big game will be broken down into much smaller packing units.

Safety First | Anything that resembles buck or bull must be disguised, lest another hunter mistake it for live game. An orange covering is ideal to hide horns or antlers.

Horse and Mule | Although most of my game goes from field to camp on my own back I am grateful for beasts of burden when available. Horses and mules are excellent packers, as are other four-legged creatures of the horse clan, such as burros.

Pack Goats | Unlike llamas, pack goats are rather friendly fellows around the evening campfire, sometimes extending their tie-cords to get close for a pat on the head. These small animals cannot be expected to pack overly heavy loads, but a little string of goats is capable of getting considerable meat from outback to home camp.

Llamas | Llamas are excellent packers, although they do have their downside, such as occasional cushing (sitting down on the trail) and spitting now and then. On one high-country deer hunt, three of us used two llamas to pack gear in and meat out. Each llama was limited to 70 pounds. We carried the remainder on our own backs. However, that's still 140 pounds—in this case boned meat—that hunters did not have to pack out.

Llamas can be rented in the West. An introductory course in handling these animals is imperative. A tip—if your llama stops on the trail to stare at something, check it out. Llamas are great at spotting big game.

The Drag | Dragging works. I was most impressed by a group of Finnish moose hunters pulling a bull more that a mile out of the forest. Each man attached a long nylon strap to the moose and away they went.

Of equal merit was a team in Maine that dragged a very large black bear along a little trail from the midst of thick trees to a lake shoreline for transporting by boat to camp.

I tried a little item called a Deer Slide that worked well. It amounted to a slick carpet affair that the deer rested on as it was tugged to camp. When the ground is covered with snow, dragging is that much easier.

In the past, horse-drawn sleds of various types were used to pull big game over the snow. Dragging with a horse, snow or not, is also effective. In the Jackson, Wyo., area there's a fellow who earns his wages pulling elk over the snow. He ties on with a rope and the horse pulls away.

Over the Water | Canoes, rafts, boats of various descriptions—darn near anything that will float and pack a load—can be used to transport game to camp. One of the more romantic pictures of the hunt is the canoe with big buck.

Two Men, One Stick | The two-man carry with deer or other game suspended on a pole does work, although a shred of balance is required, especially if the carcass begins to sway back and forth. This is a familiar method, often shown in movies where a couple stalwarts arrive in camp with badly needed meat.

The Iron Pony | There is also nothing wrong with driving right up to downed big game with a vehicle, loading it in and heading out. Driving through cultivated fields, however, or whenever the earth is marshy, can wreak havoc on the landscape. On the other hand, one drive in, one out, in most places, will not cause damage to the ground. Ask first when on ranches and farms. One good way to get uninvited on private hunting property is leaving ruts behind.

The Game Cart | Some time ago a neighbor of mine invented the most elaborate game cart I have ever seen. It was set up to work with a very long winch line. Intended for elk, it also works on all other big game, pulling carcasses out of canyons and through forests.

The regular wheelbarrow type cart is also useful for getting game out, although I'd rather pack meat on a frame when the going is uphill.

Game carts are available commercially from sporting goods stores.

The Site of the Harvest | It matters not the terrain from Southwestern desert mountains to the rich forests of the East, harvested game can lose itself in a hurry. The modern way to note a harvest site is with a GPS (Global Positioning System) unit. So marked, a hunter can return to the site of the harvest every time. It also helps to lay out blue or orange ribbon.

One time I got a Coues buck in a jumble of Old Mexico canyons. My partner had not yet connected, and so we rode our horses deeper into the mountain range, covering a great deal of territory. Without the help of the cowboy who rode with us, I am convinced that my trophy buck would not have been found again.

At one point he asked, "Do you know where your buck is? Point to the place."

I tried and failed. There were simply too many look-alike draws and rock outcroppings for us to identify the right spot. My partner tried and failed. Our cowboy, however, knew every rock in the landscape and was able to locate the buck hanging in an oak tree completely out of sight. A GPS would have taken us to the buck as surely as our cowboy did; only there was no such thing at the time.

From Camp to Home

The carcass has been kept cool hanging by night in its game bag enclosure, lying by day covered with a tarp and sleeping bags for insulation against the heat. In colder weather, the protected meat in plastic bags or the carcass can be insulated with newspapers. Now it's time to ensure that it stays cool all the way home or to the game locker plant.

Just as it was insulated in camp, it should be insulated on the way home with the same tarp and sleeping bags. Ice chests are also useful. Today's Coleman Extreme, for example, will hold a block of ice for a couple days at 90 degrees Fahrenheit. Cool or better yet cold boned meat can be packed into these modern ice chests with fine results. Dry ice is also good, but not allowed for air travel.

Lacking sufficient ice chests, Styrofoam® containers will do the job. Four such containers with frozen meat were flown 1,500 miles and when picked up the contents were still solid.

Your Way | There is no doubt in my mind that sportsmen are inventive. Hunters reading this have no doubt come up with many different means of getting game from field to camp to home. Any method is good as long as the meat arrives in top shape. The ways shown here are not the only good ones. After all, we've not even gotten into the Eskimo's dog team or the African tracker's way of dividing the meat among each person in the party.

It's Worth It | Taking a little extra time and putting out a bit of added energy to ensure that game, small or large, after proper field preparation makes it to camp and then home in perfect shape is worth it. It's part of avoiding that gamy taste that nobody likes.

10

Game Processing and Cooking Tools

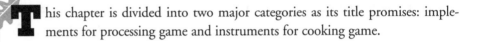his chapter is divided into two major categories as its title promises: implements for processing game and instruments for cooking game.

Meat, not Bones

Cutting meat away from the bone is the main practice outlined in the next chapter. Consider a chop normally found in the butcher shop, as well as many game processing plants. A good percentage of that chop is bone. Likewise for many steak cuts. When the meal is over, the bone, along with inedible tissue, is discarded.

So why store bones and inedible portions of the big game carcass? I say don't, and that's why Chapter 11 is dedicated to producing packages of meat without the bone, inedible tissue or fat. The following processing tools aid the boning process.

Processing Tools

Most processing of game takes place in the home, sometimes in elaborate setups, but more often on kitchen tables and worktops. A series of tools is necessary not only to do a good job, but to make the task easier. Here are some of those tools. A stroll through a first class restaurant supply house or mall cooking shop will reveal dozens more.

The following are basic. I consider them essential to my work; however, it's equally true that entire carcasses, including elk and moose, have been completely boned for the freezer with nothing more than a single folding knife. I saw the whole job accomplished with a Buck 110 folder when one of my sons decided to give it a try. The finished product was superb. However, the effort would have been reduced with some of the following implements.

The Skinning Knife for Processing | Small game and birds do not require a skinning knife; a small folder or pocketknife performs the entire job admirably. However, the big game animal's hide has to come off before any processing can be done and here's where the skinner goes to work.

A knife is no more than a wedge, as pointed out in Chapter 5. However, it can be a very sophisticated wedge designed for very specific functions. A skinning knife is unique. The blade is wide. It is thick. It is rigid. The whole idea of the skinning knife is to part the hide from the carcass.

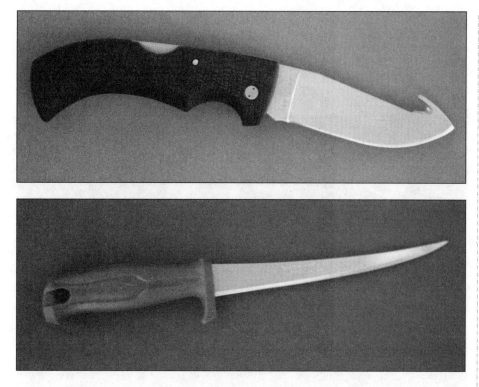

This excellent Gerber Gator folding knife with gut hook was designed for the field, but it works perfectly as a skinning knife. The blade is fairly wide and thick. While most skinning knives are not carried in the field this one can be.

This is one type of boning knife. While normally considered a "fish knife, it actually functions well in removing unwanted tissue from boned meat as well as taking meat chunks from bone.

While all knives are wedges (technically) the skinning knife is more wedge-like than other styles. Weight is of no consequence. Most skinning knives are not carried into the field, and those that are can be light, as Gerber has proved with its Gator style skinner.

The blade of the skinning knife is contoured to reduce the chance of puncturing the hide. The rounded point section serves the same purpose. Putting holes in hides that are to be discarded is not a problem; however, when a hide is punctured, hair is set free and that hair will find its way to the meat.

The Boning Knife for Processing | The opposite of the skinning knife is the boning knife. Here the blade is narrow, thin and flexible. It is narrow to work into the recesses of the carcass. The blade is thin in order to slide against bone to remove meat. And it is flexible so that it can bend around bone.

While the skinning knife works to part hide from meat, the boning knife functions to part meat from bone. Buck's folding filet knife, intended for fish, is excellent in stripping meat from bone. Many companies also have special boning knives. They are labeled as such and all have the characteristics noted above.

The Meat Saw | Although our goal is boning the big game carcass, there are some cuts that require the bone left in. A major example is the Leg O' Lope recipe that I devised a number of years ago. It's a whole section of antelope haunch, larded and marinated, then placed over hot coals or on the gas grill. As one side cooks, finished slices are removed for the table. Then the haunch is turned over for further cooking. The bone in this case is left in.

The meat saw is perfect for cutting through that bone. It's also excellent for reducing ribs to cooking and freezer-package size, although the meat cleaver is also good for this work. And the saw can be used effectively on a hanging carcass to remove portions for the cutting table.

The best meat saws are sold in restaurant supply houses, normally in two lengths. The longer one is best for larger big game, while the shorter one is ideal for deer-sized carcasses. These professional saws can be costly, but they last for ages. Buy one or two

The meat saw shown here is for the pack, but can also be used in home processing of big game. The finer tooth side of the saw is for meat and bone. The coarser teeth are for wood and other products.

The meat saw shown here is for the pack, but can also be used in home processing of big game. The finer tooth side of the saw is for meat and bone. The coarser teeth are for wood and other products.

extra blades and you're set for a lot of meat processing.

While the old-fashioned wooden-handled meat saw did the job and remains a working classic, my vote goes to the modern metal frame model. Blades are easily exchanged on the metal saw and it's also easy to clean in hot soapy water.

The Meat Cleaver for Processing | The meat cleaver is not often used on deer or other carcasses. However, it is perfect for small game and birds, lopping off the lower leg parts of rabbits and squirrels as well as grouse, pheasants and other upland birds.

There is, however, one big game application where the cleaver shines. That's ribs. The meat cleaver sections ribs fast and neatly. **Be safe: A meat cleaver can do a great deal of damage to the person using it.** Keep the non-working hand off to the side. Don't use that hand to hold whatever is being chopped.

Buy a decent-sized cleaver. The larger cleaver will work for small game as well as rib cages, while a small cleaver is good for little jobs only.

Game Shears for Processing | Game shears are wonderful meat processing tools. I've been taking a pair to camp for some time now. True game shears—not simply large scissors—have a notch for cutting bone. This notch nips through small game and bird legs quickly, precluding the necessity of a meat cleaver. I've also used game shears to cut off inedible parts of small game and birds. They really work. But buy good ones. This means heavy duty. Proper game shears break into two parts for easy cleaning.

The Steel | Mistakenly considered a knife sharpener, the steel is actually meant to straighten a knife edge, which of course does improve cutting ability, so in that regard it is a knife sharpener. But it's not intended to work the same as a stone or diamond hone.

There are smooth and serrated steels. Smooth is for only the very finest blade touch-up. I don't own one. A mildly serrated steel is my choice. Keeping a knife sharp is actually a safety as well as convenience factor. It's also important for doing a good job of boning and preparing cuts. A dull knife requires undue force to make it cut

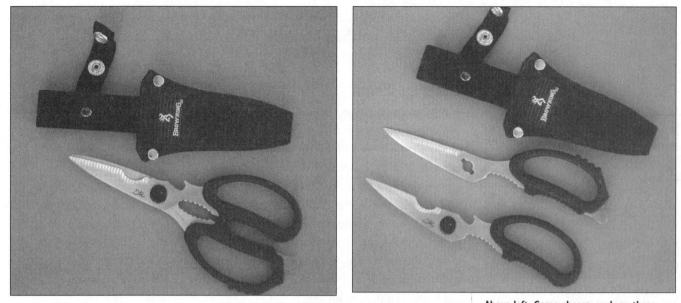

and that force can go astray. Conversely, the sharp knife glides through with minimal effort.

A proper steel has a guard. It is held point up and the edge of the knife glides evenly and lightly down the length of the steel. Maintaining angle is the key to success, as it is in sharpening a blade with stones or any other instrument.

The Butcher Knife | Large with a curved or scimitar shape blade, the true butcher knife, I believe, is essential in game processing. It's especially useful in slicing a large-boned piece of meat into sections for freezing. Tip: Don't cut steaks for freezing. Leave steak meat in larger chunks. It will last longer in the freezer that way.

Good butcher knives can be purchased without a major cash outlay. There are also high-class butcher knives available at cooking stores and restaurant supply houses. I like a long-bladed full-size butcher knife. The long blade makes clean, neat cuts from large pieces of boned meat.

Field Knives for Game Processing | Hunting knives, folders, even jackknives can be helpful in processing both small and large game. They're good for trimming ined-

Above left: Game shears, such as these, are excellent processing tools. A pair in camp is never a mistake, especially with a good carry case like the one shown here.

Above: These game shears come apart in a hinged fashion for easy cleaning.

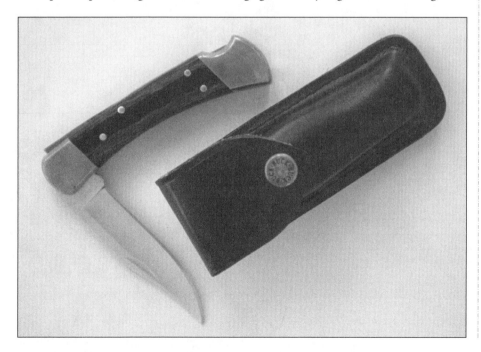

Buck's Model 110 is one of the best known folding knives in the world. While it was originally designed for dressing big game (small game and birds, too), it also serves in game processing. In one instance a Model 110 was used on an elk from field to freezer—and no other cutting instrument.

ible tissue, fat and meat from around the bullet or arrow hole. They do not, however, take the place of the boning knife. These handy knives are also useful to fill in as major knives are being sharpened.

Cooking Tools

A stroll through any good book on general cooking clearly outlines dozens of useful cooking tools. Ours is a brief look only at some of the essentials.

Cooking Knives | I find myself often using a filet knife in my cooking. Smaller portions of meat from the freezer slice up nicely with these thin-bladed knives. One special application of the filet or boning knife is larding, which means puncturing long slits into a big hunk of meat (such as the aforementioned Leg O' lope) and inserting pieces of fresh beef fat into those cuts. These slits also allow marinade to be introduced into the heart of the cut.

Butcher knives can also be used in the cooking process for cutting steaks to size as well as sectioning any variety of meat. Many other knives are also useful, of course, right down to pairing knives.

The Chef's Knife | Removed from the general category of knives (above) is the chef's. With its wide blade and long cutting surface, it's one of the most-used knives in the kitchen. I recently located a prime example of a chef's knife, more antique than modern. It rested in a perpetual garage sale in my small Wyoming community.

I was happy to part with a $10 bill for this old classic. The blade was in perfect shape. So was the wood, except for being sticky from kitchen oils. I degreased and sanded the wooden panels of the fine old knife, finishing up with a coat of tongue oil. That knife is now as good as new. It's ready to dice up potatoes, onions, mushrooms, carrots, cabbage and other foods, as well as chop parsley for that excellent red spaghetti and lasagna sauce recipe coming up later in the book.

Frying Pans | I've given in to the stick-free craze. While I still own and admire the old-fashioned cast iron skillet, there's no arguing that the modern pan is easier to cook with and to clean.

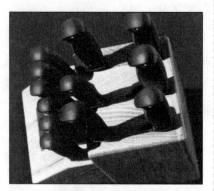

This Cold Steel knife set is perfect in the kitchen for processing and cooking foods.

This is a Buck folding fillet knife. While intended for filleting fish, it is equally useful in processing meat. Here it is shown with a backstrap. The medallions are cut away leaving the tough tissue to be discarded.

Two buying tips: Look for handles that can be tightened up if they should loosen and go for the heavier-bottom pan over the thin one. Some thicker bottom frying pans might take longer to heat, but all thicker bottom pans are also slower to warp.

The Gas Grill | Marinated elk steaks, gameburgers of every description from buffalo to whitetail deer, Leg O' lope and many other meats are perfect candidates for the gas grill. Today's models range in price from downright reasonable to "That's a car down payment!"

Beware, however, of drying meats out. Remember that game meat for the most part is lean. Carefully follow recipes that call for using the gas grill. Most will include larding and/or marinating to ensure moistness when done.

Simple as they are, good old frying pans are a must in any kitchen and a real plus for the game chef.

The Charcoal Broiler | The American cook is often a charcoal broiler expert, matching or even exceeding his or her ability with the gas grill. He or she knows how to prevent flame-ups (usually with a little water spray bottle) and the right amount of coals to get the job done.

I often take a portable charcoal broiler with me on hunts and campouts. It's perfect for preparing those oft-mentioned whitetail ribs, as well as burgers and other meats. The same warning applies to charcoal broiling that went with the gas grill: Game meat is lean so don't dry it out.

The Turkey Fryer | More than a fad, the turkey fryer has earned a place in the kitchen or on the back patio. The major value here is searing. Hot fat seals juices in. This is especially vital for wild turkeys because they are normally far leaner than domestic birds. Directions for using the turkey fryer come with it. More on the turkey fryer down the road.

Smokers | Smokers are in as they should be. They are never going away. Used properly, the smoker produces some of the finest jerky and other meats imaginable. Long-time friend Jimmy Levy was a specialist on smoking quail. We all looked forward to sitting around the campfire enjoying one (or more) of Jimmy's smoked birds. Fish, of course, also smoke perfectly.

Roasters (Electric and Oven) | As long as game recipes are followed carefully roasters produce succulent dishes, especially with what may be called a steaming process. This simply means that the meat is cooked very slowly and with plenty of broth or stock to keep it moist. The moisture in the pan actually steams the meat tender.

The good old American roast beef dinner is just as prime when the beef is wild game. Both the electric variety and old-fashioned oven roaster work perfectly for the steaming process. A big hunk of tender meat with potatoes and carrots is gourmet good.

The Pressure Cooker | I'm never without a pressure cooker. It makes fine stews and many other dishes. It's also the best parboiling pan I know of. Parboiling is both a tenderizing and clearing method. It tenderizes meat through the boiling process, but also removes unwanted elements, sometimes unsavory fluids, for example.

While parboiling in a pot is OK, the pressure cooker does a better job a lot faster. I always use the pressure cooker for parboiling rabbits and squirrels. The pressure cooker is one of favorite cooking implements. I have one in the kitchen and another in my camp outfit.

Stockpot | Since my pressure cooker makes the best stock the fastest, my stockpots are more for preparing sauces, especially red sauce for spaghetti and lasagna. The stockpot is simply a good-sized high-quality utensil, preferably stainless steel, which is costly, but also lasts indefinitely.

Meat Grinder | Some form of meat grinder is necessary for processing big game. It may be a simple hand-operated unit, a small electric model or a commercial size grinder.

The latter is expensive. Hunters who do a deer here and there will be a long time recovering the cost of a commercial grinder, which runs several hundred dollars. On the other hand, those who get an elk every year, or in the case of Canadian and Alaskan hunters, a moose, will find the commercial grinder worth every farthing. Sharing one with friends is an option.

Microwave | Lumped with pressure cooker policy in Chapter 22, the microwave can be useful for the game chef, if only for thawing meat packages quickly.

The Crock-Pot | Game cooks should rely on the Crock-Pot more often. It's a fuss-free tool capable of turning out tender vittles. See some of the Crock-Pot recipes coming up.

Wok | Stir-fry is deservedly popular. It's a wonderful means of blending wild meat and vegetables and the wok makes the dish fast and easy to prepare. The standard frying pan can be used in place of a wok, as I often do, but a true wok is a good investment.

Dutch Oven | Mastering the Dutch oven is an art. Almost anything can be cooked in one. Although usually found in camp, Dutch oven cookery is equally at home in the back yard. There are many books specifically on cooking with the Dutch oven. Owning at least one is worthwhile.

Spatula | This obvious tool would not receive mention except for one specific use, and it's not flipping burgers or fried eggs. The spatula comes into its own when frying breaded meats. Prepared in the Universal Marinade developed for this book, such meats are tender and succulent. But if turned with a fork instead of a spatula, the breading can be left on the bottom of the pan. Even stick-free pans tend to hold onto breading. The thin-blade metal spatula is a classic, but many non-stick frying pans require special spatulas that will not damage their finish.

A separator like this one is ideal for making gravy without the grease. The grease, being lighter than the stock, comes to the top. The stock is poured off and the grease discarded.

Thickener (Cornstarch, Flour and Arrowroot) Mixer | In making game stews and other dishes, as well as gravy, a container to mix the thickener, be it cornstarch, flour or arrowroot, is ideal.

Spoons | Another utensil that would normally seem too common to deserve mention is the cooking spoon. The only reason it's included here is as a reminder that the wooden cooking spoon is often ideal, not only for hollandaise sauce, which can be ruined with a metal spoon, but also various other sauces.

Strainers | For making stock as well as ensuring lump-free gravy, the ordinary strainer is ideal.

Grease Separators | This is one of the best cooking utensils to come along. There are different types, but each has the same task—to remove floating fat from stock or broth, especially when either is destined to become gravy or the juice that keeps a stew interesting.

Butcher Block | Not entirely necessary, but nice to have, is a butcher block. Its merits are obvious.

Cutting Board | Lacking a butcher block, the cutting board becomes a required piece of equipment for processing game meat. There are two basic types: wood and synthetic.

Wood is the classic and certainly the showy one to appear on a nicely set table where bread is sliced by the host. However, the synthetic cutting board is easier to clean. I recommend it not only for ease of after-use care, but it's considered more sanitary than wood, which can soak up various fluids and retain them.

Those who prefer the wooden cutting boards are strongly encouraged to clean them with hot soapy water immediately after use, followed by a thorough drying and finally a little cooking oil to prevent the wood from cracking.

Everything Else | The list of cooking tools could go on for another full book. There are literally hundreds of different utensils, such as devices to clamp onto a tomato for creating perfect slices. I found one in an old box one time and had to be told what it was.

Caring for Processing and Cooking Tools | Common sense dictates keeping all cooking utensils clean and free of abuse. Knives should not be put away wet, even if their blades are stainless steel. It only takes a few seconds to dry them.

Cutting paper as well as other materials, such as wood, with a fine knife blade can dull the blade quickly. Cut meat and other foods only with a good knife.

Wooden handles deserve a little linseed oil or tongue oil from time to time. Wooden handles sometimes require refinishing, which is little more than sanding the surface and applying a light coat of linseed oil or tongue oil.

The well-equipped game-cooking kitchen is a friendly harbor to float into any time. Cooking can be therapeutic, especially when it's not rushed. And good cooking can be accomplished with a minimum of hardware. However, cooking utensils are like hunting knives. You can never have too many good ones.

11

Processing Big Game

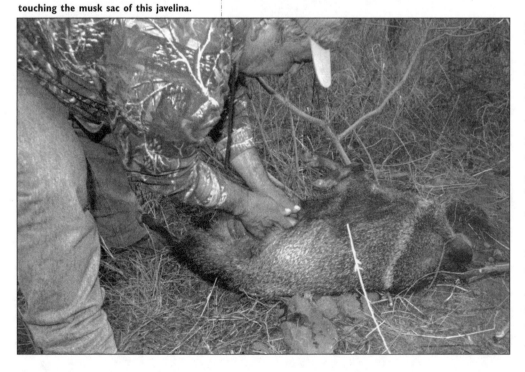

There are many ways to do a good job of processing big game. The story begins in the field (see Chapter 6). Here, a Mexican guide uses a Gerber Gator knife with gut hook to begin the process of eviscerating followed by removal of hide without touching the musk sac of this javelina.

American style butchering produces beautiful packages of meat for display at the supermarket. Most cuts are bone-in: T-bone steak, rib steak, chops. There is nothing wrong with this method of processing. However, our goal differs and there are no bones about it

The end product is pure boneless meat. Not to say that bones are without value. Cracked and boiled they create stock or broth. There is nutrition in marrow.

All the same, we do not normally take advantage of bone. It goes from dinner plate to Fido or garbage can. So why store it? Furthermore, boning meat in the back-country, when legal, is ideal for lightening the load.

The boning process I learned is of European origin, although I've seen the same style in Mexico. With a little practice, the hunter will become an absolute expert at processing big game the boning way.

Many Ways

There are many ways to process big game. Each expert will declare his the best method. For example, there are those who do not field dress game, especially when quick transportation, such as an ATV, is at hand. There is nothing wrong with this approach.

Most of my game is taken far afield in western mountains, however, and so it must be field dressed not only to reduce backpack weight, but also to prevent tainting the meat.

Teamwork

Many hands make the work light, the saying goes, and so true it is. One person, however, can easily process a deer inside an hour. But when two work at it, one can steady the carcass, which is a big help when reducing larger pieces to freezer size.

The Boning Process

Before going into the particulars of removing the hide, let's consider boning. This reversal of order is due to the fact that hides are often removed in camp. Furthermore, boning may take place in the field, which incorporates skinning. So the boning process receives initial attention with skinning to follow. That will be followed in turn by the home hanging method of processing a carcass.

Boning the Big Game Carcass on the Ground

Moose, elk, even larger deer are sometimes best boned in the field, which generally means doing the job on the ground. A come-along or hoist can lift the carcass; however, few hunters carry these tools in the field. So the carcass is boned on the spot. There are several means of accomplishing this task. Here are two:

This is a good illustration of boning. All that's left on this shoulder blade is a little scrap here and there.

Standard Method

The standard method for boning on the ground begins with normal big game field dressing as discussed in Chapter 6. The animal is eviscerated following the steps outlined in the same chapter. The field dressed carcass rests on its back. From this position, it is skinned and boned.

This Mexican guide has used the gut hook on a Gerber Gator folding knife to open this javelina cleanly. He will not remove the musk sac, however, which will come away with the hide when the animal is skinned. This work is highly important to future processing of the meat.

Steps:

1. Make a long cut under the hide of a rear leg all the way to the hock.
2. Holding the leg up, or better yet having a partner hold it, remove the hide entirely. Let the exposed meat cool a little if the carcass is still warm.
3. Observe natural muscle structure. There will be visible lines marking off the various muscles of the hind leg. These are perfect guidelines for removing the

meat from the bone in large pieces. The large hind leg bone (femur) is a guide to cutting away the muscle at that location. Connective tissue lines work for the rest of the back leg.

4. Place boned meat in plastic garbage bags for hauling to camp or vehicle.

5. Repeat process for other hind leg.

6. Remove front shoulders and forelegs, which are sliced free with a knife by pulling out on the front leg while cutting. This process is self-evident due to the structure of the front leg, which seems hardly attached to the animal.

7. Rear and front leg bones can now be cut free.

8. The carcass is rolled over slightly, but remaining on the hide to avoid contact with foreign matter, such as grass, leaves or dirt.

9. Now the entire back of the animal is skinned, exposing the spine. Here lie the filets.

10. The filets are cut out all the way into the neck by slicing as you would to remove the breast meat along the keel of a bird. This results in two long strips of pure meat known as backstraps.

11. Next, slicing deeply toward the vertebrae can cut neck meat free.

12. The rib cage may or may not be useful. Ribs on a fat whitetail buck are a delicacy. They can be sawed away from the spinal column in pieces of various sizes. A small game saw works perfectly in the field with a true meat saw for home processing.

This shows the knife cutting free one loin from the carcass by running the blade close to the spine.

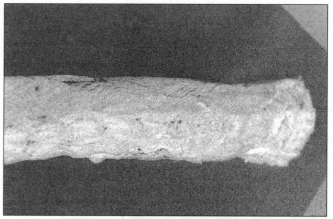

Working from the Top—Another Method

This method of field boning differs in that the carcass is not field dressed first.

Steps:

1. The carcass is maneuvered belly-down.
2. The first cut is made under the hide right along the very top of the spinal column all the way from behind the head to the tail.
3. Four more cuts are made just beneath the hide, each running down the outer center of a leg.
4. Now the hide is sliced away, spreading out on each side of the carcass to create a ground cover for the rest of the operation.
5. The first meat cut removes the entire loins—from the neck to the beginning of the haunches. These two long strips of meat are set aside to cool.
6. The front shoulders are lifted up, sliced free and set aside and to cool.
7. The hindquarters are skinned and the meat is removed from the bone as explained in the standard method.
8. The cooled shoulders are now boned.
9. The carcass can be rolled over at this point to access liver and heart, considered prime by some gourmets. A simple under-the-skin slice in the belly exposes these inner organs, which are removed from the offal.
10. Finally, a pack saw is used to cut up the rib cage.

This fine loin has been removed intact with a boning knife by carefully slicing with the blade very close to the bone.

Below left: Working from the top can begin with the caping process, as these two Mexican guides are doing here by making a cut through the hide from the top along the spine.

Below: Here is a good look at working from the top. The cut along the spine just under the hide reveals the loins at this point.

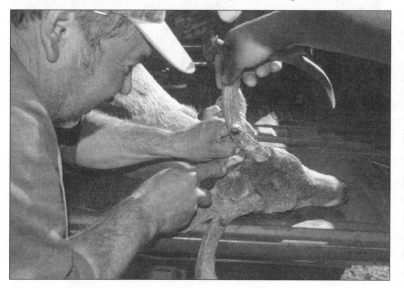

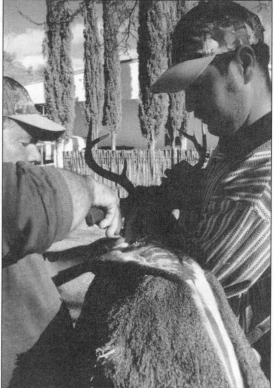

Flat Surface Boning

I've boned many big game animals on the tailgate of my pickup truck. The field dressed carcass remains on its side with the hide removed one-half at a time. Having a helper hold the legs up for skinning is a real plus because the tailgate method is admittedly a little awkward.

Once the entire hide is cut back from one side, that side can be boned by completely removing shoulders and haunches. Shoulders are easily cut free since they are not bone-attached to the frame of the animal. Rear legs are removed by sawing. These pieces are now ready for a better surface, such as a heavy table or counter for boning. Ribs are easily managed by sawing to size. Loin and neck meat are no problem to bone away from the spinal column.

Disjointing

My first experience with disjointing left me wondering about the process, but I soon learned its merits in the high country of Colorado when an experienced hunter disjointed an elk for a haul to camp on horses.

This procedure begins with normal field dressing, but the back legs are removed at the joint, hide intact. The entire back section is also removed with hide remaining. Likewise front shoulders and forelegs. The hide is left in place to prevent the invasion of dirt or other foreign matter that would attach to unprotected meat. When conditions are right, the disjointed pieces are skinned and processed.

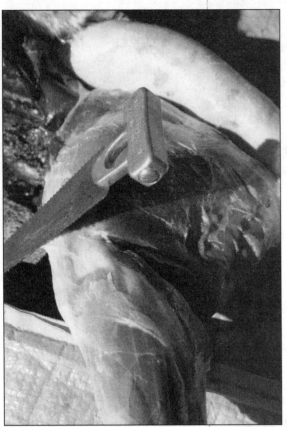

Disjointing can be done, and usually is accomplished, by cutting with a knife into the joint itself until a piece of the carcass, such as a haunch, can be removed. However, a saw is also a possibility for disjointing a carcass.

Right: Here is a haunch disjointed from the carcass and ready for further processing into boned meat for freezer or table.

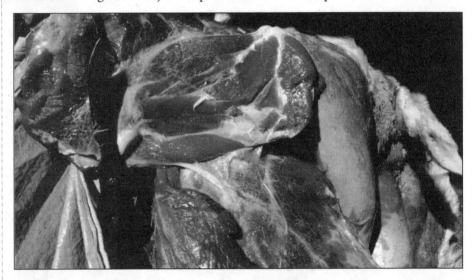

Hang'em High

I do have a come-along that can be carried to the site of a kill. Provided there's a strong limb near the carcass it can be lifted off the ground and hung by the hind legs. If a gambrel (sometimes called a ham spreader) is available to keep the hind legs apart. The carcass is hung head down.

Steps:

1. Skin the carcass completely, beginning at the insides of the hind legs and working downward to the neck. The head and neck, along with attached hide, are sawed free.

2. Remove front legs and shoulder blades.

3. Remove hams. On a large carcass the hind legs can be cut three times. First the hock is sawed through and discarded. Second, the lower half of the ham is cut away and removed to the working station. Third, the remainder of the haunch (pelvis area) is sawed free.

4. One long spinal column with neck meat, ribs and loins is all that remains hanging. Ribs can be sawed free either whole or in parcels for freezing or boning. Neck meat and loin are boned as described above.

Notes on Skinning

Although I've skinned big game animals on the ground and tailgates, hanging 'em high is easier. Removing hide from a carcass can be accomplished with almost any knife, but the best one for the job is the true skinning style. The skinning knife is right because of its design—mild scimitar (curved) shape, thick deep blade, somewhat blunt point and a more pronounced wedge than most other styles.

A wedge is required to separate hide from meat without cutting holes in the hide itself. Hides have value. Where I live deer and elk hides trade for gloves or cash, provided they are intact.

The sooner skinning begins, the easier the job. Also, tugging on the hide, as well as pushing with a fist, is useful in peeling it off.

The skinning process begins by making circular cuts at the hocks all the way around the leg bones. These initial freeing cuts, called ripping, begin the process of working the hide from the carcass. From these circular cuts, another cut is made all the way along the inside of the hind leg to the end of the hide. This cut can be made

Hanging game when and where possible promotes processing. This interesting hoist is from the Carolina North Manufacturing Company. Here it's demonstrated lifting a feeder, but it works also for big game.

This big buffalo carcass was lifted first with a front loader and after working at that level was lowered for further processing.

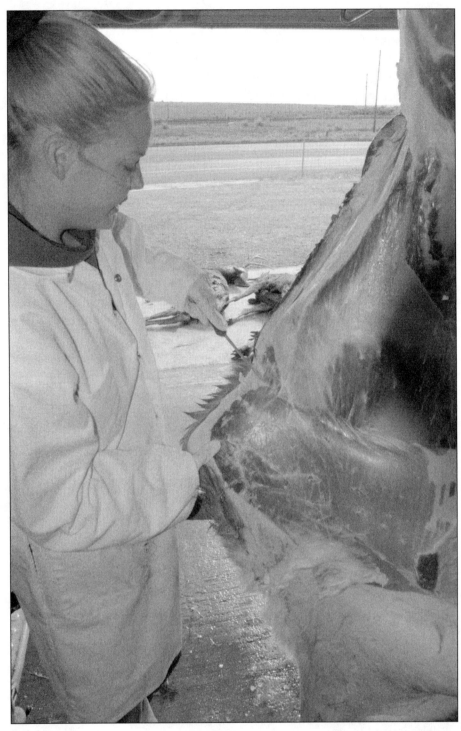

Here, the hide has been pulled downward on the carcass but a little knife work is still required to get the job done.

with a sharper pointed knife rather than the skinning knife because the more-pointed blade gets under the hide better. The tail is skinned out keeping the hide attached.

Now the hunter goes to work with the skinning knife to part the entire hide from the hams. Since the animal was field dressed there is already a cut directly center underside. The removed hide from the back legs now meets with the underbelly cut and the hide can be pulled downward to the base of the breastbone. The job is half done.

The initial cut for field dressing the animal is now extended downward. If a mount is under consideration, caping is necessary. Caping is the removal of hide from the head past the shoulder (normally) and a little beyond the sternum. Too

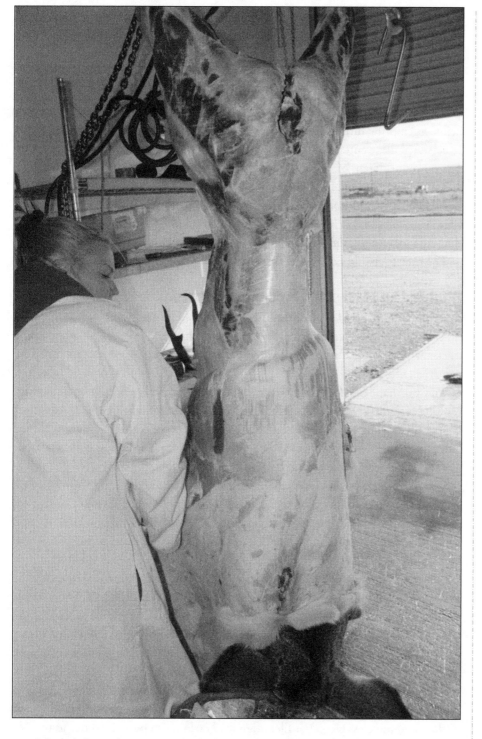

The hide is removed with judicious knife work, but also with the fist pushing hide away from the carcass as shown.

much hide left on the cape is no problem. It can be cut off. But adding hide is a little more difficult.

Our carcass, however, is not going to the taxidermist, so the belly cut is extended all the way down to the elbows of the hanging animal and then directed two ways, one cut toward each front leg. These cuts continue down the center of the back of each front leg. Now the hide can be worked downward toward the head, cutting it free all the way to the upper neck. When the head is sawed off, the hide comes away intact with it.

The end result of skinning is an entire hide attached to the head. Now the hide is cut free close to the head, resulting in one full piece.

A clean job means that the hanging carcass of meat has few hairs clinging to it. These can be brushed off with a cloth, but the carcass will be washed later regardless.

A tanner will flesh the hide, removing fat, so that step is not necessary in the processing steps.

Washing the Hanging Carcass

Before attempting further processing of the big game carcass it must be washed. One professional meat cutter that I know uses a hose at full blast to knock off any hair. The powerful stream of water also loosens outer tissue that can be quickly removed by scraping with a knife.

An alternative method is a rag and small bucket of water with a cup or two of white vinegar added. Vinegar has a cutting effect that helps remove stubborn hairs clinging to the meat. Vinegar water also works on loose outer tissue.

The carcass should be dried with a clean cloth before continuing processing.

Boning the Hanging Carcass at Home

The following process is most desirable and should be used whenever possible. It's easier than boning a carcass lying on the ground, hanging in a tree, or resting on a truck tailgate. Anyone with a little desire and interest can bone a carcass using the home hanging method.

The hide has been completely removed. The carcass is suspended, preferably with gambrel spreading the rear legs. The first step in boning a hanging carcass is removing the neck, which is at the bottom. The neck can be boned for hamburger, turned into a roast, or used for sausage/cold cuts meat. Now that the neck is gone, the front legs and shoulders can be removed.

I saw off the lower hock portions of the front legs first and discard them; they are not palatable. The front legs come off easily by simply pulling outward on the leg and cutting free all connecting tissue. The full front leg with shoulder is soon removed intact. The blades can be used as roasts or the meat can be worked off the bones using a flexible blade (filet) knife.

Next work turns to the ribs. If the ribs are to be kept and cooked they should be sawed twice length-wise. One cut parts one side of the rib cage in half. The next cut removes the ribs close to the spinal column. Now with a stout knife or cleaver the ribs can be reduced to eating dimensions or they can be wrapped and stored intact. Larger rib cages can be given three length-wise cuts per side to reduce size of pieces. And they can also be cut crossways to make smaller packages.

The carcass is now devoid of front legs, shoulders and rib cage. Showing is a long spinal column. This spinal column holds the loin, which will turn into medallions (little round boneless pieces) or filet mignon. The loin can be worked free as the carcass hangs, but this is not recommended. It's much easier to saw off the entire spinal column right up to the neck. On elk, moose, bison or other very large animals, the spine must be sawed off in sections. The full piece or sections are placed on the cutting surface and a filet knife works the loin away from the vertebrae.

The tenderloins rest on the underside of the spinal column. This piece of meat can be excellent, but not always. It is, as promised by its name, tender, but it may become tainted lying in the inner cavity. The way to tell is the nose. Remove the tenderloins with filet or boning knife. Wash well in salt water. Then take a sniff. If they don't pass the olfactory test, process them no further.

The only pieces left hanging are the hams. These are separated by sawing straight down the center of the spine between the legs. If the carcass was hung by a gambrel there will be one leg attached to each point of that gambrel. These haunches are the largest meat part of the animal and on very large carcasses must be reduced into several pieces. But on deer and antelope three saw cuts are sufficient.

The lowest hanging part, which includes the pelvic area, is cut off first. This section is easily boned. Then the large mid-section is cut off. This piece is boned by following the natural lines on the carcass that separate the muscles. Since the carcass was hanging head down, the lower leg is left. There is some worthwhile hamburger meat on this portion, but the very lowest part of the hind leg, the hock itself, can make shoe leather appear tender.

Boned Pieces

Freezing larger pieces retards spoilage. Boned meat chunks, such as pieces of the ham, can be thawed later and divided into steak or other cuts. Fat must be removed. This does not pertain to leaving some fat on the ribs of a prime whitetail buck, but even there it's a matter of taste. (Anyone who dislikes lamb chops probably won't care for whitetail ribs either. The rest of us prefer marinated whitetail ribs over hot coals to rack of lamb.) All other fat has to go. In making gameburger later, fresh beef fat can be added in varying amounts.

Aging

Chapter 17 deals more fully with this important topic. There is aging and there is spoiling. The first designed to break tissue down without rotting the meat, the second the ruination of an otherwise fine game animal. Important—do not age meat wet. After washing a carcass, if aging is desired before processing, dry it well. Moisture promotes spoilage, even at the correct aging temperature of about 40 degrees Fahrenheit.

The Processing Plant

Finally, a word about the processing plant. These professional shops range from excellent to "I wish I'd done it myself." But when time or location (hunting out of state) is a factor, the meat-processing plant is essential.

As one example only, an outfit down the road from me, Maddox Meat Processing in Medicine Bow, Wyo., does a good job, including clean skinning, cooling, *boning*, vacuum packing and freezing, along with caping and horn/antler cut-off. Maddox makes Polish, Italian, summer and breakfast sausage, and they carry interstate game tags. The out-of-state hunter is fortunate to find a good place like this one to take care of his meat.

Big game meat is only as good as field preparation and processing. The little extra time and effort it takes to do a good job will always be considered worthwhile when dinner is on the table.

12

Processing Small Game

Here are two cottontail rabbits taken with my bow. After proper cleaning they will make a fine meal.

No hunting experience matches the thrill of tagging a big game animal. However, I rank my small game hunts as the most enjoyable. The late Ted Walter and I did special survival hunts every year. The goal was striking out with only food for one day. We generally counted on our bows for food. We never went hungry, although there were a few spare days.

That 5,300-year-old man whose mummified body was found in the high Alps, had to be a small game as well as big game hunter. No mummy in history has been studied so closely and with such startling facts, such as his tattoos located at specific acupuncture points or the plants of medicinal value that he carried.

His Stone Age time was more advanced than we imagined. His people lived in dwellings, not caves. Trade routes had been established. His tinderbox spoke of his fire-making knowledge. Metal was melted and worked.

Imagine winter settling into the valleys of the high European mountains more than 5,000 years ago. It is unbelievable that small game played no role in survival.

Taking game for food today is not vital, of course, with supermarkets providing packaged foods of every description. But hunting for food, including small game, never lost favor. I learned to appreciate small game as food from the Louisiana Man.. Mullens knew why he hunted. He hunted for food.

My high school amigo and I soon learned to appreciate the true value of a bullfrog or cottontail rabbit, two targets of our mentor's Remington single-shot rolling block rifle. Muskrats, turtles, rattlesnakes and many other littler edibles were fair game to be taken with one well-placed 22 Short bullet. Anything more potent was unnecessary and possibly wasteful of meat.

Today the tradition lives on. The cottontail rabbit is the number one small game animal in North America, the tree squirrel ranking second. Both can be, and are, hunted with a variety of methods. Beagles work on rabbits. Dogs are also used in some squirrel hunting. The shotgun is popular. But where I hunt rabbits and squirrels the 22 rimfire rifle or pistol is just right most of the time. There's nothing more rewarding than bringing small game into camp for the evening meal.

But whether the feast is prepared under a canopy of trees by a lake or at home in the kitchen, proper processing remains equally important. Chapter 7 discussed field dressing small game. Rightfully, the carcass(es) will be brought into the kitchen devoid of hide, clean and cooled.

How Old is It?

Determining the age of small game is considered less important in this edition, whereas considerable space was provided to the subject in the Third Edition. The change has to do with more experience preparing both squirrels and rabbits.

Regardless of age, these and other animals are normally parboiled. (I prefer the pressure cooker method.) The only time parboiling fails is with very young and tender fare. Then the meat can be broken down too much, almost to mush.

Knowing how to determine small game age is interesting. Very young game is easily identified by size alone. A rabbit of the year, for example, will be smaller and lighter in weight than a mature specimen. Likewise squirrels and other small game.

Other ways to tell age include teeth, ears, rib cage, hide condition and hind leg. Worn and badly yellowed teeth mark a senior. Pliable ears spell young; stiff ears denote old. Rigid rib cage equals older; easily depressed rib cage suggests younger. A tough, tight hide equals older; a softer, more easily remove hide says younger. Press directly into the center of the hind leg: harder for older, easier for younger.

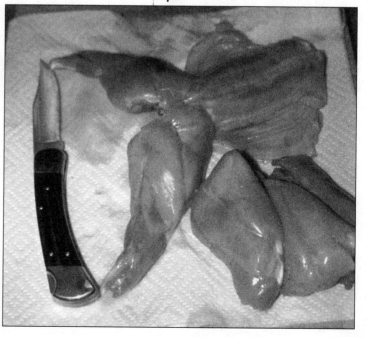

Both rabbits have been cleaned and one is cut into serving pieces. It only takes a few minutes to prepare a rabbit for the pan.

It's not a bad idea to mark a package as to probable age of small game. If Aunt Matilda is coming to supper, you might want to seek out the packages of meat that are younger and therefore more tender.

Sectioning

Rabbits and squirrels are easily divided into five parts. These parts are back, two front legs with rib cage attached to both, two hind legs. It's that simple. Anyone who can section a rabbit can section a squirrel and *vice versa*. The larger-bladed hunting knife or heavy-bladed butcher knife is normally sufficient. A meat cleaver is also useful, but it knows no difference between the hind legs of a cottontail or the hunter's index finger, so caution is the byword. Another helpful tool for this job is a good pair of game shears for snipping off leg ends. It doesn't really matter which end of the rabbit is dissected first, but here is my way:

1. Start by placing the carcass on a cutting surface, such as a butcher block, backside down.
2. With knife or cleaver, remove both back legs together by cutting straight through where they join the back.
3. Next, remove the spinal area that holds the two hind legs together. This is done with two cuts, one down each hind leg next to the tailbone/spine. Now the back legs are separated and without any attached spinal bones.
4. Next, chop or cut off the very ends of the back legs. These are tough and add nothing to an otherwise tender edible.
5. Discard the spinal column and the leg ends. This gets rid of the entire pelvic canal.
6. With the hind legs finished, turn your attention to the back. The back is cut completely through, separating it from the front legs and rib cage.
7. Now comes a very important step. Attached to the back is a tough over-skin. It has to go. Cut directly down the spine with the sharp tip of a knife blade. Now lift the flap of skin on either side of the back and simply rip each one away. It will part where the centered knife cut was made. Do this on both sides and the back is now ready to set aside.

This photo shows how to remove the flap of tough tissue that lies over the back of the rabbit. The knife has been used to slice down the center of the back right on the backbone and then the flaps of tough tissue, one on each side, are lifted away and torn free to be discarded.

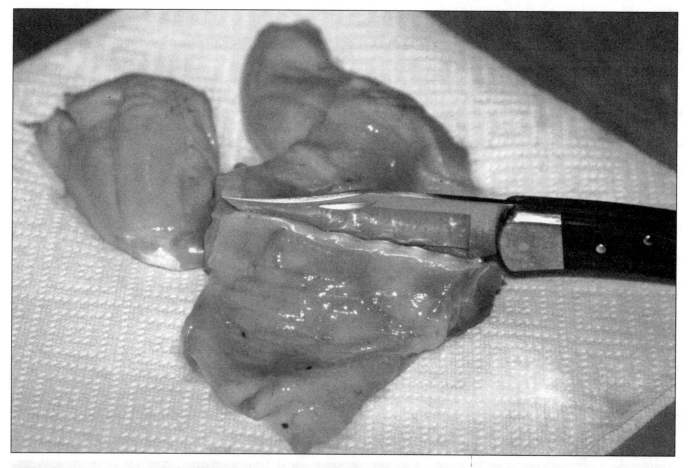

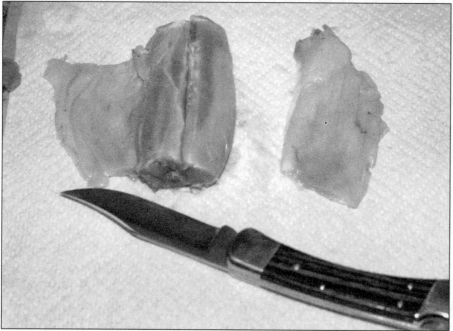

Above: Here is the knife blade going right down the center of the spine. You can clearly see the blade of the knife in the center of the spine and then the tough flap of tissue off to the side of the knife. That tissue will be cut and ripped away and discarded.

Left: Pull the tissue to remove it from the back of the rabbit.

8. The front legs with rib cage attached can be handled in one of two ways. The easiest is splitting it straight down the center, resulting in two pieces, each consisting of one front leg and half of the rib cage.

9. Chop off or cut away the very ends of the front legs. As with the hind legs, these tips are tough and unworthy of the plate. Set them out in the back yard for birds. Also, as with the sharp bony parts of the hind leg tips, these front leg

tips are even worse for tearing through the freezer-ready package. Optional: With game shears, trim away the majority of the rib cage. There is no meat there anyway.

10. The rabbit is now divided into its five cooking parts and ready for soaking out. There are one tenderloin back, two tasty front legs (not a lot of meat here) and two plump hind legs (lots of meat).

Squirrels | Squirrels are sectioned the same as rabbits, but there is no removable over-skin on the back.

Soaking

Soaking accomplishes two important goals. First, it cleans the meat thoroughly. Second, it causes over-tissues to separate from the meat for removal. Plain water works OK, but I prefer salt and white vinegar. Specific amounts of either seem to matter little. A gallon of water with a quarter cup of salt and one cup of vinegar is fine. Salt and vinegar seem to help get rid of over-tissue. And soaking results in a whiter product.

Place small game sections into the container of salt-and-vinegar water and place in the refrigerator. A two-hour soak is long enough, although I've left pieces soaking overnight with no ill effect.

Remove pieces and wash under running water. This takes away the salty vinegar water and helps get rid of the over-tissue, which often has literally bubbled up. A small scrub brush is useful here in taking off the unwanted tissue.

This is the finished product—cottontail rabbit fried served with rice and green beans. Nothing fancy, but a great meal.

Dry First

Do not package the meat wet. Dry the pieces of small game meat on clean toweling. The scrub brush normally takes care of any over-tissue, but I like to rub each piece with the toweling anyway to lift off any bits of over-tissue that might be clinging.

Processing Other Little Edibles

There is no accounting for the range of human food preference. People who happily dine on a breakfast of three-minute boiled embryos, also known as chicken eggs, curl their lips and roll their eyes at the very thought of eating the white meat of a rattler or sinking their teeth into parboiled raccoon dredged in flour/cornmeal and fried up golden brown in smoking canola oil. Here are a few irregulars for processing.

Rattlesnake is easy to manage. The head has been cut off and discarded where nothing can get to it. (Buried under a heavy rock.) Any venomous snake head remains dangerous after removal because it retains poison sacs.

Make a slit from vent to the end of the neck; peel the hide off in one piece. It can be stretched on a board, salted, allowed to dry, and then rubbed deeply with glycerin for preservation. Snake hides are useful for hatbands, covering the limbs of traditional and primitive bows, and decorations including wall hangings.

Free the spare innards, and as with a fish, use an ordinary teaspoon to scrape out the entire cavity.

Section the meat, soak as noted above, dry and package for later frying or cooked up fresh. Contrary to popular belief, rattler is very mild.

Raccoons live in many parts of America but seem most appreciated for food in the South. That's why I turn to *The Foxfire Book* edited by Eliot Wigginton for old-time information on processing the little bandit. Steps include cutting the jugular vein, supposedly to bleed the animal. The hide is removed with regard to saving it, tail intact. The pear-shaped musk sacs (glands) under each forearm are carefully removed, intact. Offal is removed. The coon is sectioned and soaked like a rabbit. The recipes from *Foxfire* are found in the recipe section.

Opossum is handled differently in different geographic areas. Bleeding out remains popular. Some folks scald the possum in boiling water along with a half cup of lime or ashes, according to *Foxfire*. Then they scrape the skin until hairless, remove the innards and musk glands under the forearms, and dissect the head. The carcass is soaked overnight in a salt-water-vinegar solution. Cooking is handled in the recipe section.

Groundhog probably sounds a little more palatable than woodchuck (East) or rockchuck (West) but it's all the same critter. The process goes like this: field dress, including skinning, remove glands from under the legs, and once again soak overnight. Sectioning follows the same routine for the rest of the four-legged smaller edibles.

Prairie dogs are treated the same as rockchucks and woodchucks. They've been food for Native Americans for ages and remain edible to this day, but are seldom cooked up. Once again, it's a matter of food prejudice and the palate.

Turtles, especially those from the sea, are good eating. I never pass up a chance to enjoy real turtle soup prepared by a chef who knows what he's doing. As for the smaller varieties found hither and yon around the country, they're edible, and as with all exotics are relished by some and avoided by others.

Here are some steps to consider. Lop head off with hatchet or meat cleaver. Drop the turtle into a pot of boiling water, well salted at about a half-cup per gallon.

Small game can be a feast and the care and preparation of these animals is easy.

Supposedly, boiling makes further processing easier. Boil for 15 minutes. Remove from water, cool a short while, and then remove shell. Cut along two shell halves to slice through connective tissues. Cut away lower shell carefully and then carefully remove meat from within upper shell.

The only way I can describe the edible parts is that they look edible. They're simply sections of meat. Meat exists also within the tail and legs, but of course claws and tail are discarded. The tail especially holds a nice morsel or two. The neck area also contains edible meat. Innards remain intact with the shell to be discarded. Cut the meat into inch square pieces and soak overnight in the usual saltwater-vinegar liquid. Drain meat, wipe dry and package for later cooking or prepare it right away.

Bullfrogs are just plain good eating and there is nothing to processing them. I learned about turning those twelve-inchers into frog legs from the Louisiana Man. Ping! One more head shot. Down the frog goes into the murky waters of the drainage canal ditch we hunted. The older gentleman remained on the bank as his son and I mucked through the muddy silt for the frog. Only the legs are kept. These are simply cut free with a sharp knife, although game shears makes the job even faster and easier. The legs can be cooked up fresh or frozen for later.

Muskrats have literally saved the lives of North Country trappers and explorers when there was nothing else to eat. They taste better when called musquash. On the other hand, water rats has the opposite effect. Of course muskrats aren't rats. They consume the same vegetation enjoyed by many other animals. Processing is the same as for rabbit with the same five edible pieces.

Porcupine, possibly due to my own food prejudice, is food for the starving hunter lost in the wild and not intended for that special meal for the boss and his wife. But that's personal opinion.

The first porcupine I tried was on a hunting trip with long-time friend Max Wilson. Max and I were both determined to see if porcupine could be cooked up into a flavorful dish. While the meat was cooked in camp, rather than a gourmet kitchen, many condiments were on hand. I deboned the quilly thing and cooked up the pieces. I use the word tolerable to explain the results. I did not give up, however, with only one cooking attempt. The quill-dog was harvested on a bowhunt but I cooked the meat at home. It was a little better. Processing follows the four-legged small game routine.

That's a general look at the processing of smaller edibles. Anyone who learns to section a cottontail rabbit has a good handle on the others, with a few exceptions, such as rattlesnake, turtle and bullfrogs.

13

Processing Upland Game

Above: Fine upland birds like these grouse taken by Sheila Cole deserve the best in field care and later processing. The processing procedure begins in the field. These freshly taken birds will be opened quickly and cooled.

Right: A highly popular game bird is dove. These little birds are best processed by first breasting them in the field. With dove the breast meat is not cut away in two steaks. They're too small for that. The entire breast is removed intact.

For our purposes upland birds include the full range from dove, snipe and woodcock to wild turkeys. As always, processing begins with field dressing, because as that goes so goes the work at home or in camp. For example, many upland birds are best handled by taking breast meat only. The spare, and often tough, leg meat is left for Mother Nature to take back, which she does with her helpers: coyotes, foxes, crows, magpies and myriad other creatures looking for a handout.

There are two general methods of breasting upland birds. One is the separation of wings/breast from legs/body/cavity. The other is boning. The first was explained at the close of Chapter 8. The bird is arranged breast upward between the hunter's legs. He or she places one foot on each wing close to the body. Grasping the legs also close to the body, the hunter then stands up, pulling away the breast and wings while leaving legs and body and offal on the ground.

The other method of breasting, which is boning, requires slicing down the center of the keel (breastbone) to part the meat on both sides into two slabs. On larger birds these slabs of meat can be cut into steaks.

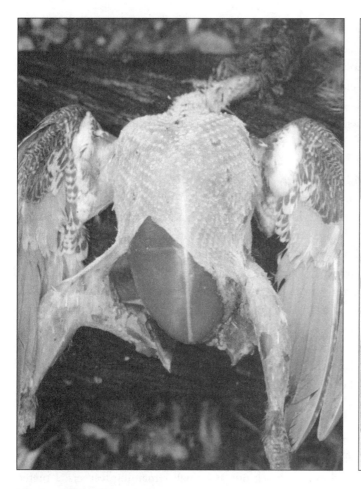

Above left: This nice grouse was plucked not skinned, although some of the delicate skin has been stripped away unintentionally.

Above: After cooling, this grouse was wrapped in clear plastic for transport to camp and further processing. Wrap keeps the meat clean.

Breasted Bird Processing

The hunter arriving home with breast meat only has very little processing left. If the entire breast is intact with bone still in, then boning takes place—simply cutting the pure meat away from the keel with a fillet knife. On larger birds, such as blue or sage grouse, the resulting pieces of meat can be turned into steaks. A full-grown sage grouse, for example, yields three steaks per side, while a blue grouse usually turns into two steaks, unless the cook wants to make them thinner. Small birds, such as dove, quail, snipe and woodcock are not boned. They're packaged or cooked intact.

Further Cooling

Cooling must take place in the field to prevent souring. A dousing with water in the eviscerated body cavity works well, as does removing innards and simply allowing the carcass to air cool.

However—especially if the hunter is close to home or camp— birds may arrive for processing with retained body heat because a bird's normal temperature is high and feathers insulate so well. Cooling is accomplished through defeathering, skinning and soaking, as described below.

Defeathering by Plucking

Plucking most upland birds is not necessary. It's a time- consuming process and the resulting benefit is minimal. Furthermore, the only advantages of skin-on breast meat are two. First, the skin can help retain juices during the cooking process, whereas peeled bare breast meat has a greater tendency to dry out. Second, the skin, especially on a wild turkey, can be browned for finished eye appeal, whereas the skinned

Ron Dahlitz poses with his Parker shotgun and a limit of dove taken on a hunt near Yuma, Arizona. These birds are enjoyable to hunt, but also prime eating when processed correctly.

bare breast meat must be covered to protect it from drying out, and therefore cannot be subjected to direct heat, as from an oven broiler. Browning the skinless breast only tends to produce a dark dry crust on the meat, not a pretty look at all.

To defeather an upland bird, simply pluck the feathers out by hand. There are machines that do this work, but they're generally confined to game bird farms and seldom privately owned. They do work, however, with little rubber projections peeling feathers off in a cloud.

Dry vs. Wet Plucking

Most upland birds can be dry plucked. This is especially true of the smaller ones, such as dove and quail. Meanwhile, wet plucking ranges from desirable to necessary. The wet plucking method has two advantages. It can help in removing the tiniest feathers and it can also save the skin from breaking open when the cook wants to retain that skin for browning. That's the desirable aspect.

The necessary part comes from the fact that some old tom turkeys of my acquaintance all but defied dry plucking. Wet plucking will also get pinfeathers that are very difficult to dislodge dry.

My method of wet plucking is simpler than tying shoelaces. Boil water in a large pot. Set the pot in a place where splashing water won't matter (not the kitchen stovetop). Dunk the bird. Let it rest in the water for a minute or two. And then go at it. Paraffin in the water is reserved for ducks. Plain water is OK for upland birds.

Singeing

After plucking a bird, especially wild turkey, a light singeing of the skin can knock out any small remaining feathers. I prefer doing a better job of dry or wet plucking rather than singeing; however, flame does work. Start up the camp stove outdoors to avoid unpleasant odors in the house. Pass the bird directly over the flame without igniting your own fingers or burning the meat and you're done.

Skinning

There is no trick to skinning upland birds. The skin is loosened at any point, such as around the keel, and lifted off—feathers remaining in place attached to the skin. Pheasant skins with feathers, called capes, have fly-tying value. But most upland bird skins with feathers are pitched out.

Soaking

Soaking upland birds is important in clearing away any possible gastric juices that may be left behind after washing in the field. This is a vital step because if the bird is processed without soaking, the bitter juices may end up on edible parts.

Shotgun pellets, arrows, sometimes bullets where mountain upland birds are hunted legally with rifle or pistol, can fly through the bird's middle, setting free those acidy juices. Ideally, the rifleman or pistol shooter will have put his projectile through head or neck. But the ideal is not always a reality. Soaking also washes away other excess body fluids.

This upland bird was skinned, not plucked, and then the breast meat was sliced away in two thick slabs from each side of the keel (breastbone). Now the cooled and boned meat goes into a plastic container to keep it clean on the way back to camp.

The soaking method for upland birds differs from small game. While saltwater remains ideal for bathing upland bird edible parts, a half-cup of salt to a gallon is sufficient. A touch of white vinegar is all right, but no more than a couple tablespoons to a gallon of water.

After soaking in the saltwater/light vinegar solution, place the birds in fresh cold water to which a tablespoon of baking soda has been added. This rids the meat of any vinegar flavor.

Body Cavity

This step is accomplished after soaking and at the conclusion of the baking soda bath.

Processed by breasting—that is removing the breast whole—this superb dove dish is ready for feasting upon.

While the cavity of the upland bird was cleared in the field, there may be some remaining tissue. During the soaking process this useless tissue is scraped away with a spoon, just as the interior of a freshly opened trout is cleaned. After scraping the body cavity, a cold-water rinse is in order. This ensures final freshening.

Crop and Windpipe

The crop should have been pulled out or cut free in the field and left behind. A hunter may forget this step, however, and if so, the crop must be removed in camp or at home. The windpipe, on the other hand, will generally remain intact in the bird. This won't happen with breasted birds because only wings and breast were taken from the field; everything else being left behind.

It is especially important to cut away the windpipe on a wild turkey. It won't taint the meat directly. The problem is spoilage.

Necks, Livers, Hearts and Gizzards

These parts (giblets) are edible on most upland birds, but so small on dove as to go unnoticed. I have, however, saved them from birds as small as quail. And they are definitely valuable on the wild turkey.

Using the pull-apart method in the field on grouse or partridge means having to go after these pieces specifically because they are left on the ground with back and legs. Soak giblets longer than main meat pieces. Overnight in the refrigerator is not too long.

Boiled or treated to strong pressure-cooking, giblets create stock from plain water, which in turn can be used in making gravy. Some of us enjoy all four pieces after boiling down for stock, consuming them with only a little salt. I like them in the Italian stuffing my grandfather taught me to make. But others do not appreciate inner meats and so I often prepare two stuffings, one with and one without giblets.

Liver | The only warning about upland bird liver—any liver for that matter—is the gall bladder. It should be removed in the field but if it was not it must be sliced out and thrown away during processing.

Gizzard | Neck meat is simply teased away from the bone after cooking to be used in dressing. Liver is cut into sections. The heart is trimmed to remove the tough part. Then it's diced up.

The gizzard, however, requires special attention; it demands different processing. It's composed of two major parts. The larger part is edible. The lesser part, comprising the interior, is tougher than shoe leather but it strips away easily. Simply peel this wrinkled tissue away with fingers and toss it to the cat.

Rinsing, Draining and Drying

An important part of upland bird processing after soaking is rinsing, draining and drying. Rinse the meat in plain cold water, allow to drain awhile in a colander or other straining vessel and then set on paper towels or a clean towel for drying. This step is especially important when the upland bird treasure is to be packaged and frozen. Freezing any meat that is wet or even damp produces an icy covering that can cause discoloration and drying out.

Hanging Up the Bird to Age

Those who remember the hero in Shogun hanging a bird to age it will recall the disgust of the gardener who cut it down and threw it away, to his ultimate punishment. The idea was hanging the bird by the neck until the weight of the rotting carcass made it fall free. That rangy flavor may have been favored in the past but today's supper guests will not appreciate it.

It is all right, however, to hang larger birds, such as the wild turkey, by the head in a cold place for a few days in camp or at home. They're hung by the neck because the body cavity is open and all drainage will be down through that cavity. Hanging does not pertain to birds that are taxidermy bound.

Determining Age

As with small game, determining the age of upland birds helps the cook decide on the right method of preparation. All wild turkeys should be cooked with the well-covered slow method, which some chefs call steaming, or prepared underground well wrapped and covered with juices. (More on the latter later.) Mature birds require longer and slower cooking to tenderize the meat. So knowing how to determine age can pay off. Here are seven ways:

First: The biologically minded hunter knows how to check wing feathers to determine if the bird is adult or younger. Most of us do not know how to do this so we turn to the other six tricks.

Second: Size is always important. A small tom turkey is younger than a big tom turkey, as a rule. Naturally, a hen bird may be small but old.

Third: The hardness of the keel is a giveaway. The keel or breastbone of a young bird is fairly pliable. The keel of a more mature bird is stronger and less yielding. Simply push with thumb pressure to tell.

Fourth: An index finger poked into the breast can help fix age. More mature birds will be firmer than younger ones.

Fifth: On wild turkeys as well as pheasants, spur size and hardness relate to age. The longer and harder the spurs, the older the bird.

Sixth: A way to tell age is the wild turkey's beard, although this is not surefire. Sometimes a younger tom will have a mature beard by virtue of genetics.

Seventh: The lower beak of an upland bird can relate to age. Here's how. Grasp the lower beak between thumb and forefinger trying to support the weight of the bird with the beak. If the beak breaks or bends, the bird is probably young. If the beak is rigid and strong, the bird is probably older.

Processed by boning or breasting, upland game bird meat can be handled in many different ways. Breasted quail are here wrapped with bacon and a bit of green chili or jalapeno and then cooked under the oven broiler.

A beautiful sight—breasted quail wrapped in jalapeno (green chili is also good) ready for the broiler. Legs and backs on these birds were not discarded. They were used to create a fine stock.

Dividing into Serving or Freezing Pieces

Most birds do not demand sectioning either for cooking or storing in the freezer. Dove and quail, for example, are cooked or packaged for freezing whole. Also, if breast meat has been boned out, there are no parts for cutting up. The wild turkey is also handled in one piece.

But sometimes an upland bird does require cutting into serving or freezing pieces. I had always heard of pheasant under glass, but when I cooked my first birds a number of years ago I didn't worry about glass. I covered them with aluminum foil to create a good seal, put them in a roasting pan and slow-cooked them to tenderness.

That was my only method until I met a fellow from Nebraska who had put more pheasants in his game bag than I had ever seen. He tested for age first and all young pheasants were fried like chicken. I was equally surprised when he treated a young wild turkey the same way.

The sectioning process reduces a bird into the same pieces as in chicken found packaged in the grocery store. The wings are cut free at the joints. The breast is removed intact, then either left whole or cut in half down the center of the keel. The legs are removed and divided into thigh and drumstick. This leaves two more pieces, neck and back. The neck is lopped off and the back is left intact. Joints determine where to make leg and wing cuts, including cutting off bony wing tips.

Leg Tendons

Methods change with time and experience. In the past I spent a good deal of effort working tendons free on various birds in camp and at home. I don't do that any longer and cannot recommend teasing each tendon free one at a time. Legs on smaller upland birds bear very little meat to begin with and are therefore returned to nature most of the time. I still save legs from large grouse most of the time, but they do not require tendon removal.

The wild turkey is the major problem. However, when cooked properly, this big bird gives up its leg tendons with little more than a good shake of the drumstick because the meat has been cooked with low temperature for a long time until tender. Literally, the cooked drumstick is given a good shake followed by finger-plucking the meat away from the bone and tendons.

Processing with a Mount in Mind

Most of the time birds bound for the taxidermist can also be eaten. On some occasions, however, they cannot. For example, removing the innards of a quail can do sufficient damage to spoil the best efforts of the artist. This is a loss, but there is also a gain. A mounted bird lasts a lifetime, even longer, to be honored, studied or simply looked upon.

All upland game birds are fit for taxidermy—without exception. Quail of all varieties are phenomenal mounted under glass to preserve the feathers. Pheasants make grand mounts. And the king of upland game birds, sometimes considered big game, makes an impressive mount. The wild turkey, of course. The toms especially, are regal mounted either standing at the alert or in the flying position. Especially handsome is a pair of birds, tom and hen together.

Newspaper Cone

Preserving upland birds for taxidermy is assured with a cone made of rolled newspaper. Its major function is to keep all of the bird's feathers running in the same, and correct, direction. The head of the bird, with wings tucked close against the body, is pushed down into the cone, thereby aligning all of the feathers. The tip of the cone is bent back to secure the beak in place. The cone of newspaper, which is several sheets thick, provides protection while at the same time soaking up fluids, should any remain.

Wild Turkey Mount

Fall birds do not make ideal mounts, especially in early fall when the bird's feathers have not grown to full potential. A wild turkey for a mount is best harvested in the spring when the bird is in full feather. This colorful avian can also be tucked into a large newspaper cone.

After taking the turkey, carry it by the legs, not the head. Hanging onto the head can ruin neck feathers as they press against your shoulder. Jammed feathers often cannot be straightened out. Obviously, the neck of the bird must not be cut or otherwise damaged.

While the newspaper cone will soak up some body fluids, it is wise to plug the throat with tissue or cotton before inserting the bird into the cone. Fluids matt feathers down and may stain them as well. Think ahead. Carry cotton or tissue, as well as newspaper for the cone.

Place bird, in the cone, on a clean surface for transportation. Once more, it's a matter of thinking ahead. Have a cardboard box, for example, broken down to serve as a platform. Give the prize a gentle ride home, rather than bouncing it all over the pickup truck bed.

Hang it up by the feet as soon as possible, or bring it directly to the taxidermist. If the bird reaches the taxidermist soon enough he can cape it, salvaging the meat. If this is not possible, then freeze it in the newspaper cone inserted into a large plastic garbage bag for extra protection until it can be taken to the taxidermist.

Processing upland game birds, including woodcock and snipe, is easy and when done correctly results in some of the best wild food on the planet.

14

Processing Waterfowl

During the early years of market hunting in America thousands of ducks were shot by professionals, not sportsmen, and not for personal use, but to sell to the public. Dissatisfied with 10-gauge shotguns, some shooters went to punt guns belching cloud-like shot charges from big bores often mounted like cannons on the bows of boats. Market hunting was rightfully outlawed before the flyways were depleted.

Between those infancy years of shooting ducks for sale and the present, waterfowl numbers fell alarmingly. Hunting was not the reason. Habitat, or rather the loss of

Waterfowl are among the most coveted of birds hunted for food. These geese represent a bounty that has through excellent management grown in numbers.

it, caused the problem. Wildlife, as with humans, must have a place to live. Through good game management and Ducks Unlimited, an organization dedicated to large and healthy populations of waterfowl, ducks and geese are back, especially geese.

In recent years many non-hunters and even anti-hunters opposed to waterfowling have complained about too many birds, especially geese on golf courses. "You can't shoot nine holes on this course," one duffer complained, "without stepping in something a goose left behind."

Handling waterfowl, as with all other game animals and birds, begins with inspired step-by-step field management, followed by careful and prudent processing for table or freezer. Here are some of the wrinkles.

Before Processing—Bleeding Waterfowl in the Field

Bleeding big game taken by a high-speed bullet or sharp broadhead is primarily unnecessary. The bullet or arrowhead has already done the job.

However, ducks are not normally harvested with sharp broadheads and cannot be taken legally with bullets. Shotguns and non-toxic pellets do the job today.

Steel shotgun loads have improved markedly since their initial debut. Ideally, these loads should be fired from a modified choke rather than full choke shotgun because steel pellets do not deform. Therefore, there are no fliers in the pattern. Fliers are flattened-out pellets that leave the pattern like little Frisbees. A modified choke provides very tight patterns with steel shot.

Bismuth is another excellent pellet, especially in shotgun barrels not intended for steel shot. Bismuth has good density, but is not destructive of standard chokes. There are various other non-toxic metals that make efficient shotgun pellets, especially tungsten-iron, as proved by the superior patterns provided by Federal Premium Tungsten-Iron High Velocity loads.

So what does all this have to do with bleeding ducks and geese in the field? Plenty. Shotgun pellets, especially harder non-toxic shot, do not create wound channels capable of evacuating body fluids. And so the waterfowl hunter who makes a neat incision at the jugular of ducks and geese is on the right track when hanging them to drain in the field.

Still In the Field – Drawing Birds

Ducks and geese get by nicely on cold days. They're built to take it because of fantastic insulation. Down covered by feathers is especially effective in retaining body heat. When a duck or goose is bagged, the prize does not immediately cool off.

Drawing the birds—removing everything from the body cavity—promotes cooling because it creates an avenue for heat to escape. It only takes a few moments to draw a duck or goose. A crosscut at the vent creates a large enough entrance to allow the quick removal of all innards. Livers and gizzards can be saved for future use.

Defeathering

Skinning | Ducks and geese destined for any dish other than roasting should be skinned. It's so much easier than plucking. Insert the sharp point of a knife under the skin at the point of the keel—that is, the farthest part of the breast toward the tail. Make a slit. Usually, the skin can be lifted away at this point, literally peeled off.

Sometimes further knife work is required, however. One of my favorite duck recipes is soup with barley. Since the duck will be boned anyway, skinning makes sense for this or any recipe other than roasting.

When dry plucking, hold the bird firmly and pull the feathers toward the head to remove them. Grasp small clumps of feathers to keep from tearing the skin.
Photo by Julie Johnson

Dry plucking is best done outside and over a trash can, for obvious reasons.
Photo by Julie Johnson

Dry plucking | Start by creating a ring around the collar by pulling feathers out circularly at the lower neck (next to the body) of the duck or goose. This leaves a ring of exposed skin around the neck about one-inch wide.

Placing the bird on a strong flat surface makes the rest of the task a little easier. Head facing toward you, begin by firmly bending the head of the bird back against the body. This step makes the skin taut. With steady pressure holding the skin tight, feathers are removed by starting at the ring around the neck. Hold the bird firmly with one hand while plucking with the other. Remove feathers from the ring around the neck down toward the tail.

Maintaining the skin tightly against the carcass is the key to this method. Feathers are much easier to pluck when the skin is taut, not loose. Rotate the bird around and around, the plucking hand ever working downward toward the tail. The best method is finger pressure against the body as feathers are pulled. Rather than pulling feathers out, they are forced free, especially with the thumb. In a sense, feathers are peeled away rather than pulled directly out.

Torch the Rest | Ideally, all feathers should be pulled out. But a few may defy plucking. A little down may also remain. Any remaining pinfeathers and down can be burned off with a propane handheld torch.

Wet Plucking | Do this job outdoors. It requires a large pot of boiling water. A camp stove is ideal. Before starting, dry pluck some of the major feathers free. Paraffin alone will not do the entire job. Remove the wings, too. They'll only get in the way. The system is just like wet plucking upland game birds with the exception of adding paraffin, which can be found at just about any grocery store, to the water. When my grandmother canned preserves she always topped the jar with paraffin and its use is still popular today.

A good formula is to use three 12-ounce cakes of paraffin dropped into six quarts of rapidly boiling water in that large pot. Now let the water cool down a little. When the water is boiling hot, the paraffin is so liquid that it

The remaining pinfeathers and down can be burned away with a torch. Keep the flame moving to protect the skin from the flame. Photo by Julie Johnson

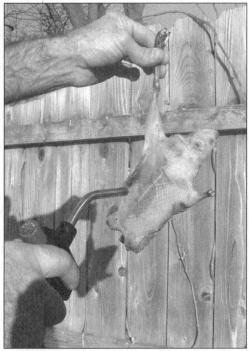

tends to run off waterfowl feathers like sheets of rain. Ideally, the birds are quite cold at this point, which helps the paraffin stick to the feathers. Dip the birds two, three, even four times to build up a wax coating on the feathers.

When wax is built up, dip the bird into cold water. This hardens the wax, making it stick more firmly to the feathers. The bird is ready for plucking. Simply pull the wax-covered feathers away from the body in clumps.

No Paraffin | The hot water method can be used without paraffin. For some birds, especially smaller ducks, simply dunking them in the hot water loosens the grip feathers have on the skin. But in my experience, paraffin helps a lot.

Nitpicking Stubborn Feathers | The propane torch noted above can come in handy burning away minor pinfeathers and down, but don't count on it for getting rid of major feathers. Tweezers can also be used to pluck away minor pinfeathers, but they're not much good on down. Singeing with the torch works better on down.

Windpipe and Body Cavity Tissues

After the bird is defeathered, cut the long windpipe free before boning or sectioning. This is best accomplished with a sharp thin-bladed knife, making a long incision the length of the neck. The windpipe is easy to spot. It's a long stringy-looking thing. If the neck is to be discarded anyway, then naturally this step is unwarranted. Lung tissue, if any remains, is removed. A toothbrush works well in scrubbing unwanted tissues from the body cavity.

Use a sharp knife to cut away any damaged tissue or excess fat.

Photo by Julie Johnson

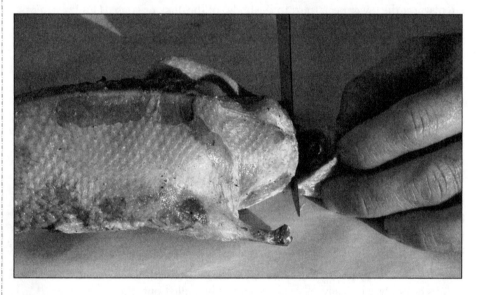

Boning

For soups or any recipe requiring pure meat, boning is the best way to go. The process is just as simple on ducks and geese as it is on upland game birds. Skin the birds. No point going through the trouble of defeathering only to remove the skin anyway.

Cut the legs off close to the body. They disjoint rather easily. Game shears do a good job of cutting away the back of the bird. This bony part can be boiled to reduce some of its juices or roasted. Breast meat is removed from the keel of the bird by cutting right against the bone, slicing the pure meat away in two large chunks, one for either side of the breast. Leg meat can also be boned with a sharp fillet knife, or if the legs are put into soup, the meat is simply cooked off. This is especially effective with a pressure cooker.

When ducks are prepared for a dish like this they do not require plucking. Skinning makes more sense. Parboiling sections ducks tenderizes pieces for slow frying with condiments.

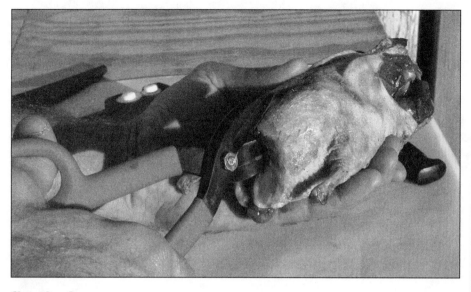

Some people use a cleaver, but game shears or snips also do a great job of cutting waterfowl into serving pieces.

This handsome dish shows just what can be done with boned waterfowl meat

Sectioning

The Chinese have a wonderful way with waterfowl, usually sectioning their birds, rather than boning them out. I enjoy watching a Chinese chef section a duck or goose. Now and then I find myself in downtown Los Angeles where I never fail to purchase a duck or two. These are cooked through and then sectioned in front of the customer. Whack! Whack! The cleaver strikes and in seconds a delicious duck is cut into serving pieces.

We can use a meat cleaver to section ducks, too, but our ducks and geese will be sectioned (usually) before cooking. It goes like this. Skin first. Once again, no sense plucking only to discard the skin anyway. Disjoint legs close to the body. Cut away bony back part with game shears. Section the breast of a small duck straight down the middle with a heavy knife or cleaver. Large duck breasts are cut into four parts with two slices, one length-wise, one across. Six to eight breast pieces for a goose. There's not much more to tell about sectioning waterfowl.

Saltwater Wash

Unlike other meats, boned or sectioned waterfowl are treated only to a light saltwater wash for thirty minutes. This prepares the meat for cooking or packaging. No white vinegar is necessary. Just add a half-cup of salt to each gallon of cold water. Rinse afterward in cold tap water. Dry the meat on clean towels before preparing or freezing.

Upland birds are easier to process, but all in all, waterfowl can be handled rapidly and without too much time or trouble invested. And the effort spent on these wonderful edibles is always worth it.

Boned duck or goose meat turns into a very fine soup cooked gently on the stove or in a pressure cooker.

15

Preparation for the Freezer

The *Fourth Edition* of this book reflects the advantage of additional time spent testing various recipes as well as facets of game care. For example, careful marking of packages with exact content and date information was tested again, proving to my satisfaction that when red meats, especially without fat, are double-wrapped, a full year in the freezer does not attack edibility. I also re-establish many points from previous experiments. Such as: keeping cottontails in the freezer longer than six months, even after double wrapping, negatively effects this excellent meat.

My so-called tests aren't tests. They're demonstrations too personal and subjective to be scientific. But I stand by my conclusions until better information is established. That's why I cook rabbit within six months after freezing, regardless of the wrapping style used. See the close of this chapter for specifics on freezer longevity for various meat types.

Another personal truth is that meat frozen in large chunks fares better than meat frozen in small pieces. That's why when I know that deer, elk, antelope or any other

Here a large chunk of meat is ready for packaging. It will first be wrapped in clear plastic, then regular freezer paper.

big game animal will reside in the freezer for up to a year before cooking, I whack off large pieces and freeze them intact to be cut into steaks or boned when defrosted.

Obviously, wrapping and storing wild meat properly is vital because to do otherwise is inviting waste as well as the complaint no game cook ever wants to hear: "This meat tastes sort of gamy" even though it was well cared for in the field and processed correctly. The few extra precautions taken in preparing meat for the freezer pay off not only in good eating, but cash in hand. Wild meat is worth a lot of *dinero*, so let's take care of it.

Freezer Taste

Some call it freezer taste. Others call if freezer burn. It's when the meat degrades in the freezer. Proper wrapping shields the product from the ravages of drying cold.

Watch Those Bones

Before wrapping any piece of meat from sectioned cottontail or squirrel to moose roast, be sure that there are no protruding bones. This is especially true of smaller game and birds. A sharp piece of leg or wing bone can pierce the best package, admitting freezer elements and air to the exposed meat, usually turning it white and unpalatable.

Double Wrapping

My own meat from small to large game, upland birds and waterfowl included, is treated to simple double wrapping that includes plastic wrap followed by freezer paper. There's no trick to it. Simply wrap the piece of meat first in plastic as tightly as possible, the goal being exclusion of all air. This tight plastic wrap continues to protect as long as the meat is in the freezer.

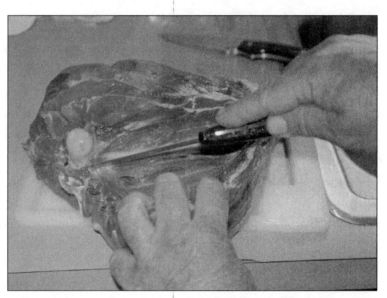

Freeze only good useful meat. Remove all the bones and fat to save space and improve taste.

Regular freezer paper finishes the package. It, too, is closely bound onto the meat with the slick side against the plastic-wrapped meat. I use ordinary half-inch wide masking tape to effect a good seal so the outer paper covering remains intact for the duration. Use whatever plastic, paper and tape it takes to bind the package into a firm and solid unit. This is cheap insurance.

Vacuum Packing

I've learned a new respect for vacuum packing over the years, although I still go with the double-wrap system for my own wild meat. Following a fishing trip in Oregon with my lifelong friend, Kelly Black, there was considerable fresh tuna, sea bass, lingcod and salmon to take home. Kelly used his vacuum-packaging machine with all of it.

Fish can fail in the freezer, as anyone knows who has pulled out a nice filet only to find that it looks mummified. The vacuum-packed fish Kelly prepared for us proved excellent for six full months. The fresh tuna seemed to soften up after that and we used the remainder right away. Salmon was next to show signs of freezer damage. Then ling cod and finally the sea bass, which came from the package eight months later tasting fresh.

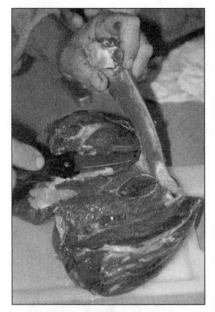

Don't freeze bones. They take up space and add nothing to the package of meat in the freezer.

This is what boned meat should look like before packaging.

Packaging Only the Best

I'm not keen on packaging bones in my freezer. My big game meat is boned, most upland birds likewise. Waterfowl—it depends upon cooking style. For soups or any recipe requiring pure meat—especially ducks—are boned. Geese and ducks destined for the oven are frozen intact. Likewise wild turkeys, which will be roasted, cooked underground or deep-fried. Small game goes into its wrap-up sectioned. I package few bones and never fat (exception noted below).

I'm convinced that fat goes first in the freezer. Since most big game animal meat is not marbled, the fat comes off intact and is easy to discard. The meat then goes into the freezer pure and lean. Burger is ground up without fat, too. Fresh fat is added later on for grill cooking, not added at all for making meatballs or for that matter fried burgers. More on gameburger in Chapter 17.

That one exception on fat? Ribs from a mature whitetail buck. Some fat is trimmed, but not all by any means. It's usually pure white and delicious—based upon what you're used to, of course. Those who are not fond of rack of lamb probably won't go for whitetail ribs on the coals either.

Bloodshot Meat

This unsavory term describes an unsavory condition, the place where the projectile—and this can include the arrow—has penetrated tissue. The effect is, pure and simple, damaged meat. Our culture is not in tune with a fowl hung by the neck until it falls free from rotting, nor are we keen on meat darkened by projectile damage.

I read with interest the words of Nessmuk, the premier outdoorsman of his day, as he described one of his favorite venison dishes. From his book, *Woodcraft and Camping*, he wrote, "Soup requires time, and a solid basis of the right material. Venison is the best, and the best material is the bloody part of the deer, where the bullet went through."

Ness, old fellow, you're the greatest, but most of us will cut away the "part where the bullet went through" rather than processing or packaging it. One point bears noting, however, and that's the fact that Nessmuk shot a modest-caliber muzzleloader with round lead ball, not nearly as destructive of tissue as today's high-speed bullets.

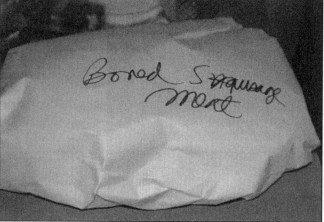

In short, package only the prime. The rest will not go to waste—sinew, bone, fat—because Mother Earth will reclaim every molecule of it. Just don't freeze it, then throw it away. Toss it first.

Above left: This package of meat is clearly marked with all the information required.

Above: Simple markings can sometimes be enough to jar your memory, but the more data you include, the better.

Information

Every package of meat must be carefully marked with pertinent information, including the type of meat, the cut, the date and even the hunter. Every shred of data can prove important.

It's vital to know, for example, whether the meat is moose, elk, deer, antelope—or javelina, the latter demanding very careful cooking. The cut is equally important. You roast a roast and make Golden Nuggets from boned meat.

The date reminds us to cook it up before it loses its best color and taste. When the whole family was home, it was important to note the hunter's name on the package because that tuned us in to the approximate age and condition of the animal. Naturally, far less information is required when the freezer contains meat taken by one hunter. Then the name of the game, such as deer, the cut and the year it was taken, suffice.

For a period of time my state game department aged animals for a study I conducted. I wanted to find out if older game was tougher or less flavorful. And so I faithfully mailed in a tooth that was studied. Then I marked the age of the animal on the package. Interestingly, older deer and antelope fared very well on the table. Older moose, elk and buffalo (bison) were a little tougher than younger ones, but still tasty.

Freezers

It's probably true that the chest freezer is, all-in-all, best for preserving meat over time. However, the upright is more convenient. When I had the former I was sure to package according to cuts—steaks, roasts, boned meat and so forth all placed together in the freezer, rather than by type of game—deer, elk, moose. Now that I use an upright, I'm not so particular. It's rather easy to locate the type of meat and cut I want.

Time to Cook

Defrosting meats is simple enough. These days we have excellent defrosting cycles on microwaves, for example, although care is still required or dark and tough cooked spots show up on the meat.

Thawing packages by simply setting them out at room temperature works, but if left for a longer period of time, bacteria can mature in meat.

Defrosting in the refrigerator is safe, but takes a lot more time.

If a cook knows well head when he or she will need the meat the refrigerator is ideal. Cooking partially defrosted meat is all right. I do so with roasts all the time. The final bit of thawing takes place right in the oven.

Defrosting meat in water is also acceptable, but of course leaving it in the water all day can reduce juices dramatically.

I prefer to put the package on the kitchen counter for awhile for partial thawing, then place it in the refrigerator until cooking time.

Refreezing Meat

I've heard that freezing a piece of meat twice ruins it. I have not found that to be the case. Recall that larger hunks of meat last longer in the freezer than smaller pieces. I often partially thaw a hunk of meat, cut off the part to be used and refreeze the rest— preferably in fresh plastic wrap and freezer paper, the new package fully taped up. I have also refrozen pieces of meat that were completely thawed. If there was a negative effect, I could not detect it.

I'm not suggesting that meat should be thawed and refrozen as a rule. However, if for some reason a piece is not used after thawing, carefully rewrap it and pop it back into the freezer. That's better than allowing it to sit out too long.

Longevity

The following is provided as a guideline only. There is nothing scientific about the information. Based upon my own experience, various meat types stand up to the freezer differently.

Small Game | As noted earlier, rabbits go about six months when properly wrapped for the freezer. However, I've had palatable cottontail that was frozen a full year earlier. The six-month notation is for general information only. It also depends upon the dish to be prepared. While tender fried rabbit, following parboiling, is best suited to meat that's been in the freezer for not much longer than six months, rabbit stew works out fine with meat frozen for as long as a year.

Squirrels seem to last longer than cottontails. I lost a package of squirrel meat in the chest freezer one time. About 14 months later, it surfaced. I made a stew of the meat that was enjoyed by all.

Upland Birds | I rank these with cottontails. Six months is quite long enough to keep them packaged in the freezer. Dove, for example, freeze up with some air around the breasts. It's almost impossible to do otherwise due to the shape of the meat to be frozen. This air probably has a lot to do with the fact that dove are best eaten a couple months after freezing and not beyond six months if possible. On the other hand, I've had boned grouse that were good eight months after freezing, but once again, why not eat it up sooner?

Waterfowl | Almost on an arbitrary basis, I give waterfowl eight months in the freezer for no loss of full flavor. I've had

These professionally wrapped wild meats are protected by heavy plastic with no air pockets.

goose frozen for a year that was acceptable, but possibly could have been better had it been roasted inside of eight months or so. Ducks likewise. Although duck meat bound for soup can probably stand a full year frozen before it loses any appreciable quality.

Gameburger | Gameburger with 10 to 20 percent fat content lasts a full eight months without loss of taste or color. I used to gauge this at six months but more recent study has prolonged that original evaluation. Keeping it frozen for eight months indicated no lack of edibility, but in some cases color waned a little. Gameburger without fat goes a full year and even longer.

Red Meat | Boned red meat, or meat in large hunks, such as full-size haunches, lasts a full year and longer with no loss of quality. This time is reduced by a couple months when fat is present in the meat. I've cooked boned red meat, frozen without fat, that was in the freezer for 18 months and it was still good.

Frog Legs, Turtle, Rattlesnake | It's much more difficult to put a freezer age marker on these and many other meats. I simply don't have the data to back up my notions. I can say, however, that I've had frog legs and rattlesnake meat frozen a full six months properly wrapped that was entirely edible.

After Two Years

We learn through experimentation and experience. I purposely refrained from cooking specific packages of meat kept in the freezer for a full 24 months. Steaked venison, boneless with no fat, was all right, but lacked some of the quality the same meat provided fresh or frozen for up to a year. Burger meat without fat was acceptable, but once again decidedly reduced in overall color and flavor. Burger meat with fat was definitely less palatable than the same gameburger frozen without any fat at all.

Conclusion—don't take a chance. Provide good field care for meat. Process it right way. Package carefully and use it up in a reasonable span of time.

Double wrap all game meat or use the vacuum packing method to ensure as close to an airtight parcel as possible. Compact the packages close together in the freezer rather than spread apart. This way frozen packages protect other frozen packages. Defrost meat carefully, never allowing a package to sit at room temperature very long beyond initial thaw.

And go ahead and use that meat. It may be a treasure, but it's not one to keep around like an heirloom.

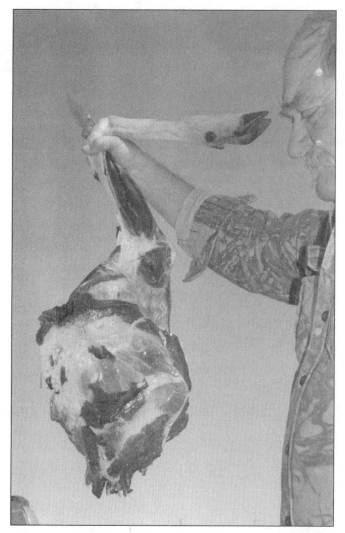

The entire haunch has been removed and will now be boned and cut into pieces suitable for wrapping and freezing. Good work here means better meat later on.

16

Aging or Spoiling?

Jeffery was a great outdoorsman, proud of his Native American heritage. I recall the day he stopped by a stream and caught a trout with his bare hands. Why, then, did he spoil six antelope harvested by himself and his family?

By aging the meat, that's how. Only in this case it was better called rotting. He hung all six animals in his garage in early fall. "They need a week to mellow out," he said.

I pleaded my case, reminding him that aging meat in temperatures in the 70s would spoil it.

"No," he concluded, "you've got to age meat for full flavor and tenderness." A week later he cut the 'lopes down and brought all six to the animal pit outside of town. They were inedible.

Game meat varies greatly in grain. Antelope is fine-grain meat. It demands no aging but can be left at 40-degrees Fahrenheit or a little colder for three or four days

The two deer hanging in the background (left of photo) are already in the aging process and will not be aged one moment further after they are transported to the locker or home processing station. They're bagged against flies and the weather is cool.

without harm. When temperatures are warm and there is no walk-in box to hang the meat in, forget aging.

The right avenue is processing soon after the meat cools. Hang overnight to rid the carcass of body heat and in the morning fetch your tools and reduce that deer, elk, antelope—whatever—into freezer packages. If it's impossible to get the meat into the home processing area, or a nearby processing plant, then hang in a protective game bag overnight, but do not leave the carcass up during the day. Take it down; place it on a tarp; cover it for insulation. I use one tarp under, one tarp over, and an old sleeping bag over it all to keep cold in and heat out.

What is Aging?

The process of aging requires a clean and protected place to hang a carcass or quarter so that air can circulate all around it. The location is fly-free and about 40 degrees Fahrenheit. It is dry, not damp. Dampness tends to spoil meat. Aging in this environment tenderizes meat by breaking tissue down.

Whether or not aging improves flavor is a personal assessment. I have eaten a great deal of game meat freshly packaged for the freezer only one day after it was taken. Taste proved excellent. I have eaten a great deal of game meat properly aged. Taste proved excellent.

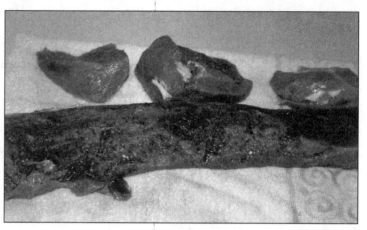

Aged meat like this loin will change color, darkening in time. Overly aged meat will turn very dark.

Aging Begins in Camp

Game hung in camp, hopefully during cool weather and in a game bag (porous cheesecloth) to keep flies off, starts to age. Hunters tend to forget this; when they get the meat home, they hang it to age when it has already aged long enough.

In a Maine hunting camp, four deer hunters got their bucks, but not on the same day. The first was dropped on day one of the adventure while the fourth was taken on the fifth day. That first buck, hanging unskinned but in a cool, dry place and in cold weather never above 45-degrees, had aged for four full days plus one afternoon, plenty long enough.

Don't forget to count camp time as part of the aging process.

Temperature

An established proper aging temperature is 40 degrees Fahrenheit; however, aging is quite probably workable down to just above freezing and up to perhaps 45 degrees, maybe even 50 degrees if the meat is not left for longer than two or three days.

Experimenting with various aging time and temperatures has been fruitless for me. I could never arrive at a conclusion on exact temperature or time for any given carcass or quarter. But I'll venture a few suggestions below for various species.

Dry Only

Water does not harm meat during the processing procedure. However, there is every indication that when aging a hunk of meat, such as a haunch, or for that matter an entire skinned carcass, the meat should be dry. Moisture tends to spoil meat, probably because dampness is a good breeding ground for unwanted biological life. So before aging, use clean toweling to totally dry a carcass or any meat parcel that has been washed with water.

Cutting into this aged piece of game meat reveals red color within but darker on the outside. Longtime aging can dry meat out too much. After all, drying is the process used to make jerky, but jerky is very thinly cut. A piece of meat this thick will not dry completely before it spoils.

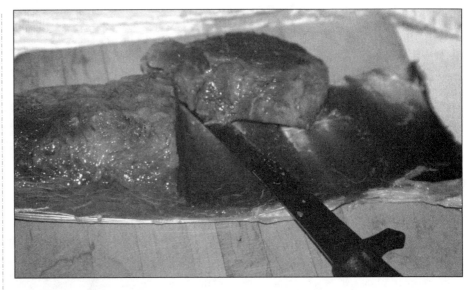

Remove the casing on a piece of aged meat with a sharp knife. Don't cut too deep, you'll waste good meat.

Larding aged meat for cooking on grill.

Clean Only

Aging meat with any form of detrimental material on it can cause spoilage. If, for example, a hunch is hung to age, ensure that the entire pelvic canal is clean and dry. Likewise the entire skinned carcass. Gastric juices, especially, will literally eat away at the good meat.

Casing

During the aging process the outer layer of meat turns into a somewhat hardened, almost leathery, texture called casing. This is not harmful. However, it is also not edible. It's just too tough. And so it must be carefully removed before cooking the meat. If the aged meat is boned out, it's easy to remove the rind with a sharp fillet knife. The casing is simply sliced away. Only the casing is removed. Going deeper into the meat wastes prime edibles. The longer meat hangs to age, the thicker casing becomes.

As a young man I worked briefly on a ranch—not as a cowboy, I'm no horseman, but as a ranch hand (lots of fence mending). When a deer was brought into the ranch it was skinned and hung during the winter. Pieces were cut off of the hanging carcass until there was nothing left but the skeleton. A deer never lasted a full week. There were too many mouths to feed. Casing became quite thick but was always easy to slice away with a sharp knife.

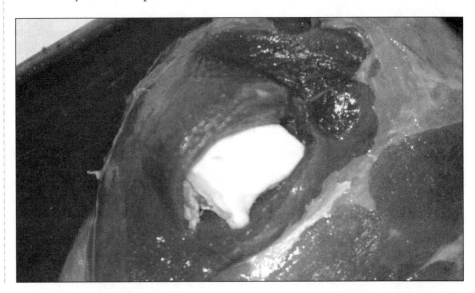

Case-Aged Meat

A dollar off this package, two bucks less for that one—this is often seen with supermarket meats. The reason is usually case aging, that is, meat aged in the display case itself. Rather than red, this meat is darker. Some people prefer case-aged meat to anything else.

Hunters who like case-aged meat can have it by simply placing a piece in the refrigerator and leaving it for a few days or until the desired darker color appears. That's all there is to case-aging meat at home. The only caution is timing. If the meat goes too long in the refrigerator it will not be case-aged. It will be spoiled.

The Walk-In Cooler

I'm surprised at the number of walk-in coolers in regular homes these days, but they pay off when a lot of meat, domestic as well as wild, is brought in for aging.

A relative who raises cattle as a service to needy families does his own skinning and quartering but has the meat processed professionally. After putting the animal down and skinning it, but before taking it to the processing plant, he hangs the quarters in his own walk-in freezer for aging at 40-degree temperature, one week for beef.

Freezer-Aged Meat

One reason I age very little meat—and when I do it is for only for short periods of time—is freezer-aging. Freezing, per se, is not an aging process. However, freezing does break tissue down, so there is a little tenderizing. In theory, freezing breaks down cell walls (I'm told) due to the liquid interior expanding. Perhaps this is so. Perhaps not. But I do believe that freezing does tenderize meat, at least to some small degree.

Aging Ground Rules for Various Species

The following notes are based on experience, not proof of any kind. However, it is definitely true that various meats differ markedly in texture and therefore require different aging times.

Antelope | My experience with antelope, which is considerable because I live in the number one pronghorn state in the nation, suggests that zero aging time for this species is correct. There is simply no need to tenderize antelope meat, and if aging promotes flavor, I've not been able to detect it in my experiments.

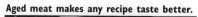
Aged meat makes any recipe taste better.

Antelope are normally hunted in early fall during warm weather. All the more reason to shoot, field dress, cool the carcass down overnight, and reduce the meat into freezer packages the very next day. Obviously, out-of-state hunters cannot run home to do their own processing. I've seen freezers in pickup truck beds and on trailers. I'm not sure if they're ever turned on (as with the latest electrical converters) or if they serve only to insulate with ice or dry ice. If there is no way to keep the skinned carcass cool, then the processing plant is the best way to save the meat.

Black Bear | Black bear meat is much coarser grained than antelope and should stand up well to aging. However, at this juncture I've had a chance to experience a number of bears and aged meat has not proved any more tender or flavorful than the bruins field dressed, cooled and processed within a day or so. Regardless, and without proof to back up my claim, I think aging for three or four days at 40 degrees is a good compromise between aging too long and not at all.

Bison/Buffalo | Only one day before penning this chapter the family was treated to a large bison roast. It was full of flavor; it created a wonderful gravy. Fork cutting—no knife required—proved its tenderness. Of course, the meat was cooked for a long time at a very low oven temperature—only 275-degrees.

This was my fourth experience with bison and I'm more convinced than ever that aging for a week, provided the temperature is constant at 40 degrees, is the way to go. One buffalo was aged for 10 days. I could determine no advantage over the week-long period.

Caribou | The longest experience I ever had with caribou came when a guide in Alaska left my hunting party of three men 30 miles off the Denali Highway, never to return for us. My two companions decided to walk for the road as I guarded camp. We all had caribou and so my main fare was caribou meat. I ate it almost exclusively for two weeks. It was good from the first to the last day and I was happy to have it. My hunger was satisfied and I had plenty of energy to range all over the general area.

Caribou meat is relatively fine-grained, not quite as fine as antelope, but definitely finer than elk or moose. If I were to age caribou it would be at the magical 40-degree level for three or four days.

Deer | Aging deer, even at 40 degrees, for two full weeks is, in my experience, too long, and yet that time frame is what I've often been told or have read. Factually, I admit that my deer seldom see any aging beyond a day or so in camp after thorough cooling. Then they're brought home and processed.

I have noticed that on out-of-state deer hunts those responsible for salvaging the meat aren't too concerned about aging. For example, on one hunt in Alabama I watched deer after deer go from field dressing to skinning to overnight hanging in a cooler to processing.

At the same time, I recall those excellent whitetail bucks (Coues deer) on that Arizona ranch of my youth. These deer were field dressed, skinned and hung in cold weather for up to a week and they were good eating the whole time.

As a compromise, I'm going with a range from zero to five days—no aging at all to five days hanging protected at 40 degrees. I'd like to say that the age of the animal makes a difference, but I've had younger and older animals that were all good with and without aging. So let's settle on five days maximum aging time for deer, with a week being all right in cold weather.

Elk | Elk meat is coarser grained than antelope or caribou, but very similar to deer. Partly due to the shear size of quarters, however, aging a little longer than deer seems judicious. The range suggested here is five to seven days at 40 degrees. I've heard and read about 14 days of aging, but cannot substantiate such claims for elk meat.

Javelina | Part of the reason for so many javelinas going to the dogs instead of the dinner table is the old wives' tale about removing the musk gland. I learned this the hard way, following old-time advice to slice the gland out right after the little wild hog buys the farm. What really happens when the gland is cut out is that musk leaks out and most likely gets on the meat.

Javelina are not easy to prepare in the first place because they are musk hogs, but to allow musk to taint the meat moves the task from difficult to nearly impossible. Aging this very fine-grained meat is not necessary and may be detrimental to cooking.

Moose | I've had the good fortune of enjoying several moose. It can be among the best-tasting wild meats in the world, as proved to me in Finland when I enjoyed it cooked to perfection. I've also had my own moose to eat, and have been graced with meat from those taken by friends.

I'm convinced that aging benefits this meat markedly. While full of flavor, moose meat has a coarser grain than elk, for example. A full week of hanging quarters at 40 degrees is about right, and I'll not argue with those who call for 10 days. I'm not sure going beyond seven days, however, does a lot to improve either flavor or tenderness. So I'm going with one week only on my next moose.

Sheep | Many hunters today and from yesteryear herald wild sheep meat as the very best available. I've eaten Rocky Mountain and desert varieties, as well as Dall, and though I cannot rank sheep ahead of mountain lion loin or whitetail ribs, it certainly is great food.

A hunter friend who has taken many sheep, mainly in Alaska, contends that aging quarters for four or five days at 40 degrees is entirely adequate. I must defer to his experience. He also informs me that sheep ribs over coals are hard to beat. And he ages these not at all.

Upland Birds | If aging improves upland birds, such as pheasants, I have not been able to prove it by my humble efforts. And I think some upland birds, namely mountain and sage grouse, are far better with zero aging. Dove and quail likewise. My plan with these is shoot, find, field dress, defeather, cool out, process or eat. Those who believe in aging upland birds are welcome to continue doing so. After all, it works for them and their taste buds. As for the rest of us, we'll process our edible avians very soon after they're harvested to the game bag.

Waterfowl | I've aged exactly one goose, and that was some time ago. My notes tell me that the meat was no better for aging. On the other hand, I recall my master chef grandfather aging a goose (completely dressed, of course) in the walk-in box at 40 degrees for two full days before roasting it. It was great, but I have no way of proving that the short aging period had anything to do with its fine flavor. It can't hurt, I suppose, to hang a dressed goose for a couple days at the correct temperature under the right conditions. But ducks I have never aged and probably never will.

Exotics | Rattlesnake, turtle, bullfrogs—you name it from raccoon to opossum— I can't see aging any of it.

It's Your Meat | As I said previously, there is no accounting for human taste. That's why some cultures love plump white grubs and others feel faint at the very thought of popping one of these wiggly creatures down the hatch.

Aging is also a matter of personal taste and choice. Nothing written here can change that. To those who age deer for two weeks, just as an example, loving the final texture and flavor, we say, "Have at it. Keep doing what works for you."

And so this chapter is one of guidelines only, not prescriptions that must be followed by every reader.

Experimenting

One thing is certain, however. Experimenting is the only way that an individual will arrive at the right aging time to suit his or her taste.

The Best Gameburger in Town

aking the best gameburger in town is simple and fast. Gameburger, processed our way is also more versatile than most store-purchased ground meat because we enjoy more options—10 percent fat, 20 percent. How about no fat at all? That's always my choice. Since game meat is not marbled, the latter is not only possible, but also advisable. So let's go.

Grinding

Fat or suet? This prime gameburger contains fresh fat taken from top grade beef steaks. Remember that no-fat gameburger is recommended for many different dishes.

When my family was growing up and we were eating game meat almost exclusively, the only choice was a commercial grinder. I found one at the local restaurant supply house. It chewed up the wallet considerably but also returned every cent with do-it-yourself economy.

A commercial meat grinder is not practical for most hunters. But there are other options. Smaller electric meat grinders work well for littler jobs. These are not costly, generally under $50. They also pay for themselves.

There are attachments for food processing machines. Some of these are extremely good, not on par with larger commercial grinders (that's not possible) but more than adequate for the average big game hunter.

There are also hand grinders. These were the only home units in days gone by. They worked in the distant past. They work today and can be purchased new or quite often found used.

Then there's the easiest method of all—the professional butcher. Check your nearest locker plant. They may grind meat for a reasonable fee. Bring only boned meat, totally free of fat, to the pro. Let him or her add fresh beef fat, if desired, at 10 to 20 percent or better yet add the fat yourself just before cooking.

Regardless of the grinder used, from arm-powered units to the finest commercial models available, the key to longevity of the unit and the best meat product lies in cleaning the machine. Problems are avoided by cleaning all parts of the grinder after every use and before storing.

The larger commercial machine may also require a little pre-cleaning before grinding meat because these grinders have motors that demand lubrication, which is often in the form of regular oil not unlike that used in an automobile engine.

It is also wise—and I think this pertains to all kinds of grinders—to put a slice or two of bread down first in order to sop up any oils that may linger around the blade area of the unit. The first cargo of meat through the grinder will push out any remaining bread, which is summarily tossed away because it could be tainted with oil.

Any red game meat is a candidate for gameburger, including elk, moose, antelope, caribou, and of course deer. This fine burger meat is being prepared for Italian spaghetti meatballs.

Fat or Suet?

Let's get this one out of the way before proceeding with processing tips for making gameburger. Suet is interior fat. Ordinary fat we simply call fat. Suet, as found around kidneys and other organs, is clean and pure. There is nothing wrong with it. However, trimmed fat, from a T-bone steak, as one example, is tastier. That's pure opinion but I'll stick by it. I purchase fresh, trimmed beefsteak fat from my butcher. At home I trim off and discard the outer layer, retaining only the solid white. My grocery store also sells pre-ground fat frozen in packages.

Processing Fat

Remember to remove all fat from the carcass before processing. Game fat is not bad. It's simply unfamiliar and best trimmed away. It can be used as a treat for Fido the dog or Tom the cat, or put out for birds in the back yard, especially during winter when many of these visitors are looking for something to eat.

Crows and ravens come to my backyard regularly for these handouts, and more than once I've had the pleasure of seeing a full-grown golden eagle landing for a free meal.

Freezer longevity for game meat was discussed in Chapter 15. Meat frozen without fat lasts longer in top shape than meat frozen with fat content. That's why I process beef fat separately to be added to ground game meat just before cooking time. Grinding fat requires nothing more than a small home machine, especially since very little will be done at any given time.

Suggestion: Try fat-free gameburger first, especially if patties are fried in some form of oil, such as olive or canola oil. Spiced normally, these no-fat burgers are very good.

There is also no reason to add fat to pure gameburger intended for meatballs, chili dishes and so forth. But for the grill, adding 10 to 20 percent beef fat produces the sizzling and minor flaming that most of us are used to and desire. To be exact weigh both the ground meat and the fat, kneading in the desired amount of fresh beef fat by hand.

What Meat?

Red meat is the general answer but not a complete one. I've had wonderful gameburger from deer, whitetails, blacktails and mule varieties. Moose makes superb gameburger. Likewise elk. Caribou turns into top grade ground game meat. Antelope is good, too, especially if spiced slightly before grinding. More on this approach later in this chapter and in Chapter 22.

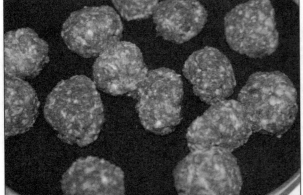

Trimming is the key to great gameburger. While it may seem wasteful to discard parts of a carcass that may be tainted in any way, it's actually economical. Better to lose some meat than a lot by incorporating the bad with the good.

I've had good wild boar, not-so-good ground javelina or bear meat. And while it's entirely possible to grind up small game and upland birds—and I suppose waterfowl as well—my personal experience here is zero. It's red meat all the way with the exception of javelina and bear.

I'm also against grinding mountain lion, being too fine as it is to process any further than boned meat for medallions or steaks. And the meat on my whitetail ribs will be enjoyed over the coals or gas grill, not trimmed and ground up.

The key to prime gameburger is trimming to get rid of any and all discolored meat as well as sinew and tough tissue. The very best gameburger is made of the very best meat. While a large commercial grinder will integrate most of this material, it only makes sense to trim closely.

Trying to save bad scraps is poor economy in the long run because the end product is less desirable than it could be. I'd much rather have a third-pound prime gameburger than a half-pound patty with gristle. So would everyone else.

A boning or fillet knife is perfect for the job, its thin blade working around bone to remove meat. The same knife is ideal for slicing away the bad from the good, that is, the solid red meat from sinew and connective tissues as well as any dark product.

Hold a piece of meat firmly against the cutting board with the bad stuff downward. Then slide the blade of the knife in between the good and the bad, the good above the blade, the bad below. Then use a slicing motion to separate the keeper from the throwaway.

Boned meat for gameburger is derived from various parts of the carcass. Rib cages on moose and elk are good candidates for boning. The reader knows by now that I never bone the rib cage of a whitetail buck because those ribs are great as is. Sometimes mule deer will have sufficient rib cage meat to be worth trimming, sometimes not. Antelope do not. Trying to trim good useable meat from a pronghorn's rib cage is an exercise in frustration. I'd rather devein shrimp.

The front shoulders (shoulder blades) can be fully boned out for ground meat. This is not a given. Sometimes those blades are great for roasts or the boned meat can be used for chili con carne or stews. Main pieces for grinding emanate from odd-shaped cuts. For example, processing a haunch into steaks always yields pieces from both ends that are good for boning and not much else. Neck meat can also be used for grinding. Remember that home meat grinders won't do much with sinew or tough connective tissue, so trim, trim, trim. And forget lower shanks. While commercial grinders can turn some of this flak jacket stuff into burger, home grinders cannot.

Rut Meat

It all depends upon the animal and I suppose personal taste as well. I've never had a problem with rutting elk or antelope, likewise moose.

I cannot say the same for rutting deer with regard to neck meat. The nose knows all here. If there is the slightest hint of musky aroma from neck meat, use it for pets or backyard birds or at the very least separate it from other meat to be ground now but tested later.

Do not mix it in with chunks of boned meat known to be prime. This is only inviting waste. Imagine tainting 20 pounds of super boned meat with five pounds of bad stuff.

Sausage and Gameburger

Boneless game meat can be prepared with pork and spices to make several different types of sausage. These can be made at home or the job can be turned over to a professional.

Down the road about 20 miles from my residence is a game processing plant that specializes in breakfast sausage, Italian sausage and Polish sausage as well as summer sausage. Maddox does an especially good job with the latter, which is not prepared like salami, but rather fried like patties. These patties make an excellent breakfast with eggs and hash browns or home fries, as well as turning into that "something different" for supper on Saturday night. (Serve with sourdough pancakes.)

Ground meats can also be used to create numerous special prepared cold cuts. However, readers of the previous three editions have told me that preparing bologna and headcheese along with many other specialized cold cuts is not popular. And so this edition does not provide information on these. However, there are books specializing in producing these treats.

Clean Only

I appreciate the candidness of one professional meat processor when he admitted that, "No, I cannot guarantee that the meat will be entirely 100 percent free of hair. I do my best. I work hard to ensure that every single one is located, but then—oops. There it is. That one single hair standing straight up in boned meat ready to drop down into the blade of the grinder."

Washing boned meat, followed by drying, ensures that hair is removed—most often down to that one single piece. I suggest wearing reading glasses for this work. A magnified view of the meat helps locate that vagabond and almost microscopic piece of offensive hair that almost got away.

Spicing Boned Meat

Using great restraint, four condiments can be added to boned meat before that meat is ground. These are either soy sauce or teriyaki sauce (not both), garlic powder (not

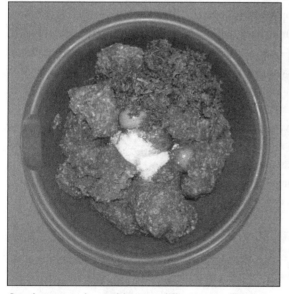

Gameburger can be used in many different ways. This is gameburger being turned into Italian meatballs with spices, Parmesan cheese, and egg.

Gameburger has been treated to beef fat and then used in recipes requiring very little to no fat in the meat the fat can be reduced as it was here using a microwave.

Above: This is Chef Sam's special turkey dressing going together. It includes prime gameburger along with hardboiled eggs, celery, onion, and other ingredients as described in the recipe.

Above right: A pan of meatballs ready for frying and then adding to a red spaghetti sauce. Gameburger that has been well cared for is perfect for this sort of use.

salt) and pepper. All four will impart good flavor to ground game meat. They will also become stronger with age. Using very little is the key to success.

I find adding a touch of garlic powder and soy or teriyaki does nothing to preclude the use of gameburger in any dish and can go a long distance in imparting a more familiar flavor to the meat. Likewise ordinary black pepper. See Chapter 22 for further details.

Freezer Smart

Same tune, different day. Chapter 15 said it all but a reminder is imperative here. Every package of ground game meat bound for the freezer must be secured first in thin plastic sheeting (sandwich wrap) and then protected by regular freezer paper with the slick side inward. As always, the idea is to expel air. A tightly wrapped package of fat-free gameburger stays perfect for a long time when stored in a quality freezer. This ground meat can be used for anything just as if it were prepared only hours earlier, including the ever-popular hamburger. See Chapter 15 for approximate storage longevity of gameburger.

A Few Gameburger Uses

In closing this chapter it's appropriate to consider a few uses for gameburger. First in line is the All-American hamburger with trimmings: tomato, onion, lettuce, pickle, relish, mustard, mayo, ketchup—there's no end to it. Meatballs in soup as well as red spaghetti sauce are created perfectly with fat-free gameburger. The list goes on: chili, meatloaf, Chef Sam's Special Turkey Stuffing (see recipe section), ground meat (with a little Italian sausage) in spaghetti sauce in place of meatballs.

Mix wild and domestic for varying flavor: gameburger and sausage, gameburger and beef hamburger meat, gameburger and ground lamb—let your imagine fly free. There are also ground sirloin steaks to consider. These are excellent in the skillet made with fatless gameburger or prepared on the grill with a little integrated beef fat.

Finally, there are entire books on cooking with ground meat. Gameburger works in all of these recipes.

18

Trailside and Campfire Cookery

Sometimes we make friends with people we never met. I have several such friends. They're mostly authors from times well in the past. Nessmuk, the grand old camper/hunter, is one. I enjoy his philosophy. He wrote in *Woodcraft and Camping* that "We do not go to the green woods and crystal waters to rough it, we go to smooth it. We get it rough enough at home; in towns and cities, in shops, offices, and stores, banks—everywhere . . . with the necessity always present of being on time and up to our work, of keeping up, catching up, or getting left." And so he took on a quiet way of visiting the great outdoors with simplicity foremost.

As we will see in Chapter 26, lucky are we to have the grand high-tech camping gear and tools of the era. With these we can "smooth it" better than any outdoors person of yesteryear.

Nessmuk said we do not go to the outdoors to rough it. We go to "smooth it." Campfire cookery helps to smooth it. A fine meal can be prepared in camp with only a few utensils. Here, there's even a Coleman table to sit at to enjoy the feast.

Staying Over

Hunters who stay over in the field for a given time increase their odds of success. That's because they're in the habitat of the game animal rather than on the fringe—or back home. While this notion may seem simplistic, it's a valid judgment.

There are two ways to sleep in the niche. The first is backpacking. The second is building a camp not that far from a road, but far enough to locate undisturbed game.

With hot spot located, the hunter sleeps over rather than returning to base camp or home, waking in the morning in the midst of the action.

I've backpacked into many honey holes in my time, going joyfully like the tortoise with my home on my back. My Coleman Inyo™ 2 backpack tent weighs only four pounds. It packs like less due to compactness. My backpack sleeping bag from the same company is the Summit™ 2 at little more than five pounds. For under 10 pounds, I have both shelter and sleeping warmth.

For those who prefer a more complete camp—and I've come to appreciate those creature comforts—it's a mere matter of packing gear in a half mile, mile, maybe two. It's amazing how different the habitat can be not that far from a vehicle path. My last pack-in was only a half-mile. I brought in everything but the kitchen sink in multiple trips, staying a week and filling three deer tags (necessary to keep the herd in balance in that region).

I saw, heard and even felt things that running back and forth from a motel room would not have allowed, including my last day in the mountains when a light snow fell in late afternoon just after I'd made a Marlin 38-55 shot at a 75-yard deer. The quiet that came with the snow made its own special sound. This time my camp consisted of a Coleman Outdoorsman™ 10x8 tent with 72-inch center and high walls that I at 5' 11" could stand up in. Mr. Heater frightened the chill away when I dressed in the morning. It was the Hilton of camps, well-lighted with a Northstar lantern outside and a Lazer Stik from Essential Gear for night light inside.

The real beauty of staying over is pure enjoyment of the outdoors. But it's also a chance to harvest great game for camp and home. I always plan to have small game or upland birds by the campfire and it has worked out that way for many years now.

Of course, game taken back in must be packed back out. But there are many ways to accomplish this, as discussed in Chapter 9. There may even be a legitimate four-wheel-drive trail to the campsite for hauling a camp in and getting game meat out. And where legal and prudent, boning and backpacking the prize to the vehicle is a good way to go.

The Survival Hunt

My amigo, the late Ted Walter, and I spent many days on the trail in what we called survival hunts. They weren't grim tests of courage and skill, but rather restful times away from civilization, smoothing it Nessmuk style.

We usually carried bows and arrows. Initially our packs were homemade, terrible things compared to the commercial models available today. But we were young and enthusiastic and didn't mind the burden. We strolled from one lonesome spot to another making camp and hunting for food.

Those simple times of trailside and campfire cookery made lasting memories. We went hungry only once, that being in the high mountains when for two days our rations were slim. But mountain grouse put an end to that brief fasting and we were full again with rich meat provided by the big birds. While no one should embark on such an adventure without proper preparation, the survival hunt remains interesting as a cooking as well as exploring time.

Going way back into the outback can be a great experience for the prepared meathunter, who is especially wise if he has along with him utensils to cook up fresh camp meat.

Backpack Cooking

The MRE—Meal Ready to Eat—of the day of the United States armed forces, is far better than K-Rations and C-Rations of the past. These are balanced meals well sealed against the elements. Gourmet they are not—how could they be? But they are nutritious and I have no problem with anyone who places a few in his packsack.

There is, however, nothing quite like cooking wild game taken along the trail. From cottontail to grouse the meat is delicious and easy to prepare with minor utensils.

Heat comes from any fire safely built and allowed to run down to coals. Or backpack stoves can be used when fires are not prudent, possible or legal. I can fix up cottontails or grouse with one stick-free skillet, a small container of canola oil, touch of garlic powder, paprika and black pepper, and sprinkled lightly with salt after cooking. I guarantee the results.

There is no need for a meat-only meal. Freeze-dried vegetables as well as packaged soups that require nothing more than hot water to bring them to life are abundant and easy to carry. There's no meal better than freshly taken game cooked with a little side food along a trail away from the crowd. A walk through outdoor catalogs reveals numerous trailside cooking utensils including stoves and other useful gear.

Adding a simple and fast meal to backpack cooking is perfectly all right. However, having along the means to prepare small game and birds taken on the trail is always a treat.

The open campfire is not only for light and heat, but can also provide for excellent cooking. Wood varies greatly across the country. In the Southwest a blaze like this soon turns into hot coals for campfire cooking.

The Open Campfire

Cooking on the open campfire requires special care beginning with the right type of fuel and flame. Too much fire and pots/pans go black with the same fate sometimes befalling the food they contain. Too little fire and the job doesn't get done.

Nothing more than a simple rock corral to retain flame and concentrate heat is required for good open-fire cooking. Flat rocks arranged along the sides of the formation are perfect platforms for cooking utensils. Sometimes it's necessary to set a pot or pan aside as the fire calms or builds or to keep contents warm.

My open-fire cooking utensils have changed over time. I still have black-bottomed pots and pans but the cast iron skillet has been retired. In place of the heavy utensil is a less romantic, long-handled stick-free fry pan with lid. So much easier to clean up afterwards; good ones live up to their reputations.

Potholders

No campfire cooking site is complete without potholders or large cooking gloves that allow handling hot utensils without burning a hand. These are not frills. They are cooking tools.

The secret to successful open-fire cooking is moving the utensils to various places with different flame temperatures. It's no big trick because anyone can see when the contents of the pan or pot are cooking too fast and in jeopardy of burning. Potholders make moving utensils safer and faster.

The Dutch Oven

Dutch oven cookery is a world of its own deserving of the many books written about and for it. Some cooks pride themselves in being experts at this kind of cooking. They know exactly how much heat to allow underneath the oven and precisely how many coals to ladle on top. Cobblers, soups, stew—every dish comes away in perfect doneness.

I make good Dutch oven soup but claim no special expertise otherwise. Soup is easy. Ingredients go into the Dutch oven, which can be set down into open flame provided there is a flat base on which to place the oven. The broth is allowed to boil and then the oven is retrieved from the center of the fire and placed on the fringe to slowly roll and bubble until cooked into a savory dish.

Duck soup is great this way. Boned breast meat is braised in the oven, and then the broth is added. Add vegetables after the meat is cooked through. It doesn't take long to soften thinly sliced carrots, for example. Barley is my favorite in duck soup, but instant rice is also good. Perhaps it's only imagination, but it seems that Dutch oven duck soup tastes better than the same made at home on the kitchen range.

Types of Wood

Strange that the better woods are found in warmer climes. Where I live in Wyoming pine is king. Pine is a lot better than no wood at all, but it's certainly all wrong for broiling meat over coals. Aspen is a little better. Going south to Colorado oak is available, although not statewide. Continuing into the Southwest there is not only oak, but also mesquite, which burns hot and long, and instead of imparting a turpentine

Many kinds of utensils work well at the campfire, including an old coffee pot like the one in the foreground.

flavor, mesquite lends a unique and positive bouquet to meats cooked directly over its coals.

For open-fire cooking, any wood is fine. Faster-burning fuel simply requires special feeding, adding pieces to maintain even heat, whereas a nice coal bed of mesquite, oak or other hardwood works long and hard to produce ideal results.

Pots and Pans on Coals

In most instances, even with softer woods, my goal is a bed of coals for pots and pans to rest directly on. A bed of coals is much the same as cooking on a regular stove at home, provided it is flat and it can be maintained for heat. With softer woods the ideal is a side fire with fresh coals added as the cooking bed cools down. Many foods are well prepared by starting with higher heat that is reduced as the food cooks, which is just what happens automatically with a coal bed.

Hardwood coals maintain heat throughout the cooking process. Once again the key to success is moving the pan or pot to hotter or cooler spots on the coal bed. When I get to hunt in the Southwest I always carry a grate, which is placed directly on the coal bed as a separator between the hot coals and the bottoms of utensils.

Broiling Over Coals

This is an entirely different process from cooking on a coal bed. Whereas the coal bed takes the place of a gas range, electric stove or griddle, cooking food over coals takes the place of an oven broiler. Heat comes from above the food with an oven broiler, whereas heat arrives from below when cooking over a bed of coals. But the result is the same.

The major difference in cooking over coals is the imparting of flavors from the smoke. That's why greasy woods don't work well for broiling meat. Exception: I have seen meat broiled with fires made literally of desert greasewood. The cooks were doing a whole goat as part of a religious ceremony. The fire was intense and constantly fed. The meat, however, was kept on the leeward side, the wind never blowing smoke on it.

Some type of grate is necessary. There are lightweight backpacking grates plus a huge variety of different types for camp and backyard use. The grate holds the meat (as well as many other foods from tortillas to corn on the cob) over the source of heat, which is the coal bed. In some instances, the coal bed is so hot that pots and pans can be put directly on the grate, as noted above. The grate in this case is nestled directly down on the coals or raised to whatever level necessary for proper heating of the pots or pans.

One of the better campfire meals my brother and I enjoy is larding a roast (see Leg O' Lope recipe for details) along with marinating and cooking that roast on a grate directly over a coal bed. The roast is turned often. Cooked meat is sliced off thin and eaten hot while the roast continues to cook. Along with Mexican refried beans and corn or flour tortillas this meal is hard to beat after a day of hunting Coues deer or javelina.

Griddle on Coals

A griddle is simply a heavy piece of metal, preferably of a material that can be easily cleaned after cooking. Most griddles for outdoor use are made of heavy metal. They do require seasoning and a proper coating of oil to prevent food from sticking. The griddle is placed directly on a coal bed for heating.

Watch for Sparks and Hot Rocks

In Finland, as the hunters cooked a prime cut of moose meat directly over coals, I was reminded of a lesson I learned years before—about sparks popping like bullets. One shot directly into my eye. Luckily, there was a medical facility down the road and a typically good Finnish doctor removed the cinder in no time. Zero harm done, but I now have a pair of clear lens eyeglasses that I wear in camp and in the field.

Rocks can all but explode in the fire, too, sending sharp penetrating slivers in all directions. Smooth hard rocks are not so bad. It's composite stones, for lack of a better description, that fragment with heat.

In all types of cooking, but especially around open fires and hot coal beds, safety is the byword.

Aluminum Foil Cooking

On a float trip along the Platte River near Saratoga, Wyo., our guides made a meal of fresh trout for sons, friend and me. They put the cleaned fish—dried thoroughly, rubbed with a little oil, sprinkled lightly with garlic powder, paprika and black pepper, a touch of salt and with lemon juice (in the cavity)—into aluminum foil, sealed the package and placed it directly into the coal bed. The aluminum foil pouch came out of the heat sizzling hot with steaming cooked trout.

On our survival hunts my partner and I always took a modest supply of staples. Aluminum foil coupled with a coal bed proved perfect for corn and potatoes. The good news is that there are no dishes to wash. The foil is both cooking utensil and plate. Naturally, all foil is packed back out, not left on the trail.

The Camp Stove

As with all camp gear, the gas cookstove is better than ever. For a base camp there is nothing better than a large stove. There are good ones that burn white gas (unleaded gasoline). These also burn Coleman fuel. The fuel itself is a matter of personal choice.

There are many different styles and sizes of stoves, including a compact one-burner from Coleman that I rely on often. It's essentially a single burning unit that attaches to a 16.4-ounce propane cylinder. It's exceedingly handy and will cook up everything from scrambled eggs to boiled soup. I can slip it in my pack if I wish or keep it handy at the campsite.

Along with everything else, campstoves have climbed into the high-tech realm. For example, there's the Coleman RoadTrip™ Grill with 20,000 BTU capability and a 285-square-inch-cooking surface. It'll grill darn near anything and it's highly portable with detachable side tables.

The Metal Box

That's about all they really are, those wall tent stoves intended mainly for heat. One of the worst camps I survived was in a wintry setting in a dismal dark wall tent saved only by the woodburning stove inside. These stoves are also useful for warming food and can be relied on as a cooking surface if necessary.

I like to keep a kettle of water on the surface for a little boost in humidity. It can get pretty dry inside a wall tent with a fire going. Of course when wet clothes are hanging on the line inside, dry is what you want.

The Cookie Tin

This is a unique cooking tool and it's essentially free. Cookies, especially imported, are housed in these metal containers for freshness and to withstand long travel from port to port. When the cookies are gone, the tin turns into its own little stove.

It's simple. Fill the cookie tin with coals. When ready to cook, remove the airtight lid and stoke the coals up with a little help from charcoal lighter fluid. When the coals are hot, place a grate directly over the cookie tin stove and go for it. Meat can be broiled over the coals. Pots or pans can be placed directly on the coals. When cooking is done snap the lid back on to snuff the coals. It's not unusual to get two to four cooking sessions from one load of coals.

The Jack-Knife Cookery Book

James Austin Wilder penned one of my favorite cookbooks. He called it *Jack-Knife Cookery*, printed in 1929 by the E.P. Dutton company. The theme is simple yet profound. The author explained it this way: "For it is really astonishing how many good, hearty, wise, stick-to-your-ribs dishes can be well cooked, deliciously cooked…scientifically cooked…with only your jack-knife for a kitchen implement."

While cooking with jackknife alone is essentially for fun, it does teach how much can be done with the barest of implements. For example, author Austin digs a "plug hat hole," as he terms it, so called because you can plug it with a tophat, the sort of headgear worn in Abraham Lincoln's day. A mound of dirt is left near the hole to hold a kabob.

Wilder advises lining the bottom of the hole with small hard stones to hold the heat in. He warns, "Choose 'non-pop' stones the size of an egg. Certain kinds explode." Place small dry twigs upon the egg-size stones in the hole. Leave air space around the wood to encourage a draft to fan the fire.

As the wood reduces to coals, fix up a kabob. Wilder wasn't fussy about what he stuck on his skewer, including lizard. We'll go for boned quail, duck, rabbit and similar fare. The skewer is a bark-peeled sharpened green twig. String chunks of half-inch boned meat on the stick with a trace of sunlight between each. Roll the kabob lightly in flour to coat the meat. It's time to cook. Stick the kabob in the mound of dirt by the hole and let the meat cook slowly over the coals.

I like the spirit of the Wilder book, but I modify it to suit my fancy. For example, before running meat onto the green wand skewer, why not marinate to ensure moistness? Lace with a bit of soy or teriyaki sauce. Lightly flour or flour not at all and stick the kabob's end into the dirt mound to hold it firmly in place. A sprinkle of garlic powder won't hurt. Likewise a little pepper. Have salt standing. For less cooked meat, run each boned square right up against the next one. The plan is utter simplicity in trailside cooking. A bannock can be made in the same hole by wrapping the dough around a green wand stick.

The Nested Cook Set

Armies the world over have provided cooking kits of one sort or another, usually nested to save space. Camping supply stores have similar kits. They're a good idea. Example: Coleman Exponent cooking kits are lightweight stainless steel. The backpack outfit at two pounds has two "sporks," two 5 1/2-inch plates, an 8-ounce cup, a 16-ounce bowl, 1-quart pot, 1 1/2-quart pot, 1 3/4-quart pot, a 3-quart pot and a wind screen (good idea), all in a nylon stuff sack.

My only complaint is that some are made of metals that are difficult to clean or allow food to stick to the cooking surface if not watched closely.

The Possibles Box

There are grub boxes and what I call possibles boxes, a word stolen from 19th century mountain men referring to larger bags of goods perhaps because it was possible to find many different things within from tobacco to galena (lead) for making bullets. The term is misused today for shooting bag.

Any box loaded with cooking equipment is a mess or grub box. When the container goes to cooking plus campside tools, it's a possibles box. There's also an emergency or survival box, which is a different outfit. It contains food along with sleeping bag and even a heater should a person become stranded.

The whole idea is self-sufficiency, being able to prepare food along the trail and/or by the campfire. I find a certain adventure in it, along with a good feeling that comes from having shelter nearby with good food to eat, but no supermarket in sight for miles and miles.

19

Managing Compressed Fire

The sagebrush plains provided little cooking fuel. But I knew that going in. I had a handful of charcoal briquettes carefully wrapped first in cling plastic covered by a strong layer of aluminum foil in my backpack. Runaway charcoal can cause considerable sooty coloration of equipment. Also along: the Purcell Trench lightweight compact grate. A generous chunk of marinated venison, also wrapped tightly against leakage, soon smoked heartily on the little grate over a bed of hot coals.

And why not? There's nothing wrong with an MRE or any other quick and hearty food item on the trail, but for mere ounces of carry weight I had fresh meat. The same arrangement of grate and coals has charcoal broiled many other edibles in the outback, including grouse, but you have to have cooking oil (such as canola) for that as well as a touch of teriyaki marinade for best results. Both of these carry well in daypack, fanny pack or backpack contained in leak proof plastic bottles.

A favorite grate of the author is the Purcell Trench, which is not only very light in weight for backpacking, but also compact in its own nylon case, as shown here.

Charcoal cooking is not for every day. Some people contend that too much of this smoky delight is harmful. Of that I'm not sure. I am sure, however, that foods from corn tortillas to red meat turn into tasty dishes prepared over hot coals.

Hardwoods

Often I've paused to wonder why the stunning landscape from Badlands to above timberline where I live in Wyoming is bereft of solid hardwoods for warmth and cooking, while the warmer climes, such as the Southwest, abound in the best. Start a strong pine fire at night in softwood country and long before morning the night has claimed its power. The same fire created of mesquite or oak on the desert promises hot coals when the sun's rays climb over the eastern horizon.

And so hunters enjoy hardwood where they have it, carrying charcoal briquettes to camps where only softwoods grow. When I visit hardwood territory I make a good-sized fire, larger than normally recommended by owl-wise camp experts. That's because my fire serves two masters—one demanding warmth and light, the other glowing nuggets for cooking.

As one cook put it—coals are *compressed fire*. When raked away from the main hardwood fire, coals turn into hotbeds where cooking takes place directly on them or just above the body of intense heat.

The Rock Corral

Many devastating forest fires began as little blazes for warmth or cooking. The rock corral, a simple arrangement of hard rocks that won't explode into shrapnel when superheated, prevents this problem. A rock corral can also become a cook's kitchen by simply arranging rocks within the circle. One side of the pit can serve for the blaze itself while the other side is reserved for raked-out coals. A flat rock on one interior edge keeps food warm. A simple metal rod extended over the top of the rock corral holds pots with handles directly over the heat source.

Imagination alone limits the possible arrangements of the rock corral. And so the interior of the rock corral becomes a holder of both open fire and those nuggets of *compressed fire* we call coals. The modern campstove is addressed in the next chapter. There is no doubt that high-tech models of this old-time cooking unit are ready for action faster than coal beds and essentially easier to work with. But on long stays, especially in the backcountry, the rock corral earns its keep not only for cooking but also warmth and light after the sun goes down.

Coal Heat Management

Managing the amount of heat on the electric or gas range at home is as simple as turning knobs. Managing the amount of heat emanating from a coal bed is not quite that simple, but almost. Two methods work well: water and dirt.

A spray bottle filled with water tames flames and cools coals. Flare-ups are attacked the moment they occur or super hot areas are hit with a few squirts that do not quell the heat, but control it.

Then there's ordinary dirt. Applying a layer of dirt on top of coals requires a little more care than the water bottle because air can be completely shut off and the coals will die out. A judicious covering works perfectly. Oxygen is not denied but intense heat is mastered.

Utensils for Coal Cook0ing

The Frying Pan or Skillet | Long handles are nice for the obvious reason of retrieving a frying pan or skillet from intense heat. Heavy-bottom skillets heat slower naturally, but also retain heat longer. These are far from ideal when backpacking, but weight means nothing in the regular camp. I've gotten spoiled with stick-free pans. Cheaper ones don't last long over hot coals but if proper non-metal spatulas are used even less costly stick-free skillets survive many camping trips. The stick-free pan not only lets go of the food cooked in it, but also cleans up fast and easy. On the other hand, a well-seasoned cast iron frying pan can work just as well. It's a camper's choice.

The Coffee Pot | A teakettle (not teapot, but kettle) heats water for any use, but so does a coffeepot. Remove inner parts and the coffeepot is nearly ideal for dispensing boiling water because of its spout, which pours out an easily directed stream. I have an old coffeepot that manages hot water. It can be set directly upon the hottest coals without incident.

The Teakettle | A teakettle in camp is not necessary if there's a coffeepot handy. However, there are some who prefer the kettle if only for the usual whistle that it makes announcing boiling water for tea, hot cereal, cocoa or mixing with cooler water in a plastic basin for a quick face and hands washing. Teakettles come in various sizes. Some have very thin bottoms and will eventually burn out on a bed of coals, but secondhand stores have a good supply of replacements.

The Teapot | Coffee is number one in restaurants across America, but in a cold north country camp—make it Alaska or Canada—hot tea is often chosen over the darker brew. The only secret in making good tea that I know of is hot water—really hot water—boiling water, which is no problem over a hot coal bed. Boiling water bursts the leaf to fully release its bouquet and flavor. Some campers are turning to herbal teas in place of regular leaf. They prefer the flavor. Tea is high in caffeine, which pleases some and turns others away.

The Grate | Already noted, the grate is essential in cooking over hot coals, especially for broiling meats. It also serves as a platform for holding pots and pans over coals. Essentially, there are two types: light and heavy. Light is for backpacking. I have one that only weighs a few ounces. Stove racks, barbecue racks from old grills and even refrigerator racks, as well as commercial grates of different sizes and weights can be used in the regular camp.

The Dutch Oven | Cooking with the Dutch oven is an art in itself as proved by the many books on the subject. Coal management is essential here. I watched a Dutch oven master work her magic with several different sizes over coal beds. She used briquettes because she had, through trial and error, found the exact number required not only underneath, but also on top of the heavy lid, to cook specific meals perfectly.

A full-blown grate like this special unit designed for heavy duty campfire coal cookery will last lifetimes. It's large enough to serve as a range for utensils as well as roasting pieces of meat.

Another excellent cooking instrument along the line of the Dutch oven is the African potjie. Dutch settlers brought the iron concept of cooking to Africa and over several hundred years the potjie was refined. Today, it's a round cast iron pot with three legs that keep the belly off the coals. Noted for even heating over coals, the potjie is sold today be the Cheaper Than Dirt! Company. (See Directory.)

Pots and Pans | Blackened, beaten, downright ugly pots and pans that would repel the home cook are at home on coal beds. There's rarely a secondhand store in the country that doesn't have one or more of these for sale. Most of the dedicated campers I know have their own special pots and pans, some looking like refugees from a junkyard.

Aluminum Foil | Given a nice coal bed and a sheet of aluminum foil, the camp cook can prepare a number of food items. Potatoes, carrots, corn and other vegetables are buttered then wrapped in foil and thrust into the coals. Likewise freshly caught trout. Rub a hunk of meat with oil. Ladle on a few tablespoons of teriyaki sauce along with condiments—a sprinkle of garlic powder, pepper and salt. Seal package, bury in the coal bed and the show is on the road.

Use cooking glove or hot pads, retrieve the package from time to time to check doneness. Not cooked enough? Rewrap and thrust back into the coals.

The Cookie Tin | The cookie tin filled with coals was touched on in Chapter 18. A small grate turns the cookie tin into a compact charcoal grill.

The Griddle | Any sheet or plate of metal can become a griddle. Cowboys in Sonora, Mexico, prepared flour tortillas on a piece of roofing metal. They were the best I'd ever tasted. But the real griddle has a smooth (sometimes modern stick-free)

Above: Coal management often relates to the cooking unit itself. Here is a charcoal grill, compact in size, and just right for cooking in camp.

Above right: Letting the fire burn down for coals. Soon, the flame will disappear and in its place will lie a cooking bed almost as manageable as a stove top for those who know how to deal with coals.

surface. It goes directly on the coal bed ready to prepare pancakes to go with those whitetail ribs smoking over the coals.

Safety

A night chill playfully poked at us as we huddled around the rock corral. A friend and I had our families along for the campout and everyone was enjoying a jolly good time until one little boy leaned too far over the pit with his marshmallow on a green stick and literally fell in, hands out.

He was snatched away before deep burns developed, but the episode put a damper on that night's fun. A first aid kit in camp contained an after-burn agent and the lad's hands were soon comforted. It could have been a lot worse. Coal management includes respecting the intense heat that is generated.

There are also several safety tools to consider. Simple potholders are essential. A metal bar with a hook on the end is useful in lifting utensils from the coal bed. Pots with bales are good. The bale can be hooked or handled with cooking glove or potholder and a bale is far less subject to get hot than a protruding handle settled directly over the coals. But most importantly, respect for hot coals is the best safety measure.

On The Trail

Any safe container for hot coals can be arranged on the trail to prepare a number of foods, especially meats. I've made quail, for example, over hot coals. But attention must be paid to drying out non-marbled game meats.

Coal Smoke

The quail mentioned above are more smoked than cooked over direct heat, although certainly it's the heat that does the cooking. By simply managing the height of food, such as quail, above the coals, smoke can become an important part of the cooking process. One time I smoked a half dozen birds over coals on a backpack trip. The meat remained safely edible for three days.

Game Meat Over Coals

Sometimes a piece of game meat with a layer of fat cooks up well over coals without marinating. Whitetail ribs and bighorn sheep require no special treatment other than a little salt and a light sprinkle of garlic powder.

Non-marbled meats cooked over coals can be mummified into leathery non-chewable chunks. There are four ways to prevent essentially fatless meat from drying out over coals.

Marinating | The Universal Marinade so important to tender and palatable game meat is not right for coal cooking. Universal Marinade with milk and eggs requires that the meat is cooked in butter or oil.

And so we turn to marinades that penetrate but do not of themselves burn up over hot coals. Teriyaki and soy sauce work well. A simple hand rubbing of olive or other oil helps, too, in preventing game meat from drying out over hot coals. I've cooked venison steaks directly over coals by marinating them for an hour or two in a mixture of teriyaki and Worcestershire Sauce.

Larding | Larding does not mean that lard must be used in the process. Slender strips of fresh beef fat work well, for example. Larding is cutting narrow slits in the meat with a fillet knife and then inserting some form of moisturizing element into those cuts. Heat from coals causes the strips of beef fat, for example, to cook, but the resulting liquid will not invade the meat. Mostly, it's cooked off. Fat used in larding is discarded, not eaten.

Injection of Juices | Most of us will not have a meat pump along on a camping trip. However, especially for backyard coal cooking, injecting juices into the meat is a good way to prevent drying out. Stock is ideal as a juice, but if not available, a can of broth will work. Liquid is introduced to the chunk of meat just like an injection—that's exactly what's happening—to prevent drying out. Meat pumps can be found in professional restaurant supply houses.

If the hunk of meat has been larded then a basting syringe can be used to inject juices into the slits. Cabela's (see Directory) offers a Commercial Injector in 2-ounce and 4-ounce capacities, perfect for delivering juices into a large chunk of meat.

Basting | Basting is another good way to prevent game meat from drying out over coals. Basting is especially important in preparing Leg O' Lope, where the huge chunk of meat is cooked directly over coals. Basting is simply ladling juices on the meat as it cooks.

Combing | Leg O' Lope, as only one prime example, combines all four methods of preventing drying out. The meat is marinated overnight. Then it is larded. It can be treated to injection of juices with a meat pump as well; although basting works well enough here because of the slits cut into the meat for larding. Basted juices flow directly into these slits to penetrate the heart of the antelope haunch. The end result of combining the four methods is a tender and juicy piece of game meat.

In Closing

Of course there's some natural crossover between chapters 18 and 19, because some camp cooking takes place over coals. Meanwhile, managing compressed fire is an art form all its own. Dealing with these hot nuggets is simple, but when the rules are ignored the result can be disastrous. Food gets burned up instead of properly cooked and in some cases cooks and campers can also make unhappy contact with coals.

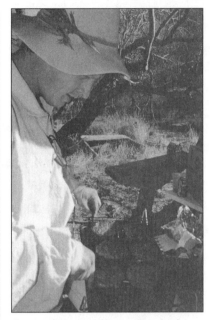

Shannon Thomas cooks up a batch of burgers on his charcoal grill. Managing compressed fire means getting coals good and hot, but also maintaining the right cooking temperatures.

20

Camp Stove Cooking

While campfire cooking is a wonderful way to get a good meal going, the modern camp stove or grill like this Coleman Road Trip can make cooking in a hunting camp faster and easier.

Below: While the author's favorite use of a camp stove is for cooking in camp, the modern unit works perfectly in many other settings.

Campfire cooking with curls of smoke caressing tree leaves overhead is far more aesthetic than turning the knob on a camp stove and lighting a match to a burner. But everything serves in its own place and while I enjoy raking a pile of coals into a veritable cooking range or broiling a prime piece of marinated venison on a grate, I'm grateful for the speed and ease of cooking on a camp stove when convenience outruns romance.

This is especially true today with the finest stoves the world has ever seen. They're sold coast to coast, border to border, and at reasonable prices. These stoves are efficient, sufficient for a multitude of cooking jobs, easy to set up and ignite and are entirely reliable. Safe, too, when used properly.

Breaking camp stoves down into various categories leaves us with compact models for backpacking, medium-size units for average camps, super size for outings with larger groups. There are many choices of fuels as well, including gas (propane and butane), gasoline (unleaded), specially formulated liquid (Coleman Fuel), jellied and solid combustibles. Each type has its own merits and I suppose demerits as well. The specific use of camp stoves is either self-evident or covered in product literature.

The value of this chapter is apprising the reader of the many available camp stoves and related cooking tools because the hunter/cook needs to know what types of camp/outdoor stoves are available. So let's go.

Where and When

Where? Anywhere in the great outdoors as well as cabins and travel trailers (with proper venting). Even back yards and for power outage emergencies (again with proper ventilation). Camp stoves are at home on the open range, in the heavy forest, in the valley and up the mountain. They cook up meals inside of tents, on the ground, and in liaison with the various camp kitchen options of the day. They also work along the trail.

When? Any time food needs preparation from full-scale meals to boiling water for coffee, hot cocoa—or a bath.

What they Burn

There are many suitable fuels for camp stoves, such as butane, propane, blend of butane and propane, commercial fluid (Coleman Fuel), gasoline, Sterno™ and various solid fuel pellets and bars. Propane bottles come in a compact 16.4-ounce size. Propane tanks are available in 5-, 11-, 20-, and the big 40-pound unit. Cabela's sells all of these tank sizes.

My Sierra backpack stove burns bits of wood, cow chips, just about anything combustible, which comes in handy on the High Plains where there is so little wood to burn. The Sierra works with a single AA battery that operates a fan below to feed the firebox.

Sheepherder type stoves burn wood, charcoal and other combustibles. While intended for heat, these stoves, as seen in sheepherder wagons, can be used to cook food.

Cooking Utensils for the Camp stove

Before we can cook anything on our camp stoves we must have the right utensils. Mostly, these are pots, pans, skillets and just about any other implement that serves in the average household kitchen.

But there are a few special items as well. For example, the Coleman company offers Exponent™ Cookware in several different packages including the Backpacker Cook Kit, Outfitter Cook Kit and Solo Cook Kit. These are made of lightweight stainless steel. The larger Outfitter set goes three pounds. Cabela's has its Non-Stick Complete Outdoor Cooking Kit consisting of 12 pieces complete with burner. Army/Navy surplus houses sell good camp stove utensils and they can also be found at backpack and general sporting goods shop, mall outlet stores and discount houses.

Compact Stoves for Backpacking

Literally dozens of compact cookstoves for backpackers and general camp use are sold in a variety of places. I have a single-burner Coleman propane stove that has heated gallons of water in camp and on the trail, plus cooking countless meals in both settings. When only one vessel is necessary for the task at hand, this little stove does the job regardless of camp size or location.

Camp stoves are at home just about anywhere now, including the back yard or regulated campground as well as wilderness setting.

What do camp stoves burn? Many different fuels. The Sierra Stove shown here consumes bits of wood and just about any other combustible.

Compact camp stoves work hard and they don't take up much space. This little Coleman stove burns a special propane/butane mix. It works with many different cooking utensils, even a coffee pot.

A quick break on a deer/antelope hunt in Wyoming brings out some vittles and a compact stove to cook things up.

For those who prefer liquid fuel, Coleman has a one-burner unit that runs on commercially prepared Coleman Fuel or regular unleaded gasoline. It pumps up for pressure just like a gasoline lantern. There's also an X-Series stove from Coleman that uses Powermax® fuel cartridges (blend of propane and butane). It's made of aluminum and magnesium alloy components. Primus is another big name in compact camp cookstoves.

Medium-Size Camp stoves

Field Products, Inc. (see Directory) has an interesting medium-size camp stove called the Power Stove Modular Cooking System. It's designed with a removable, fully adjustable burner that puts out up to 65,000 BTUs per hour. It's called modular because it folds flat. It works on propane. It stands alone or can be used with up to four units combined in one cooking range.

Coleman's RoadTrip™ Grill is another medium-size stove. It runs on propane, either the 16.4-ounce bottle or the larger tank. The RoadTrip™ is highly portable but sets up medium-large with 285 square inches of cooking surface.

Larger Camp stoves

My own larger camp stove is a Coleman Guide Series with three burners. It runs on propane. I use the big bulk tank in camp both for economy and convenience. A 20-pound bulk bottle normally lasts for a week of general cooking.

Coleman's 3-Burner Dual Fuel™ model is like mine, but it uses Coleman prepared fuel or unleaded gasoline.

New as this is written is another Coleman camp cooking stove. The Outpost™ operates on propane tanks for heat output ranging from 5,000 BTUs up to 200,000 BTUs. It comes with an integral stand. This big boy weighs 69 pounds.

The Outdoor Kitchen

I have the Campin' Kitchen, a field cooking center from Campin' Stuff, which is the Field Products, Inc. company (see Directory). A major selling feature on this kitchen, for me, was the double lantern holders, one on either side of the work area. I have two Coleman NorthStar lanterns and when these light-givers are set up with the Campin' Kitchen, cooking at night is a pleasure instead of a hardship.

The Campin' Kitchen is 93-inches long, 26-inches wide, with a 36-inch high counter height. It folds down into suitcase-size 40 x 22 x 6 and weighs 25 pounds. It features cutting boards, a large working surface, ice cooler storage area, paper towel holder (I use a lot of paper towels in camp), side shelf for stove, the aforementioned double lantern holders, utensil hooks and a food storage area.

Hunters can also fix up a kitchen with a large sheet of plywood temporarily secured to a tree with stout picked-up branches for legs. But the commercial camp kitchen is hard to beat.

Whipping the Wind

Wind is the biggest villain in camp stove cookery. It's whipped in several ways, the first being built-in guards that shelter stove burners. Even with guards, setting up where a barrier thwarts the zephyrs is never a mistake. The rest of the story writes itself. Turn the knob. Light the burner. Adjust flames to suit the task at hand, from boiling water as fast as possible to frying marinated venison steaks, and pretend you're home cooking on the electric or gas range in your kitchen.

Setting up Camp stoves

The only warnings about setting up camp stoves inside of closed-in areas, such as tents or cabins, are having proper ventilation and guarding against fires. Otherwise, camp stoves set up easily and securely.

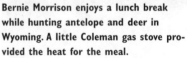
Bernie Morrison enjoys a lunch break while hunting antelope and deer in Wyoming. A little Coleman gas stove provided the heat for the meal.

My little one-burner stove normally rests outside my sleeping tent. If the area is clear of combustibles, it may go directly on the ground. If duff and other burnable materials are present, a scraped-out area is imperative. A rock corral around the stove is another possibility, mainly for wind protection, since flame is restricted to the stove burner itself.

Other setup possibilities are the camp kitchen, which prevents having to bend over a cookstove placed on the ground, a camp table, or a plywood sheet workplace set up about waist high to the cook. The latter must be a hundred percent secure, not only to prevent the supper from diving earthward, but also to safeguard against a dropped stove starting a fire.

Once again, the rule about clearing a cooking area prevails. It only takes a few minutes to scrape out a place beneath a camp cook stove and a few more minutes to rake natural elements back over the scraped area before breaking camp.

Cooking Shelter

An overhead tarp or awning is ideal, especially when a cooking station, such as the Campin' Kitchen is set up in a semi-permanent manner. Cooking in rain or snow is less than fun, and having moisture come down into the food seldom makes the final result more palatable.

How to Cook on a Camp stove

There's not much to say about cooking on a camp stove, with the exception that sometimes we fail to set the unit up properly, causing ourselves problems. We may also fall short in basic management of the stove. After all, these are entirely adjustable cooking tools. There is no more excuse to burn food in camp than there is to burn food at home on the standard gas or electric range.

The hunter/cook needs to study the full potential of his camp stove in order to get the most from it. This is a simple matter of reading the instruction sheet that came with the stove.

The Alcohol Stove

I still have and use a little alcohol stove that has served well for several years now. Mine is a Safesport model. It weighs only nine ounces and measures 2.75 inches by 3.5 inches. Housed in its own leather case, this little stove burns denatured alcohol, which is available at hardware stores and discount houses. It'll work with rubbing alcohol, too, but not as efficiently.

Double wall construction makes this alcohol camp stove turn softly wavering flame at initial lighting into jetted multiple flames like a stovetop burner in a short time. A full tank of alcohol burns for about 22 minutes. I've boiled lots of water with this little stove as well as cooking up considerable food.

A wind guard is required. I've used this little stove in the back of my camper-shell pickup truck with open window. It does not give off the same type of offensive odors commonly found with stoves burning other types of fuel.

Solid and Jellied Fuel Stoves

Army/Navy surplus houses sell military stoves that burn solid or jellied fuel. These are simple but effective camp cookers. Sterno™ is a famous name among this type of cooking tool. Sterno™ cans contain a combustible fuel that appears to be jellified.

The Illex camp stove is a favorite with the author for what he calls roving, driving around to find a suitable hunting spot or doing a little off-season scouting.

Another interesting little stove along the same lines is handled by the Cheaper Than Dirt! company. The Folding Personal Stove sells currently for two dollars. Folded, it's about the size of a deck of cards. It uses Trioxane fuel, which is a solid bar or "heat tab" 3?- inches long, 1?-inches wide, 3/8-inch thick. One bar, which comes sealed in a waterproof container, burns for seven to nine minutes depending upon oxygen supply and other atmospheric considerations.

Illex Gas Range

The Illex Model ISR-5000 has its own little spot because it's not a backpack stove and yet it weighs so little that it goes with my roving camp— a pickup truck with camper shell. Camp is wherever the truck stops that night. The compact Illex has a solid platform, its single burner just like the one found on a regular home gas range. It has spark ignition and burns on a butane bottle. Sold by Fundicion Callao (see Directory). I purchased butane cartridges at Big 5 sporting goods store, where I also saw a nearly identical butane stove for sale.

Many More

Many other camp cooking stoves are available in various styles, as a stroll through the Campmor (see Directory) proves. Campmor sells the afore-

Here is the Illex stove showing its butane cartridge installation. The cartridges are inexpensive and can be found at sporting goods stores such as Big 5.

mentioned Sierra Stove, for example, as well as the Kwik-Cook Metal Folding Stove that burns Sterno or other canned heat. Also several MSR models including the little Dragonfly multi-fuel stove.

On the Home Ground

While our major interest in this chapter is stoves for camps, back yard-cooking machines deserve mention as well. My grandfather and namesake, Chef Sam Manetta had a special custom-built gas range assembled in his backyard. My grandmother loved it because it kept her kitchen a lot cleaner. This was essentially a counter top range that burned natural gas. I have one slated for my own back yard. It, too, will work on natural gas, with a barbecue grill option.

Cooking stoves for outdoor use have developed along with other high-tech equipment. This chapter simply brushes the edges of the total concept. Many companies are working toward more efficient stoves. There is no doubt that we will see additional innovations. But if the world of outdoor cooking stoves were to grind to a halt this very day we couldn't complain because there are already dozens of unique, interesting, easy-to-use stoves available.

21

Pressure Cooker and Microwave

Two of my most-used implements are the pressure cooker and microwave, the first for parboiling, making soups, stews, stock and numerous other important cooking tasks, the second mainly for thawing, heating and grease removal, with some cooking.

Pressure Cooker

The modern pressure cooker | My latest pressure cooker, a present from my wife, is a Farberware NutriMaster. There is no pressure regulator to lose. Rather than the jiggling dance of a regulator on a stem, the new model has a sliding lever with three settings—full steam, partial steam and relief. There is a pressure button on the forward part of the handle that shows when the cooker is under steam or fully relieved. Other than the modernized no-pressure regulator design, cooking with the new model is just like the old one.

I like the fact that there is no pressure regulator to lose, but I've not discarded my older model. It's now packed with the camp gear and has proved to be one of the most useful tools for outdoor cooking, from tenderizing rabbit pieces to fry for supper to making full-scale soups.

Unit size | I'm familiar with 4-quart, 6-quart, 8-quart and 10-quart pressure cookers. There are larger ones, but these serve mainly for canning. Mine is the 6-quart size and it does everything required of it.

Construction | Aluminum and stainless steel are the two major metals that go into pressure cookers. I have both. Both work fine. I'm partial to my Farberware stainless steel pressure cooker in the home kitchen, while the aluminum cooker goes to camp.

Time and timing | The pressure cooker is all about time and timing, two different things. It saves time and in order to cook well with one properly, timing must be right. About the first: I can have the finest mashed or whipped potatoes on the table in only minutes with the pressure cooker. Mine cooks chunked raw potatoes perfectly in four minutes. A stew that would take a couple hours boiling away on the stove is finished in a quarter of that time. Refried beans have gained favor nationwide. On a ranch in Sonora, Mexico, a lady prepared as fine a dish of frijoles refritos as anyone could want.

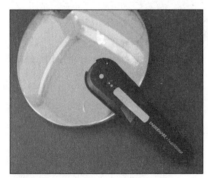

This excellent modern pressure cooker has no protruding stem with pressure regulator. The regulator is built in and a sliding bar sets pressure to low, high, or open.

This is a good look at the interior of the author's most-used pressure cooker. It has no top stem with pressure regulator. The regulator is built in.

Later on the same hunt my own pressure-cooked refried beans from scratch were almost as good and I had 'em on the table steaming hot in a half-hour. So the pressure cooker is a wonderful time saver, but it does demand timing, which follows another trail altogether.

Timing varies with the specific pressure cooker. While mine cooks Irish potatoes perfect for mashing in four minutes, another might require a little more or less time. Fresh vegetables can be cooked very rapidly in a pressure cooker, their juices contained and concentrated in very little water.

This excellent example of ranch beans was created quickly with the pressure cooker. Both beans and meat were fully cooked in the unit.

How does it work? The pressure cooker functions with captured steam. Cooking takes place with super heat in a sealed vessel. Of course some steam escapes or the cooker would eventually rupture. But the rubber ring on the inside of the lid ensures that most of the pressure remains inside.

One of the biggest mistakes with pressure cooking is the amount of water used. It varies with the dish. Parboiling rabbits and squirrels, for example, means just covering the meat with water and no more. Cooking fresh vegetables in the pressure cooker demands even less water. Only enough to prevent burning. The veggies won't be in the cooker for more than a couple minutes anyway. Carrots, for example, are soft in less than two minutes in my cooker. Stews and soups use much more water.

Pinto beans soak up a lot of liquid, so the cook must be careful. The initial water level goes over the top of pintos or other dry hard beans by an inch or two. The cooker is brought up to steam and allowed to go for 10 minutes. Then steam is carefully released and the lid removed to check the beans; more water will be needed. And the beans are brought under steam again.

Parboiling with the pressure cooker | Parboiling means plopping meat, usually sectioned, into water with or without condiments to render that meat more tender. The liquid is strained off and discarded. The meat is then fried, baked, broiled— whatever. I use parboiling especially with rabbits and squirrels. Not only does parboiling tenderize the meat perfectly; it also has a washing effect. Rabbit meat, after parboiling, is pure white.

I don't parboil game in the usual pot. I rely on the pressure cooker to do the job just as well or better and in a fraction of the time. The end result of pressure cooker parboiling is rabbit or squirrel that follows the well-worn cliché that goes "it melts in your mouth." I especially like to parboil (pressure cooker style) rabbit or squirrel destined for the frying pan.

Pressure cooker advantages

- *Speed* — In these busy times, the pressure cooker saves time. Follow directions with the specific pressure cooker. Each one comes with recommended times for various foods.
- *Captures nutrients* – Especially with vegetables, the pressure cooker retains nutrients within the cooker itself. Very little food value escapes in steam.
- *Tenderizes* – While there can be meats too tough for anything short of an explosion to tenderize, the pressure cooker does an admirable job of rendering tough meat tender.
- *Makes stock* – The pressure cooker reduces meats and bones to stock. Longer periods of cooking literally remove juices from any products destined for broth.

- *Good taste* – Condiments introduced to the pressure cooker tend to literally invade cooked foods, including meats.
- *One-pot meals* – One-pot meals, such as soups and stews, cook up perfectly in the pressure cooker.
- *Fat-free cooking* – The pressure cooker requires no fat or oil. It cooks splendidly with clear broth or water.
- *Gravy maker* – Giblets and meat scraps that may otherwisego unconsumed turn into wonderful gravy juice.
- *Simplicity* – The pressure cooker is truly simple to operate. Instructions are clear. Completely close the lid; set the pressure regulator; use medium heat—and the show is on the road.

Pressure Cooker Safety

One of my uncles, a full-blown engineer, decided to use his ailing wife's pressure cooker to fix her a nice soup. He managed to knock the regulator from the top of the cooker in his efforts and steam attacked the ceiling of the kitchen. My aunt didn't mind. She wanted to repaint the kitchen anyway.

Every pressure cooker that I know of comes with instructions. These are to be followed to the letter. Pressure cookers are dangerous only when used dangerously. Mine requires setting the sliding gauge before heating the unit. As noted above, the three settings are steam escape, medium contained steam and full steam. To release steam the sliding gauge is ***not*** engaged before the unit is cooled down. I place the cooker in the kitchen sink under a small stream of cool running water. When the pressure button falls, that tells me the steam is down and then I push the sliding gauge forward to open the cooker.

Other cookers require a different approach. Read the directions before beginning to use the cooker.

Obviously the pressure cooker is all about pressure—but that pressure must be regulated. The top of this pressure cooker shows the removable regulator that allows some steam escape out of the unit (see stem with hole going into body of pressure cooker). There is also a pressure valve that is geared to give when pressures are not properly regulated.

This ultra modern pressure cooker does not have a regulator resting on a steam valve. It operates with a sliding regulator in the handle.

Pressure cooker safety cautions

- *Read and follow instructions carefully* – As with most cooking tools, pressure cookers vary in proper use. Read all instructions before attempting to cook anything.
- *Pressure regulator* – Must be installed correctly every time the cooker is used. On some modern models without a separate regulator, the proper setting must be made before heat is introduced to the unit.
- *Lid* – The top of the pressure cooker, with interior rubber ring, contains the steam within the unit. The lid must be properly and fully engaged for safety.
- *Use only correct pressure regulator* – Pressure regulators are not universal. Use only the pressure regulator made to go with the specific pressure cooker and no other.
- *Watch pressure indicator* – Pay attention to the pressure indicator on the lid of the pressure cooker. It shows when pressure within the cooker is present or absent.
- *Do not disturb* – Don't bump the pressure cooker when it's under steam. The regulator may be knocked off the stem allowing steam to escape.
- *Never remove regulator under steam* – Be certain to cool the pressure cooker before removing pressure regulator or moving the sliding regulator to the open position.

- *Do not remove lid under pressure* – Never attempt to take the lid off of the pressure cooker until all of the steam within has dissipated.
- *Fast cooling* – Sometimes it's perfectly all right to turn the heat off and allow the pressure cooker to simmer down on its own. In fact, this is a preferred method when making pinto or other dry, hard beans and it also works well with stews and soups that get a little extra time under steam as the unit naturally cools off. But fast cooling is often called for. Example: Carrots are under way requiring two minutes of cooking time. When that time is up the pressure cooker must be cooled rapidly or the carrots will turn to mush. Place the cooker in an empty sink where it will sit flat. Then run a small stream of cool water on the lid until the safety button shows that all steam within the unit has dissipated.
- *No kids* – Teaching children to cook is great, but youngsters and pressure cookers require constant supervision. Instruct children that a pressure cooker has a great deal of hot steam inside and they can get burned if they do not use the cooker properly.
- *Never overfill* – Overfilling the pressure cooker with water can cause the undue escape of steam or hot liquid. Use only the amount of liquid necessary to accomplish the cooking task.
- *Maintenance* – As with any tool, maintenance is imperative. Loose handles, for example, can be a disaster. As the cooker is removed from source of heat to water for cooling the handle falls off and the cooker hits the ground under full steam. Loose handles can also cause the cooker to rotate in the hand when it's removed from the stove, causing the pressure regulator to falling off, resulting in escaping steam.
- *Replace worn sealing rings* – Locate the correct sealing ring for your specific model when a ring requires replacement. There are generally numbers that correspond. New rings can be found at appliance centers and some hardware stores and discount houses.
- *High heat warning* – It's OK to start a pressure cooker on higher heat levels, but heat should be lowered as soon as the unit is under pressure. Continuing on high may cause dangerous steam escape.
- *Consider upgrading* – Very old pressure cookers work well; however, newer models may be safer. Check it out.
- *Keep it clean* – The pressure cooker must be kept clean. Any clogged port may cause a problem. Do not put oil on the sealing ring unless instructions call for it. Some rings may actually deteriorate when oiled.

The pressure cooker is ideal for many applications. Here a chunk of moose meat is not only tenderized, but the cooker also provides a wonderful stock for gravy.

Microwave

This invention of the 1940s is everywhere now. Few kitchens are without one. But I have backed off of certain dishes fully cooked in the microwave. This tool has gravitated to its own level in my kitchen. It serves important functions, none of which is making a full meal from scratch. This in no way throws cold water on microwave recipes. Some are excellent. Poached eggs, for example, come out perfectly in the microwave. But its other uses, in my particular kitchen, outweigh cooking meals fully.

Power | Microwaves can vary greatly in output. The smart cook learns how to time-manage his specific unit regardless of how strong or weak it may be. Time required to boil water is a good gauge. Put a vessel of water in the microwave at different full power timings and keep a mental note of how long it takes to boil that water in a specific machine and at specific power settings.

Side dishes | There are those who contend that they can taste the difference between an Irish potato cooked in the microwave and one baked in an oven or foil wrapped in coals. I cannot. Baked potatoes cook up perfectly in the microwave—a great time saver. Likewise many different vegetables.

I seldom cook green beans, for example, on the stove. The microwave does the job too well with far less fuss. Corn is fine in the microwave. I tightly wrap each husked ear in slightly dampened wax paper and cook for two and one-half to three minutes. Cooking time depends upon microwave power, the size of the ear, as well as toughness or tenderness of the corn.

Rice is perfect from the microwave. In a large microwave safe bowl add an equal volume of water and rice. For example, a quart container of water requires the same container filled with white rice. Stir. Cover the bowl tightly with plastic wrap. Microwave for five minutes. Check for doneness, stirring rice/water with a large spoon. Return to microwave for brief intervals until fluffy cooked rice results.

Heating | There's more to heating foods than just popping them in the microwave. There's also timing. For example, I prepared a breakfast of antelope sausage, eggs and French toast for several people. I cooked several slices of French toast first. Then as the eggs and sausage finished up, the microwave heated two or three slices of French toast for each plate. In other words, all of the food went to the table equally hot and ready to eat thanks to the microwave.

Finishing | The microwave is great for finishing foods. An omelet is a good example. When the outside is perfectly browned the inside could still require further cooking. A half-minute or a little longer in the microwave finishes the job without overcooking the outer part of the omelet.

More important to me is finishing up meatballs. I prefer totally cooked gameburger meatballs as well as sausage balls for my red spaghetti sauce. The microwave finishes up the inside of meatballs perfectly.

Grease reduction | The microwave does a perfect job of degreasing meat. Recently, I prepared a huge red Italian sauce for spaghetti to feed a large gathering. Buffalo burger meat made meatballs; antelope sausage made sausage balls. After browning meatballs and sausage balls on all sides, the microwave knocked out any unnecessary fat. Moisture in the meat is also reduced through microwaving.

The process is simple | Place browned meatballs or sausage balls on a dish with two paper towels to soak up grease and/or moisture. Microwave on high for one or two minutes (time depends upon power of unit). Check doneness by pressing. If the meatballs and sausage balls are done through, degreased and moisture free, they'll feel solid. If they're spongy, remove, place on fresh paper towels, return to microwave and whack 'em again. Then dry each before placing in the sauce by squeezing gently with a paper towel to soak up any grease or water bombed by the microwaves.

Thawing | One of the best services rendered by a microwave is thawing of meat and other foods. Today's sophisticated machines have automatic settings for thawing.

A chunk of meat like this can be cooked in the pressure cooker in short order. This boneless piece is destined for thin slicing into sandwich meat.

This is a terrific service to the cook, especially when a meat meal requires fixing on short notice.

Most meat does not demand total thawing for cooking. This is good because thawing in the microwave can become cooking, where edges or outside parts of the meat are browned into small leathery spots. For making New England boiled dinners (in the pressure cooker) the hunk of roast need not be fully thawed. Pressure cooker heat will eventually reach the center of the roast, cooking it thoroughly.

Likewise steaks thawed partially cook up fine. As do meats to be marinated, especially in the Universal Marinade. These can be placed partially thawed in the mixture and left at room temperature to complete the remainder of the thawing process while marinating at the same time.

Sauces | Some sauces can be made from scratch in the microwave, just as many grain serials are cooked perfectly. Ingredients are blended in proper sequence and with proper power levels.

Microwave Methods

- *Cook and look* – One of the easiest, as well as safest, methods of cooking with the microwave is blasting food, whether heating, thawing, or actually cooking, for half the prescribed time, then taking a look to see how things are coming along. You can always cook longer, but uncooking is a little more difficult—like impossible.

- *Motion* – Move food from one spot in the microwave to another when using the cook and look method. While most microwaves today have stirrers or turntables, even distribution of microwaves is best accomplished through moving a cooking item from time to time.

- *Stir the food* – When cooking anything that can be stirred, or for that matter heating a dish (such as stew or beans), use the cook and look way and in between stir contents in the microwave-safe dish. This helps distribute heat evenly.

- *Rest periods* – Some foods do well given a final resting period after cooking or heating. For example, bombing a dish of Mrs. Kane's Ranch Beans (see recipe) to warm them up for lunch does well with the cook and look method—and also allowing the food to rest for a few minutes after the dish is hot. There's a little residual heating and cooking with this method.

- *Food arrangement* – Modern microwaves aren't too temperamental about how food is arranged on the dish because the waves are more evenly distributed than ever before. However, I still find that the edges get hot first. Food should be arranged on the dish with colder or thicker portions ringing the outside of the cooking vessel.

- *Cover it* – The rice noted above requires covering for best results. Covering concentrates heat. It also holds in steam, which for is important when cooking rice. I use plastic wrap for this job. However, covering food is also important to keep the interior of the microwave clean. For this I prefer ordinary wax paper. It's economical and it serves the purpose.

Safety

Cooking demands heat and the microwave is designed to provide plenty of that. A major safety feature is the door-activated shutoff. Or to look at it another way, the microwave will not function with the door open. This is vital. Small hands especial-

Above: Today's crock-pots are better than ever—easy to use and just about foolproof. This handsome crackpot is a perfect example of the species.

Above right: This slow cooker comes in three pieces—a heating shell, interior crock, and lid.

ly can investigate with curiosity. The microwave will not turn on should little fingers enter the interior of the unit. All the same, the heat factor remains. Microwaved foods can emerge super hot, hot enough to cause a burn.

Two more safety factors are maintenance and proper utensils. The microwave must be maintained in perfect working order for complete safety and microwave-safe utensils are imperative. Don't put metals in the microwave. And though glass is OK, ensure the right kind of glass. While an exploded glass cup or dish is contained within the microwave behind a closed door, dealing with the shards afterwards may be hazardous.

Speaking of explosions, certain foods cooked in the microwave can blast apart. Potatoes, for example, should have their skins pierced before cooking to allow heated air escape. Likewise sausages.

Limits

There are definite limits to microwave cookery and while a multitude of microwave books suggest preparing all manner of full meals in the machine, there are some items best prepared in regular ovens or on standard stoves. Large stuffed birds can be microwaved. But not in my kitchen. I'll stay with the ordinary roaster, well-covered, using the slow-cooking steaming method.

Many Others

These days there are dozens of different cooking tools. The remainder of this book could be filled with various electric grills and griddles, deep fryers, broilers—on and on. One tool, however, cries out for mention and that's the Crock-Pot, a slow-cooking implement which is ideal for stews, chili dishes and so forth. But the focus in this chapter is the pressure cooker and the microwave. They represent two important tools for the game chef because both save time and each one turns out good food when used properly.

22

No Gamey Taste

The term itself is flawed, but everyone knows what it means. "Oh, I can't eat wild meat. It tastes gamey."

No, it tastes either unfamiliar or lousy, or the meat is the victim of food prejudice. The first reason, unfamiliar taste, is because most people normally get very little game meat. They simply aren't used to it. Interestingly, the reverse can be true. When my youngest daughter, Nicole, tasted her first beefsteak she said there was something

Personal taste always plays a role in what foods we like. Javelina can be difficult to prepare. But this Mexican cowboy was thrilled to have this one for his wife, who will turn the meat into chorizo, a spicy Mexican sausage great cooked together with eggs and potatoes.

The smile on Memo's face is not there altogether for the fact that the hunter he guided got a javelina. This Mexican guide knows how good the meat will be. Handling is the initial key to no gamey taste. This little musk hog will be carried back to camp, skinned, bagged, and soon processed.

Mixing wild and domestic meats is a good way to impart that familiar flavor. Here, chicken and game bird meats blend to create an excellent soup.

wrong with it. That prime chunk of expensive New York strip tasted awful to her. In time she got used to the flavor of beef, but having been raised on deer, antelope and elk, domestic meat had a decidedly unfavorable flavor to her.

Along with being something people aren't used to, game meat can actually taste lousy because of bad field care and/or processing, including aging that was actually rotting. Any meat would taste awful after being dragged through dirt and hauled home on a car fender in the heat of the day.

Lastly, there is pure and simple food prejudice. I fixed two roasts for a large family supper. I wasn't trying to fool anyone. One was beef. The other game. And I said so, separating the two on the table. Someone accidentally reversed the two roasts. When I noticed that, I made mention of it. Two people at the table quietly stopped eating, fearing they had gotten wild instead of domestic meat, which they had. The funny part is that both had praised the game meat roast boldly. They really liked it—until they found out that it was game. Such is unfounded food prejudice. And we all suffer from it—unless we're starving to death. Then everything tastes good.

Having enumerated the three major reasons for meat tasting gamey to people—poor handling, lousy cooking and food prejudice—let's consider ways to eliminate the first two. Food prejudice is not based on logic, so it remains difficult to deal with. Previous chapters covered taking care of game in the field with proper processing afterwards.

The middle problem, however, cooking wild meat to avoid what diners might call gamey flavor can be addressed with high hopes of success. Example: A friend and his wife were over for dinner. She had overcome previous game meat prejudice and happily ate it at our home. Her husband remarked that the meat tasted fine, but it had been disguised. "When I eat venison I want to know that it's venison," he remarked.

His wife chimed in, "And that's why nobody likes the game meat you cook."

Some may call it disguising. I don't believe that. Cooking game meat so people enjoy it is not disguising. It's using sound methods to create the best possible dish. There are several ways to accomplish this worthy goal. Chapter 23 deals with spices and sauces. Both go a long way in defeating unfamiliar flavors. Chapter 24 goes into wines and other liquids designed to enhance foods, including game meat. And Chapter 25 discusses marinades and marinating to impart familiar flavors the average consumer enjoys.

This chapter does *not* deal with spices, wines or marinades because each has its own forum. Instead, it covers mixing wild and domestic meats, making sausage, which is related to mixing game and tame, points on larding, injecting juices into meats, chili con carne, chili and beans, pit cooking, barbecuing, basting, using tomatoes, cooking with beef fat, bacon and brine bath.

Mixing Wild and Domestic Meats

As this was written I had a batch of antelope sausage made for me by a local butcher. He does a great job of it. But his antelope sausage is very mild. That's why I mix it 50/50 with regular Italian, Polish or breakfast sausage. The end product is excellent. The familiar sausage flavors of Italian, Polish and breakfast stand out, but they are milder when blended with antelope sausage.

Another excellent mix of wild and domestic meat is lamb roast with antelope, deer, elk or other venison-like meat. How about a rack of lamb with interlaced strips of game meat? For those who like lamb this dish is a special treat.

Adding beef fat to game for hamburger is another example of mixing wild and domestic meats. Curling strips of beef fat around pieces of game meat is another way of mixing wild and domestic, especially for cooking over coals or on the gas grill.

Sausage

There are literally dozens of different sausage types that can be made with game meat. This is not the aforementioned mix of game sausage with domestic. It's making sausage from scratch with just about any red game meat from deer to moose. The spices that go into preparing sausage impart their special flavorings. Pork is added to create this sausage. So this is truly a mix of wild and tame in one blend. The result is sausage that most people find taste-friendly.

Important: Game sausage must contain a significant amount of pork if that familiar flavor is to be achieved. It won't work by making the sausage mostly of game and sausage spices. Watch out for packaged game sausage kits. If they don't call for pork, consider adding it anyway.

Javelina, considered difficult to cook, is here turned into an excellent Mexican sausage cooked to perfection.

Larding

As explained elsewhere and as included in some of our recipes, larding does not mean using lard, although lard, salt pork and other domestic meats, including side pork and bacon will do the job. In this case larding means creating pockets in hunks of game meat and then inserting into those pockets strips of domestic meat, especially fresh beef fat preferably from choice cuts, such as Porterhouse, New York Strip or rib eye steaks.

Larding is ideal for making game roasts over coals or on the gas grill with familiar juices dripping down through the game meat. The domestic meat is usually discarded before the dish is served. Or in the case of Leg O' Lope, which is sliced off in fillet pieces as the large hunk of meat cooks, the diner removes fat pieces, which are found within the boneless piece of meat.

Larding works with oven-cooked roasts, too. Some of the best game roasts are made with strips of beef fat or other domestic meats poked into pockets.

Larding (also injecting juices) is a wonderful way to add that familiar taste. So is charcoal or gas grill broiling. This beautiful leg o' lope has been treated to both measures—larded and injected, then cooked on the gas grill to perfection.

Juice Injection

Cabela's Cajun Marinade Injector is a perfect example of the tool that does the job of installing various juices directly into the cut of meat. The same company offers a marinade kit with various juices to be injected. The kit has a meat injector and four 16-ounce marinades: Creole Butter, Creole Garlic, Honey Roasted Garlic and Herb and Teriyaki Honey. Sold separately from the kit are other flavors, including Lemon Butter Garlic, Cajun Hot and Spicy Butter, and Honey Butter BBQ. Cabela's also offers King Kooker injectable marinades, such as Italian, Teriyaki, Lemon-Pepper, Praline, Steak House, Cayenne Garlic, Butter-Garlic and Hot & Spicy Butter Garlic.

Injectable flavor enhancers are almost endless in number and include ordinary stock, beef broth, chicken broth, oil and garlic mix, soy sauce, teriyaki sauce, along with literally dozens of other sauces found on the grocery store shelf. When a hunk of meat is injected with any one of these, that cut naturally takes on the flavor of the additive.

Mostly for roasts, the process also works for steak meat before it is sliced. A large hunk of boneless game meat destined for steaks is injected, set aside for several hours or overnight in the refrigerator, and then cut into steaks.

Chili Con Carne

I've traveled the northern state of Sonora, Mexico, a good deal, also visiting parts of Baja. And I've eaten red and green chili con carne from just over the border all the way down to Libertad, where my friends and I fished for many different species from sardinera to sharks.

While this book includes chili recipes using strips of red meat, rather than hamburger, making note of chili con carne here is important to the subject of imparting a familiar flavor to game meat. In this dish, strips of fresh meat are cooked in red chili powder or with green chilies. The blend of either one of these popular chilies overtakes any other flavor, making this another way of producing a dish with a more familiar flavor for diners who don't eat very much game.

Chili con carne—the Mexican way with chunks of meat rather than hamburger— is a fine way to avoid any hint of the so-called "gamey taste" some consumers complain of.

Chili And Beans

What we Americans generally label simply as chili is not chili con carne. It's really chili beans made with ground meat. Gameburger of all types from antelope to moose work well in this dish, which is relatively simple to prepare. How to make chili beans is included in the recipe section, however, as with chili con carne, it deserves special mention here as one more way to prepare game meat in a way that will be familiar to those who order chili at the local diner.

Complete the game meat meal with attending foods. These flour tortillas were served with chili con carne and refried beans, both of which complemented the main meat dish.

Pit Cooking

Many fine meals can be prepared in a pit, from wild turkeys to great hunks of red game meat, especially larger pieces from the bigger species such as moose and buffalo (American bison). There are various means of pit cooking. Where hardwoods grow these are used exclusively for cooking in the pit. Where these woods do not exist, commercially purchased charcoal briquettes do the work.

Essentially, pit cooking is nothing more than digging a hole in the ground large enough to contain the meat along with coals for cooking. The hole is dug. Hardwoods are burned down to hot glowing coals right in the pit, or briquettes are ignited and allowed to finish to hot coals.

My method of cooking in a pit is to first remove the hot coals from the pit and then line the bottom with a single layer of flat rocks just sufficient to form a base. On top of this rock surface goes a solid bed of coals. The wrapped meat package is placed upon these coals. Then the rest of the coals are ladled into place all around and on top of the meat package. Place a sheet of metal—or if that is lacking a couple stout layers of aluminum foil—over the topmost layer of coals to protect the meat from invasion of dirt. This is important because the hole is now refilled with the dirt that came out of it. At this point, the cook simply goes away. The work is done, except for digging the meat up later.

It's impossible to give an exact pit size or number of coals because these vary with the meat to be cooked. With wild turkey or a very large game roast, I lay down a bed of coals about two inches deep. Then what amounts to almost a bucket of coals goes all around the meat package and on top of it. Covered with a piece of sheet metal first, dirt is replaced in the pit and that's that. I've yet to uncover a burned roast or turkey, but I'm sure this could happen with an overkill of coals.

The most important aspect of cooking underground is the meat package itself. This, too, varies considerably with the chef. My packages are created from aluminum foil, but first the meat, regardless of type from turkey to moose, is well treated to a coating of pure lard along with condiments. The meat is placed on the aluminum sheeting and a cup of broth or water is ladled in before wrapping. Then the meat is completely wrapped in foil with each succeeding layer taking on a little water. Finally, the well-wrapped and dampened package is ready for the pit.

One of my relatives pit-cooks huge chunks of meat. He wraps his meat only once in foil, using wet burlap bags for the remainder of the package.

Timing is not terribly essential in pit cooking. So far every pit-cooked turkey or huge roast has emerged from the hole in the ground cooked to tender perfection.

The hot hole is the key to success. There must be sufficient heat to cook the meat, of course, but as time goes by the heat dissipates. So the coals are steadily cooling off and yet the ground around the meat remains hot for hours. I've put a large turkey in the ground at 9 a.m. taking it from the pit at 3 p.m. completely cooked with meat falling off the bone, but not one burned spot.

Barbecue

Another way to impart a familiar flavor to game meat is to barbecue with regular barbecue sauce. There are many excellent prepared sauces available at any local grocery store. One of my favorite barbecue meals consists of chicken along with strips of game meat. This mix is perfect for the diner who seldom gets game meat partly, I think, because the chicken gives it a domestic appearance.

Chicken tends to flare up considerably over coals or on the gas grill. So a good trick is to apply condiments such as a judiciously small amount of garlic powder, some paprika, along with the usual poultry spices, then rub every piece well with olive oil, then wrap each in wax paper. Microwave the chicken for a few moments on about medium power. This reduces fat content, which in turn cuts down on flare-up.

Another way to impart familiar flavor is barbeque sauce, which is applied toward the latter fourth of the cooking process as the meat (strips in this case) is broiled over coals or on a gas grill.

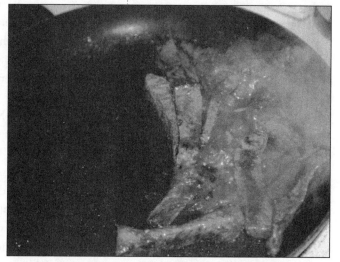

This aged game meat, sliced as shown, is now treated to Mexican salsa while the meat is cooking — about three-fourths finished before salsa is added. This is just one way to add familiar flavor to game meat.

The strips of game meat are prepared at least two hours before it's time to put them over the coals or on the gas grill. They're made very much like the chicken pieces, but without microwaving. Each strip is treated to condiments first, then rubbed with olive oil. When it's grilling time, the chicken is put on first. When it's roughly half finished the game meat goes on the grill alongside the chicken. When both chicken and meat are nearly cooked the gas grill temperature is reduced to low, or if coals are used they're tamed down with water. Caution: Take all meat and chicken pieces off before spraying water on coals. Otherwise the upshot from the hot coals may cover the chicken and meat.

Replace each piece on the grill and coat with barbecue sauce. Close the lid on the grill and let the sauce bake on with attending smoke. Don't let the barbecue sauce burn, however. Turn all pieces and coat the other side. Smoke 'em up again. Remove from grill and serve.

Basting

As simple as basting is, the method can be useful when imparting a familiar flavor to game meat. Basting can take place in the oven, on the grill and in the frying pan. It's a simple matter of first preparing a proper basting mixture. When making a game roast ensure that there is broth or stock in the roasting pan. Add spices. The resulting liquid at the bottom of the roasting pan becomes a perfect basting product that is simply ladled over the roast from time to time.

Important: Turning a piece of meat over is equivalent to basting. I turn my roasts a few times during the cooking process, while also basting from time to time with a syringe.

On the grill—and this is especially vital with Leg O' Lope—the basting sauce rests in a nearby vessel. A little is sucked up with a syringe and introduced directly into the pockets that were created for larding the meat. This puts the sauce directly into the meat itself.

In the frying pan, turning meat over brings it into contact with the juices in the pan, but there is nothing wrong with spooning a little juice over the meat as it cooks.

Tomatoes

We're all guilty of failing to record fine recipes created by the older members of our family. When these people are gone the excellent dishes they made are gone with them. So it is with a javelina recipe my maternal grandfather, Chef Sam, created. All I recall is his statement that "You have to use tomatoes. Tomatoes can change the flavor of any meat." On that he was certainly correct.

My mother makes a stew with canned tomatoes and it tastes very different from one made without the tomatoes.

The challenge for all of us is to work on recipes using canned tomatoes to affect a taste to the finished dish that more people will find palatable.

Javelina, for example, is very hard to cook. This is not Porky Pig. This is a musk hog. And due to the old wives' tale about cutting the musk sac out many javelina are ruined when the fluid from the sac permeates the meat. Even when the sac is correctly removed intact with the hide javelina meat, while beautifully white and tender, can be tainted. People who shunned wild meat raved on about my grandfather's javelina in tomato dish.

Here is a finished meal using one of the many methods of avoiding the so-called "gamey" flavor. Meat strips have been treated to salsa during the latter fourth of the frying process and now served with beans and flour tortillas.

Beef Fat

We've discussed beef fat strips cut fresh from prime steaks but another way to impart the familiar beef taste is rendering beef fat on low heat in a frying pan and then using the resulting juice for cooking. A little rendered beef fat—straight—in a frying pan can be used to fry any red game meat. Adding broth to beef fat creates another cooking medium for roasts or to baste meat on the grill. Certainly beef fat is a familiar flavor to modern diners and there is nothing wrong with using a little to dress up game meat. Finished fried meat is normally drained a little on paper towels, so we're not adding back fat that game meat doesn't have in the first place. Cooking with beef fat is a flavoring process only.

Bacon

I believe that cooking with bacon is overdone in creating game dishes. I've had quail, for example, double-wrapped in bacon strips and roasted so that this superior meat tasted more like bacon than prime upland bird. I like bacon, but I like quail better.

On the other hand, there is nothing wrong with judiciously using bacon, as well as a little rendered bacon fat, to add the familiar flavor we're after as game cooks. I've cooked floured red game meat steaks in canola oil and a tablespoon of bacon fat with good results. The bacon fat does not overcome the meat. It just touches it up. Also, a couple strips of bacon laid down on top of a game roast are all right.

The idea is flavoring only, not overcoming the dish with bacon taste.

Brine Bath

Soaking out any game meat in a brine bath is perfectly acceptable. White vinegar may or may not be added to the brine. This method reduces some of the natural juices within the game meat, but it will not invade the meat unless left for a very long time.

Soaking game birds from dove to ducks and geese is never a mistake. It's not so much to bleed them out, but more to ensure getting rid of any gastric juices that may have been introduced to the meat via a shotshell pellet passing through the body cavity and then the breast.

Another positive aspect of soaking in brine is removal of unwanted outer tissue. I always soak my rabbits for a couple hours. This lifts outer tissue away from the meat so these can be pulled free and discarded.

These are a few methods the wise cook can use to create dishes that will please people who normally don't get much game meat. I employ them all the time regardless of who will be eating the meat because I have never found any of them to harm game flavor unless abused, such as smothering game meat with bacon taste. I don't worry about my game meat being disguised. My only concern is that people enjoy eating it.

23

Condiments That Make a Difference

This nice rack of spices on a Mexican ranch in Sonora was adequate, but it takes an even greater range of spices to do a wide variety of cooking. For example, paprika was lacking here and unavailable for the author's favorite universal marinade.

As far as I can tell the big deal about finding a trade route to the West Indies from Europe had a lot to do with spices and not much else. I can understand why. It's hard to think of a single major meal that serves well without spices, herbs or other condiments.

Today we don't have to set sail over the ocean to find these flavor enhancers. They grow in our back yards if we wish, but most of us buy ours in the supermarket or specialty grocery store where a mind-swimming plethora graces the shelves.

Spices are mainly aromatic or pungent vegetable products that originate in tropical climates. Herbs, associated with temperate climates, are classified as plants with woody tissue that withers and dies after flowering. The resulting herb tissue has been used for eons as medicine as well as in cooking. The often-mentioned Iceman had his own little medicine bag when he met his fate more than five centuries ago.

For our purposes spices and herbs are not separated into their own specific niches. Our interest is condiments in general and all we care about is knowing what to do with each one to lift our game dishes one more notch on the good-eating scale.

Celia, cook on a Mexican ranch during a Coues deer hunt, made this wonderful chorizo. She used javelina for the meat. Spices made this Mexican sausage delicious.

Testing Condiments

Sniffing is a major test of any condiment. For example, when I crush rosemary between my fingers and smell it I know that this herb of marriage is going to be used judiciously. That's personal, of course. The next cook and his guests may prefer a bigger jolt of this pungent herb.

Light and Heat

Herbs and spices are best kept away from light and heat. I secure some of mine in the freezing compartment of the refrigerator, near at hand, but in the dark and very cold.

The Condiments That Make a Difference

Basil | Sacred in India, basil, also known as sweet basil and basil leaf, is a major ingredient in red spaghetti sauce. I have never made red spaghetti sauce without basil and don't plan to. Great fresh, it's just about as good dried. My brother raised a batch in his garden and gave me some, which I hung in the kitchen.

Basil also works in certain marinades as well as side dishes such as kidney and green beans.

Bay Leaf | Essential in red spaghetti sauce (in my opinion), bay leaf is also great in many soups. I put several leaves into the liquids used in cooking a game roast. I think bay leaves enhance the resulting juices for gravy. Also good in juices for stock.

The leaf is removed and discarded after cooking. Being large, it's easy to find.

Bell Peppers | Not really a spice or an herb bell peppers can be used as either one. Green or red, these peppers wed favorably, or we might say flavorably, with many dishes, especially stir-fries with cubes of red game meat.

Caraway | Another useful condiment for game cookery when employed judiciously is caraway. A pinch in stews and soups adds flavor. Well-known for enhancing sauerkraut.

Celery Salt | Celery salt does not qualify in the herb/spice list either, but it works miracles in game soups. It's especially handy in camp where fresh celery is seldom found.

Chili Powder | I prefer the red chili powder that comes in cellophane packages, usually from a chili powder country such as parts of New Mexico. This is the heart of

Above left: Sometimes spices are incorporated within a meat product. This sausage is a perfect example. There is no need to spice any further. Celia, cook on a Sonora, Mexico ranch, created several fine dishes, including homemade sausage by using the correct spices.

Above: Celia, the cook on a Coues deer hunt in Mexico with Holehan Outfitters, prepared this fantastic soup called albonidgas from javelina meat. Spices made it perfect.

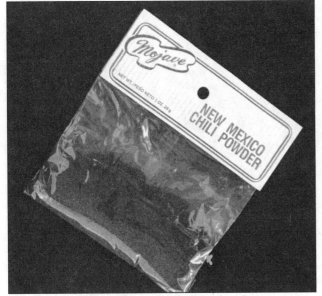

This chili powder from New Mexico is ideal for chili con carne and other authentic South of the Border dishes.

Red Chili Con Carne. It's available in mild, medium and hot.

Coriander | See juniper, below, for a good use of this herb. Cooks of India use coriander in curry powder. Fresh coriander leaves are also known as cilantro or Chinese parsley.

A small amount is useful in certain dressings, such as stuffing for geese and ducks. Also worthwhile in homemade sausage.

Cumin | I always associate this seed with Mexican dishes, where it is often included in the recipe. Experimentation is the heart of cooking. But sometimes the experiment fails, as mine did when I put a dash of cumin into red spaghetti sauce.

Curry Powder | Curry powder is a mixture of spices blended through pounding on a flat hard surface. Brands differ in flavor and intensity and therefore the cook must experiment in order to find one he or she prefers.

East Indians use a lot of curry powder, which for them is almost as common as salt is to us. It can actually mask a dish entirely, which is good or bad depending upon the dish.

Mild curry powder can be made at home by grinding with mortar and pestle—carefully. Resulting dust and volatile oils caused by grinding can severely irritate the eyes and nose. Ingredients to grind together are: 3 tablespoons black pepper, 4 tablespoons coriander seeds, 2 tablespoons caraway seeds, 1 tablespoon cumin seeds, 1 tablespoon whole cloves, 2 tablespoons cardamom seeds, 1 tablespoon cinnamon, and 1/4 teaspoon hot chili pepper. Store in freezer in tightly sealed jar.

Fennel | Good in some fish dishes, fennel can be lightly applied before cooking. Some cooks believe that it sets fish off the same way lemon does with its slight acidity.

A touch works well in some soups, but not everyone will appreciate its flavor.

Garlic | Many game meat recipes would suffer without this wonderful perennial bulbous plant. I employ it every way it comes—fresh, powder or salt. Fresh garlic can be placed on top of a game roast as peeled cloves. It can also be crushed or bought pre-crushed.

Garlic salt imparts a saltier taste to game meat meals, while garlic powder renders the same effect without increasing salt taste. Minced garlic cooked in oil creates a wonderful base for frying game meat. My Universal Marinade (Chapter 26) would be nothing without garlic.

Ginger | Native to China, gingerroot is found in many recipes originating in that country. It can be hot and biting. Especially good fresh, as found in most oriental grocery stores.

Since a little goes a long way, it's wise to freeze the gingerroot; its bouquet will not be harmed at all. Or place root in a glass container with sherry wine, where it will take on a new flavor. A little ginger in a game stews and soups can be refreshing, but experimentation is advised.

Green Chilies and Jalapenos | My wife makes a special South American chili relleno with game meat. Green chilies can be used in game soups. They turn into excellent salsa that goes great with many game dishes. Jalapenos can be added to chunks of game meat for those who like things hot, as most, but not all, jalapenos are.

Green Onions and Chives | Not the same, but they work similarly; both are excellent in sauces and soups. Nice flavor, fine coloring for food, too. Chopped, green onions top off many soups added uncooked in the last few moments of preparation.

Garlic is one of the most important spices in game cookery, as well as general culinary efforts.

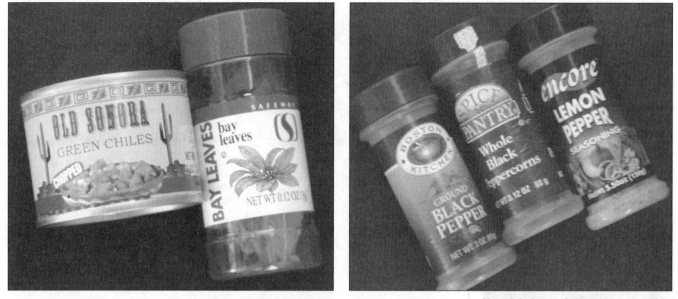

Horseradish | Credited with stimulating the appetite and aiding digestion, horseradish root has a peppery, pungent flavor either freshly grated or in commercially prepared form.

A touch in cream sauce is well advised, while overuse has the potential of ruining a dish. Can be very hot! It's most often applied afterwards, such as on a finished game roast.

Horseradish is at home in various sauces, especially for fish when mixed with catsup or what I call grocery store chili sauce.

Juniper Berries | Juniper berries are the fruits of the juniper evergreen and can be the heart of certain game meals. For example, the berries crushed and mixed with an equal amount of crushed coriander are useful with antelope meat.

For roasting game meats, such as antelope or venison, the resulting juices can be enhanced with a dozen or so crushed juniper berries soaked in a little gin overnight.

Lemon Pepper | This is highly useful condiment for making jerky, especially oven jerky. It's also wonderful on game, not only red meat but birds as well from quail to ducks and geese. A little is also good in certain soups.

Mustard | Credited as both herb and spice, mustard comes in many different forms, including mild yellow which is essentially a mixture of mustard, ground turmeric, vinegars, glucose and salt. Commonly used on hamburgers. Also a part of many barbecue sauces.

Mustard can be heated up by adding horseradish. English mustard is also hot—simply a mixture of dry mustard and water.

Onions | Fresh, dried, powdered or as onion salt, regular or white, this is a condiment that finds its way into countless recipes. I can't imagine red spaghetti sauce without diced onion lightly browned first in canola or olive oil.

Whole onions cooked alongside game roasts are another treat. A must for game soups, great in stir-fries, onions/bacon/liver—the list goes on.

Oregano | Oregano can be overwhelming but it's vital (in my opinion) in red spaghetti sauce and used judiciously can enhance some marinades. A touch can also dress up fried game meats. Optional in Universal Marinade (see Chapter 25).

Oregano is also excellent in Mexican salsa when added in a small amount to the chopped green chilies, tomato and onion. A light touch of oregano leaf on grilled fish is nice (subject to personal taste).

Green onions can turn a ho-hum recipe onto a taste treat. Here, the onions are chopped using a Cold Steel chef's knife.

This slab of fine fish would have half the taste without spices. Mainly, lemon pepper and paprika have been used to bring out the best in flavor.

Paprika is another highly useful spice in game meat cookery. Hungary is known for its excellent paprika.

Marjoram | This herb works with some game meat, but should never be overused in any dish. A hint in a game meatloaf, for example, is worthwhile, while a large dose can overwhelm.

Paprika | While paprika is used mainly to color food, such as sprinkling over deviled eggs, I find it useful in cooking. It goes well on wild turkey and red game meat roasts, and is excellent on grilled gameburgers. It is added to the raw product and cooked right into the meat. Also nice on fish.

Paprika is made by grinding the dried stemless pods of a mild capsicum pepper. A famous spice in Hungary.

Parsley | I never cook red spaghetti sauce without this herb. It's always added not only to the sauce itself but also mixed into the ground meat for meatballs. It's OK as a colorful garnish, but better cooked in dishes such as soups. My choice is fresh, which is available all year long.

Hint: Put the bunch under hot water for a couple seconds; wring some of the water out by hand; wrap in paper toweling and hand-squeeze more water out. This is called bursting and it helps bring out the bouquet.

Chop parsley finely on a cutting board using a chef's knife. I also used a large bowie knife in the kitchen for this task. Include the flavorful stems, although the bottommost of these can be discarded by slicing the end off squarely.

Pepper | About as common as air, pepper, black or white, adorns almost every game meal either during or after cooking. I think white pepper is a little stronger and therefore better in certain dishes but black pepper is the all-around king. Ground

Parsley is normally chopped, either coarse or fine, for cooking. Here is has been chopped fairly fine with a Cold Steel chef's knife.

Far right: Parsley is important in making an excellent red sauce with game meat. Here the parsley has been hit with hot water and squeezed by hand to remove some of that water.

fresh as peppercorns there's even more flavor and peppercorns can also be used whole with some roasts (discarded by straining the resulting broth).

Rosemary | I'm not a super fan of rosemary, but my brother, who is a good cook, uses rosemary with antelope as well as antelope/lamb dishes. A little crushed between the fingers before adding to the meat goes a long way.

Sage | This woody plant, employed with minute application on antelope steaks, for example, can be an enhancer. Sage is recommended for sausage and can dress up wild birds as well.

It also works in small amounts with certain stuffings (optional in Chef Sam's Dressing). Homemade sausage is also nicely dressed with sage. As with any spice or herb, this one can overtake instead of enhance.

Salt | I don't cook with salt very much. Salt does not harden arteries, but some people are not supposed to consume much of it for other health reasons. And it's so easy for a person to add salt to taste at the table.

However, some dishes just don't cook up right without a little added salt. When I make venison steaks cut right off the standing haunch; salt is definitely applied to the meat before it hits the pan. A little salt in refried beans is warranted as well—sprinkled in just before mashing the cooking beans.

Tarragon | This is another powerful herb. It can add an extremely unique flavor to stews, and is useful also with fish. A sprig of fresh tarragon in white vinegar adds a distinctive flavor.

Thyme | A good herb at home in various recipes, but not one of the main ingredients in most of the recipes used in this book. I have used it successfully as a fish dressing—juice of one lemon, ? teaspoon dried thyme, rubbed, ? cup olive oil, ? teaspoon salt, sprinkle of black pepper.

Not a spice, but cheeses, such as these, can be used as condiments, especially complimenting a rich red sauce made with game meat.

Camp Condiments

Truly there is no limit to the spices, herbs and other condiments that can be carried on the trail or brought to camp. However, there are a few that work well in general. Of course there's salt and pepper. But lemon pepper is another good one in camp. I'd not be without garlic powder. A little bottle of teriyaki marinade will enhance many in-the-camp game dishes. Bouillon cubes, plus teriyaki marinade and any kind of broth make a fine cooking base for fried upland birds as well as rabbits.

Ishi, the last member of his Northern California tribe, cooked his venison boiled in plain water. There's no doubt about his healthy method, but exciting dishes become that way mainly through the addition of herbs, spices and other condiments. Imagine a restaurant that cooked without them. It would be out of business in no time.

24

Spirits for Flavor

Spirits, including wine, have a tenderizing effect in marinades but added to a hunter's stew or any other recipe flavor is the bonus. Alcohol content is essentially cooked out so there truly is no other reason to cook with spirits other than taste enhancement. Even specific bouquet is overcome, or almost so, during the cooking process.

As one cook put it, "The alcohol in the wine [and other spirits used in cooking] evaporates while the food is cooking and only the flavor remains."

There are special recipes that include spirits for their flaming effect (flambéed), but these are not part of basic game cookery. This chapter forks in the trail, taking two distinctly different branches. One road leads to what spirits can do in game cookery—in other words, how to use them. The other deals with specific spirits and their cooking value.

Wines and other spirits can have a tenderizing effect on meats. They also enhance sauces.

Many different spirits work in game cookery. Experimenting is always worthwhile, when done judiciously. Don't take chances when guests are coming over.

Spirits for Cooking

First, what not to use. Avoid cooking wine sold on the grocery store shelf. Content generally includes salt and other additives that do nothing to further the flavor of a recipe. The best spirits for cooking are the kind that normally find their way onto the dinner table or into the living room after supper.

Expensive and exclusive wines and other spirits (such as high-dollar cognac) for cooking represent a waste of money (in my opinion). Port wine, for example, is a good choice for many recipes. This wine can be purchased for a few pesos or a hundred dollars a bottle. I harbor grave doubt that when used in cooking there would be much difference in the overall effect of either.

At the same time, some inexpensive spirits should be avoided. Overly sweet wine can almost caramelize in a dish; certain very dry red and white wines lend an acidy taste.

All in all, a medium wine, such as medium sherry, works well in game cooking and at nominal expense. Likewise other spirits—middle price range is best. Gourmands will not agree with the last statement, insisting that high-class spirits impart the finest flavor.

Not Wine Alone

I'm sure there are some products from the spirits world that don't belong in any kind of cooking but I don't know what they are. I figured vodka would be worthless, but a visitor from Finland taught me otherwise in a poached salmon dish. Bourbon works well in certain recipes. Even gin. I've had some luck with a few cordials as well, but they've been hit and miss. Regardless, experimentation is always worthwhile (plus interesting) and I plan to try an array of different spirits with a few harder-to-cook game meats, such as javelina.

Substitutes

Although alcohol content is generally dissipated in spirits cookery, some consumers still prefer avoiding its inclusion in their meals. While nothing fully takes the place of wine, for example, in a recipe, some juices substitute in a minor way. Grape juice is a natural since many wines began as grapes in the first place. Apple juice is another excellent choice. Pineapple juice can greatly change the final flavor of a game dish. Also try a half-cup of water with the juice of one medium to large lemon as a replacement for each cup of wine called for in a recipe. Lemon serves to balance the acids but it does not take the place of wine *flavor*.

And then there are the more exotic juices. I once rendered a few pomegranates for their juice and the result was recipe worthy. But take the place of sherry? I don't think so. I've also used flavored vinegar in a few recipes that called for gin or similar alcoholic beverage. Results were acceptable if not exciting.

There are very few wines that have no value at all in game cookery, and for those who do not want the alcohol content, remember that the alcohol cooks off—most of it anyway—in most recipes.

Proper Application, Amounts and Timing

Splashing spirits into a frying pan full of breaded venison medallions that have been prepared in Universal Marinade is a fairly good way to destroy an otherwise prime dish. It's a matter of proper application. Not every recipe, in other words, is escalated by the addition of spirits.

Amount is also important. Once more we tread on personal ground. Some appreciate the strong influence of spirits, such as bourbon, while others prefer a hint instead of a hit.

Timing is highly important. Adding spirits to a hunter's stew, for example, is best done toward the end of the cooking cycle, not the beginning. If added too early, it can overtake the natural flavor of the meat and vegetables in the stew. Conversely, adding wine to game recipes after cooking can be a real disaster, with the exception of so-called fortified wines and aperitifs. These differ chemically from other wines and serve more as seasoning than cooking agents.

Remember that wine is mostly water to begin with, so adding wine takes the place of about an equal amount of water. Good to know when making a stew or other dish requiring a liquid base or body.

Spirits in Cooking

Wine Splash | To be ladled over game meat at the table and not for direct cooking, this is basically canned broth, consommé or hearty stock plus wine. Add one cup of medium port or sherry wine and a half lemon diced to five cups of boiling liquid. A stick of butter is optional. Allow mixture to simmer for a few minutes to blend. Serve in a bowl with a spoon for ladling over cooked meat.

Experiment with different wines. Also try leaving out lemon or adding other fruit, such as cherries or orange sections during the boiling stage. This little addition to game meat on the plate is best served very hot. Otherwise, it tends to cool off the meat.

Marinating and Cooking with Wine | Marinating with various wines is well established. Sometimes the marinade is discarded. But in some recipes the marinade can be cooked with the meat rather than tossed away.

Basting | Basting with wine directly can greatly enhance a dish or ruin it. A roast, for example, can be lifted several notches on the good-taste barometer with judicious wine basting. Recommended: Baste with wine during the middle cooking time, not at the beginning of a steamed (cooked in a tightly covered roasting pan in the oven) roast nor after it is finished. Wine or other spirits introduced in the middle of the cooking time tend to blend nicely with juices in the pan.

Remember that resulting gravy will take on wine flavor. In some cases strained juice from the roaster used as the above wine splash may be a better choice than gravy when a roast is cooked with wine.

Roasting with Spirits | This differs from basting because the proper dose of spirits, such as a full cup of wine or other beverage, is added at the midpoint of the cooking time for the covered roast. The spirits cook right into the roast as well as the roast juices.

Deglazing | Deglazing with wine takes place after the meat is finished. It occurs in the same vessel that cooked the meat, such as an oven roasting pan and especially a frying pan. Personal preference is a medium sherry or port wine for deglazing but some cooks will prefer one of the white wines.

For roasts, remove cooking juices to another container. Strain the liquid. Return strained juices to original cooking/roasting pan and heat on the stove. When the juice begins to boil, add wine. Amount varies with personal taste. About two-thirds juice and one-third wine one is good.

For fried steaks, do not strain the juice in the pan. Here a single cup of wine usually works since the meat was fried with a little canola oil, olive oil, butter or margarine. Once the pan is very hot—smoking—splash in the wine and stir constantly. Add a couple tablespoons of butter and keep stirring. The well-combined juice/wine mixture is strained and served separately to be ladled over game meat. Slice steaks or roast meat thin for better invasion of the mixture.

Frying | Regular fried meats can be enhanced with a splash of spirits toward the end of the cooking process. A little bourbon, white or red wine or other alcoholic beverage works here. As soon as the meat is cooked, remove from the pan, set aside. Raise the temperature under the pan. Add the spirits.

Above: Sweeter wines can be used in various sauces and other cooking applications, but may be all wrong for certain recipes.

Above right: A wine sauce is distinct in flavor and can enhance many different game meat meals.

Here is where deglazing and frying with spirits differ. Let the spirits release their alcohol content for a couple minutes and then add the meat back to the pan, turning each piece two or three times. The end result is spirits cooked to somewhat gravy-like consistency rather than a watery liquid. The meat is served with these juices. They are not ladled on afterward.

Stir-Frying | Using spirits in a stir-fry is simple. When the food in the wok or frying pan is very hot add spirits according to taste. The alcohol is cooked off, leaving the flavor of the spirits. Experiment, beginning with a half-cup or less for a larger amount of stir-fry meat and vegetables. Once again, medium red wine works well, but trial and error, as always, is encouraged. Using small portions, in case the dish fails, try bourbon or other liquor in your next stir-fry.

Stews | Toward the end of the stewing cycle, add the spirits. Continue cooking until alcohol has evaporated. There are two ways to test this. The aroma coming from the stew reveals when the alcohol is cooked off by mellowing. Tasting is the other test. If the stew liquid tastes like uncooked spirits, further cooking is required. The goal is a blended liquid that is normally thickened somewhat to a gravy-like consistency.

Soups | There is nothing more natural than adding spirits to soup. As usual combining toward the middle or late in the cooking time is best. Added too soon, spirits may overwhelm the soup. Added too late, they do not reduce to a properly blended liquid.

Gravies | Spirits can be added to finished gravy but it's best to use juices from roasts that were treated with wine or another beverage during the cooking stage. The gravy is made directly from these juices. Juices heavily ladened with spirits can produce unsavory gravy. See Chapter 26 for more on gravy making.

Sauces | Spirits cook up well in various sauces while absolutely destroying others. There are many sauces, for example, that are designed around spirits. Consider orange sauce with wine. Combine one cup orange juice, 1/4 cup orange marmalade, 1/2 cup port wine and 1/2 teaspoon ginger with two pinches of ground cinnamon. Bring to a boil. Immediately lower heat to a simmer, thickening with cornstarch well blended into the mixture. This sauce goes well with roast wild boar and other whiter meats. Double or triple all ingredients for larger portions.

Sautéing | Sautéed meats are well dressed with spirits by simply adding a tablespoon or so of butter, raising the temperature under the pan to medium-high, and

adding wine, stirring constantly. The burst of aroma at first will be fully wine-centered. However, a more blended juice and spirit mix soon follows. As always, we don't want the spirits to take over the dish.

These are some ideas on the art of cooking with wine. Now let's look at some of the available spirits available to the game cook.

A Few Spirits for Cooking

Since there are hundreds of different alcoholic beverages suitable for cooking, the following is nothing more than a skeletonized list, but it's a start.

Beer | Beer is a brew fermented from hops and cereal grains that are fermented with yeast. Alcohol content is relatively low compared with other spirits. In fact, some would not call beer a spirit at all. This brew can be added to various meats during the cooking process.

I watched one cook prepare excellent moose steaks over hot coals while pouring a modest amount of beer directly on the meat as it cooked. He probably hit the steaks with beer four to six times per side as he turned them over on the grill.

Beer can also be used in certain stir-fry dishes and has been known to compliment fried rabbit at the end of the cooking cycle; the beer mainly cooked off.

Ale is related to beer but is a malt brew normally containing a little higher alcohol volume. It, too, can be used for cooking, but it may result in more leftover flavor than beer.

Bourbon | Bourbon is a whisky distilled from grain mashes, the majority of which is normally corn. Bourbon can add flavor to just about any red game meat when applied judiciously. While some wines can be added by the cupfuls this is not true of bourbon.

As always, experimentation is recommended. After all, that's what good cooking is all about—experimenting bravely with all kinds of ingredients, even if it means relegating some dishes to the garbage disposal. That's how many great recipes were created.

Brandy | Brandy is a liquor prepared through the distillation of wine or fermented fruit mash. At one time the term referred only to a liquor made from grape wine. Brandy can compliment a game roast to perfection when not overused. In one instance, for example, a mere quarter cup was cooked into a six-pound elk roast toward the end of the cycle. Cooking continued until the alcohol dispersed.

A few dishes do well with special brandies, such as apricot or peach. Grand Marnier has a brandy base, but it's distinctive orange flavor makes it very special. Red and yellow varieties are available. Great with waterfowl, especially painted on a roast duck or goose toward the end of the cooking cycle.

Cognac | As one connoisseur pointed out, all cognac is brandy, but not all brandy is cognac. Cognac is brandy distilled from special grapes grown mainly in the region around Cognac, France. It is carefully aged in casks of Limousin oak. Cognac is simply a high-class brandy and it can merit the price, sometimes a hundred dollars a bottle and higher, but usually much less. Cognac can be used wherever brandy is included in a recipe.

Armagnac is a brandy produced in Gers, not far from the famous French town of Bordeaux. It has a drier and heavier taste than cognac for those who want to give a particular game meat dish a real spike.

Gin | Seemingly unlikely for cooking because of its strength, gin is a liquor made with what is known as natural spirit base, another way of saying alcohol. It is flavored with various seeds including juniper berries.

A little gin is a flavor enhancer in rabbit and some upland game dishes. It's to be used in much smaller quantities than wine. Added toward the end of a gamebird stir-fry or just about any gamebird, gin adds a flavor all its own that will not be mistaken for any other cooking spirit. Gin can also be used in some fish dishes. But then so can many other spirits.

Rum | Rum is also a liquor. It's distilled of fermented sugarcane. Three popular types of rum are dark, light and Jamaican. Mexico exports good rum, as does Cuba. Rum, often used in bakery products such as rum cake, is used the same as wine. The only caution is amounts. Rum can readily overtake a dish.

Wines | There are hundreds of excellent wines available to the game cook. Among them ordinary sherry is hard to beat, especially medium. Darker sherry (sweeter) is also good, but can turn somewhat syrupy when cooked down.

Another great cooking wine is port. It works about anywhere sherry is welcome, but has a different flavor.

Madeira is a superior game-cookery wine. It imparts a flavor enjoyed by many.

Vermouth is an aromatic herb-flavored wine that my grandmother gave us in eggnog when we had a cold. It comes sweet or dry. Both work for game meats but with different final flavoring. Sweet is generally dark in color, but there is also a colorless Vermouth that is very sweet. Dry Vermouth is light in color, but not colorless.

Although television chefs may have us in awe of their culinary abilities in the kitchen, there is really nothing tricky about cooking with spirits. Follow the recipe at first, adding more or less spirits to successive attempts. This is the way to arrive at that personal level of appreciation where adding spirits to the game being cooked is an enhancer and not a takeover. The reverse is equally true. Too little does just that—adds too little value to the recipe. Just remember one thing: Cooking with spirits is all about flavor.

Marinating Game Meat

My favorite venison/antelope steak recipe of all time is not fancy. It's simple, basic and terrifically successful in changing the minds of many who believed that game meat had to taste gamey. Simply frying the steaks would be useless without using what I call Universal Marinade first. Universal Marinade can be prepared with only four ingredients: eggs, milk, garlic powder and paprika. Optional ingredients include sweet basil, oregano—plus an invitation to the reader to add whatever he or she thinks might work.

Game steak meat—usually venison or antelope for me—is sliced about a half-inch thick. A little thinner is OK. Thicker will not marinate as thoroughly. Universal Marinade is created by breaking eggs into a bowl, adding milk, a sprinkle of garlic powder, a similar hit of paprika, then whipping into a mixture. Exact amounts are difficult to list because that depends upon how many steaks are to be marinated. An egg per pound with sufficient milk to provide enough liquid to treat the steaks is about right.

The last time I cooked marinated venison steaks with Universal Marinade I had a four-pound chunk of boneless meat. The marinade included four eggs, two cups of

Below left: A beginning for many marinades is a soak-out of the game meat in saltwater as shown here. Soaking reduces fluids in the meat and also takes care of that stray hair that slipped by inspection.

Below: Universal marinade is so important in game cookery that the entire sequence of preparation is illustrated in this chapter. This is step one—adding to a mixing bowl the milk, eggs, and condiments.

Using a whip, blend the ingredients of the universal marinade well.

Above right: Medallions or other boned meats, including game steaks, are settled into the universal marinade for several hours before cooking.

milk, about an eighth teaspoon of garlic powder and the same amount of paprika, all combined with a whip.

The steaks (not shaped with a meat hammer first) were marinated in this mixture for six hours before cooking. Tip: Pound tougher meat into submission with a meat hammer before marinating. The steaks were breaded just before frying in a 50/50 mixture of thoroughly powdered (with a rolling pin) saltine crackers and ordinary white flour. The breaded steaks were fried in an open pan (a cover can cause mushy coating) on medium heat in a mixture of canola oil and butter, just enough of the first to coat the bottom of the pan. The steaks emerged cooked just through—no running juices—golden brown. Guests who said, "I don't eat game meat" were daring enough to give these venison steaks a fair try. Every diner returned for more.

Marinade Purposes

A marinade is a liquid that serves three main purposes: flavor enhancement, some tenderizing effect (depending upon the ingredients of the marinade) and infusion of oils for grilling. The marinade is either left in its original mixing dish, meat added directly, or transferred to a large sealable plastic food bag for steaks. The plastic bag works especially well, requiring less marinade to saturate the steaks. The term itself comes from the French word meaning to pickle in brine. Marinating preserved meat on board ships.

However, for our purposes the process has nothing to do with preserving and everything to do with flavor, possible tenderizing and preventing meat from drying out when cooked over coals or on the gas grill. Marinades are also used to sharpen the flavor of otherwise dull meats. But game meat is marinated to lend a friendly taste that most diners will enjoy.

Marinade Makeup

No single list of marinades can be considered complete. Weekly—if not oftener—a new marinade comes along. That's because the only limit on marinades is the cook's imagination. Everything from brandy and beer to flavored vinegar and ginger ale has been used for marinating meats. Marinades may consist of oils and wine, wine and condiments, wine vinegar and condiments, lemon juice and condiments, canned broth or stock plus condiments, oils and diced garlic cloves mixed together, onion and oil—and many other combinations.

Ordinary Italian dressing from the grocery store can be used to marinate meat. Likewise soy sauce, teriyaki sauce or glaze, Worcestershire, Yoshida's Original Gourmet Sauce—these and many other liquids combined with spices and herbs turn into good marinades for game meat.

Cooked and Uncooked Marinades

Most marinades are uncooked. Universal Marinade, so-called because it works well with a huge variety of game meats, falls into another niche. It works uncooked but also serves as part of the coating with saltine cracker/white flour that gets fully cooked as a breading on the meat. Part of the golden brown color of game steaks treated to Universal Marinade and breading comes from the egg/cracker/flour combination on the meat. On the other hand, there are a few marinades that are cooked before use. Several marinades are listed below to get the game cook started.

Author's favorite fried venison begins with a 50/50 mixture of saltine crackers and flour, the crackers pressed fine with a rolling pin.

After the meat has marinated for the proper length of time in the universal marinade it's thickly breaded with the flour/cracker mix and placed on a cookie sheet awaiting frying.

After every piece of meat is well covered with flour/cracker meal the remainder of the meal is sifted on top as shown here.

The meat, after soaking in universal marinade and well covered with the flour/cracker mix, is fried on medium heat. Half canola oil, half butter makes a good combination to fry in. The pieces of meat here are cooking on the first side.

The marinated and coated venison has been cooked on one side and is now finishing up on the other side. The color here is perfect—golden brown. The meat will be cooked just through and served very hot.

Here is the contrast between the marinated and coated meat on the right and the finished product on the left.

After Marination

After soaking raw meat in a marinade that marinade must be cooked or discarded. I'm opposed to saving marinade because raw meat was soaked in it. Universal Marinade becomes part of the finished cooked product. Leftover Universal Marinade is poured down the drain. Marinade for Leg O' Lope is cooked on the grill or over coals as meat is sliced off in relatively thin steaks. Be safe. Discard all marinades after they've done their work.

Hand Rubbing Spices and Herbs

Most marinades call for spices and herbs. Dried examples of either should be hand rubbed. This means just what it says—the spice is placed in the palm of the hand and rubbed to break it down further, releasing more flavor.

A Few Good Marinades

Beer | Used straight from the container, beer can have a tenderizing effect. I'm not big on leaving meat soaking in beer for more than three or four hours. But it is interesting that the actual flavor of the brew does not seem to permeate the meat to any real degree, yet the flavor of the meat itself is improved in many cases. Beer also tends to clear the meat, working somewhat as brine in reducing unwanted juices.

Beer Marinade | This is a full marinade recipe using beer as the body. Slowly pour one can of beer into a bowl large enough to contain the uncooked game meat. Add 1/2 cup of canola oil, a medium size onion sliced thin, 2 tablespoons of lemon juice, 1/4 teaspoon white pepper (black is also OK), one large garlic clove cut into four pieces and 1/2 teaspoon of salt. These ingredients are married by mixing with a fork and allowing to rest for an hour.

Dove breasts treated in this marinade for two hours turned into tasty treats in the skillet. Experimentation with other meats as well as fish is called for with beer marinade.

A Base for Marinade | Two parts olive oil, 1 part wine vinegar, an onion diced small, 1 garlic clove cut into 4-6 pieces and a little salt and pepper make a base for marinade. Added to this base are various spices and herbs to the cook's delight: sweet basil, oregano, parsley—let the imagination run wild.

Basic Marinade | This is not a base for marinade, but actually a simple marinade. Add 1/2 teaspoon of crushed garlic to 1/2 pint of prepared teriyaki sauce straight from the bottle. Mix well and apply to meat with a brush or simply dab on. Leave for 2 hours and then cook up the meat in stir-fry, fried as steaks, braised for stews, and so forth. This simple marinade turned cubed hunks of fresh venison into a real taste treat fried in olive oil.

Upland Marinade | Good with pheasants, this marinade is a glaze more or less painted on the meat. It consists of 2 crushed garlic cloves, 1/2 teaspoon salt, 3 tablespoons olive oil, the juice of 1 squeezed lemon or lime, 1/2 teaspoon of crushed peppercorns, 1/4 teaspoon of basil leaf, 1/8 teaspoon oregano and a pinch of tarragon. This will make enough marinade for 2 pheasants.

The marinade is painted on the uncooked birds, which are then set aside in a covered dish in the refrigerator overnight. The bird(s) are then roasted using the steaming method—roasting pan covered with tight-fitting aluminum foil followed by the cover. The roasting pan should contain juices for moisturizing the meat, especially 1 or 2 cups of apple juice plus 1 can of chicken stock for waterfowl and game birds.

White Wine Marinade | Ideal for red game meat, this marinade is built with 3 cups of white wine as the base plus 1 cup of olive oil and 2 cups of stock or one can of broth. Add 2 white onions, sliced, plus 2 mashed garlic cloves (pressed flat with the side of the chef's knife). Add 4 large bay leaves plus 1/2 teaspoon of salt and 1/4 bunch of chopped fresh parsley. Drop in 10 unbroken peppercorns and 8 juniper berries well crushed. Mix these ingredients in a large bowl and allow to rest for a few hours. Then add meat. Let this marinade work on the meat for 12 to 24 hours. Ideal for a game meat roast.

Butter/Margarine Garlic Marinade | Add 1 sliced garlic clove to 1 full cup of either melted margarine or butter. Cover container and place in the refrigerator to cure overnight. For cooking, strain garlic pieces out (optional) and paint meat with the marinade. Good on game meat steaks cut no thicker than a half inch.

Butter/Margarine Sherry Marinade | One cup medium sherry wine blends with 1/2 cup melted butter or margarine for this marinade. Canola oil may be substituted for the butter or margarine. Add 1/4 teaspoon rosemary, the grated rind of 1 orange, the grated rind of 1 lemon or lime, 1/4 teaspoon ground sage and 1/2 cup freshly chopped parsley. This marinade is best suited to ducks, but experimentation on other game is encouraged.

One of the author's major standby products for cooking game meats is Mr. Yoshida's Original Gourmet Sauce.

Orange Duck Marinade | Orange sauce is ideal for ducks. (See Chapter 30.) This is not orange sauce, but rather an orange marinade. Combine 1 cup of orange juice and 1/2 cup of sweet vermouth wine. (1/2 cup of limejuice may be substituted for the wine.) One-half sliced white onion, 16 juniper berries, crushed, 1/4 bunch of parsley, chopped, 1/2 oregano finish this marinade. Mix and allow to rest overnight.

Add pieces of duck and allow to marinate for about 6 hours. Fry duck pieces in margarine or butter, adding 1/4 cup of medium sherry when skillet is hot. Toss actively. Cook wine down, but do not allow pieces to go dry in the pan.

Upland Bird Tarragon Marinade | This marinade calls for tarragon vinegar, which is nothing more than a cup of white wine vinegar and 1/4 teaspoon tarragon mixed together and set aside in the refrigerator for at least 24 hours. Optional: sweet vermouth with added tarragon. Pour 1/2 cup of the resulting tarragon-flavored vinegar into a mixing bowl. Add 1 cup of olive oil, 1/4 teaspoon tarragon leaf, 1/4 bunch of chopped parsley, 1/4 teaspoon thyme (dry and hand rubbed). Mix ingredients thoroughly and ladle over pieces of game bird, especially pheasant. Cook pieces in 2 to 4 hours after applying the marinade. Tarragon can overwhelm the meat if allowed to work too long.

Stir Fry Marinade | This marinade ends up cooked in the wok or skillet. It begins with 1/2 cup of soy sauce. Add 1/2 cup medium sherry. Canned beef broth may be used in place of sherry. Add 1 large crushed garlic clove, 1/2 teaspoon ginger, 1/2 cup of Mr. Yoshida's Original Gourmet Sauce. Stir well.

Marinate cubed meat for 2 or 3 hours. Remove meat from marinade with fork. Heat wok with canola oil. Brown meat pieces. Add marinade and cook meat until just done. Serve over rice.

Red Meat Wine Marinade | Begin with a cup of medium or dry sherry. Add 1/4 cup canola oil, 1/4 cup olive oil, 1 large chopped garlic clove, 1 chopped medium white onion, 1/4 teaspoon salt and 1/4 teaspoon sweet basil. Mix well. Marinate game meat for 2 to 6 hours before cooking.

Wild Boar Marinade | Combine 1 cup white vinegar, 1/8 cup olive oil, 2 large mashed garlic cloves, 1/2 teaspoon marjoram, 4 bay leaves, 1/4 teaspoon oregano, 1/4 teaspoon white pepper (black pepper OK). Allow to rest for 2 hours. Add meat and marinate for 4 hours before cooking.

Cooked Game Meat Marinade I | Bring 2 cups water to full boil in a saucepan. Add 1 1/2 cups honey, 2 tablespoons cider vinegar, 1/4 teaspoon rosemary, 6 peppercorns. Boil hard for 2 or 3 minutes. Allow to cool before marinating meat.

Cooked Game Meat Marinade II | One quart water, 1 cup red wine vinegar, 2 chopped onions, 1 thinly sliced large carrot, 4 diced celery stalks, 2 small white onions sectioned, 1/4 bunch fresh parsley bursted (see Chapter 23 for bursting), 1/2 teaspoon thyme, 6 crushed juniper berries, 6 peppercorns, 1/2 teaspoon salt. Bring to a boil. Then simmer very slowly for 30 minutes. Allow cooling and resting before use. Marinate meat for 2 to 6 hours. Drain off marinade before cooking meat.

Barbecue Marinade | Combine 1 cup catsup, 1/2 cup grocery store-style chili sauce (comes in a catsup-like bottle), 1/2 cup cider vinegar, 2 tablespoons Worcestershire sauce, 2 tablespoons lemon juice, 2 tablespoons orange juice, 6 tablespoons brown sugar, 2 teaspoons dry mustard, 1/4 finely chopped onion and 2 cups prepared barbecue sauce. Marinate meat to be cooked over coals or on gas grill in this mixture for 2 to 4 hours

Remove meat. Strip marinade off of the meat pieces back into the bowl. Rinse meat pieces in plain water, dry on paper towels. Rub meat with canola oil. Place over

medium coals or gas grill. Baste with marinade. Be sure to cook marinade on meat. Do not consume this marinade uncooked after raw meat has rested in it.

Apple Juice Marinade for Ducks and Geese | Start with 1 quart of apple juice. Add 1 pint orange juice, 2 garlic cloves, halved not crushed, 1/2 bunch parsley cut, but not chopped, 1/2 onion sliced. Place in plastic food bag with duck or goose, seal and allow to marinate for at least 4 hours before cooking.

Fish Marinade I | Combine 8 tablespoons canola oil, 3 tablespoons wine vinegar, 1/4 bunch chopped parsley, 1/8 teaspoon thyme, 1/2 teaspoon salt, 1/2 teaspoon pepper, 1/4 cup lemon juice, rind of 1 lemon (optional) and 1/4 bunch chopped green onion. Marinate fish fillets for 2 to 4 hours before cooking. Fish fillets marinate better than uncut fish in this marinade. Yields sufficient marinade for 4 to 6 slabs of fish fillets. Multiply ingredients for cooking more fillets.

Fish Marinade II | This marinade is strong on soy sauce. Add 2 crushed garlic gloves to 1/2 cup soy sauce. Add a little water to thin marinade (2 or 3 tablespoons). Marinate fish to be *broiled* in this mixture. While broiling, apply fresh, if available, lime juice over fish.

Marinades are major means of preparing game dishes that will please people who don't get to each all that much wild meat, which includes most of us. Marinades impart familiar flavors. Some may call it disguising. But is it? Cooks are not accused of disguising flavors when they add all manner of sauces, spices, herbs and condiments to domestic meats.

To marinate is not to mask, but rather to enhance. And the few marinades presented here are perfect examples of starting with a good product in the kitchen—wild meat—and making it even more palatable.

Sauces, Gravies, and Stock

Strolling hand-in-hand with Chapter 22 on no gamey taste, partnered with Chapter 23 on condiments that make a difference, and associated with the use of spirits in Chapter 24 and marination in Chapter 25, this chapter talks about sauces, gravies and stock that turn ordinary meals into gourmet tablefare both at home and in the field. Sauces, gravies and stock are given a full chapter because of their important role in game cookery.

Sauce and gravy serve the same general purpose of dressing up a meal after it's cooked, such as ladling pan gravy over chicken-fried game steak and mashed potatoes, or covering foods with sauce.

Stock, on the other hand, is a base that constitutes the body of soups, stews, gravies, sauces and other dishes. Full-blown sauces, such as Chef Sam's Red Spaghetti Sauce, are in the recipe section. The following is a basic look at sauces, gravies and stock designed to provide a strong foundation for the game cook.

Gravy is, after all, a kind of sauce, and it was the gravy that made this meal special in a Kentucky hunting lodge.

Above: Thickening a sauce gives it gravy-like consistency. This brown sauce was thickened through the addition of arrowroot and further cooking.

Above left: This Northern Italian gamebird dish is essentially built upon a white sauce.

Sauces

On a special occasion I had the pleasure of dining at a somewhat exclusive (at least it was expensive) French restaurant. My particular portion was sized to feed a canary on a diet. Furthermore, everything on my plate, what there was of it, was smothered with sauce. The sauce was good but as with all cooking too much of a good thing goes awry. I enjoyed the meal, filling up at home with an honest peanut butter and jelly sandwich and a glass of cold milk.

Sauces are intended to enhance, not overcome food. Here are a few basic examples. Hint: Pay attention not only to ingredients in a sauce, but *how* those ingredients are blended. A true sauce has body. It is not a liquid. Sauces are intended to compliment just about any cooked meat as well as fish.

The Roux | A base to start various sauces is the roux, a French name that translates into a simple 50/50 mixture of oil and flour. The roux eliminates a raw flour taste in subsequent sauces made from it. Cooking the flour and oil together also promotes blending with ingredients later when a sauce is built. The roux is made in a saucepan over low heat. The oil is heated first (canola is good) with flour added slowly as the oil heats. The result is a white base when the mixture is just blended.

The longer the roux cooks the darker it becomes which is fine for brown sauces, but not white. The end result should be very smooth regardless of the color. A roux is a good start for a true sauce thick enough to look like a fine gravy.

More Body | Sauces are thickened to create more body. The game cook needs to know how to create a sauce that is not simply juice to be ladled on food. One way is simple reducing, which means slowly boiling a sauce on very low heat until it thickens, making sure it doesn't burn. Often boiling is sufficient to thicken a sauce.

Butterballs can also be used to thicken a thin sauce. These are prepared with equal amounts of butter and flour pressed together into little balls. These are dropped into a thin sauce and blended with a whisk.

Another thickener is made of cold milk and cornstarch. Two to four tablespoons of cornstarch or arrowroot can usually be added to 1 cup of milk. The finished product should look like cream with no lumps. This mixture is added to a sauce and blending with a wire whisk as the sauce lightly boils.

Finishing a Sauce | My grandfather finished some sauces with the simple addition of butter. He removed the hot sauce from the stove, added a tablespoon or so of butter and mixed thoroughly with no further cooking. This gave the sauce a pleasant glossy shine. Sometimes he used whipped cream instead of butter, using three times the amount of butter, i.e., a tablespoon of butter becoming three tablespoons of whipped cream.

A Few Good Sauces

Brown Sauce | There are elaborate brown sauces that deserve their honor, but they are not in keeping with our basic rule of great food without too much fuss. For example, one brown sauce calls for baking with meat bones and several vegetables. If our brown sauce receives a sideways glance from TV chefs—oh, well! It's made by taking the aforementioned roux and adding a few ingredients. That's it.

The roux should consist of 2 cups flour and 2 cups canola oil. Add 2 cups of canned beef broth or strong stock; bring to a simmer. Add 1/2 cup of Mr. Yoshida's Original Gourmet Sauce or similar substitute. The former is widely available, especially at large discount facilities such as Costco. Optional ingredients include a little minced onion along with a tablespoon of vermouth or medium port wine.

White Sauce | This sauce requires more chef time than simple brown but it's not too much trouble to prepare. Its body is a roux with flavored milk. The roux is small, 1/2 cup of flour, 1/2 cup of oil. Pour 2 cups milk or half-n-half into a saucepan. Add 1/8 teaspoon salt, 2 bay leaves, 1/8 teaspoon nutmeg (optional), 1/4 of one sliced onion. Simmer for about 30 minutes. Strain and add to the roux blending with a whip and cooking to a creamy texture. Finish with the butterball treatment noted above. Optional: Instead of milk use 1 cup light cream and 1 cup white wine. Finish with butterballs. White sauce is just right for topping off certain gamebird dishes.

Another White Sauce | This white sauce calls for 4 tablespoons butter and 4 tablespoons flour (sound familiar—like the beginning of a roux?) 2 cups milk, a pinch of salt, a pinch of pepper preferably freshly ground. Melt the butter first in a saucepan over medium heat. Maintain color. Do not brown. Add flour, stirring in with a whisk to blend well. Meanwhile in another saucepan heat milk to very hot but not boiling. While continuing to blend flour and butter mix, add milk all at once. When this new mixture reaches the boiling point it will thicken on its own. Simmer for a few more minutes and it's ready to serve.

Hollandaise Sauce | This sauce is not for red meat although it can be used with Eggs Benedict in which some form of cured game meat takes the place of Canadian bacon. It is, however, a fine sauce over many vegetables that go with the game meal. It's also good with poached fish and waterfowl.

Hollandaise is not difficult to prepare, but becomes a disaster unless certain rules are followed. Forget double boilers and other fancy cooking implements. Some recipes insist on a heat resistant non-metallic bowl. I use a saucepan successfully but always with a wooden spoon for stirring. Cooks who get gray hair making hollandaise sauce are victims, generally, of applying too much heat.

Before going forward with the recipe, here are three ways to recombine hollandaise that has separated. One: Add an ice cube and stir the sauce. Two:

There's nothing wrong with getting a little help with sauces. These packaged mixes prepare quickly.

Add a few drops of cream and stir. Three: Add a few drops of boiling water and stir. If one trick fails, go immediately to the next. These steps do not cancel each other, so one can be tried right after another has failed.

Hollandaise ingredients are simply egg yolks, lemon juice and butter or margarine. The egg yolks become the body of this somewhat amazing sauce. Place 4 egg yolks, pierced with a fork but not stirred, into bowl or saucepan. Have 2 sticks of cold butter or margarine standing by. Emphasis on cold. Also have 6 tablespoons of lemon juice in a small dish. Over low heat—emphasis on low—stir egg yolks and lemon juice together with the wooden spoon. Add 1/2 stick margarine or butter. Continue on low heat until butter or margarine has melted. Add another 1/2 cube of butter or margarine. Stir in again. Add another 1/2 cube. Stir again. Add remaining margarine or butter, continually stirring with wooden spoon until sauce is a very light golden color, rich and thick. Orange rind may be stirred in for duck or goose topping. Likewise various berries, such as cranberries warmed and broken up.

Simple Orange Sauce | This sauce is almost a necessity with roast duck or goose. And it's not hard to prepare. This amount is for a large roast duck or roast goose supper.

In a saucepan mix 2 cups of regular white granulated sugar with 4 tablespoons cornstarch or arrowroot and 2 pinches of salt. Stir in 2 cups of orange juice and 1/2 cup lemon juice. Add 1 1/2 cups boiling water, scalding hot. Boil the mixture from 1 to 2 minutes until it attains a sauce-like consistency. Remove from heat and add 2 teaspoons of grated orange rind and the same amount of lemon rind along with 3 tablespoons of butter or margarine. Blend well.

Madeira Sauce for Roasted Game Meat | This recipe calls for 4 tablespoons butter, 4 tablespoons finely chopped green onion, 3 cups of brown sauce (see above), 4 tablespoons lemon juice and 1/2 -cup of Madeira wine. The blending is simple. Melt butter in a saucepan. Sauté green onion in the butter for 2 or 3 minutes to wilt the pieces. Maintain a low enough heat so butter is not browned. Add brown sauce and lemon, blending with wooden spoon. As soon as the mixture comes to a boil add the Madeira wine and simmer gently for 5 or 6 minutes. Serve hot.

Gravy

While there are hundreds of sauces with a multitude of variations, only three gravies are necessary to game cookery: brown gravy, white gravy and pan gravy.

Brown Gravy | This gravy is built of juices from a game roast. The roast will have been made with plenty of stock or canned broth to provide a blend with the natural meat juices coming from the cooking roast. These juices are the body of brown gravy. They are removed from the roasting pan and strained into a separator.

Fat content rises to the top of the separator. When the juice is poured from the separator into the saucepan for cooking, the prime liquid flows out while the fat remains behind to be discarded.

This golden brew is now ready for thickening into gravy. If it looks a little light in color, add 1/4 cup or so of Mr. Yoshida's sauce. Beef bouillon cubes are also good for adding flavor and color, but will make the resulting gravy saltier.

In a bowl combine 2 cups beef broth or 2 cups stock with about 4 tablespoons of arrowroot or cornstarch. Do not use water. Mix to a milk-like consistency. Bring juice to a boil in the saucepan. Add 1/4 cube of butter or margarine and 1/4 cup of cream or milk. Return to a slow boil. Add the cornstarch or arrowroot mixture slowly, stirring all the while. When the gravy is thick enough, pour into a serving boat. If

One of many packaged sauce helpers, this one is especially good with game meat.

the cornstarch or arrowroot mixture is not enough to thicken the gravy, simple make a little more.

White Gravy | The only difference between white and brown gravy is the color, which is provided by the stock or juices used as a base for the gravy. Some gamebird roasts, for example, result in a light-colored juice in the pan. Color is maintained by preparing the thickener of arrowroot or cornstarch, as mentioned above, but with milk, not broth or stock. Add clear stock or chicken broth to extend the amount of gravy. Add butter or margarine as above. This will not darken the resulting gravy.

White gravy works exceptionally well with breaded game steaks that were treated to Universal Marinade before breading.

Pan Gravy | The name says it all. This is a good gravy made right in the pan—the frying pan, that is. After the meat is cooked it's removed from the skillet and set aside. Breaded meat works very well for pan gravy, leaving the skillet bits of cooked breading that fell off of the meat in the skillet. If there is enough of the oil, butter or margarine that was used to fry the meat remaining in the pan, then milk can be added at this point. If there's not enough base, add a little extra oil, butter or margarine. With the pan hot, milk is added. Amount depends upon the size of the skillet, but a cup or so is normally enough in a skillet holding meat for 2 or 3 people. Blend the meat juices with the milk. Carefully sift flour into the milk. Blend with continual stirring as the flour thickens the mixture into pan gravy. Pepper is a good addition. Careful with salt. The pan gravy might have sufficient salt left over from the juices the meat was cooked in and any bits of leftover breading.

Stock

Stock can be made at home or purchased in the can as broth. Both chicken and beef broth make ideal helpers in preparing game gravies.

Stock is nothing more than rendered juices from cooked meat. It can be made from just about any meat. Some of the best stock has many different vegetable products added to meat juices. The plan is to boil the ingredients long enough to reduce their content into the liquid. If stock is prepared correctly, the products used to make it, meat or vegetable, are rendered useless and discarded.

Stock also requires seasoning, but with caution. Seasoning can continue working so that stock stored in the refrigerator for a few days gains more and more power, especially if garlic or onion is part of the recipe.

Stock has been used as a soup in itself but it's best employed as a soup base, gravy base or sauce base. Strong well-prepared stock promotes good-tasting sauces, soups and gravies.

Stock is also economical. Instead of tossing out bones after processing game for the freezer, they can be used for stock. Caution: Never attempt to save anything that is tainted. Use only good clean products for stock.

Stock ingredients include many products that may otherwise be tossed out. A good example is chicken parts, especially wings and backs, along with livers, hearts and gizzards. Upland game birds offer the same parts for stock, which is very accepting. It gets along fine with mixes of different meats and vegetables. Those chicken parts, for example, blend perfectly with clean scrap from boned elk, deer or just about any other big game.

There is no single recipe for stock. It's built from whatever is at hand but not without thought. I like to begin with the pressure cooker, breaking down the products quickly but not completely. After the pressure cooker has done its work the juice, with all products, is placed in a standard pot and boiled slowly. This makes a richer broth because some of the water is wafted away as steam, producing a more concentrated juice.

Let's consider a standard stock with a multitude of products cooking down in plain water. It all begins with a pressure cooker about half full of water. This particular—and I might say imaginary— stock is built of clean meat scraps from the recent processing of a big game carcass. However, the butcher just happened to have a batch of beef bones available at little cost so they're in the brew as well. And that roast chicken last week surrendered a back, wings, gizzard and heart, which were frozen right away and now thawed and added to the makings in the pressure cooker.

Tossed in for good measure we have about 1/4 bunch parsley, 1 small onion quartered, 12 peppercorns, 1/2 teaspoon dry mustard, 3 bay leaves, 1/4 teaspoon oregano and the same of sweet basil. Oh, look, there are 4 celery ribs in the refrigerator. In they go. How about those 2 carrots? Why not? Dice and toss them into the pot. After pressure cooking for 30 minutes the entire content of the cooker is dumped into a stockpot and simmered for a couple hours.

When everything in the pot seems to have given up all it has to sacrifice the liquid is strained off, cooled and saved. I've had stock frozen in jars for three months without ill effect.

This little stroll through the forest of good game cooking has but stirred the leaves and yet it contains golden nuggets of useful information. Sometimes those few extra moments spent creating a special sauce to grace a dish can turn an ordinary meal into a memorable one. A hearty brown or white gravy tops off game steaks, potatoes and vegetables for hungry folks. Hollandaise sauce over vegetables or fish shows everyone that the cook cared enough to add a little flair to that evening's dining. And how much effort was any of it to make, really? Meanwhile, a simple stock that required almost no attending, unless the cook insisted on watching the pot boil, serves as a base for other good things, including game soups.

Bouillon in various forms is important in preparing many different game gravies and sauces.

Canned tomato products are ideal for creating red sauces. And they're especially handy in camp cooking.

27

Fishing for the Pan

High in the Colorado Rockies I lay in my tent one night listening to the peaceful flow of liquid diamonds making their way to the river below. I got up and went outside. The moon, full and bright, highlighted the scene with pine trees black against the sky, the moving water a shining ribbon.

Nearby many camps just like this one lie streams and lakes ready to give up delicious fish for hunters who take a break from the action.

Before making it back to the warmth of my sleeping bag, something occurred to me. "There are fish in that stream," I whispered to myself. "How come you aren't catching a few for supper?" The answer came simple and direct: I had not purchased a fishing license, never even thought about it.

Chalk up one more hunter among thousands who ends up near river, creek, lake or pond without the means of pulling a few finny fellows from the water. There is no excuse for it and it never happened to me again.

I love to fish but I am a hunter not a fisherman. Fishing tackle seems to tangle all by itself when I get my hands on rods and reels. At the same time, when I fish I do all right, probably because I don't know any better. Landing a fish on line that resembles a spider web is great sport but when I'm fishing on a hunting trip the goal goes beyond playing a fish to landing one—can't eat the fun.

Hunters who fish incidentally require not only special tackle but also a different slant on the adventure. My own tackle is compact and easy to carry, except when the fishing is close by. Then full-size rods and reels are put into service. My attitude includes enjoying the fishing as an important part of the hunt but always with a feast in mind. Furthermore, both out-of-state and local hunters double their investment when they add fishing to the adventure.

What fish? Where? What tackle? Which methods? What about bait?

What fish? That's easy. All fish. Mainly brook trout, lake trout, browns, rainbows, golden trout and cutthroats where I go for elk and deer. But I've caught catfish as well as smallmouth and largemouth bass along with other pan delicacies. Crappie, pike, rock bass, grayling—you name it. All are fair game in season.

Hunting near a large reservoir one time I flipped a lure into the deep water and got a snag. No, wait a minute. It was a fish. Out came a walleye, certainly one of the most edible fish on the planet if not the greatest fighter. The only thing a sportsman has to know is which fish are in his area and in season so he can bring the right tackle, bait and lures.

Where are these fish? Everywhere. While most of my fishing on hunting trips happens in the West, catchable edibles are available all over the globe from bass in

A daypack like this one will "hide" a complete fishing outfit, especially one like the South Bend outfit mentioned in the text.

Far left: A happy wandering bowhunter can find delicious fish over the next hill or in the valley below. Fishing is an enjoyable adjunct to hunting and its bounty in camp and home food is welcomed.

Left: Where are the fish? Everywhere. There are few hunting areas that have no fishing within reach. This small lake gave up a mess of fine-eating trout.

Incidental fishing gear is compact. Here bowhunter Herb Meland prepares to catch a few trout for supper.

Africa to bluegills in a little rural America pond. Mule deer hunters in Baja can even fish the ocean. On an antelope hunt in rolling sagebrush country I located a small lake on a topographical map. Couldn't be fish in it, could there?

The answer came at the edge of the water. Should have been picked up, of course, but there on the bank lay convincing evidence that at least one other person thought fish were in the water. The giveaway was an empty nightcrawler container.

Smallmouth bass inhabited the pond and they were hungry. I soon had enough for myself as well as sharing with a camp of hunters down the road. Catching the lively little fish on lures was fun. So was dining on them by campfire that night.

As a hunter my fishing gear is basic. Last time out my wife and I hiked from our camp to a small lake at an altitude of 9,500 feet. The limit on brook trout was 10.

All kinds of fishing tackle works for hunters. Here, the author uses a lightweight outfit to fish a small stream.

We both had compact fishing kits, mine a South Bend Professional Adventure PAC AP-701 Ultra Light Spinner Kit, a long name for a short outfit that fits into a little pouch too small for a good-sized handgun. Our telescoping rods flicked out to full length and reels were attached, Judy's a closed-face spinner, mine open-face. We were in business.

On my second cast I moaned, "Drats," as W.C. Fields would say. "Double drats." I thought I had a snag. Then the snag began to fight and out of the water latched onto a piece of nightcrawler came a beautiful brook trout. Action continued that way for an hour with a number of smaller fish returned safely to the water. Once again we had neighbors to share with so we felt justified in taking our full limits from the seldom-fished lake.

Fishing equipment for hunters must be easy to use, widely applicable to varying situations, and portable for pack-ins. One-piece rods are generally, but not always, impractical for hiking in. Those who crave the action may opt for a two-piece rod since every added section of a takedown sacrifices a little life along with some strength. Meanwhile, a one-piece six or seven foot rod with matching reel is fine for fishing near camp or where the hike to water is not fraught with brush or other obstacles.

Tackle must be in good shape. Going back to town for a new rod ferrule is normally out of the question, a broken reel likewise. Some form of carrying case affords protection not only on the trail, but also during transport in the vehicle. The reel should balance with the rod. Drag should be easy to set. Spinning reels are good. Casting reels may be less practical, but today the better levelwind models have been refined into excellent tackle used with all but the lightest of lures for casting jigs, spinnerbaits, spoons, topwater baits, jerk baits, crankbaits, plastic worms and more.

Gear includes the must-have stringer to keep fish alive as long as possible. A compact landing net is good for larger fish. Transporting fresh fish from water site to camp is best accomplished with a wet burlap sack that breathes to keep the fish cool by evaporation. Adding dead plants of any kind to the sack is an invitation to decomposition. Before carrying the catch to camp the fish should be pan-dressed—gilled and gutted. When possible it's also nice to have a cooler with ice waiting at the vehicle or in camp. A compact tackle box should carry assorted split shot, small floats, swivels, and snaps, as well as hooks in sizes 6 to 12.

Line is the link to the fish. Light line reduces wind deflection. I know that. Light line is also easier to cast farther. It has less resistance in the water, too, so a lure is presented more naturally in currents, eddies and pools. Another plus for thin line is less visibility in the water, which is ideal in clear mountain streams and lakes. However, whereas 6-pound test may save lure or bait, get a snag with 4-pound line and kiss the package goodbye.

This bounty of trout caught on a high mountain lake during a bowhunt were welcomed in camp by all.

Nessmuk warned not to go into the woods without a few angleworms. Good advice. This fine little brook trout was caught on a worm and worms are not dangerous to the fishery, as some live baits can be.

Right: Fishing for hunters can get quite serious. After game is tagged, there is nothing wrong with looking for action in nearby waters, even the ocean.

Far right: Panfish? Actually, yes. These fish were caught for the pan. A hunter who gets near some fine fishing but fails to take advantage of it is missing a good bet.

Great strides in technology have produced high-test lines of small diameter but spider webs are not necessarily right for hunters who fish. My regular spool for pan-fishing carries 6-pound test with 8 pound on the backup spool when the undersurface is full of snags and requires stronger line. Forty-pound fish are caught on 20-pound-test line all the time, but heavier line reduces loss. And remember—we're fishing for food.

Live bait is OK as long as it isn't dangerous to the fishery, such as minnows that could escape to introduce trash fish into a wonderful little spot. Bringing night-crawlers is never a mistake as that great outdoorsman of long ago, Nessmuk, suggested. "Do not go into the woods on a fishing tour without a stock of well cleaned angle-worms." (Woodcraft, 1819) Sometimes mealworms work, too, carried in dry cornmeal to keep them cool in the hunting camp, especially if there is ice handy.

On a deer hunt my partner and I hiked down-canyon into a fast-moving stream in northern Arizona. I prepared a swatter from a fallen tree branch and we soon had a multitude of grasshoppers. We couldn't keep the native trout off our hooks.

I've collected grubs from rotten stumps and under rocks and worms along stream banks. On a dove/quail hunt near Yuma, Ariz., I caught catfish by first reeling in a couple of carp on doughballs. Carp meat works great for cats because it's tough and not readily chewed off the hook.

Commercial baits are almost endless. One of my hunting partners caught a 40-pound king salmon, an eight-inch yellow perch, plus Dolly Vardens, all on salmon eggs. Yellow, red, orange, garlic, anise and other marshmallow types are a possibility, along with many different kinds of Power Bait. Why wild trout bite on Power Bait they have never seen before is a mystery to me, but they do. Prepared catfish bait is good, and Velveeta cheese can also work.

Flies can be real killers. A fly attached three feet from a small float was used to land a limit of trout on one mountain lake. I have a bowhunter friend who never passes up a chance to fly-fish wild waters, which is out of my league. Along a tiny creek in Wyoming he landed beautiful cutthroats with his fly rod as I sneaked up on the stream presenting a wriggling worm to the fish, much less romantic, but his fish and mine tasted the same back in camp.

There are many fishing methods for hunters. Most of the author's incidental fishing occurs in the high country of Wyoming and other parts of the west with compact tackle.

Spoons and spinners of all kinds can be deadly. On one trip we ended up on a pristine lake in Alaska. The fish showed no interest in anything we presented. At the time the Herter's company had a giant catalogue advertising "the best in the world" on all manner of outdoor-oriented supplies. I had a Herter's Eskimo Wobbler, which was guaranteed irresistible to northern pike. I flung it out as far as I could upon the calm lake and began to reel in when suddenly—wham! I knew I had the king of the lake on the line. I didn't. Two fish had fought for the lure and both were hooked.

Dardevles can be good. I've done well with Z-Rays and small Mepps, too. Panther Martin spinners have accounted for various panfish, including trout, bass, walleye, pike and salmon, especially with slow retrieval. Cabela's sells lure kits loaded with various types.

Being an amateur fisherman, I was surprised when a real pro told me to carry various jigs on my next fishing-for-hunters expedition, especially if I ended up near bass, crappie, trout or bluegill waters. While the jig is good for bottom fishing, it can also be used in streams. Starting it upstream, the jig drops into holes downstream where fish are lying.

Fuzz-E-Grub Jigs caught walleye, small mouth bass, crappie and a variety of pan fish for my amigo Kenn Oberrecht, who is an expert on fishing with jigs. His excellent book on the subject, *Angler's Guide to Jigs and Jigging*, Stoeger Publishing Company, is filled with solid information. Jigs of 1/16 to 1/4 ounce are good for smaller streams, lakes and ponds. Mini Tube Tail Jigs of only 1/32 of an ounce are useful, as well as Unrigged Flat Foot Jigheads at 1/8 ounce, 1/4 ounce and 3/8 ounce. Cabela's advertises its Marathon Jig as having "breathing, living, pulsating action attractive to most freshwater gamefish."

Methods begin with attitude. Although I've preached that my own fishing on hunting trips is for food alone, that's not entirely true. Hunting and fishing go

Sometimes a good hunting trip ends with a good fishing trip, even on the ocean. Judy Fadala landed this fine tuna off the coast of Oregon.

together as naturally as inhaling and exhaling, and trading rifle or bow for rod and reel has saved more than one mediocre hunting safari.

Fly-fishing is probably the king of all methods, but remains the most difficult means of procuring camp fare, with sport often outweighing the pan. Ultralight tackle also escalates the experience, while standard lightweight rods and reels, along with standard tackle, are more practical for the incidental fisherman. Dunking nightcrawlers, mealworms, grubs, salmon eggs, cut baits and commercially prepared baits is also rewarding.

Skilled anglers fight the fish with rod, not strength of line, using reel drag for control, while the rest of us are content putting another fish on the stringer. But even those of us who fish mainly during hunting season are required to know a few tricks, such as going slower with more patience when colder waters slow fish activity, as well as sneaking up on small streams.

I recall my first attempt at removing trout from a trickle of water in the Rockies. I strolled boldly up to the bank to take a look. As I did, silver bullets fired both upstream and down in the water. I had frightened every trout away. I soon learned to stalk little streams, presenting bait carefully over a brush screen to keep my body out of sight.

I have a permanent hunting list that is consulted before every big game trip. It includes everything from guns, ammo, bows and arrows, to daypack, weather radio and toothbrush. But one thing is certain. That list of vital gear would be a fleshless skeleton without fishing tackle. Once a tag is filled, as well as during in between times, out come the rods and reels. I wouldn't be without them. Neither should any other big game hunter.

28

Caring for the Catch

My mini-bible on caring for the catch is Kenn Oberrecht's *Fish & Shellfish Care & Cookery*, a Stoeger Publishing Company book devoted to its title and referred to in this chapter simply as "the book." Just as this work includes both game care and cookery, Kenn's deals with fish care and cookery.

Cooking is like a computer—good in, good out—bad in, bad out. Use low-grade ingredients in a recipe—suffer low-grade results. That's where care comes in. We were concerned about field care for big game followed by proper processing, wrapping and freezing. Now let's look at waterside care for fish followed by proper processing, wrapping and freezing. The author of *Fish & Shellfish Care & Cookery* begins with contaminants and toxins, a good start for our own chapter.

Contamination of the Catch

All foods are susceptible to some form of contamination. That's why we're told to use protective gloves when field dressing a game animal—or domestic stock for that matter. Few of us heed this message. I'm just beginning to build a habit of wearing gloves. Most of the time I forget, but I'm working on it. I have no fear of poisoning by either meat or fish because the danger of contamination is low in either case. Furthermore, heat (as in cooking) destroys most harmful elements. So what can lurk in fish that may cause a problem? But before that, how would we know?

So How Would We Know?

Fishing for hunters is incidental to this book. We are not died in the creel fishermen. We're nimrods, to use the old term. We love to catch fish more than we enjoy fishing. So how would we ever know if our fish were contaminated?

Most of us wouldn't. Luckily, there are agencies at work studying game and fish for safe eating. The word goes out from these

Caring for the catch begins with a good attitude about equipment and its use. The author prepares here, in the middle of a bowhunt, to capture a few brook trout for supper.

A fine mess of fish caught on a hunting trip in the author's home state of Wyoming. Odds of such fish being contaminated in this high country stream are small, but checking with the officials never hurts.

Keep 'em cold or eat 'em now. These fish will be consumed only a couple hours after being caught.

agencies to us, provided we're astute enough to ask. So we ask. This means dropping into a game and fish department office or information booth to glean the latest information on contaminants—if any have been identified for areas and species we hunt or fish. That's how we find out about any potential problem. There's also the Internet as well as published materials.

PCBs

Oberrecht's discussion of contaminants in *the book* includes PCBs—polychlorinated biphenyls. These are liquid chemicals on the order of DDT and dieldrin. Levels of this toxin are dropping. If a lot of PCBs are consumed a person could end up with skin rashes, nausea, fatigue and other symptoms. PCBs can be especially threatening to pregnant women who should therefore avoid eating fish they know is contaminated with this chemical.

Mercury

The word on mercury contamination has been spread worldwide for decades. Mercury is in just about everything at some level, including our own bodies as well as vegetables, fruits and other organisms on the planet. Regardless, the hunter/fisherman is obligated to check with local fish and game agencies for the latest information on mercury or any other potential threat. And he or she must always heed locally posted warnings.

Swordfish and sharks may contain more mercury than panfish, so don't eat these species more than once a month. Not much risk there, but as always, check with the proper agencies for latest information.

All the Rest

There are other fish contaminants lurking in both salt and fresh water. I place my faith in game and fish departments as well as the Environmental Protection Agency (EPA) and various study groups and universities, trusting that we will be warned if any of these toxins become truly dangerous.

Parasites

Just about every living creature has something in its system that survives on that system. That's what a parasite is. Sometimes this condition is harmless. Sometimes it's even beneficial.

And sometimes it's dangerous to the host organism—like us. Flu bugs and nasty bacteria are only trying to make a living when they invade our bodies. Unfortunately, using us as a grocery store can make us ill, so we take medicine to fight these no-see-'em critters.

Parasites are present, but easy to destroy, in fish. Their major enemy is heat. Most of my fish cooking in the wild is over a bed of coals or in a hot skillet. Since parasites succumb to heat higher than 180 degrees Fahrenheit, I'm not too concerned.

Keep 'em Cold or Eat 'em Now

We know from game-care rules that cold retards bacterial growth and so we keep meat cold to prevent spoilage. Likewise fish. Either keep them cold or consume the catch soon after the fish are caught. My own fishing during hunting season is for food, although I admit the fun factor is always dancing about the stream or lake, especially when tags have been filled and there remains field time to enjoy.

Oberrecht says in *the book* that nothing beats ice for making fish cold. He recommends packing the bottom of a cooler with about four inches of crushed or shaved ice. The rules are simple. Place gilled and gutted fish directly on this ice bed, separating each by a couple inches. Pack ice into the open cavities. Cover fish with more ice. This cools them down fast and also keeps them cold. The latest coolers (ice chests), such as Coleman's Xtreme™ line, do a fine job.

Transportation

The parallel between game and fish care rises to the surface again. Our Chapter 9 deals with proper transportation of game from field to camp and then onward to a processing location. Fish must also be transported from water to camp or home with care. If fishing close to camp, no problem. Catch, clean, eat or put on ice.

My wife and I fished a high-country Wyoming lake one hunting season. Since we had others to share with and the waters were seldom fished, taking a full limit was

Keeping the catch on a stringer until transported maintains freshness.

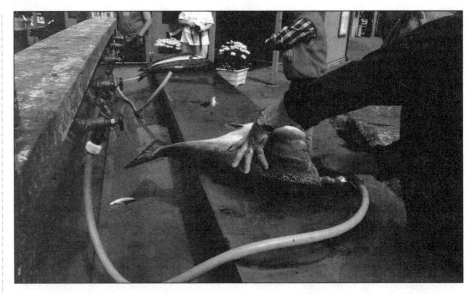

A processing station like this one in Oregon is ideal for caring quickly for the catch. While this one is on the ocean-front, there are many others near rivers and lakes close to hunting territory.

Above right: Caring for the catch always means cleaning and plain water is ideal for the task.

Kelly Black, author's fillets a salmon. The fillets went from this cleaning station to wrapping and freezing in short order. The fish fillets never had time to get warm.

ethical on this particular lake. The catch had to be transported two and a half miles from lake to vehicle and then several miles back to camp. Waiting at the vehicle was our ice chest. We cleaned our fish not far from the lake for two reasons. First, we wanted to get to them fresh. Second, what was left behind would be consumed by animals and returned to Mother Earth. I like that.

Our Coleman Xtreme cooler held a block of ice. Crushed or shaved ice cools everything much faster, be it a can of soda or a fish. However, this form of ice also melts quickly. Our fish were packed on the ice for less than one day before we could give the bulk of them away. We ate four, presenting 16 brookies—clean and cold— to a nearby camper whose eyes lighted up. His camp of six hunters would make short work of the fish that very day.

Usually, fishing for hunters means catching only what can be eaten in camp. Now and then, however, fish are transported from field to home. This occurred when bowhunting with Herb Meland, the man who makes those fantastic Pronghorn bows from his shop in Casper, Wyo. We were finished hunting but near prime trout waters. And so we wet our lines, capturing two limits. We had almost 300 miles to drive. Now what?

Time for dry ice—if it can be located. Not every town has it, but in hunting and fishing areas it's surprising how many little villages have dry ice on hand.

Dry ice is solid carbon dioxide and must be handled with care. It will damage skin. It may even penetrate the walls of an ice chest if not carefully wrapped first. And if it does that to human flesh and ice chests, how about fish?

The idea is to secure the dry ice so it will not attack skin, coolers or the catch. This means several wraps of newspaper. A five-pound chunk of dry ice will keep fish that are already cold perfectly chilled for a full 24 hours. Of course, more dry ice can be added during a very long trip from field to home.

On another trip my wife and I enjoyed a huge catch of fish off the coast of Oregon with our friend Kelly Black. Kelly is a fisherman among fishermen. He lives to fish as many of us do to hunt. And so he wanted us to enjoy eating our bounty back home, which included an air trip. How would that work out? Our catch included lingcod, coho salmon, several species of rockfish and Pacific albacore, a testy member of the tuna family.

With a razor-sharp fillet knife, Kelly deftly transformed it all into skinless, nearly boneless slabs of gamefish-cum-foodfish at an Oregon State fish cleaning station.

Later we vacuum-packed the fish fillets at Kelly's lodge in town and froze them solid. For the plane trip home, we used standard disposable coolers, first wrapping the packages in newspaper, then stacking them into the foam coolers secured with duct tape to prevent opening on the flight home.

Those great-eating fillets made the journey of a thousand air miles without thawing in the least. That was partly due to the coldness of the airplane's hold, but mainly because of *insulation*. Just as we hang a big game animal by night to cool it, taking it down and covering it with tarps and sleeping bags by day to keep the carcass cold, the wrapping and coolers preserved the catch.

Coolers

Coolers, also known as ice chests, have been noted several times in this chapter. Regardless, they're so important in protecting game and fish from spoilage that a few special remarks are in order. There are many brands to select from with good models in each make.

As this is written, however, I'm compelled to state once more that the most efficient cooler I've come across is Coleman's Xtreme line. The 36-quart model is a good size. Coleman says it will keep a block of ice for up to five days at temperatures as high as 90 degrees.

The same company also offers a thermoelectric cooler with 12-volt adapter for vehicle use. Plug the cord into what we used to call a cigarette lighter—now known as a power point in some vehicle literature—and this cooler brings food down 40 degrees Fahrenheit below the ambient (outside) temperature. The 16-quart Thermoelectric model denotes its internal volume. The cool thing about this cooler is that reversing the power cord heats the interior 100 degrees Fahrenheit above ambient temperature to keep food warm.

Coleman also offers its Activity Coolers. The Event™ model holds 16 beverage cans plus ice, but can also be used to keep fish cool from water to camp.

Processing

Oberrecht's recommendation in his book goes, "Food fish should be killed as soon as possible after they're landed or brought aboard, then bled or gutted and gilled and promptly chilled." This does not mean that fish cannot be kept alive, as on a stringer or in a livewell. It's simply a point of good management—just as field-dressing game soon after it drops is good management.

Fish that are drawn and gilled soon after taking need not be bled. But go ahead and bleed fish that are to be kept for awhile before processing. Bleed the fish, according to *the book*, by severing the gill rakers. Gill rakers are "the red comblike appendages under the gill covers," to quote *the book*. Use a fillet knife to slice the gill rakers on both sides of the fish. After the fluids evacuate (does not take long) ice the fish or fillet them. Fish that are to be filleted soon after they're caught need not be drawn and gilled as long as they're kept good and cold.

In drawing a fish, make a shallow cut with a sharp knifepoint from anus to gills, just deep enough to allow entrance to the entrails. This, to us hunters, is field dressing. Dump out everything inside the fish including the gills.

I have long used a strong teaspoon for scraping out the interior of trout and other smaller game fish destined to be cooked whole in the pan. Raking along the backbone with the spoon clears away organs and extraneous fluids. Cut the fins off and follow with a cold-water rinse.

In camp, I scrape the exterior of trout more to clean than to scale. A knife blade works here. Then I cook the fish whole (minus head, which is lopped off beforehand for a better pan fit). The cooked fish is easily deboned right in the dish by making a cut down the lateral line (center of the fish's side) and parting the meat away on either side of that line. Once the meat is removed in two slabs from one side, the skeleton of the fish can be lifted right out of the remainder of the carcass in one piece, leaving the other side mainly boneless meat.

Roe

Roe is simply a term for fish eggs. While my friend Jeffrey, the American Indian outdoorsman, consumes these on the spot, I'm more inclined to save roe for bait, especially trout roe. That's either a case of simple food prejudice or a mere matter of taste preference. After all sturgeon roe, after curing and processing, is caviar and caviar can cost a pretty penny. Other fish eggs may be turned into caviar but only sturgeon, according to *the book*, is the real thing. Roe can be cooked, too. An ice fisherman friend of mine in Wyoming saves roe all year, freezing packages for winter use.

Roe is not offal. It's useful either as food or bait and should be so treated and not discarded on the ground.

Filleting

I'm not very good at it, but filleting fish isn't that difficult. Deferring again to *the book*, filleting steps include first placing the fish on its side on a cutting board. Make a semicircular or diagonal cut behind the gill cover and pectoral fin. Then run the blade of the knife full length along the backbone all the way to the tail. The fillet is now free except for attachment to the tail.

Flip it over so that the skin of the fish is on the cutting board, meat upward. Put the slender blade of the fillet knife to work again slicing the meaty fillet away from the skin. "Carefully cut into the flesh at the tail end of the fillet down to but not through [the skin]," says *the book*. Glide the blade from the tail end to the gill end of the fish to remove meat from the skin. Repeat on the other side of the fish. Trim the fillets.

The tuna required a different method. Kelly cut along the lateral line of each one, removing four pieces, two from each side, which in this context are called loins, not fillets. It's not necessarily the size of the fish that dictates this method but rather the anatomy of the fish.

Here's a nice fish ready for processing. It's been thoroughly washed and of course completely dressed with all innards now out and discarded.

An initial cut in the filleting process occurs behind the head of the fish.

The fillet knife follows along the backbone in this second step cut in the filleting process.

The fillet knife cut has continued in this illustration all the way to the tail section.

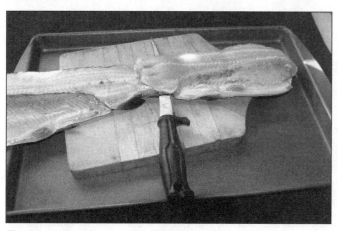

The slab representing one side of the fish is now turned aside and the skin is trimmed away from it to create a fillet.

This is the finished fillet ready for cooking.

Oberrecht points out that whether he's dressing a 1-pound crappie or 40-pound chinook salmon, he cuts one fillet from each side of the fish. But he removes four loins from any member of the flatfish or tuna family. Warning: Use a protective glove to prevent cut fingers and hands when filleting or removing loins. (Normark has a good one.)

Wrapping and Freezing Fish

I use the same process described in Chapter 15 for wrapping and freezing fish, especially fillets. The object is the same—exclude air and protect from dehydration (loss of moisture). Air is kept out with plastic food wrap, which also fights dehydration. The package is protected with regular freezer wrap. As stated in *the book*, oxidation and dehydration, known collectively as freezer burn, are the two major enemies of frozen food.

Freezer life for fish is generally shorter than red game meat and much more in line with cottontail rabbit, which I like to use up inside of six months. The large cache of frozen ocean fish mentioned earlier was beautiful for six months. After that signs of failure set in mainly signaled by a little mushiness in place of firm flesh.

Of course there's a ton more to caring for game fish. However, the mission of this chapter is fulfilled—first to remind hunters that fish are waiting to be caught in many areas and second to lay down a few basics about caring for this valuable catch.

Basic Fish Recipes

This fine fish is being cut into deep fry pieces, which will be treated to a tempura batter.

This short chapter exists only to complement the two chapters that precede it on fishing for hunters and caring for the catch. After hunters have successfully caught a few finny fellows and taken proper care of the bounty, it's time to cook up a meal or two.

There are countless fish recipes in equally countless cookbooks. The few here are aimed more at camp than the home kitchen. But they'll work in either place just as well. This next statement is ironclad: Game meat is great in camp, but so are freshly caught fish. So hunters—let's go fishing and dine on the catch!

Simple Pan Fry

It's simple, and good, too, frying freshly caught fish—never mind what kind from trout to walleye—right in camp. My aforementioned bowhunting partner, Herb Meland, and I caught a mess of brook trout one day after unsuccessfully hunting for the elusive wapiti in the Rocky Mountains of Wyoming. A good friend was camped only a few hundred yards away. Maybe it was the aromas drifting on the early evening breeze that brought him over with a hungry look in his eye.

"Have one," I coaxed. "We have plenty. I'll put another pan on the fire right now."

"No, no," he said. "Well, maybe just one."

"How about just one more?" I asked.

"No, no," he said. "Well, maybe just one more."

After eating six fried trout our friend pulled up a stump and sat contentedly, hat thrown back as he studied the first stars of the night.

That's the usual response to freshly caught fish in the frying pan. Chapter 28 dealt with processing a fish to be cooked whole, as these little brookies were handled. Lop off the head to fit the pan, draw and gill the fish, using a spoon to scrape the inside clean and a knife to scrape the outside. Wash and dry the cleaned fish with paper towels. The fish may be floured or not. If floured, a good mixture is a cup or two of flour and a few shakes of salt, pepper, paprika and garlic powder. If not floured, then sprinkle both inside and outside of the fish with garlic powder, paprika and a light shot of pepper.

Now into the pan they go where canola or olive oil is just beginning to smoke. If the pan is too hot the outer part of the fish will brown up or even burn before the meat is cooked. So after the first hit in hot oil, lower the heat or move the pan to a cooler spot on the coals. The skin must come out crispy, but the meat must also be cooked done through but not dried out.

Deep Frying

This is another way fish can be cooked in camp. A deep fryer is not necessary. A frying pan, preferably the no-stick surface type, is more than good enough. Make a batter with tempura, a boxed powder easily found in the grocery store. It can be used by itself as a fish coating, but is far better after a doctoring.

"Just start tossing spices and herbs in." That's the advice I received from friend Kelly Black on my first attempt with tempura. And it's not far off the mark. But that makes talking about a recipe a little difficult, so I'll narrow it down a little.

Consider only two diners in camp this fortunate night after a morning of successful hunting closed with a fine afternoon of fishing. The kind of fish does not matter a lot, but it has to be filleted as described in Chapter 28. That's because tempura batter in this recipe calls for chunks of boneless (as close as possible) fish.

Combine and shake into the tempura, which is of flour-like consistency, 2 or 3 strong sprinkles of salt followed by a little garlic powder. We're not finished. Add 2 pinches of sweet basil. Want to try a pinch of oregano? Go ahead. A minute pinch of tarragon is OK, but not too much. It will overpower the tempura. Let's see. What else is handy? A couple shakes of lemon pepper. That'll do unless the reader has thought of something else. Oh, a touch of celery salt? All right. And a sprinkle of onion powder? Maybe. I've never tried it.

Mix the dry tempura with just enough milk (canned is fine) to make a thick doughy batter. Coat fish pieces with this batter and fry away. Each chunk is introduced to the hot oil in the frying pan and cooked until done through. If the pieces are not too large, the heat can be fairly high, because before the tempura coating burns the interior meat will be cooked. But be careful with larger chunks. Cook on lower heat to ensure that the middle is done without overly browning the tempura coating.

Foil cooking fish is simple. Adorn with spices; add a little margarine or butter and lemon or lime juice; wrap in foil and place on coals to cook just through. Check from time to time to ensure doneness by simply opening the foil package during the cooking process. Also, skin can be removed from the fish followed by a little longer foil cooking, as was done here.

Fish in Foil

This is another simple way to make fish. Rub each whole cleaned fish with cooking oil and place separately on a generous sheet of aluminum foil. Douse the inside with lemon juice, which is an easy product to keep in camp either as lemons to be squeezed or bottled. Hit both sides of the fish with condiments: pretty much open choice. I like to keep it simple: a sprinkle of ever-present garlic powder, another of paprika, a couple pinches of sweet basil.

Secure foil package. The foil package should be suspended a little above the coals rather than placed directly on them unless the coals have cooled down considerably. Super hot coals may burn the fish because the foil covering offers very little insulation, which is good when trying to cook something inside. That's about all there is to preparing freshly caught whole fish in camp using foil. Advantage—no plate required. These fish are eaten right out of their aluminum foil packages. Many options are available in this recipe: a little minced parsley for flavor, diced green onion, a dash of medium sherry.

Fish Over Coals

Again, a simple camp recipe for making delicious fresh fish. This time treat each fish to an oil rubdown both inside and outside. The skin and oil prevent drying out. Pepper and salt are usually sufficient condiments because smoke from the coals will also impart flavor. However, it's a chef's choice. Don't overcook. Peek into the cavity for color change. When the raw appearance of the flesh is replaced with a finished look it's time to check things out. Pull one fish off the grill. Poke a fork into the thickest part to see if it's done. If not, put it back on the grill and let the coals work a little longer.

Poached Fish

Poaching is another easy camp method for cooking fish. It is nothing more than cooking in water, but not boiling in water. The major differences are the amount of water and the utensil.

Poached fish can be excellent. Here, poaching is done with quartered limes.

The water level for poaching is only enough to cook the meat. This is not a job for a boiling pot, but rather a frying pan, just as poached eggs would be made.

Done correctly, fish is wrapped in cheesecloth before poaching, the ends of the cheesecloth becoming handles to remove the fish from the pan. However, I've gotten by in camp by putting the whole fish, minus head for space, directly into the hot water. If the fish is to be cooled and used for sandwiches, little or no condiments are necessary. The sandwich mix (below) provides the herbs and spices.

It's a different story when poaching fish to be enjoyed immediately. Consider a prepared base for poaching rather than plain water. Put 1 or 2 cups of water in the frying pan (amount depending upon size of pan and number of fish to be cooked). Add 2 to 4 beef bouillon cubes to the water; the number depends upon pan size and fish. Boil bouillon cubes down to create a broth. Sprinkle in condiments and boil for about a minute to burst the flavor of the herbs and spices. Consider a couple bay leaves and pepper. No salt; bouillon cubes lend a salty taste. A little dry onion is good, perhaps a light hit of garlic powder. Once again, condiments are a chef's choice because so many work well in this recipe. Now that the brew is bubbling away, lay the fish into the pan, cover and simmer until cooked through. More liquid may have to be added. Options include soy sauce, Madeira, gourmet sauce, teriyaki and others.

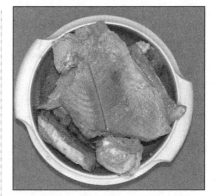

This cooked fish will turn into excellent fish sandwiches by breaking the meat down, removing any possible bones, and then treating very much like canned tuna.

Fish Sandwiches

Any cooked fish can be used to make a spread. Poached fish is especially good because the meat is normally well cooked and soft for breaking down. Crumble cooked and cool (cold) fish meat in a bowl. Remove all skin. Break the meat down with a fork. This is the time to search for bones when they are easiest to locate and remove from the crumbled meat. When the deboned fish is thoroughly broken down, it's time to create a spread with a mayonnaise binder.

If I know fish sandwiches are a possibility in camp my ice chest contains a jar of mayonnaise, which must be kept cool for safety. I'll also have a little fresh celery and green onion on hand. A dash or two of paprika, a little pinch of sweet basil, chopped celery, chopped green onion and mayonnaise are sufficient to create a good fish sandwich spread. Mustard can also be added to taste, but a little goes a long way.

After the fish is fully fried, it can be filleted in the dish. The initial cut is made along the lateral line in the middle of the fish's side.

Fish and Chips

The English style fish and chips I've had were fried fish with pieces of fried potato alongside. Here's an American angle on it: fish and potato chips. This can be done in camp, too, but I recommend a deep fryer with an interior basket. The fish can be fried in any style. I prefer plain, not breaded. The only difficult part of this recipe is the requirement of two cooking utensils working at the same time, one for fish, the other for potato chips. Also, it's difficult to feed everyone at once.

Bring the oil in the pot to hot. When the oil is hot, or nearly so, put

The fried fish, fully cooked and on the plate, has been filleted in the dish by cutting along the lateral line and lifting away the meat on both sides of the cut. This exposes the skeleton which is lifted off in one piece with almost all of the bones intact to be discarded.

Deep fried fish coated with tempura batter makes a delicious meal in camp.

the fish frying pan into play. The idea, remember, is to have pieces of fish and homemade potato chips emerge simultaneously in goodly amounts. Both are best when eaten hot. Place the fish in the pan as the oil heats. When one side is done, turn. It's time to make chips. Hold a potato above the hot oil. Work fast with a potato peeler, slicing off chip after chip into the hot liquid below.

Fresh potato chips are so good that I've had to keep the pot going for a long while to satisfy the people sitting around the stove. As soon as a batch is finished lift the chips from the hot oil and drop into a basket, if available, or a large deep dish lined with with paper towel to absorb a little oil. Immediately hit those hot chips with salt. This meal is not a dieter's delight. It's for special enjoyment. The diet continues tomorrow, hopefully along with exercise hiking for game.

These little fish recipes are essentially foolproof. They're designed to take very little of the cook's time, with the exception of fish and potato chips, which are fun to make anyway. And they're especially good in camp after a day's hunt, pleasing just about anyone, even if he or she is not a dedicated fishianado.

30

A Meathunter's Equipment and Camp Gear

No hunter is better than his equipment. And as the camp goes, so goes the hunt. Unreliable hunting equipment often brings negative results in the field. And a cold, dismal, camp can take the starch out of any sportsman's collar. This chapter addresses these two important topics—equipment for hunting and camp gear.

I'm reminded of Nessmuk, that intrepid outdoorsman of yesteryear who left home with his Billinghurst muzzleloader and knapsack, living off the land for extended periods of time. He got by with very little but his equipment was the best of the day and his camps were strongholds against the elements. We're luckier than Nessmuk with our high-tech hunting and camp gear. Had these been available in his era, he would have used them.

By choice, I enjoy hunting with basic tools of the harvest, such as traditional archery tackle and 30-30s instead of mechanical bows and super magnums, although I have strong admiration for both of the latter. A Marlin 38-55 was this season's major rifle. That lever-action and old cartridge lifted the experience like a hot air bal-

Harris Bipod

Moses Stick

GPS

loon. Regardless of my tool of the harvest, however, be it Pronghorn Ferret IV recurve bow, muzzleloader or 30-30, my field and camp equipment are high tech all the way.

For Hunting

The Bipod | The hunter should always go for the steadiest possible shot. There are several ways to accomplish this important goal from resting across a tree limb to prone on the ground. One of the best field rests is the bipod. Mine is a Harris, uniquely designed to promote one well-placed bullet. This American-made marvel attaches to the fore stock of the rifle. It comes in different models to accommodate various firearms and shooting conditions.

Anyone can test for himself its worthiness by shooting with and without it. With it, groups shrink like new dungarees in hot water. Shots that may have gone astray are placed spot on with the Harris bipod.

The Moses Stick | I will not hunt without a Moses Stick unless I've gone by air and could not take mine. This lightweight staff, named after the Old Testament figure, is mainly for hiking—adding a third leg. The stick prevents falls and promotes hiking distance.

It also serves many other purposes. It's ideal for steadying binoculars for a game-finding view. It can be used standing or sitting as a rifle rest. I've also steadied my 22 pistol on it for ideal shot placement on camp edibles. The stick is good for signaling by ringing a hat over one end and holding it high in the air so it can be seen from a distance. It's also a probe in grassy snake country or when hiking in the dark.

My sticks are made of the agave stalk, a cactus much like the century plant but far lighter and more slender in the hand.

The PoleCat | The PoleCat from the Stoney Point Company is a portable staff that collapses to fit into tight places. It's highly portable for air travel or going into the backcountry with a horse and mule pack train. It serves the functions of the Moses Stick in a commercially made tool. This is my hiking/shooting/binocular staff when the Moses Stick is impractical.

GPS | This amazing instrument can change a hunter's style all by itself. I am not a pathfinder. When sense of direction was passed out I thought it was cents and asked for only a nickel's worth. I am not confident in black timber where no landmarks show for miles. However, with a GPS (Global Positioning System) I'll roam the extra miles knowing that the way home will be provided on the little handheld device. My personal unit is from Magellan, easy to use and reliable.

One afternoon on a high and rugged mountain my wife and I were making our way through a jungle of dense timber. She was operating the GPS. We could not see 50 yards ahead. Suddenly, we popped out on a road with the little GPS arrow pointing directly at the side of our blue Chevy pickup truck.

The Portable Blind | I've been a pursuit hunter all my life but in the past few years was introduced to tree stands and ground blinds. Portable ground blinds are like real estate. The three most important aspects are location, location and location.

I have a Game Tracker blind. This blind is roomy with shooting ports. It's also a cozy nest against the weather. Whereas I may have retreated if a squall invaded my brush blind, I sit tight in the Game Tracker. It defies wind, snow and rain. And it's warm when the next mentioned high-tech piece of equipment is humming quietly inside.

Mr. Heater to the Rescue! | Heater ventilation remains vital at all times. But the Mr. Heater portable propane heater can be used in close quarters provided the company's warning is heeded: "This is an unvented gas-fired portable heater. It uses air (oxygen) from the area in which it is used. Adequate combustion and ventilation must be provided."

It has an oxygen-depletion sensor pilot for additional safety. Mr. Heater comes with full instructions that must be followed. And it works, promoting hunter comfort, which is always important.

Binoculars | I rank binoculars with my Moses Stick. I do not go hunting without a pair at my neck. Currently, my most-used is a 12x50 Bushnell reverse porro prism with high optical resolution. With walking stick or any other solid stance, 12X is not too much magnification. I've made many finds with the glass and located game before it sees the hunter. In the woods the old standard 7X glass is adequate and I have a 6X set for small game and bird hunting.

A tip: To each his own, as the cliché goes, but for me a short strap is better than a long one, preventing bounce when walking. Another tip: Finding game with the glass requires a steady view, slowly focusing and refocusing to sharpen the image.

Binoculors

The Spotting Scope | Spotting scopes are great for locating far-off wildlife and determining species and sex. I've spotted deer with my 12X binoculars so far in the distance that it was impossible to determine if the game was legal, which is especially vital in buck-only areas. My Bausch & Lomb Elite spotting scope with 80mm objective lens and high magnification tells me to stalk or keep on looking.

The Spray Bottle | I carry a small plastic spray bottle for both calling game and stalking. The little pump is filled with lure/scent and water, one small bottle of either one into about a half pint of water. A few mists in the air can help fool the keen nose of an incoming elk or a stalked deer.

Lures and Scents | In hunting, few tactics work all the time. But that does not preclude using many different approaches. Lure/scent is not a piece of equipment. But it can work as one. I use cover scent around my blind. I use lure in a spray bottle to fool keen noses.

Spotting Scope

Daypack

And I've experienced some success building a scent trail and fake scrape. I've had deer, both does and bucks, stop to investigate these phony scrapes. Active Scrape, supplied by the Wildlife Research Center, laced into a roughed up ground surface, stopped two barren whitetail does for clean 38-55 harvests 75 yards from my portable blind this past season.

The Turkey Vest | I don't use a turkey vest in the high mountains but I do use one for river and creek bottom whitetail and wild turkey hunting. Mine is the 3-D model from RedHead , available through Bass Pro Shops. A great deal of thought went into its design. It's full camouflage with detachable front and back blaze orange bibs. The twin carry straps are padded. There is also a waist belt, two slate call pockets up front on one side plus a snap lock and zipper pocket. The other side has a large snap pocket and oversized zipper pocket with interior pouches. Inside there are two extra large zipper pockets.

The game pouch on the back is large enough for a wild turkey but also works for packing extra gear. There is a padded seat that snaps free. The seat is a great boon, protecting not only from cold ground but also rocks and other poking intrusions. The turkey vest does not take the place of a daypack or fanny pack, but it is ideal for many applications.

The Daypack | Whenever a lazy streak winds its way through me and I elect to leave my daypack at camp or vehicle, I pay the price—every time. My daypack from the Cheaper Than Dirt! Company is all-inclusive. It carries small scissors, tweezers, first-aid kit, spare ammo, fire starting material, emergency kit, food, water bottles (pint U.S. Army never-leak), rope, spare gloves, Woolrich wool sweater at the bottom and much more.

The Fanny Pack | There are a number of super-designed fanny packs today, some with shoulder straps for extra comfort in various sizes. The fanny pack has many fans, and deservedly so. Fire starters, lunch, rope and spare gloves carry handily in the fanny pack.

The Packframe | My Freighter packframe from Camp Trails is modified to suit my needs. I've attached protective panels on either side for carrying rifles without scratching stock or metal. There are sling hooks

Pack frame

on both sides bolted to strut. That's better than carrying slung on shoulder slipping and sliding until you want to leave the rifle perched against a tree just to be rid of it. The extra hook is for carrying a partner's rifle as he packs meat to camp. The shelf is set level and reinforced with aluminum bars. This packframe stands straight up when set down.

A daypack is slung over the top struts. Often, I have a nylon tarp between the back of the frame and the daypack, this for an emergency shelter against a sudden cloudburst or snowstorm. Many game animals have traveled from field to camp or truck rope-tied on this packframe.

The Rangefinder | I have three rangefinders. A Bushnell Ranging® 800-yard model is for long-range sport shooting. The Bushnell Yardage Pro® Compact 600 is small enough to carry in my pack. Recently, a third rangefinder found its way onto my belt. It's the seven-ounce Nikon Laser 400 Water Resistant, only 3 1/4-inches long, 2 1/2-inches high, 1 1/4-inch thick.

Rangefinders are good hunting tools. They help teach us how to judge distances, which we think we're pretty good at until put to the test as I was one afternoon on a patch of Wyoming badlands. My first guess was on the money. "I think that fence is 175 yards away," said I confidently. And it was. Looking at another fence line sharply uphill I proclaimed, "That one is almost 300 yards." It was also 175 yards from where we stood. The angle created an illusion of distance.

The rangefinder is also useful from any kind of stand, especially for bowhunters. Knowing the distance from broadhead to rock, bush, log or edge of waterhole pays off.

The rangefinder is also supreme for game in the distance. One afternoon I spied a little party of Coues whitetails making it across a ridge. Using a Bushnell rangefinder, there was plenty of time to get the exact range from my location to a point where the deer would pass. I knew exactly how to hold for the shot.

Wind Detectors | Being found out by game depends upon the animal itself and the habitat. For example, on moonscape western Badlands, mule deer depend on eyes first, nose second, to foil an oncoming hunter. When Badlands' deer are bedded on a promontory, eyes detect the hunter.

Bedded in draws, the nose captures a hunter's ambiance. Whitetails in the thicket, elk coming into a call and many other big game animals in various niches smell out a hunter before spotting him.

This is where wind detectors come in. A talcum-like powder in a plastic bottle sends a jet of white into the air that detects wind and behavior. Windfloaters® (see Directory) is fuzzy material in a plastic container. Small bits are plucked free and turned loose. These tiny fiber packages float on the air showing wind direction and action perfectly.

A hunter who knows wind behavior puts those zephyrs in his face as he still-hunts or stalks, rather than allowing his scent to announce his coming.

Wind detector

Clothing | The protective shell we wear against the elements is imperative to good, safe hunting. I've come to appreciate more and more the fine outdoor garb now available. Like my Woolrich soft flannel shirt and warm vests from the same company. A finger-walk through catalogs reveals the many excellent outdoor clothes we're privileged to have today, such as RedHead socks with the wild guarantee that they'll be the last pair a hunter will have to purchase—ever.

Boots | There's no end to the fine boots available from many different companies. I own several for different hunting conditions, including Woo Davis fishing shoes

from the Georgia Boot Company. They were designed for catching the finny fellows but they don't seem to know it on High Plains for antelope or rolling hills for deer.

Among many other useful foot coverings I have a pair of high-top boots from Bass Pro Shop that defined a new way of whitetail hunting for me. Waterproof, these boots allowed me to walk right down a shallow stream flowing between two ridges where I hunt the flagtail. Deer cannot hear me coming, the rushing waters capturing every step I take.

For Camp

Weather Radio | My Midland weather radio goes to every camp. It's an early-warning device against storms. Mine has an alarm setting that rings out if the weather service issues a warning or alert.

Regular Radio with Tape Deck | September 11, 2001, I lay in my tent atop a tall mountain listening to my radio when the report came in of the disaster in New York City. I like a radio in camp. When bad weather confines me there I can listen to a talk or sports programs, or perhaps a book on tape.

Sleeping Bag | Two models from Coleman treat me well in camp. One is the Elk, a heavy bag that guards against the icy spears of cold weather hunting. Outfitted with sweat suit and watch cap, plus heavy socks, tucking down into the Elk model ensures a warm night. The other is for backpacking.

I've learned that staying over instead of heading for camp in late afternoon can sometimes be the answer to success, waking up in the hot spot rather than hiking back to it in the morning. For this type of hunting my Coleman Exponent™ Summit™ 0 is the cat's pajamas.

Tent | We enjoy a large family-style tent for long camps. It stays warm with heaters and provides ample shelter against Mother Nature's sometimes-bad temper.

For backpacking, however, a Coleman Exponent™ Inyo™ 2 fills the bill. It's light and compact and if there's a wind that can invade it, I hope I'm inside four walls at home when it strikes and not in the outback.

Camp Shoes | Don't forget 'em. Camp shoes, that is. I have a slip-on pair to replace my hiking boots for enjoying an evening at the campfire.

Heater | Mentioned above, the Mr. Heater portable is excellent for maintaining a comfortable temperature in camp. Another good one is from Zodi. It throws a lot of

hot air, but requires a car battery for operation. A good point—the unit itself remains outside of the tent during operation. No venting problem.

Portable Shower | Zodi also offers a portable shower that works on dual propane bottles. In seconds hot water pours out of a showerhead on the end of a hose, somewhat like those found in self-contained trailers.

Refreshing is the word for a good hot shower in camp and a refreshed hunter is a better hunter, also safer because he or she is more alert.

Camp Lantern | There are many good ones. I'm partial to my North Star from Coleman because it burns regular unleaded fuel from the gas station and it chases away the darkness of night with superior illumination.

A fairly fat book could be penned on all of the great gear available to today's hunter. But the little ink spilled here in closing this book will have to suffice for now.

And so good hunting—straight shooting—and fine game meals to each of you!

Directory

Benchmade Knife Company, Inc.

300 Beavercreek Road, Oregon City, OR 97045
503-655-6004 (Phone)
800-800-7427 (Phone, toll free)
E-MAIL: info@benchmade.com
FAX: 503-655-6223
WEB SITE: www.benchmade.com

Makers of excellent knives, including the author's Model 80602, which has a permanent place in his daypack. This folding knife has a very sharp point that serves many applications, from field dressing big game to boning meat in camp, as well as working on birds and small game.

Buck Knives

1900 Weld Blvd., P.O. Box 1267, El Cajon, CA 92022
ORDERS: 800-326-2825
FAX: 619-562-5774
WEB SITE: www.buckknives.com

Long history of fine knives for sportsmen with new designs seasonally, plus the retention of specific styles that have served hunters for many years, such as the Model 110 Folding Hunter used by the author over numerous seasons. Also many heavy-duty fixed blade knives as well as numerous knife sharpening and maintenance items.

Bushnell Performance Optics

9200 Cody , Overland Park, KS 66214-3259
Important Phone Numbers:
In Kansas City area - (913) 752-3400
CONSUMERS: (800) 423-3537
DEALERS: (800) 221-9035
FAX: (913) 752-3550
WEB SITE: www.bushnell.com

Among the finest optics for the serious meat hunter, including the 12x50 reverse porro prism binocular often employed by the author in finding game, as well as the Bausch & Lomb Waterproof 80mm spotting scope with Rainguard protection and ED type lens for high optical resolution.

Cabela's, Inc.

One Cabela Drive, Sidney, NE 69160
ORDERS: 800-237-4444
FAX: 800-496-6329
WEB SITE: www.cabelas.com

Huge catalog of outdoor equipment including firearms for the meat hunter and an endless supply of camping gear and outdoor clothing. Cooking supplies as well, including the Ultimate Turkey Frying Kit, along with several kits and tools for deep injection of fluids into meats.

Campin' Stuff Field Products, Inc.
P.O. Box 296, La Mirada, CA 90637-0296
714-739-5329 (Phone)
ORDERS: 800-600-7423
FAX: 714-739-8243
E-MAIL: info@fieldproducts.com
WEB SITE: www.fieldproducts.com

The author's Campin' Kitchen came from this company, with its double lantern posts, large work surface area, stove holder, paper towel holder and many other features. Also camping tables, tents and much more for the camping meat hunter.

Campmor
28 Parkway, Box 700, Upper Saddle River, NJ 07458
ORDERS: 888-226-7667
WEB SITE: www.campmor.com

Campmor's catalog includes a few hundred items for the outdoorsman, including numerous gas operated camp stoves, along with the Sierra Zip Woodburning Camping Stove that burns bits of wood and other fuels with a battery powered fan providing extra oxygen.

Camp Trails
Johnson Outdoors, Inc.
1326 Willow Road, Sturtevant, WI 53177
262-884-2500 (Phone)
ORDERS: 800-345-7622
FAX: 262-884-1703
WEB SITE: www.camptrails.com

Home of the author's Freighter packframe used in carrying field dressed game from field to camp. Also internal packframes, along with various packs for frames. Johnson is the home of Silva compasses and Eureka! tents as well as packframes and packs.

Cheaper Than Dirt! Company
2524 NE Loop 820, Fort Worth, TX 76106-1809
800-421-8047 (Phone)
24 HOUR FAX: 800-596-5655
WEB SITE: www.cheaperthandirt.com

Interesting company catering to hunters and sportspeople, including numerous daypacks both military and commercial, as well as the Bush Rag™ Ghillie Suit to hide hunters. Ammunition, knives, clothing, camp gear, tents, all at reasonable prices.

Cold Steel, Inc.
3036-A Seaborg Avenue, Ventura, CA 93003
800-255-4716 (Phone)
FAX: 805-642-9727
WEB SITE: www.coldsteel.com

Cold Steel makes some of the most rugged cutlery in the industry in a myriad of designs. The company's Mini-Tac, while intended for tactical work, is one of the author's favorite camp knives. The Kitchen Classics line includes several excellent blades for game cookery with a Kitchen Classics Set in an oak counter-top stand. The latter is a favorite of the author, receiving considerable use in the kitchen.

The Coleman Company
P.O. Box 2931, Wichita, KS 67201

Makers of Xtreme coolers (ice chests) the author considers the ultimate in keeping foods, fish, and game cold in camp and on the road, along with many different up-to-date camp stoves, backpack style as well as larger units, plus many different tents and sleeping bags of high quality.

Essential Gear, Inc.
171 Wells Street, Greenfield, MA 01301
413-772-8984 (Phone)
ORDERS: 800-582-3861
FAX: 413-772-8947
WEB SITE: www.essentialgear.com

Essential gear is a good name for this company because it offers outdoor-oriented equipment that can indeed be essential for safety, such as the VP Signal Light which reveals camp location to a hunter coming in after dark. There is also the Windmill® Stormproof Lighter. One of the author's favorite Essential Gear products is the Ultra 7 Led mini headlamp which leaves hands free when field dressing game after sunset or finding your way to camp in the dark.

Field Products, Inc.
P.O. 296, La Mirada, CA 90637-0296
714-739-5329 (Phone)
ORDERS: 800-600-7423
FAX: 714-739-8243
E-MAIL: info@fieldproducts.com
WEB SITE: www.fieldproducts.com

This company makes several interesting and useful camping tools, including the Campin' Kitchen. Also special stainless steel coffee pots in 8- to 36-cup sizes, a variety of sleeping bags and cots—even a gasoline powered blender as well as Cookin' Stuff, promised as the "Ultimate Turkey Roasting System" with burner and Dutch oven.

Fundicion Callao

15500 N. Coronado Forester, Tucson, AZ 85739
520-825-7013 (Phone)
FAX: 520-825-7013

Distributor of the interesting Illex Model ISR-5000 butane fired camp single burner camp stove as discussed in Chapter 20.

The Game Tracker, Inc.

P.O. Box 380, Flushing, MI 48433
810-733-6360 (Phone)
ORDERS: 800-241-4833
FAX: 810-733-2077
WEB SITE: www.thegametracker.com

Top-grade ground blinds to hide the meat hunter, including the Model 9732 RealTree® Advantage Timber™ with scent eliminating system and multiple shooting mesh screens and windows. The carbon coating on this blind is automatically activated when exposed to direct sunlight, even during cold winter months.

Garmin International

1200 East 151st Street, Olathe, KS 66062
913-397-8200 (Phone)
FAX: 913-397-8282
WEB SITE: www.garmin.com

High-tech GPS (Global Positioning System) units for hunters who want to branch out with a lot less worry about finding the way back to camp. Also highly useful for marking game down and finding it again even in vast territory. Many different models with numerous features.

Georgia Boot

1810 Columbia Avenue, Franklin, TN 37064
800-251-3388 (Phone)
ORDERS: 800-251-3388
FAX: 615-790-4229

Author's Woo Davis Fishing shoe has become one of his favorites for hunting antelope and deer. Georgia Boot also has a multitude of footgear for the outdoorsman in many different styles for different applications in the field.

Gerber Legendary Blades

14200 SW 72nd Avenue
P.O. Box 23088, Portland, OR 97224
ORDERS: 503-639-6161
ORDERS, TOLL FREE: 800-950-6161
FAX: 503-684-7008
WEB SITE: www.gerberblades.com

Numerous cutting instruments as well as the excellent Multi-Plier® from this company, including author's favorite hand axes made of high-quality steel in various styles. Also a complete Big Game Cleaning Kit with Gerber's Back Paxe™ and other tools all in one rugged kit. Gerber's Folding Spade is a wonderful camp tool.

Harris Engineering Company, Inc.

999 Broadway, Barlow, KY 42024
270-334-3633 (Phone)
FAX: 270-334-3000

The Harris Engineering Company produces the excellent bipod of the same name, with numerous models for various applications. Made of top grade components, well designed and constructed, the Harris bipod is useful from prone as well as sitting shooting positions.

Magellan

960 Overland Court, San Dimas, CA 91773-1742
909-394-5000 (Phone)
FAX: 909-394-7050
WEB SITE: www.magellangps.com

Superb state of the art GPS systems that enable hunters to venture farther into the niche with the assurance of being able to find the way back to camp. No single piece of equipment is to be relied on for lifesaving, and so maps and compasses are always included with a GPS. But the author says his GPS has added greatly to his hunting style.

Midland Radio Corporation

1120 Clay Street, North Kansas City, MO 64116
816-241-8500 (Phone)
FAX: 816-241-5713
WEB SITE: www.midlandradio.com

Along with two-way radios, Midland is noted for its special weather radio, which is a comfort to hunters in deep country camps as they listen to news about any incoming storms that may be brewing.

Mr. Heater

This excellent camp heater, noted in Chapter 30, is sold widely in discount stores and through catalogs, such as Campin' Stuff Field Products, Inc.

Nikon

1300 Walt Whitman Road, Melville, NY 11747-3064
631-547-4200 (Phone)
FAX: 631-547-4040
WEB SITE: www.nikonusa.com

Maker of top quality riflescopes, binoculars, spotting scopes and cameras.

Outland Sports

4500 Doniphan Drive, P.O. Box 220, Neosho, MO 64850
417-451-4438
800-922-9034 (Phone)
FAX: 417-451-2576
WEB SITE: www.outlandsports.com

Various companies exist under the Outland Sports banner. Three of the author's favorites, however, are Lohman, M.A.D and Big River game calls. There are calls for just about every huntable species one can think of. Fadala often uses the Lohman antelope challenge call with success. Lohman's Turkey Locator is another outstanding call.

RedHead Bass Pro Shops

2500 E. Kearny, Springfield, MO 65898-0123
800-227-7776 (Phone)
FAX: 800-566-4600
WEB SITE: www.basspro.com

The RedHead name from Bass Pro Shops has long standing among serious hunters and outdoors people in general. It was RedHead that came up with the All-Purpose Lifetime Guarantee sock advertised as "The Last Hunting Sock You'll Ever Have to Buy." RedHead also has its well-designed Striker Turkey Vest as well as a large collection of Bone Dry hunting boots.

Stoney Point Products, Inc.

P.O. Box 234, New Ulm, MN 56073
507-354-3360 (Phone)
FAX: 507-354-7236
WEB SITE: www.stoneypoint.com

Interesting products from an interesting company, especially the Polecat® "Hike 'N' Hunt" comprised of two four-section Navigator staffs with carbide tips, detachable wrist straps, bipod cradle, snow and tundra boots and more; a super lightweight, strong, portable multi-tool for hunting and hiking. The staffs go from only 18 to a full 62 inches in length.

Wildlife Research Center, Inc.

1050 McKinley Street, Anoka, MN 55303
800-655-7898 (Phone)
763-427-3350 (Phone)
E-MAIL: info@wildlife.com
WEB SITE: www.wildlife.com

Developers of numerous lures, as well as various cover scents, especially fresh earth, which is one of the more effective concoctions in foiling the sharp noses of deer and other game.

Woolrich, Inc.

Attn: Customer Service
2 Mill Street, Woolrich, PA 17779
800-966-5372 (Ask for customer service)
800-995-1299 (Phone)
FAX: 570-769-6234
WEB SITE: www.woolrich.com

Simply one of the finest sources of good hunting clothing on the planet, with a multitude of well-designed garments intended to keep hunters warm and comfortable in the field.

XX Sight Systems

(Formerly AO Sight Systems)
2401 Ludelle Street, Forth Worth, TX 76105
817-536-0136 (Phone)
ORDERS: 888-744-4880
FAX: 800-734-7939
WEB SITE: www.aosights.com

The author relies on this company's Ghost-Ring sight on two of his most-used game-taking rifles, a Marlin 336-A 30-30 and Marlin 336CB Cowboy 38-55. The Ghost-Ring, coupled with a White Line front sight, provides a clear sight picture. There's also an excellent Power Rod™ with accessories that the author likes for his muzzleloading rifles.

Foreword to the Recipes

The recipes in this Fourth Edition of Sam Fadala's *Complete Guide to Game Care & Cookery* are all new or revised and refreshed following further work in the galley. Each one has been kitchen-tested by the author and his diners. The grand old recipes, such as Leg O' Lope and Chef Sam's Turkey Stuffing, remain, but with alterations.

The goal is gourmet cooking without the fuss. These are meals that guests think must have taken hours when actual hands-on time was but a fraction of that. Remember that recipe ingredients cannot be copyrighted, so enjoy adding the recipes in this book to your own files along with changes to suit personal tastes.

The book contains general recipes that have come down the pike over many years, perfected by trial and error. Where a recipe is credited to Sam that refers to the author. When credited to Chef Sam that is the author's grandfather, Master Chef Sam Manetta. I have also included many side-dish recipes, but will not recommend which side dishes should accompany a given entrée. That I will leave up to you.

Timetable for Game Meats

This timetable for game meats is based on domestic cuts. Therefore, care must be taken with the unmarbled meat. In many cases larding with fat will be required to prevent drying out. However, the time chart can be used as a frame of reference.

Cut	Approximate Cooking Time (Minutes per pound)	Meat Thermometer Reading
Rolled Rib Roast		
(4 to 5 pounds)	32	140 (rare)
	38	160 (medium)
	48	170 (well)
Rib Eye*		
(4 to 5 pounds)	18 to 20	140 (rare)
	20 to 22	160 (medium)
	22 to 24	170 (well)
Sirloin Tip		
(3 1/2 to 4 pounds)	35 to 40	150 to 170
Rolled Rump		
(4 to 5 pounds)		25 to 30 150 to 170

* Roast at 350 degrees.

Big Game Recipes

Sam's Leg O' Lope

I came up with this recipe to allow grilling of a large piece of meat without drying it out. Antelope is hard to beat in this recipe but other game meat can be substituted.

Place haunch in a deep pan, such as a roaster. Poke long slits in roast with narrow bladed knife. Force half of Gourmet sauce and broth or stock down into slits. Cut beef fat in strips. Put a strip of beef fat in each slit. Put one slice of garlic in each slit. Sprinkle meat with paprika and pepper. Ladle rest of broth or stock over meat. Cover and set aside for an hour or two in the refrigerator. Remove. Turn over in pan. Sprinkle with paprika and pepper. Ladle juices from pan over meat. Set aside again. Turn in pan now and then. Marinate for at least 6 hours and up to 24. Place entire haunch on grill. Slice off pieces length-wise as they cook to medium and serve hot. Turn haunch over and cook the other side, slicing off pieces of meat when cooked medium. Continue turning and slicing until the meat is sliced from the bone. Cook's choice of side dishes, such as green beans and salad.

INGREDIENTS

1 antelope haunch (whole meaty part of hind leg)

1 1/2 pounds fresh beef fat

2 cups Mr. Yashida's Gourmet Sauce or equivalent teriyaki sauce

4 garlic cloves, sliced

3 cups beef or chicken broth or equivalent other stock

Paprika to sprinkle on

Pepper to sprinkle on

Marinated Venison Steaks on the Grill

This recipe works with elk, moose, buffalo, antelope and other meat as well as venison. The plan is to marinate the meat sufficiently to prevent drying out over coals or on the gas grill. Remember that game meat is not marbled.

Shape steaks with a meat hammer to consistent thickness of a little less than one-half inch. Sprinkle on pepper, garlic powder and onion powder. Drop meat into mixture of soy or teriyaki sauce, sherry and broth or stock. Marinate for 2 to 4 hours. Place over medium coals or medium gas grill. Baste with juices while cooking. Cook to medium doneness. Good with baked beans and greens of any kind. Mashed potatoes, too.

INGREDIENTS

2 to 4 pounds of boned big game meat
1/4 cup soy or teriyaki sauce
1/4 cup medium sherry, optional
1/4 cup beef or chicken broth or stock
Sprinkle pepper
Sprinkle garlic powder
Sprinkle onion powder

Floured Pan Fried Steaks

This simple recipe is fast and easy. I used it with caribou when hunting in Alaska.

Lay steaks out on a butcher block or stout cutting board. Sprinkle with flour, paprika, garlic powder and pepper. Now shape with meat hammer, driving the flour and condiments right into the steaks. Heat pan to medium. Add 1/4 cube of butter. Before butter smokes or burns, add meat to pan. Brown and turn. Lower heat and continue to cook steaks until done just through. Serve with standard side dishes.

OPTIONAL | When meat is browned it can be finished with teriyaki sauce and/or sherry by simmering until juices are thickened.

INGREDIENTS

2 pounds venison or other red game meat
Flour
Sprinkle paprika
Sprinkle garlic powder
Sprinkle pepper
1 cube butter or margarine

OPTIONAL

2 ounces teriyaki sauce
2 ounces sherry

Lemon Pepper and Garlic Wild Boar

Wild boar can be excellent meat, especially from farm areas where they have all of the best possible feed. This recipe calls for tender loin meat.

INGREDIENTS

10 wild boar medallions (full loin size)
1/2 cup olive or canola oil
1/2 cup lemon juice
1/2 teaspoon tarragon
1/4 cup broth or stock
1/2 teaspoon sweet basil
Paprika
Lemon pepper
Butter or margarine for basting

Marinate medallions in oil, lemon juice, tarragon, broth/stock and sweet basil, with sprinkle of paprika and lemon pepper. Marinate overnight. Remove from marinade just before cooking. Place medallions on double thick sheet of aluminum foil on a cookie sheet. Oil foil to reduce sticking. Place under broiler and cook to medium doneness while basting with butter or margarine.

Golden Nuggets

This little gem is another easy-to-fix recipe that results in a gourmet dish.

INGREDIENTS

2 pounds any red game steak meat
1/4 cup teriyaki sauce
1/4 cup Mr. Yashida's Gourmet Sauce or equivalent
2 beef bouillon cubes
2 cups broth
2 garlic cloves, halved
Canola oil
1 cup flour
Sprinkle pepper
Sprinkle paprika
1/4 teaspoon sweet basil
Butter or margarine

Cube steak meat. Brown lightly in canola oil. Deliver to pressure cooker with beef/chicken broth (or stock) plus gourmet sauce and teriyaki. Add bouillon cubes and garlic cloves. Pressure cook for 20 minutes. Strain off juice. Place meat in paper bag with flour, paprika, basil and pepper. Shake well, coating meat. Cook cubes in butter or margarine until just done. Cooks's choice of side dishes. Consider applesauce with cinnamon sprinkle and salad.

So Simple American Hamburger

The all-American hamburger, which didn't start in America and is eaten on all seven continents, can't be left out in spite of the fact that everyone knows how to make it.

Turn meat into four patties, which will cook up to be about one-third pound each. Rub each side of patty with a little canola oil. Sprinkle with a little paprika, pepper and garlic powder. Cook to about medium over coals or gas grill—or any manner. Serve on fresh buns with onion, lettuce and tomato, along with mustard and/or catsup to taste. All burger makings are optional, even the bun. At the same time, dozens of other makings are acceptable, including sauerkraut, chili beans—you name it.

INGREDIENTS

2 pounds lean gameburger
Canola oil
Paprika
Pepper
Garlic powder
Burger makings

TO FEED FOUR HUNGRY PEOPLE

Another Game Stir-Fry

This is one more good game meat stir-fry that can be made in your camp home on the range or on the cooking range at home. It's tasty and fast.

Slice meat into very thin strips. Heat one tablespoon oil in skillet over medium heat. Add meat strips in two batches and stir-fry until browned. Set meat aside. Add remaining oil, vegetables and garlic powder and stir-fry over medium heat until tender crisp. Mix cornstarch, broth and soy sauce until smooth and add to cooked vegetables stirring constantly until mixture boils and thickens. Return meat to the pan and heat through. Serve over the cooked rice.

INGREDIENTS

1 pound boneless steak, about
    3/4-inch thick
2 tablespoons cornstarch
1 can beef broth
2 tablespoon soy sauce
2 tablespoons vegetable oil
3 cups cut-up vegetables
    (combination of broccoli florets,
    sliced carrots, green or red pep-
    per strips—other—cook's
    choice)
1/4 teaspoon garlic powder
4 cups hot cooked rice

Judy's Fajitas

This is one of several methods for making what has become an American favorite, although the recipe arrived from south of the border many decades ago.

INGREDIENTS

1 pound boned game meat, sliced thin

1 tablespoon vegetable oil

1 large onion, sliced

1 green pepper, sliced

2 teaspoons chili powder

1 teaspoon garlic salt

6 flour tortillas

Heat oil in a medium skillet. Lightly sauté meat. Add onion and green pepper. Cook until onions are clear. Stir in seasonings. Serve rolled in warm flour tortillas. Tip: Flour tortillas can be warmed and also finished on the open flame of a gas stove burner or on an electric stove burner. Keep the tortilla moving to prevent burning and watch out for burned fingers as well.

Sukiyaki Game Meat

Another recipe designed to impart familiar flavors, this time with an Oriental touch. It has relatively few ingredients and can be prepared easily in camp as well as home.

INGREDIENTS

4 tablespoons margarine or butter

1 pound boned game meat cut in thin slices

2 stalks celery, cubed

2 medium onions, diced

1 can French-style green beans

1 green pepper, cut in rings

4 green onions, chopped

1 can beef broth

1 cup sliced mushrooms

2 tablespoons soy sauce

4 cups cooked hot rice

Slice boned meat into thin steaks. Brown meat in margarine or butter. Drain green beans, saving the liquid. Simmer meat in green bean liquid until tender or pressure cook to parboil. Add vegetables and cook until crispy done. Add 1 cup beef broth, 1 cup mushrooms, 2 tablespoons soy sauce, and simmer 3 minutes. Serve over hot rice.

Judy's Tamale Casserole

A favorite Southwestern treat, this recipe puts gameburger to another excellent use. It uses a lot of ingredients, but comes together faster than a cook might think. Using one of the good cornbread mixes available today, the recipe is even faster and easier to prepare.

Preheat oven to 400 degrees. Heat oil in a large skillet; brown meat and onion. Add chili powder, garlic, green chili and tomatoes. Simmer on low heat for 5 minutes. Add corn and beans; simmer an additional 8 to 10 minutes. During this time make the cornbread mix according to the directions on the box. Evenly coat a Pyrex casserole dish with cooking spray. Layer meat mixture and cheese in dish; cover with cornbread mixture and top with cheese. Bake until cornbread is golden brown.

INGREDIENTS

1 pound ground game
1 tablespoon cooking oil
1 small onion, chopped
1 tablespoon chili powder
1 teaspoon garlic powder
1/4 cup chopped green chili
1 cup whole kernel corn, drained
1 can chopped tomatoes
1 can pinto beans
1 box Jiffy cornbread
2 cups grated Colby Jack cheese

Judy's Tasty Tostadas

Here is another good way to employ gameburger in a dish enjoyed by a wide range of people.

Preheat oven to 350 degrees. Heat oil in medium skillet; brown meat stirring constantly; remove and drain excess oil. Salt and pepper to taste. In same skillet combine beans, milk, 1/4 cup cheddar and Monterey Jack cheeses. Heat until bubbly, stirring regularly. Place tostada shells on cookie sheet and heat both sides. Spread 2-3 tablespoons bean mixture and 1/4 cup meat over each tostada shell. Layer with sour cream, chili, tomatoes, lettuce and remaining cheese. Serve immediately.

INGREDIENTS

2 pounds gameburger
Salt and pepper to taste
1 tablespoon cooking oil
1 can refried beans (canned or homemade)
1/4 cup milk
2 1/4 cups cheddar cheese, shredded
1/4 cup Monterey Jack cheese, shredded
1-2 packages tostada shells
1 cup sour cream
1 (4-ounce) can diced green chili, drained
2 cups tomatoes, chopped
1/2 head lettuce, shredded

Chef Sam's Italian Lasagna

INGREDIENTS

Sam's Spaghetti Sauce modified (see page 244)
1 pound lasagna pasta
1 pound ricotta cheese
1 pound mozzarella cheese, sliced thin or grated
1/2 cup Parmesan cheese, grated
Oregano
1 bunch parsley, chopped

There is nothing wrong with American lasagna, a tasty casserole. But it has little to do with the Italian version. This recipe is the Italian version. It was originally from Chef Sam Manetta but modified slightly for easier preparation without loss of quality.

Make Sam's Spaghetti Sauce recipe as shown elsewhere, but not with meatballs or sausage balls. Use the optional method as outlined in that recipe, which is to cook both meats in a frying pan, breaking them down so that they mix with the sauce as part of it. Omit primavera sauce. There will be leftover sauce. This can be frozen for use later over spaghetti. Be sure to remove bay leaves when the sauce is finished. Set sauce aside. Boil lasagna pasta until done. Drain well and set aside. Use a 11x16-inch pan sufficiently deep to make lasagna about 2 to 2 1/2-inches thick. Layer ingredients into pan in the following order exactly: sauce, lasagna pasta, ricotta, mozzarella, oregano (sprinkle only), Parmesan, light parsley. Then start over: sauce, lasagna pasta, ricotta, etc. until the pan is full. Finish with sauce on top of the layered ingredients. Sauce, in other words, will be the top of the finished lasagna. Bake for 30 minutes and let stand for 15 minutes more to blend cheeses.

Game Meat Pepper Steak

INGREDIENTS

2 pounds boneless game steaks
Freshly ground black pepper
Paprika
Butter
Olive oil
2 ounces brandy or teriyaki sauce

This is a rather ordinary dish, but it works well for many different game meats with the exception of javelina.

Dry steaks on paper towel and grind the fresh pepper on them to taste. Since this is pepper steak, more pepper than usual is the rule. Shape the steaks with a meat hammer, which at the same time incorporates the pepper into the meat. Sprinkle with paprika. Mix butter and olive oil together (half-and-half) in a skillet over medium heat. Olive oil helps prevent butter from burning. Place steaks in skillet and cook over medium heat. When steaks have a nice brown color, reduce heat and continue cooking to just done or until the center is slightly pink. Remove steaks from pan and increase heat to high. Add 2 or 3 tablespoons of butter. As soon as the butter is melted drop in brandy or teriyaki sauce. Blend well. Use as a sauce over steaks.

Wild Boar Bake

Wild boar meat is compatible with chicken flavor and that's why this recipe works so well. Another meat that is good in this recipe is cubed mountain lion fillet.

Heat canola oil in skillet while warming the oven to 350 degrees. Dust cubed meat with garlic powder and paprika; brown in hot oil. Remove meat and place on paper towel. Place meat in casserole dish with all remaining ingredients. Bake uncovered in oven until noodles test done with a fork.

INGREDIENTS

4 cups cubed meat
2 tablespoons canola oil
1 cup uncooked noodles
2 cans cream of chicken soup
2 (16-ounce) cans corn
1 cup cheddar cheese, shredded
1 cup diced green peppers
Dash paprika
Dash garlic powder

New England Boiled Big Game Dinner

This recipe is about as old as the country, and has been offered over the years in many different forms. The pressure cooker makes it fast and delicious. Venison, moose and elk are ideal meats. Vegetable content varies with individual taste.

Place meat and broth in pressure cooker, being sure that there is enough broth to fully cover meat. If necessary add extra broth or water to cover meat. Add garlic cloves, paprika and pepper. Pressure cook meat for 20 minutes. Let steam off naturally. Probe meat with slender fillet knife to check doneness. It will probably not be cooked through. Pressure cook for another 10 minutes. Let steam off naturally. Add potatoes. Pressure cook for half the amount of time for normal cooking (should be about 2 minutes). Let steam off rapidly under cold water tap. Add carrots and green beans. Bring pressure up for 2 minutes. The meal should be done to perfection. Serve with bread to soak up those good juices.

INGREDIENTS

3- to 4-pound chunk of boned game meat
4 to 6 medium potatoes cut into 6 pieces
6 to 10 carrots
1 to 2 cans green beans
3 cans beef broth or same amount stock
2 garlic cloves, quartered
1/2 teaspoon paprika
1/4 teaspoon pepper

Thyme Game Meat

If thyme is not a favored flavor of the cook or his diners, this recipe will not please. Conversely, thyme lovers will appreciate this dish. Useful with stronger-flavored game meats. Worth trying with javelina, but experiment in the kitchen before serving to guests.

INGREDIENTS

2 pounds boned game meat in strips (any red game meat)

1 cube butter or margarine

1/4 cup medium sherry or teriyaki sauce

1 small splash Worcestershire sauce

2 large onions, sliced into rings

1/2 teaspoon thyme

Drop quarter cube butter or margarine into frying pan, add onion as soon as butter or margarine melts. Cook onion tender and set aside. Add half cube of butter to pan. As soon as butter heats, add strips of boned game meat. Brown for a minute or two. Add wine or teriyaki sauce along with Worcestershire. Add last of butter cube with thyme. Stir. Cover pan and finish over low heat turning meat frequently. Add onions to pan only to warm them. Serve with white or wild rice and green vegetable along with a salad.

Javelina Creole

Javelina is difficult to cook. However, when the musk sac has been properly removed with the hide rather than cut out separately the meat can be good. It has fine grain and in some dishes cooks up white and tender. This recipe is designed to give the meat a tangy flavor. Double the recipe for more guests. Freshly ground black pepper is a bonus.

INGREDIENTS

2 pounds boned javelina meat

1 teaspoon salt

1/2 teaspoon black pepper

1 small onion, diced

1 green pepper, diced

2 beef bouillon cubes

8 tablespoon uncooked white rice

2 regular size cans of stewed tomatoes

Canola or olive oil for frying

Stock, broth or water as needed during cooking

Cut boned meat into bite-size pieces. Sprinkle with salt and pepper and place in frying pan with canola or olive oil. Brown over low heat until almost done. Add onion, green pepper, rice, bouillon cubes and stewed tomatoes. Cover. Simmer on low heat until meat is cooked through and all ingredients are blended. Add stock, broth or a little water to maintain juices in pan. Do not allow to dry out.

Sam's Simple South of The Border Venison

This dish takes about 10 minutes to prepare. Although it's totally simple, the results are good.

Ingredients are difficult to pin down with this recipe because it's good for 1/2 pound of meat up to at least four pounds. Drop cubed meat into medium-hot canola oil in a skillet;, turn with spatula constantly to brown all sides. Pepper to taste while cooking. Add crushed garlic while continually stirring with spatula. Add salsa, about 1/4 cup to each pound of meat. Continuing cooking just long enough to heat salsa. Do no overcook salsa. Add canned pinto beans directly to the skillet. Continue on stove until beans are piping hot. Remove and eat with flour tortillas. Tip: Finish flour tortillas over gas flame or electric stove burner to both heat and remove any raw flavor.

INGREDIENTS

*1/2 to 4 pounds of boned and
cubed red game meat*
Pepper
Salsa
Crushed garlic to taste
Canned pinto beans

Sam's Venison South of the Border

This older recipe has many ingredients, but it prepares easily. The cook is invited to try many different meats, including wild boar and javelina, as well as antelope. The little bit of cumin in this recipe changes the flavor significantly and therefore is listed as optional.

Mix flour, chili powder, salt, pepper, and if desired, cumin. Coat meat heavily with mixture. Heat oil in skillet. Brown coated meat well. Add broth or stock to pan, along with celery, onion and green pepper. Simmer covered until blended. Add carrots and pinto beans. Simmer until meat is tender. Serve with flour tortillas. Tip: Finish flour tortillas on gas stove flame or electric stove burner. This removes any raw taste while also heating the tortillas.

INGREDIENTS

2 pounds game meat, cubed
4 tablespoons flour
*1 tablespoon Mexican red chili
powder*
1/2 teaspoon salt
1/4 teaspoon pepper
1/8 teaspoon cumin, optional
4 tablespoons olive or canola oil
1 cup broth or stock
1 cup celery, chopped
2 medium onions, chopped
2 carrots, sliced thin diagonally
2 green peppers, sliced thin
2 small cans pinto beans

Chef Sam's Game 'n' Noodles

This is another recipe aimed at simplicity and thriftiness of time. It's best with either Chef Sam's Red Spaghetti Sauce or Sam's Red Spaghetti Sauce, but prepared (from a can or jar) sauce will work. And it's another good use for gameburger meat.

INGREDIENTS

2 pounds gameburger

1 quart red spaghetti sauce

1 1/2 cups broth or stock

1/2 teaspoon crushed garlic

1/2 teaspoon oregano

6 ounces uncooked noodles

1/2 cup pitted olives, diced, optional

1 cup cheddar cheese, shredded

Canola or olive oil for browning

Brown gameburger in skillet with canola or olive oil. There should be very little oil remaining with meat after it is browned. If oil content is readily present, remove meat to dish with paper towels and wipe pan dry. Return meat to pan. Stir in all remaining ingredients except the cheese. Reduce heat to simmer contents of pan. When noodles are tender, remove from skillet to bowl. Stir in cheese immediately. Good with green salad.

Elk Charcoal/Gas Grill Broil

This simple recipe is good with moose, too, or any other larger-grained wild red meat. The secret is crisscrossing the meat with a sharp knife blade to score the surface deeply to take on the flavor and tenderizing benefit of the marinade. It's another good way to grill game meat.

INGREDIENTS

1 large boneless piece of meat, thick

1 cup prepared Italian dressing

Paprika

Pepper

Garlic salt

Onion salt

1/2 ounce Worcestershire sauce

Make deep crisscross cuts on both sides of the meat, but do not cut so much as to separate into pieces. The piece of meat must be intact to cook on the grill. Place meat in shallow dish and season with condiments, including Worcestershire, not overdoing any of them. Allow to marinate in the refrigerator from morning to evening. Place meat on grill over medium coals or gas flame. Turn frequently and baste with leftover marinade juices. Cook until done through, but not well done. Good with Speedy All-Day Baked Beans side dish.

Venison Steaks with Butter Sauce

Yet another good way to serve venison without the fuss. It's the butter sauce that makes this dish different.

Season steak with garlic salt (not powder). Cook cubed meat in appropriate amount of canola oil (or olive oil) until browned and medium done. Remove meat. Set aside. Add butter, mustard, lemon juice and Worcestershire to the pan. As soon as butter is melted, add green onions. When onions are soft, stir in sherry (if desired). May substitute teriyaki glaze for sherry.

INGREDIENTS

2 pounds boned game meat cubed

Canola or olive oil

1/2 cube butter

Garlic salt

3 tablespoons lemon juice

2 teaspoons Worcestershire Sauce

1/2 bunch diced green onion

1/8 teaspoon mustard

1/4 cup medium sherry, optional

Antelope and Herbs

Antelope meat is not as difficult to prepare successfully as javelina, but it can be more challenging than venison. This recipe helps impart flavors that most people seem to enjoy. Herbs make the difference.

This dish is prepared under the oven broiler. Rub boned antelope pieces with canola oil. Place meat on broiler pan covered with aluminum foil to facilitate cleaning pan. Rub a little canola oil on aluminum foil to avoid sticking. Butter the top of the meat as you would a piece of toast, not too heavily. Sprinkle garlic salt and oregano on meat. Broil to about half done. Turn meat over. Sprinkle the rest of the condiments on the meat and continue to broil until just done through.

INGREDIENTS

2 pounds boned antelope meat – large cubes

Canola oil

Butter or margarine

1/8 teaspoon garlic salt

1/4 teaspoon oregano

1/4 teaspoon sweet basil

1/4 teaspoon rosemary

1/8 teaspoon marjoram

Pepper

Antelope With Pineapple

Since antelope has a less familiar flavor than many other big game meats a recipe like this one works well.

2 pounds boned antelope meat
1 large can pineapple bits
4 tablespoons soy sauce
1 teaspoon white vinegar
1/4 teaspoon dry mustard
Canola or olive oil
4 tablespoons brown sugar
4 tablespoons cornstarch
3 cups cooked rice
Parsley

Place meat in plastic sealable refrigerator bag. Drain juice from can of pineapple and add to bag. Mix soy sauce, vinegar and mustard together. Pour into bag with meat. Marinate meat in refrigerator for at least 4 hours but not longer than 8 hours. When ready to cook, remove meat from plastic bag. Save juices. Heat oil in skillet. Add meat. Brown meat over medium heat. When meat is browned, add marinade and simmer while turning from time to time. Mix sugar and cornstarch together in small sauce pan. Stir in rest of marinade. Heat mixture to blend sugar and corn starch. Ladle resulting sauce over cooked meat. Color with a little parsley.

Buffalo Roast

The American bison, which we know simply as the buffalo, is beef-like while at the same time much more lean than his domesticated brother. Its meat must be cooked with that in mind. Otherwise buffalo can come out dry.

1 large buffalo roast
1 cup Mr. Yoshida's Original
   Gourmet Sauce (or 1 cup
   teriyaki glaze)
2 garlic cloves, crushed (or 1 teaspoon prepared crushed garlic)
Paprika
8 peppercorns
4 cups broth or stock
1 pound fresh beef fat
1/2 teaspoon salt
6 large potatoes, peeled
2 large white onions, whole,
   peeled
10 carrots, peeled

Put broth in roasting pan along with peppercorns. Add roast to pan. Dispense crushed garlic on top of meat. Slowly pour Gourmet Sauce or teriyaki glaze over meat. Sprinkle with paprika. Place beef fat on top of roast. Cover pan with aluminum foil and then roasting pan cover. Roast at 250 degrees. Check every half hour for liquid level. Add stock or broth if necessary. Turn roast over after two to three hours of slow cooking. Place beef fat on top again. Return to oven. Cook until tender (may take several hours on low heat). Cooking more rapidly at higher temperature can cause shrinkage. Slower cooking makes the roast more tender. Remove roast and set aside. Strain juices from roasting pan. Save bulk in the oven for gravy. Add some juice along with potatoes, onions and carrots to pan. Cook vegetables until almost done. Put meat back in roasting pan. Cover and finish vegetables. A feast.

Orange Boar

If a javelina has received supreme field care, musk sac removed intact with hide rather than separately, the little peccary could be a candidate for this recipe. However, it was designed around wild boar.

Slice salted boned meat thin and brown in skillet containing canola oil. Add half of broth, onion slices on top of meat. Combine orange juice, sweet basil, brown sugar and lemon juice with rest of broth and pour into skillet with meat. Heat to boiling then immediately cover pan and reduce heat to simmer for 30 to 40 minutes. Cook sweet potatoes or yams in microwave until done through. Lay sweet potato slices and sliced orange on top of meat. Return to simmer, covered, until meat is tender and juices are blended. Add a little extra broth, stock or water if necessary to prevent juices from becoming too thick.

INGREDIENTS

5 pounds wild boar meat, boned
1 teaspoon salt
1 can broth
1 large onion, sliced
1 can frozen orange juice
4 tablespoons brown sugar
1/4 teaspoon sweet basil
4 tablespoons lemon juice
2 sweet potatoes or yams
2 oranges, sliced

Chef Sam's Game Liver

Liver is loved by many and disliked by the same number. No recipe can, or should, completely disguise liver. However, this recipe does impart familiar flavors. In spite of that, it is not recommended for those who simply do not care for liver in any form.

Place thinly sliced liver in Universal Marinade (Chapter 25) overnight—or up to 24 hours before cooking. When ready to cook liver, drain and sprinkle with garlic salt. Then bread liver slices with flour. Brown liver in olive oil in a skillet over medium heat. Lower heat and add sauce, pepper slices and onion slices. Cover and simmer slowly until liver is cooked completely through. Cook pasta (about one-half pound). Remove liver from skillet. Serve liver and sauce over pasta. Sprinkle with Parmesan cheese.

INGREDIENTS

1 pound thinly sliced game liver
Universal Marinade
1/2 teaspoon garlic salt
Flour
Olive oil
1 can primavera sauce
1 green pepper, sliced thin
1 onion, sliced thin
Pasta
Parmesan cheese

Venison Shish Kabobs

Boned venison, cubed
Prepared Italian dressing
Small whole onions
Pineapple chunks
Green peppers, cubed
Red peppers

The secret to good shish kabobs is cooking the meat to desired doneness without ruining the tidbits on the skewer. This is accomplished by sizing the cubed boned meat to different dimensions. A 1-inch cube, for example, will normally turn out about medium to medium rare without ruining the other food items on the skewer. Larger cubes are more rare, smaller less rare.

NOTE | Amounts are not included with this recipe because any amount of boned meat may be used along with the appropriate number of onions, pineapple chunks, peppers and other vegetables (and even fruits). Small chunks of peeled orange, for example, can be used. The success of this recipe lies with the cook's imagination.

Marinate boned venison chunks in Italian dressing for at least 4 hours and up to 8 hours. Alternate meat and other items on skewers. Broil over hot coals, gas grill or roast uncovered in the oven.

Chef Sam's Game Meatball Soup

Homemade chicken broth
2 pounds gameburger
1 can chicken broth
1/2 bunch parsley, chopped
2 eggs
Parmesan cheese
1 onion, halved
3 stalks celery, halved
Pepper
Paprika
Salt
Garlic powder
Sweet basil
1 or 2 cups barley

This is a hearty dish well suited to a fall or winter camp as well as at home by the hearth. And it's another good use of gameburger.

Place one chicken, one can chicken broth, sufficient water to just cover chicken, pepper, celery, paprika, salt, onion and garlic powder to taste in pressure cooker. Pressure cook chicken until meat comes off bones. See Chapter 21. Strain juice and return to pressure cooker. Set chicken meat aside for future use, as in sandwiches and salads. We're only after the broth in this recipe. Prepared broth can be used in lieu of chicken; however, there is nothing like fresh chicken broth for this recipe and the chicken does not go to waste. Place gameburger in large bowl. Stir in two whole eggs; mix well. Blend in parsley. Sprinkle with Parmesan cheese and blend in. Make meatballs. Fry meatballs to done in canola oil. Add meatballs to broth in pressure cooker. Pressure cook 10 minutes. Cook barley— 1 to 2 cups as desired—and add to broth.

Wild Boar in Sweet and Sour Sauce

*Other meats can be used in this recipe, but whiter varieties seem
to work best.*

Brown boned meat slices in canola oil in medium skillet. Mix flour, corn-starch, baking powder and salt with stock or broth in a bowl. Add two tea-spoons olive or canola oil. Make a smooth mixture (may require beater). The result is a basting mixture. Dip browned meat into basting mixture and return to skillet to fry until done. Sauté green pepper and onion until soft and blend into sweet and sour sauce after it is cooked. The sauce has been prepared ahead. Ladle sauce over cooked meat. Good with white rice.

SWEET AND SOUR SAUCE | Mix 1/2 cup brown sugar and 4 tablespoons cornstarch or arrowroot in saucepan. Add liquid from pineapple with sufficient broth or stock to create a smooth sauce-like texture. Add 1/4 cup vinegar and 4 tablespoons catsup to this sauce. Cook and stir constantly until mixture thickens. Stir in pineapple bits and cooked peppers and onions. The finished sauce is ladled over the cooked meat as noted above.

INGREDIENTS

Sweet and Sour Sauce (Below)
2 pounds boned meat, sliced
1 green pepper, diced
Canola or olive oil
1 cup flour
1/2 cup arrowroot or cornstarch
1 teaspoon salt
1 cup broth or stock
1/2 teaspoon baking soda

Venison Steaks Viennese

*While this dish sounds like a time-taker, it's really not. In fact
can be cooked up in the camp skillet. A good ice chest will hold
all of the perishable ingredients for several days and the venison
may come into camp fresh.*

Pound venison steaks to very thin, about 1/4-inch. Treat with Lawry's Seasoned Salt and Lemon Pepper. Heat olive oil in skillet. Fry steaks over medium-hot to hot heat, turning constantly. Dust cooked steaks with both grat-ed cheeses. Add garlic. Reduce to medium heat, stir in onions, butter and Madeira wine. Return heat to high to blend wine and butter into a sauce. Add whipping cream. Serve immediately. Minute Rice works well as a side dish in camp—easy to prepare and good tasting with some of the sauce created by this dish.

INGREDIENTS

2 pounds boneless venison steaks
Olive oil
Parmesan cheese, grated
Romano cheese, grated
1 clove garlic, crushed or 1/2 tea-
    spoon prepared crushed garlic
3 bunches green onion, chopped
2 pats butter or margarine
Lawry's Seasoned Salt
Lemon Pepper
1/4 to 1/2 cup Madeira wine
    (to taste)
1/2 cup whipping cream

Mother's Venison Stew

This recipe in a somewhat different version was served often in our kitchen as we were growing up. It's simple enough to prepare in camp. The addition of Lawry's Seasoned Pepper takes the place of original pepper. Can be made in slow cooker or pressure cooker in camp or home. A pressure cooker is used here.

Apply Lawry's Seasoned Pepper and dusting of garlic powder on meat. Brown cubed meat in mixture of 3 parts canola oil and 1 part lard. Put meat and juices from skillet into pressure cooker with can of chicken broth. Cover meat with cold water. Pressure cook for 20 minutes. Cool pressure cooker down (See Chapter 21.) Check meat for doneness. Add stock, broth or a little water if necessary. Return pressure cooker to heat. Add all spices, including bay leaf and cook meat until done. Cool pressure cooker. Add tomatoes and potatoes. Pressure cook again for about 4 minutes, which should cook potatoes through. Serve with Italian bread.

INGREDIENTS

5 pounds boneless venison, cubed

1/8 teaspoon Lawry's Seasoned Pepper

Garlic powder

1 can chicken broth

1 large can Italian tomatoes

1 can green beans or equivalent amount of fresh cut green beans

4 potatoes, peeled and cut into serving pieces

1/8 teaspoon oregano

1/8 teaspoon sweet basil

4 large bay leaves

Canola oil

Lard

Chef Sam's Elk Medallions

This is the Carbonari style but with modifications. The resulting dish is rich and tasty.

Sauté green onion, quartered mushroom pieces and garlic in butter. Remove from pan and set aside. Add gourmet sauce to juices remaining in pan and bring to boil. Immediately reduce to simmer. Add brandy and cook off alcohol. Remove rich sauce from pan and set aside. Sauté green and red peppers in butter until tender. Put sauce back in pan with peppers. Add cream. Blend in well. Set aside. Salt and pepper elk medallions with dusting of paprika. Fry in fresh skillet with butter until just done. Add sauce to pan and blend with meat. Place medallions on individual plates with sauce. Serve with pasta, green salad, potatoes—cook's choice.

INGREDIENTS

2 pounds elk tenderloin

Salt

Pepper

4 tablespoons butter

1 bunch green onions, chopped

2 garlic cloves crushed or 1/2 teaspoon prepared crushed garlic

1 pound mushrooms

1 cup celery, peeled and finely diced

1/2 cup green pepper, diced

1/2 cup red pepper, diced

1 cup Mr. Yoshida's Original Gourmet Sauce (may substitute 1 cup teriyaki glaze)

1/2 cup brandy, optional

6 tablespoons heavy cream

Paprika

Sam's Javelina Roast

There is no way to cook javelina satisfactorily if the meat has been tainted with musk, which is most often caused by cutting out the musk sac individually rather than removing it intact with the hide when skinning the little wild hog out. However, if the meat is musk-free and pure, this recipe works.

Place roast in pan with vinegar and sauce or teriyaki glaze, plus beef broth or stock. Apply crushed garlic to top of roast only. Add bay leaves, cloves and a liberal sprinkling of paprika. Seal meat with aluminum foil between roast and top of roasting pan. Cook on low heat, 250 to 300 degrees. Every half hour turn roast over in juices. If juices are low, add more stock. After meat is cooked tender, remove and slice. Coat with horseradish sauce and serve.

HORSERADISH SAUCE is quickly made by combining the following in a saucepan: 1/2 cup prepared horseradish, 1 teaspoon dry mustard, 1/2 cup mayonnaise, 1/4 teaspoon paprika, 1 tablespoon lemon juice. Heat through in saucepan and remove to serving dish.

INGREDIENTS

Roast (usually most of one hind leg on these small animals)
1 tablespoon vinegar
2 cups Mr. Yoshida's Original Gourmet Sauce (or equivalent amount of teriyaki glaze)
2 cans beef broth or equivalent amount of stock
4 garlic cloves, crushed, or 1/2 teaspoon commercial crushed garlic
6 bay leaves
2 cloves
Paprika
Horseradish sauce

Sam's Antelope/Lamb Roast

Mixing wild and domestic meats works perfectly with many different recipes. In fact, there are only a few recipes where wild and domestic do not happily wed.

Bone the lamb haunch (sold as a roast in the meat department of the grocery store) into neat slices about 1/2-inch thick. Bone the antelope haunch into neat slices about 1/2-inch thick. Sprinkle salt, paprika, pepper, garlic powder, and a touch of onion powder on each slice of meat. Stack meat slice by slice—one lamb, one antelope, one lamb, one antelope. Wrap together with string into a bundled roast. Place in roasting pan with beef broth or stock. Pour teriyaki marinade over top of bundled roast. Layer aluminum foil between roast and lid of roasting pan. Cover. Cook on slow heat, 250 to 300 degrees, for about 2 hours. Add carrots. Cook for 15 minutes. Add potatoes. Cook until potatoes are done. Alternate slices of lamb and antelope on serving plate.

INGREDIENTS

3- to 5-pound lamb haunch
3- to 5-pound antelope haunch
Salt
Paprika
Pepper
Garlic powder
Onion powder
Teriyaki marinade
3 cans beef broth or stock
8 carrots, peeled
8 potatoes, peeled

INGREDIENTS

~~~~~~~~

3 pounds elk ribs

2 teaspoons salt

1 can beef broth or equal stock

1/4 teaspoon garlic powder

1/4 teaspoon sweet basil

1 pound carrots, peeled, cut in
    four pieces each

4 to 6 potatoes, peeled and
    quartered

INGREDIENTS

~~~~~~~~

2 pounds gameburger

Canola oil

1 green pepper, chopped

1 red pepper, chopped

1 onion, chopped

1 large can of Italian tomatoes

2 cups broth or stock

1 teaspoon Lawry's Seasoned Salt

1/4 teaspoon red chili Mexican
    chili powder

1/2 pound bacon

1/2 pound noodles

Simple Elk or Moose Ribs

This meal almost cooks itself. The ribs must be meaty, however, or the end result is disappointing.

Section ribs and put in pressure cooker with salt, garlic powder, sweet basil and broth or stock. Or boil in pot for about two hours on low heat. Remove cooked ribs to baking dish. Add potatoes and carrots with one cup of stock from pressure cooker. Bake for about one hour at 325 degrees.

Gameburger Noodle Bake

This recipe is a one-dish affair, and it imparts familiar flavors to gameburger.

Boil noodles and drain. Set them aside. Coat skillet with canola oil; place gameburger in skillet and cook until just done. Remove from pan to paper towels. Wash pan. Cut bacon into small squares and cook until done. Return gameburger to skillet adding peppers and onion. Mix in tomatoes, stock or broth, chili powder and seasoned salt. Cover skillet and add cooked bacon pieces and noodles, simmer for about 15 minutes.

Elk or Moose Ribs in Baked in Barbecue Sauce

I first had this dish with beef ribs. It was disappointing because the fat from the ribs mingled with the barbecue sauce, reducing its flavor. But game ribs, trimmed, turn out fine.

Pressure cook sectioned ribs in beef broth or stock with condiments until tender Remove from pressure cooker and place in baking dish. Add full bottle of barbecue sauce, place in oven and cook on low heat, about 225 degrees, until ribs and barbecue sauce are well mingled. Serve with baked beans or potato salad.

INGREDIENTS

4 pounds elk or moose ribs
Small bottle barbecue sauce
Paprika
Pepper
Salt
1 teaspoon Worcestershire Sauce
1 teaspoon A-1 Meat Sauce
2 cans beef broth or equal stock

Chef Sam's Spaghetti Sauce

This recipe is for a full-blown spaghetti supper served with garlic toast and a green salad. Sam's Spaghetti Sauce recipe is a little less involved.

Combine gameburger, ground pork, cheese, two pinches of salt and two pinches of pepper. Form into meatballs and place in a skillet; brown all sides. Remove; place on dish with two paper towels and microwave for 1 to 2 minutes. Set aside. Puree tomatoes in a blender and pour into pot large enough to hold all ingredients. Add basil, bay leaves and oregano. Slice and sauté garlic until clear. Sauté onion. Add to pot. Simmer for 5 minutes. Add meatballs to tomato mixture. Add salt. Bring to slow boil then lower heat immediately. Cover pot and cook 30 minutes on low heat, stirring occasionally. Taste for salt. Add more if needed. Cook uncovered for an additional 30 minutes on low heat until somewhat thickened. Tip: Use a stove ring (metal ring between electric burner and bottom of pot) to prevent scorching sauce.

INGREDIENTS

2 cans Italian (pear-shaped)
   tomatoes
3 small cans tomato sauce
1 medium onion, diced
2 garlic cloves, diced
1 bunch fresh sweet basil, chopped
4 bay leaves
1 teaspoon oregano
1 teaspoon salt
1 teaspoon pepper
1 1/2 pounds gameburger
1/2 pound ground pork
1/2 cup grated Romano cheese
   (or Parmesan)
Salt
Pepper

INGREDIENTS
〜〜〜〜〜〜

Boneless meat (any amount)
Butter
Prepared or home crushed garlic
Paprika
Pepper

Quick Broiled Medallions

This ultra simple recipe works with loin meat or other tender cuts. Good with elk, moose, deer and antelope.

Shape meat with meat hammer only to create uniform thickness, not to tenderize. Dust each piece with paprika and pepper. Combine butter and crushed garlic. Butter the cuts with the garlic butter combination as you would a piece of toast. Cook under the broiler to just done or a little rare.

INGREDIENTS
〜〜〜〜〜〜

*1 (106-ounce) can crushed
    tomatoes*
1 can primavera sauce, optional
*1/4 teaspoon garlic powder or
    crushed garlic*
1 teaspoon sugar
1 teaspoon sweet basil
6 bay leaves
1/2 teaspoon oregano
1 onion, diced and sautéed
1 bunch parsley, chopped
2 pounds gameburger
1/4 teaspoon pepper
1 egg
1 pound Italian sausage
*4 tablespoons Parmesan cheese,
    grated*
1 medium can tomato paste

Sam's Spaghetti Sauce

This red spaghetti sauce takes more stove time but less cook's time. It can be made with meatballs and sausage balls or with meats cooked and blended in.

Put crushed tomatoes in cooking pot such as 6-quart stainless steel pressure cooker without lid. Add primavera only if that flavor is desired. Warm sauce on low heat with stove ring between bottom of cooking vessel and electric stove burner. Add garlic, sugar, sweet basil, bay leaves, oregano, onion, Parmesan cheese, half bunch chopped parsley. Stir. Cook on low for 30 minutes. Meanwhile add two teaspoons Parmesan cheese plus pepper and rest of parsley and raw egg to gameburger. Mix thoroughly. Form meatballs. Make sausage balls half the size of meatballs. Brown meatballs and sausage balls. Microwave meatballs 1 minute on paper towels, sausage balls 2 minutes. Add meatballs to sauce in pot. Cook on low for 2 hours. Optional: Cook gameburger and sausage, microwave both on paper towels, add directly to sauce and cook in. Use more or less condiments to taste. Tip: Cover pot with mesh splash guard with paper towel on top to capture moisture rising as steam.

Chicken-Fried Game Steak

This is especially good with boneless venison steaks, but can be prepared with other game meats as well, such as antelope. If antelope is used, soak meat in brine/vinegar for 10 minutes before cooking. Dry thoroughly before breading.

Shape steaks with meat hammer to about 1/4-inch thickness, not over 1/3-inch thick. Pepper to taste. Bread in 75/25 mixture flour/saltine crackers. Fry steaks to just done in canola oil with pat or two of butter or margarine. Prepare pan gravy (see recipe). Cook potatoes (amount to match number of steaks), ideally in pressure cooker with only enough water to prevent burning. Drain all water from cooked potatoes. Add butter and milk (amount up to cook). Whip potatoes smooth. A whip or mixer can be used for lump-free whipped potatoes. Serve meat and potatoes under pan gravy. Serve green bean dish on the side (see recipe for green beans).

INGREDIENTS

Game steaks — any number
Canola oil
Butter or margarine
Pepper
Breading
Whipped potatoes
Pan gravy

Chef Paul's Apple Venison

Chef Paul is a hunter as well as professional in the kitchen. This is one of his favorite venison recipes. It's gourmet all the way.

Heat oil in frying pan on medium-high. Lightly flour venison and fry until just cooked, not overdone, turning meat in pan. Remove meat from pan. Leave a little oil in the pan to sauté shallots or green onions until soft. Add vinegar and brown sugar. Cook two minutes. Add AppleJack, maple syrup, stock or broth and apple cider. Stir in apples. Bring to a boil; cook for 2 to 3 minutes. Mix 4 tablespoons butter with 2 tablespoons flour in pan used for meat. Cook on low until sauce thickens. Add meat back to pan, heat through. Season with salt and pepper to taste. To serve: Pour sauce on platter and top with meat. Serve with wild or white rice.

INGREDIENTS

3 pounds boned venison (steaks)
1/3 cup shallots or green onions, chopped fine
4 tablespoons apple cider vinegar
1 1/2 tablespoons dark brown sugar
1 tablespoon maple syrup
3 ounces Laird's Applejack
8 ounces chicken broth or stock
4 ounces apple cider
2 medium Golden Delicious or Granny Smith apples, sliced thin
4 tablespoons butter
2 tablespoons flour plus flour on the side
Corn oil (do not use olive oil)
Salt
Pepper

Hot Game Sausage Open Face Sandwich

This little gem is another quickie that really pleases at the table. It's great for lunch. It's normally made the day after a big spaghetti dinner because it requires spaghetti sauce. The ideal sausage for this recipe is half Italian game sausage and half commercial Italian sausage. Most diners prefer mild, but hot Italian sausage is a possibility.

INGREDIENTS

Game/domestic mix sausage links cut in half length-wise
Mozzarella cheese
Italian bread
Red spaghetti sauce

After cutting sausages in half length-wise, cook until done in frying pan. Microwave for 30 seconds on paper towel to reduce fat. Slice Italian bread generously thick. Toast the bread to taste—light or dark—or not at all. Place halved sausage links on toast, cover links with thin slices Mozzarella cheese to taste (some like more, some prefer less). Ladle spaghetti sauce over cheese. Place on serving dish in microwave and heat until cheese just melts. Do not overheat. The microwave time will also heat spaghetti sauce. Can be served as a sandwich only or with salad or pasta.

OPTION | If there is no homemade spaghetti sauce, consider a commercial substitute.

Good Old Gameburger Meat Loaf

This is one way to make a fast meat loaf from gameburger that shows well on the dinner table. Leftover is cut into sandwich slices.

INGREDIENTS

3 pounds gameburger (prepared as in Chapter 17—no fat)
2 raw eggs
5 hard-boiled eggs
Half bunch parsley, chopped
Half onion, chopped
1/4 teaspoon garlic salt
Paprika

Thoroughly mix raw eggs, parsley, onion and garlic salt with meat. It's the egg content that holds the meat loaf together for neat slices on the dinner table and afterward for sandwiches. Divide the meat into two equal parts. Shape like two small loaves of bread. Place peeled hard-boiled eggs in a row lengthwise on one layer of meat and put the other layer firmly on top. Mould into shape as a meat loaf with the hard-boiled eggs secured inside. Sprinkle with paprika. Bake at 325 degrees on a cookie sheet covered with aluminum foil to make cleanup easier. Cook until done through, never rare. When sliced crosswise the center of most pieces will have a ring of cooked egg showing. Serve with the old standby side dishes such as the fast baked bean recipe or potato salad.

Go Away Game Roast

This dish is ordinary, nothing special, but it works well with the Crock-Pot. Add ingredients and go away. Come back later and supper is ready. The cooker I use is a Rival Oval Crock-Pot® Slow Cooker. Directions for cooking time and arrangement of ingredients in recipe the are taken from Rival recommendations. Meat can be venison, elk, moose, antelope—just about any red game meat. Do not add salt to the pot. Bouillon cubes will impart salt taste.

Place onion, potatoes and carrots on bottom of stoneware Crock-Pot. Add bouillon cubes and broth. Cover pot and cook on low setting for 10 to 12 hours (about right for starting in the morning for the evening meal).

INGREDIENTS

3 pounds boneless game meat

1/2 cup canned beef broth

2 beef bouillon cubes

2 carrots, sliced thin

2 potatoes, sliced thin

1 onion, sliced thin

1/4 teaspoon pepper

Vegetable Beef Soup – No Beef

This is a hearty soup for camp or home. The pressure cooker makes it fast and easy to prepare, but it can also be made in a regular pot on the camp or kitchen stove. The Crock-Pot is also ideal for this dish. Instructions below are for pressure cooker. Just about any red game meat is good—deer, elk, moose, buffalo, caribou—whatever is on hand.

Cut boned meat into bite-size cubes. Melt lard in skillet. Brown meat on all sides. Remove from pan. Place meat in pressure cooker with just enough water to cover pieces. Add garlic, onion, bouillon or beef base, salt and pepper. Pressure cook 10 minutes. Add broth or stock plus soy, gourmet sauce, or teriyaki. Pressure cook another 10 minutes. Add potatoes. Pressure cook 1 1/2 minutes. Release pressure immediately under small stream of running water. Add carrots. Pressure cook 1 1/2 minutes. Release steam right away. Mix in cooked barley.

INGREDIENTS

2 pounds game meat

2 tablespoons lard

1/4 teaspoon crushed prepared garlic or fresh cloves crushed

4 cups stock or broth

10 carrots, diced

2 potatoes, diced

2 cups cooked barley

1/4 cup soy, Mr. Yoshida's Original Gourmet Sauce, or teriyaki glaze

1 small onion, diced

2 beef bouillon cubes or equivalent beef flavor base

1/2 teaspoon salt

1/4 teaspoon pepper

Crock-Pot Antelope

Venison works in this recipe as well, which began as a Rival dish for that company's Crock-Pot. The rosemary is the heart of this recipe taste-wise. The beauty of the Crock-Pot is combining ingredients, turning the pot on, and walking away to other chores.

Large chunk of boned game meat (will take up most of the space in the Crock-Pot)

4 potatoes, cubed

1/4 teaspoon garlic salt

4 garlic cloves, peeled and crushed

1/4 teaspoon oregano

lemon zest*

4 sprigs fresh rosemary

1/2 cup dry white wine or 1/2 cup teriyaki sauce

Olive oil

Rub garlic salt into chunk of boned meat then brown game meat in olive oil in a hot skillet and set aside. Place potatoes on the bottom of the stoneware. Mix salt, garlic, lemon zest, oregano and rosemary in a small bowl. Rub all sides of meat with seasoning mixture and place meat in stoneware. Add wine or teriyaki and cook for 5 to 6 hours on low setting.

*Grate the rind of 1 full lemon down to the meat. Set meat aside and use rind as zest.

Venison Mushroom Sauté

This is a stir-fry that takes only minutes to prepare. It tastes great and can be made in camp with nothing more than a source of heat, such as a camp stove or coal bed and a skillet.

2 pounds boned venison, cubed

3 tablespoons olive or canola oil

1/2 teaspoon crushed or finely sliced garlic (cloves or prepared)

1/8 teaspoon oregano

Mixed vegetables*

1 1/2 pounds fresh mushrooms, buttons halved, larger quartered

1/2 bunch green onion chopped

Heat skillet. Add olive or canola oil. Lightly brown garlic, stirring constantly with spoon or spatula. Sprinkle oregano on cubed meat. Drop meat into skillet, turning all sides. When the meat is partially cooked, add onion and mushrooms. Cook 2 or 3 minutes. Add vegetables. Cook until all ingredients, including meat, are done. Serve over rice. Minute rice works well in camp.

*Mixed vegetables in camp can be canned, but frozen taste better in this dish. Frozen vegetables can be kept on ice in cooler for a day or two.

Simply Fried Venison Loin (Fillets)

This little recipe is wonderful in camp with a deer carcass hanging cold. Strip a loin out for campfire dining. Be sure to have a generous piece of fresh beef fat in the ice chest. This recipe was originally intended for venison but has proved its worth with other meats including antelope and elk.

Heat olive oil in skillet. Render nice piece of fresh beef fat (about 1/4-inch to maximum of 1/2-inch thick) on medium heat. Add garlic to rendered fat in skillet. Cook garlic to light brown. Drop in venison loin medallions. Immediately salt and pepper. Cook meat to just done. Add teriyaki glaze and cook to a somewhat thickened consistency. Remove meat from pan. Serve with fast-cooking minute rice in camp.

NOTE | I've been known to eat a little of the well-cooked beef fat mixed with slices of fresh hot venison fillet medallions by the light of the campfire.

INGREDIENTS

Venison loin medallions
Olive or canola oil
Salt
Pepper
Fresh beef fat
1 clove garlic, diced
(or garlic powder or salt)
Teriyaki glaze

Big O Venison Barbecue

Kenn Oberrecht is known for his fishing articles and books plus freshwater and seafood recipes, but this recipe for big game barbecue is just right for our book. This recipe works with any red game meat.

In hot skillet brown stew meat in olive oil. Drain meat on paper towel. In heavy Dutch oven add meat, garlic, 1 diced onion, pickling sauces in tea ball. Add water to just cover mixture. Simmer 2 hours or until meat can be shredded. Drain liquid off meat. Reserve half of strained liquid. Shred meat. Transfer reserved liquid back to Dutch oven. Add green pepper, celery and remaining onion. Boil vegetables until tender (about 5 minutes). Add barbecue sauce. Place tea ball with pickling spices to Dutch oven. Add Worcestershire Sauce and fines herbs. Simmer for 30 minutes, stirring often.

INGREDIENTS

2 tablespoons olive oil
4 pounds boned venison stew-cut
4 garlic cloves minced
2 onions diced
Tea ball filled with pickling spices
2 green peppers, diced
5 sticks celery, diced
1 regular size bottle hickory-
    flavored barbecue sauce
2 tablespoons Worcestershire Sauce
1 teaspoon fines herbs

INGREDIENTS

2 pounds gameburger, no fat
1 cup regular rice, uncooked
1 1/2 tablespoons onion, chopped
    fine
1 teaspoon salt
1/4 teaspoon pepper
1/4 teaspoon paprika
Two pinches of garlic powder
2 cans tomato soup
1 1/2 cups water

INGREDIENTS

3 pounds boned meat
4 tablespoons brown sugar
1 cup concentrated orange juice
4 sweet potatoes, halved
5 tablespoons lemon juice
8 whole cloves
1/4 teaspoon oregano
4 sweet potatoes
Canola or olive oil (for browning
    meat only)
Cornstarch
Broth or stock

Porcupine Meatballs

This recipe has been around since Washington cut down the cherry tree. It continues to please and it's not hard to make, especially with our often-recommended pressure cooker.

Combine soup and water in pressure cooker and set aside. Combine meat and condiments and mix well. Make medium-small meatballs. Place these gently into the soup in the pressure cooker. Pressure cook on lower setting for about 9 minutes depending upon specific cooker. Remove cooker from heat source and allow to rest for five minutes. Then release steam safely under stream of cool water.

Javelina Orange

As always, the warning is sounded about javelina: If the musk sac has been allowed to drain on the meat, chances of a tasty dish later are remote. This recipe is recommended to impart good flavors to javelina, but it also works with other boned meats, including wild boar. Instructions for pressure cooker are given. An ordinary pot will work, only much slower.

Brown cubed boned meat in oil and place in pressure cooker. Drop in cloves, brown sugar, orange juice and oregano. Add enough water to cover meat, usually about a cup. Cut sweet potatoes in half and add to cooker. Pressure cook 10 to 12 minutes, depending upon specific cooker. Let steam off carefully under running water. Check meat for doneness. Remove meat from pot. Add lemon juice to liquid in pot and bring liquid to a boil. Lower heat and thicken mixture with cornstarch and stock or broth mixture. Start with 1 cup of broth or stock and 2 or 3 tablespoons cornstarch mixed into a milk-like consistency. Pour cornstarch/stock mixture into liquid stirring constantly to create the sauce.

Game Chili Con Carne

This recipe is easy to make and very good. It uses real Mexican ground chili powder, which is found normally in sealed plastic containers. Mexican chili powder is available in mild, medium and hot. Cook's choice. This is not standard chili powder in the spice tin. Just about any game meat works in this dish. It's authentic and simple to make. Use a pressure cooker to save time. Serve with refried beans and flour tortillas. Finish the tortillas over gas flame or on the electric stove burner to both heat and cook.

INGREDIENTS

3 pounds red game meat, boned and cubed bite size
3 cans beef broth
Mexican red chili powder
Cornstarch
Lard

Brown cubed meat in lard. Remove meat from skillet and drain on paper towels. Place meat in pressure cooker with 2 cans beef broth. Ensure that meat is just covered with liquid. Add a little water if necessary. Add red chili powder to taste (such as 2 tablespoons). Pressure cook for 20 to 30 minutes checking liquid level after first 20 minutes. Meat should be cooked soft. After carefully releasing steam, remove lid of cooker and thicken liquid with mixture of cornstarch and broth to make a rich red sauce.

Simple Game Meat Stir-Fry

The grocery store has many different types of frozen stir-fry vegetable packages. They're good and they save time. Those who wish to do their own vegetables are welcome to choose the ones they prefer. Venison, antelope, moose, elk and other red game meats work well for this dish. There are numerous Oriental sauces that can be added to this stir-fry. Specialty Oriental markets, as well as the local grocery store, have these on hand.

INGREDIENTS

2 pounds boned and cubed game meat
2 tablespoons Worcestershire Sauce
1/2 cup Mr. Yoshida's Original Gourmet Sauce (or teriyaki glaze or other Oriental sauce)
1 cup chicken broth
1/4 teaspoon crushed garlic
Olive or canola oil

Parboil (or pressure cook) cubed meat until tender in water to which Worcestershire Sauce has been added. Drain meat and discard liquid. Heat oil in skillet. Place drained meat and garlic in skillet over medium heat and brown all sides while stirring constantly. Increase heat to high. Add broth and bring to a boil. Add vegetables. Cook for about 2 minutes on high. Add gourmet sauce, teriyaki glaze or Oriental sauce(s) and cook until vegetables are just done (somewhat crispy, but not cold).

Bryce's Game Sausage Biscuits and Gravy

This is the same sausage and gravy recipe your favorite local café or restaurant serves for breakfast, only made with game sausage. One of Bryce Judd's favorites.

INGREDIENTS

1 pound game sausage
Flour
Milk
Pepper

Cook sausage until done in skillet, breaking into small pieces as it cooks. Sprinkle flour over meat in skillet and blend in (about 1/3 cup). Stir until meat absorbs flour. Add milk slowly and bring to a boil in the skillet. The goal is gravy made in the skillet and combined with the sausage. Amount of milk varies—usually about 1 quart, but may take as much as 1 1/2 quarts to bring to desired consistency. If too much milk was added, in a separate container blend 1 spoon of flour with warm water to a creamy, no-lump consistency. Add flour/water mixture to gravy in skillet to thicken the mixture. Serve over biscuits. Biscuits are easily made with prepared mix.

Wild Game Stroganoff

This recipe qualifies under the heading of "familiar taste." It can be made with any boned red big game meat; however, as always, the meat should be soaked for 20 to 30 minutes in brine or brine combined with vinegar.

INGREDIENTS

1 medium onion, thinly sliced
1 tablespoon salad oil
4 steaks, cubed
4 tablespoons flour
4 tablespoons salad oil
1/2 teaspoon salt
1/2 cup dairy sour cream
1/2 pound mushrooms
1/2 cup beef broth

In large skillet, cook and stir onion in 1 tablespoon salad oil until tender. Remove from skillet and set aside. Coat cubed steaks with flour. Heat 4 tablespoons of oil in the same skillet. Cook steak over medium heat, about 4 minutes on each side. Sprinkle with salt to taste. Place steak on warm platter. Drain oil from skillet. Add onion, sour cream, mushrooms and broth to skillet. Heat, stirring occasionally. Serve sauce on steaks.

Gameburger Tacos

This is another great recipe for gameburger. The familiar theme of wild without a wild taste is honored here. Double or triple the gameburger for guests, but do not double or triple the onion, oil or condiments. Use your judgment. For example, if the meat is doubled, consider 1 1/2 medium diced onions rather than 2 onions, adding only a little more garlic salt.

In large skillet add oil and diced onion; cook and stir until onion is tender. Add ground venison; cook and stir meat until brown. Drain off excess fat. Stir in tomato sauce, garlic salt, chili powder and pepper. Simmer uncovered for about 15 minutes. While meat mixture simmers, heat taco shells as directed on the package. Divide the meat mixture equally among the 12 prepared taco shells. Top each taco with lettuce, cheese, chopped tomato and salsa as desired.

INGREDIENTS

1 medium onion, diced
1 1/2 tablespoons vegetable oil
1 to 1 1/2 pounds ground venison
1 (8-ounce) can tomato sauce
1/2 teaspoon garlic salt
1 teaspoon chili powder
1/4 teaspoon pepper
1 dozen taco shells
1 cup shredded lettuce
1 cup shredded cheddar cheese
1 cup diced tomato
Salsa as desired

Herbed Game Medallions

This recipe began as chops, but since most of our game meat in this book is boned, any boneless piece of meat, especially loin cuts (medallions) will work. It's a simple—but good—recipe.

Set oven control at broil and/or 550 degrees. Place chops on rack in broiler pan. Sprinkle selected spices on chops. Broil about 3 inches from heat, turning once until brown and meat reaches desired doneness. After meat is cooked, season with salt and pepper.

INGREDIENTS

4 chops (antelope or deer), cut
    1-inch thick
1/4 teaspoon oregano, rosemary or
    marjoram
Salt and pepper to taste

Minute Venison Steaks with Butter Sauce

This is another easy recipe that turns out gourmet good on the table. It's the butter sauce that makes the difference.

INGREDIENTS

1 tablespoon salad oil

4 venison steaks

Garlic salt to taste

4 tablespoons butter or margarine

2 teaspoons lemon juice

1 teaspoon Worcestershire sauce

1 teaspoon dried chives

1/2 teaspoon dry mustard

Heat salad oil in large skillet. Cook steaks over medium heat until brown, about 4 minutes on each side. Season to taste with garlic salt. Remove steaks from skillet and keep warm. Drain fat from skillet; melt butter and stir in remaining ingredients until heated. Place steaks on dinner plates; pour butter mixture evenly on each steak.

Big Game Meat Loaf

This is just one of many excellent meat loaf recipes the cook can prepare for family and guests. Sliced cold it turns into excellent sandwich meat.

INGREDIENTS

3 eggs

1 cup milk

2/3 cup dry bread crumbs

3 pounds ground game meat

1 medium onion, finely chopped

1 teaspoon salt

1/2 teaspoon pepper

1/2 teaspoon dry mustard

1/2 teaspoon garlic salt

2 to 6 peeled hard-boiled eggs

Heat oven to 350 degrees. Mix all ingredients except the hard-boiled eggs thoroughly. Divide the meat mixture in fourths. Spray two 9x5x3-inch loaf pans with cooking spray. Press 1/4 of the meat mixture in the bottom of each loaf pan. Place three eggs, end to end on top of the meat; press the remaining meat mixture around the eggs. Be sure the eggs are buried in the meat. Bake for about 45 minutes.

MAKES 4 OR 5 SERVINGS

Southwestern Game Steak

The chili peppers earn this dish its name. Add to taste. Good dish served with flour tortillas and refried beans.

Cut several small slits in meat with tip of a knife; insert a garlic slice in each. Heat oil in a large skillet; brown meat on both sides over medium heat. Drain off oil. Add salt, marjoram or basil and water to the browned meat. Reduce heat, cover tightly and simmer until tender, 1 to 1 1/2 hours. Add small amounts of water if necessary.

Melt butter or margarine in small saucepan. Add raisins and tomatoes; cook over low heat, stirring occasionally, until hot. Remove steak to a serving platter, pour raisin-tomato mixture around steak and garnish with chili peppers.

INGREDIENTS

2 pounds game steaks, 1 to 2 inches thick

2 cloves garlic, thinly sliced

1 tablespoon salad oil

1 teaspoon salt

Dash marjoram or basil

1/3 cup water

1 tablespoon butter or margarine

1/2 cup raisins

2 tomatoes, peeled and cut into wedges

Green diced chili peppers—one small can or to taste

Italian Game and Noodles

This dish can be made spicier if desired. It's also easily altered by using different spices and herbs. Store-bought sauce works out well here because of the added oregano and sweet basil.

In large skillet heat oil; add meat, cook and stir meat until brown. Stir in spaghetti sauce, garlic, sweet basil, oregano and olives. Reduce heat; cover and simmer about 15 minutes. Stir in cheese; cover and simmer an additional 5 minutes.

Cook spaghetti as directed on package. Drain noodles; serve meat sauce over hot spaghetti.

INGREDIENTS

2 pounds ground game meat

2 tablespoons cooking oil

1 (32-ounce) jar meatless spaghetti sauce

1/2 teaspoon instant minced garlic

1/2 teaspoon oregano leaves

1/2 teaspoon sweet basil

1/2 cup sliced pitted ripe olives, optional

1 pound package spaghetti noodles

3/4 cup shredded Cheddar cheese

SERVES 8

Broiled Elk or Moose

This recipe works well for the larger game species such as elk and moose. But other red big game meat can be substituted.

2 pounds moose or elk steak
3/4 cup Italian dressing

Score 2 pounds elk or moose steak; place in shallow glass baking dish. Pour 3/4 cup Italian dressing on steak. Cover and refrigerate at least 8 hours, turning meat occasionally. Remove steak; reserve dressing. Set oven temperature to broil and/or 550 degrees. Broil 3 to 4 inches from burner until medium rare, about 4 minutes on each side, brushing with reserved dressing several times. To serve: Cut meat across the grain at a slanted angle into thin slices.

Orange Wild Boar

The wild boar has done so well that in many areas this clan is considered a threat to farm fields, gardens and the land in general. Some ranchers and farmers offer very reasonable access to their lands for wild boar hunting. The orange flavoring goes well with this dish. Javelina may be substituted. If so, double lemon juice.

8 wild boar chops, 1/2 to 3/4 inch thick
2 tablespoons cooking oil
2 teaspoons salt
1 small onion, sliced
1 (6-ounce) can frozen orange juice concentrate, thawed (may experiment with more juice)
1/4 cup brown sugar
1/4 teaspoon allspice
4 tablespoons lemon juice (may experiment with more juice)
3 tablespoons broth or stock

MAKES 4 OR 5 SERVINGS

Heat cooking oil in a large skillet. Brown chops on both sides over medium heat. Drain off fat. Sprinkle chops with salt. Arrange onion slices on chops. Mix orange juice concentrate, brown sugar, allspice, lemon juice and broth; pour into skillet. Heat to boiling. Reduce heat; cover and simmer for 35 minutes.

Savory Game Stew

This dish can be made in camp. It's not difficult to prepare in spite of the long list of ingredients.

Heat oil in large skillet or Dutch oven; brown meat. Add the beef broth, garlic, bay leaf, salt, allspice and lemon juice; heat to boiling, stirring occasionally. Reduce heat, cover and simmer until meat is almost tender, 1 to 1 1/2 hours.

Add onions, potatoes, carrots and celery; heat to boiling. Reduce heat; cover and simmer 20 to 30 minutes or until the vegetables are almost done. If desired add peas; cook until vegetables are tender.

INGREDIENTS

2 tablespoons cooking oil

2 pounds of meat (venison, elk, moose), cut into 1-inch cubes

2 cans beef broth

1/2 clove garlic, finely chopped

2 bay leaves

2 teaspoons salt

1/4 teaspoon allspice

1 teaspoon lemon juice

1 large onion, cut into chunks

5 medium potatoes, pared and cut into 1-inch cubes

4 medium carrots, cut into 1-inch pieces

3/4 cup chopped celery

1 (10-ounce) package frozen green peas, optional

MAKES 5 OR 6 SERVINGS

Swiss Steak

The pressure cooker tenderizes the meat in this dish, but it's best to cook in stages—pressure, test, pressure, test—because the meat should be tender, but not mushy.

INGREDIENTS

2 pounds of round steak, 1/2- to 3/4-inch thick (any wild meat)

3 tablespoons flour

1/2 teaspoon salt

1/4 teaspoon pepper

3 tablespoons cooking oil

1 (14.5-ounce) can stewed tomatoes

1 large green pepper, sliced

1 large onion, sliced

1 teaspoon salt

Cut meat into serving size pieces. Heat oil in large skillet. Mix flour, 1/2 teaspoon salt and the pepper; coat meat with flour mixture. Brown meat over medium heat; add tomatoes to skillet. Transfer to the pressure cooker. Pressure cook for 15 minutes. Check for doneness. Remove from pressure cooker. Place cooked meat with juices in a covered skillet. Add green pepper, onion and remaining salt. Cover and continue to simmer until all ingredients are cooked, about 20 to 30 minutes. Add small amount of stock or broth if necessary. Serve with noodles.

Sweet-and-Sour Game Ribs

This dish can be spiced up with additional chili powder and pepper if desired. Works well with buffalo, moose or elk. Personal: I'd rather save whitetail ribs for Sam's Whitetail Ribs over Coals.

INGREDIENTS

4 pounds meaty ribs cut into serving pieces (elk or moose)

1 cup catsup

2 tablespoons brown sugar

1/3 cup vinegar

1/4 cup Worcestershire sauce

1 teaspoon celery seed

1 teaspoon chili powder

1 teaspoon salt

Dash pepper

MAKES 4 TO 5 SERVINGS

Parboil sectioned ribs first, ideally in pressure cooker with 2 beef bouillon cubes for flavor. Place tenderized ribs meaty side up on rack in foil-lined shallow roasting pan. Mix remaining ingredients; pour 2/3 of the sauce on the ribs. Bake uncovered in 350-degree oven until done, 1 1/2 to 2 hours, basting 3 or 4 times with the remaining sauce. If ribs are browning too quickly, cover loosely with aluminum foil.

Barbecued Sirloin Steak

This is another of our marinated dishes. If steaks are not tender to begin with, consider pressure cooking them for 15 to 20 minutes before marinating them. Marinate for a minimum of 1 hour; 2 to 6 hours is better.

Place steak in a shallow glass dish. Mix all remaining ingredients and pour onto the steak. Place meat and marinade in freezer bag. After completely marinated, remove meat from the marinade with tongs (a fork releases the juices). Place on a hot barbecue grill. Grill 1-inch steak 4 to 5 minutes on each side for rare, 7 to 8 minutes on each side for medium. Make a small slit near the center of the meat to test for doneness. To serve, cut meat across the grain at a slanted angle into thin slices.

MAKES 4 TO 5 SERVINGS

INGREDIENTS

2 pounds boneless venison steak,
    1- to 1 1/2-inches thick
1/4 cup olive oil or salad oil
1/4 cup vinegar
1/4 cup apple juice
2 teaspoons soy sauce
1/2 teaspoon rosemary leaves
1/2 teaspoon dry mustard
1/4 teaspoon minced fresh garlic
2 tablespoons catsup

Braised Wild Boar Medallions

The prolific wild boar now roams many states in large herd numbers. It's a tough and adaptable animal not always loved by ranchers and farmers. This simple recipe is one way to prepare the meat. If commercially butchered into chops, use chops for this recipe. Otherwise use boned steak meat or loin medallions.

Heat cooking oil in a large skillet, brown chops over medium heat. Sprinkle condiments on chops. Add juice or water and Worcestershire sauce. Reduce heat; cover and simmer until chops are done, about 30 minutes. Add small amount of broth or stock if necessary.

INGREDIENTS

6 to 8 chops, boned meat, or loin
    medallions 1/2- to 3/4-inch
    thick
2 tablespoons cooking oil
2 teaspoons salt
1/4 teaspoon pepper
1/4 teaspoon garlic powder
1/2 cup apple juice, pineapple
    juice or water
1 tablespoon Worcestershire sauce

MAKES 5 TO 6 SERVINGS

Boar or Javelina Medallions Creole

Javelina does well in this recipe because of the stewed tomatoes and green pepper rings.

8 boneless steaks or medallions,
   1/2- to 3/4-inch thick
2 tablespoons cooking oil
2 teaspoons salt
1/4 teaspoon minced fresh garlic
1/2 teaspoon pepper
10 onion slices
12 green pepper rings
8 tablespoons uncooked instant
   rice
1 (14.5-ounce) can stewed
   tomatoes

Heat cooking oil in a large skillet; add chops and brown over medium heat. Sprinkle with salt and pepper. Top each chop with onion slices, green pepper rings, garlic, 1 tablespoon rice and 1/4 cup tomatoes. Reduce heat; cover and simmer until done, about 45 minutes. Add small amount of broth or stock if necessary.

MAKES 4 TO 5 SERVINGS

Mexican Game Steak and Beans

Just about any game meat works in this recipe. Since there is chili powder and cumin (optional) in this dish, it joins the ranks of familiar flavor recipes.

2 pounds of boned steak 1/2- to
   3/4-inch thick (any wild game)
2 tablespoons flour
1 1/2 teaspoons chili powder
1/2 teaspoon salt
1/4 teaspoon pepper
1/8 teaspoon ground cumin if
   desired
2 tablespoons cooking oil
1 cup water
1/2 cup chili sauce
1 cup celery, diced
1 large onion, chopped
1 carrot, cut diagonally into 1/4
   inch slices
1 medium green pepper, cut into
   1/4 inch strips
1 (16-ounce) can pinto beans

Cut meat into 1-inch pieces. Mix flour, chili powder, salt, pepper and cumin; coat meat with flour mixture. Heat oil in large skillet; brown meat over medium heat. Drain off fat. Stir in water, chili sauce, celery and onion; heat to boiling. Reduce heat; cover tightly and simmer 1 hour. Add small amount of water if necessary. Add carrot; cover and simmer until carrot is crisp-tender, about 10 minutes. Stir in green pepper and beans (with liquid); cover and simmer until green pepper is crisp-tender and beans are hot, about 10 minutes.

MAKES 4 TO 5 SERVINGS

Boned Game Steaks Hawaiian

Pineapple is the key to this recipe, imparting a familiar flavor to just about any game meat.

Place meat in shallow glass dish. Mix reserved pineapple syrup, soy sauce, vinegar and mustard; pour on meat. Cover and refrigerate at least 6 hours, turning meat occasionally. Remove meat from marinade (reserve marinade). Heat oil in large skillet; brown meat over medium heat. Pour 1/2 cup of marinade on steaks. Cover and simmer until tender, 30 to 40 minutes. Mix sugar and cornstarch in small saucepan. Stir in remaining reserved marinade. Heat to boiling, stirring constantly. Reduce heat; simmer 2 to 3 minutes. Stir in pineapple; heat through, about 1 minute. Serve meat with pineapple sauce and rice.

MAKES 4 TO 5 SERVINGS

INGREDIENTS

6 game steaks, 3/4- to 1-inch thick
2 (16-ounce) cans pineapple tidbits, drained (reserve syrup)
5 tablespoons soy sauce
2 tablespoons vinegar
1/2 teaspoon dry mustard
4 tablespoons salad oil
1/2 cup brown sugar
2 to3 tablespoons cornstarch
5 to 6 cups hot cooked rice

Gamburger Barley Stew

Being a huge fan of barley as a wonderful grain product, I'm partial to any recipe that uses it. This is one of those recipes. Duck is another winner. Double or triple for more guests. But do not double chili powder unless more of that flavor is desired.

Heat oil in large saucepan; cook and stir meat and onion until meat is brown and onion is tender. Drain off any fat. Stir in remaining ingredients; heat to boiling. Reduce heat; cover and simmer until barley is done and stew is of desired consistency, about 1 hour.

MAKES 4 TO 5 SERVINGS

INGREDIENTS

1 pound ground game meat
1 tablespoon cooking oil
1 cup chopped onion
1/2 cup chopped celery
4 cups tomato juice
1 cup water
2 teaspoons salt
1 tablespoon chili powder or to taste
1/4 teaspoon pepper
1/2 cup uncooked barley

Game Liver Italiano

There is something interesting about game liver. Some people, even those who do not normally eat beef liver, love it. And others do not. It's a matter of personal taste. This recipe was exceptional, however, with moose liver.

Mix flour and garlic salt; coat meat with flour mixture. Heat oil in large skillet; brown meat over medium heat. Stir in tomato sauce; add green pepper and onion. Cover and simmer until done, 8 to 10 minutes. While meat simmers, cook spaghetti as directed on package. Serve meat mixture on spaghetti. Sprinkle cheese on top.

MAKES 4 TO 5 SERVINGS

Salisbury Game Steak with Mushroom Sauce

This meal is intended to lend a special flare to supper, but it can actually be cooked up without much fuss in camp.

Mix meat, salt and pepper; shape mixture into 4 oval patties. Heat oil in medium skillet; cook patties over medium heat, turning occasionally, until patties are done. Remove meat to a warm plate. Cook and stir mushrooms in same skillet until light brown. Stir in flour; cook over low heat, stirring until mixture is bubbly. Remove from heat; stir broth into flour mixture. Heat to boiling, stirring constantly. Boil and stir 1 minute. Pour over meat.

MAKES 4 TO 5 SERVINGS

Delicious Gameburgers

A different take on ordinary American hamburgers and a good use for gameburger. Best done with gameburger containing some fat.

Mix all ingredients. Shape into 4 patties about 3 inches in diameter and 1-inch thick.

TO BROIL | Set oven control at broil and/or 550 degrees. Broil 3 inches from heat 3 to 4 minutes on each side for rare, 5 to 7 minutes on each side for medium.

TO PANFRY | Heat 1 tablespoon cooking oil in large skillet; cook patties over medium heat, turning frequently, until done.

TO GRILL | Heat barbecue grill, place on grate. Cook over medium heat, turning frequently, until done.

VARIATIONS

CHEESEBURGER | About 1 minute before burger is done, top with a cheese slice; continue cooking until cheese is melted.

CALIFORNIA BURGER | Top each cooked patty with lettuce, onion slice, tomato slice and dab of mayonnaise.

BARBECUED BURGER | Mix 1/4 cup catsup, 2 tablespoons brown sugar, 1/2 teaspoon dry mustard and a dash of nutmeg; brush mixture on patties before and after turning. Cook until done.

INGREDIENTS

1 pound ground game meat
2 tablespoons onion, finely chopped
1 teaspoon salt
1/4 teaspoon pepper

INGREDIENTS

1 pound ground game meat

1 tablespoon cooking oil

1 (5.5-ounce) package au gratin
   potatoes

1/2 teaspoon salt

MAKES 4 TO 5 SERVINGS

INGREDIENTS

1 pound ground game meat

1 tablespoon cooking oil

2 large onions, sliced

1 large green peeper, chopped

1 (14.5-ounce) can stewed
   tomatoes

1/2 cup uncooked regular rice

1 teaspoon chili powder

1 teaspoon salt

MAKES 4 TO 5 SERVINGS

Gamburger Au Gratin Skillet

One more in a series of useful recipes for gameburger. This one adds potatoes to round out the meal.

Heat cooking oil in medium skillet; add meat and cook and stir until brown. Drain off any fat. Add potato slices and salt to meat. Sprinkle sauce mix on top. Stir in half the amounts of water and milk called for on package. Heat to boiling, stirring occasionally. Reduce heat; cover and simmer, stirring occasionally, until potatoes are tender, about 30 minutes.

Texas Gamburger Hash

Some hunters like to have a good deal of their game turned into ground meat. And so this book contains several recipes that include gameburger, even Chef Sam's Special Turkey Dressing. This is another gameburger recipe to enjoy.

Heat oven to 350 degrees. Heat oil in medium skillet, cook and stir meat, onion and green pepper until meat is brown and vegetables are tender. Drain off any fat; stir in remaining ingredients; heat through. Pour into ungreased 2-quart casserole dish. Cover and bake until rice is tender, 30 to 35 minutes.

Macaroni-Gameburger Sauté

In keeping with the promise to offer game cooks a series of useful recipes for their gameburger meals, this is another good one.

In large skillet, cook and stir meat, macaroni, onion and green pepper in oil until meat is brown and macaroni is light yellow. Drain off any fat. Stir in remaining ingredients; heat to boiling. Reduce heat; cover and simmer until macaroni is tender, about 20 minutes. Uncover and simmer until sauce is desired consistency.

MAKES 4 TO 5 SERVINGS

INGREDIENTS

1 pound ground game meat

1 cup uncooked elbow macaroni
  or similar pasta

1 medium onion, chopped

1/2 cup green pepper, chopped

3 tablespoons cooking oil

3 cups tomato juice

1 teaspoon garlic salt

1 teaspoon salt

1/4 teaspoon pepper

2 teaspoons Worcestershire sauce

Viennese Big Game Steak

Some of the nicest game meat recipes with big sounding names are truly on the easy side to prepare. This is one of those recipes.

Cut meat into serving size pieces. Heat oil in medium size skillet; brown meat over medium heat until brown. Add water; sprinkle with salt and pepper and top with onions. Reduce heat; cover and simmer until tender, about 1 hour. Add small amount of water if necessary. Remove meat to warm platter; keep warm. Drain off any fat from skillet. Stir in soup and heat; pour on meat to serve.

MAKES 4 TO 5 SERVINGS

INGREDIENTS

2 pounds game steak, 1/2- to
  3/4-inch thick

3 tablespoons cooking oil

1/2 cup water

1 teaspoon salt

1/2 teaspoon pepper

2 large onions, thinly sliced

2 (10.5-ounce) cans condensed
  cream of mushroom soup

Braised Antelope and Vegetables

Antelope meat can be difficult to prepare. This is one of several helpful recipes, although nothing takes the place of Leg O' Lope to please diners who generally don't care for wild game.

INGREDIENTS

2 tablespoons cooking oil

2 pounds of boned antelope, chunked

1 cup water

2 tablespoons lemon juice

1 teaspoon salt

1 teaspoon crushed rosemary leaves

1/2 teaspoon lemon pepper

1 small clove garlic, crushed or 1/4 teaspoon garlic powder

2 bay leaves

2 large onions

12 small carrots, cut into halves

4 medium potatoes, pared and cut into halves

1 (16-ounce) package frozen Italian green beans, broken apart

1 teaspoon salt

MAKES 4 TO 5 SERVINGS

Heat oil in Dutch oven; brown meat. Add water, lemon juice, 1 teaspoon salt, rosemary, pepper, garlic and bay leaves. Cover tightly and simmer on range top or in 350-degree oven for 1 hour. Add small amount of water if necessary. Add vegetables and 1 teaspoon salt; cook until meat and vegetables are tender, 40 to 60 minutes.

Roast Buffalo or Moose
with Oven-Browned Potatoes

This dish is ideal for larger grain wild meats, such as buffalo and moose, which are both supremely good in many other recipes. The potatoes are an important ingredient.

INGREDIENTS

1 large roast
Fresh beef fat
4 baking potatoes

Place roast on rack in shallow roasting pan. Lay fresh beef fat on top of roast. Season with salt and pepper before, during and after roasting. Insert meat thermometer so tip is in center of thickest part of meat. Roast uncovered in 325-degree oven until done using thermometer reading as your final guide. About 1 1/2 hours before roast is done, pare 4 medium baking potatoes. Make thin crosswise cuts almost through potatoes. Heat 1 inch salted water (1/2 teaspoon salt to 1 cup water) to boiling. Add potatoes. Cover and heat to boiling; cook 10 minutes. Drain.

Place potatoes in meat drippings in roasting pan; turn each potato to coat with drippings. Or brush potatoes with melted butter or margarine and place on rack with meat. Turning potatoes once, bake until tender and golden brown, 1 1/4 to 1 1/2 hours. Season with salt and pepper.

Roasts are easier to carve if allowed to rest 15 to 20 minutes after removing from oven. Serve with meat juices or pan gravy.

Mint-Glazed Roast

Most of our recipes are geared to lend a familiar flavor to game meat. This is another of those recipes.

INGREDIENTS

1 large game roast
Beef fat
Mint glaze

Make long narrow cuts in game roast. Insert slits of fresh beef fat. Place roast (elk, moose, venison or antelope) on rack in shallow roasting pan. Season with salt and pepper before, during and after roasting. Insert meat thermometer so tip is in thickest part of the meat and does not touch bone or rest in fat. Roast uncovered in 325-degree oven to desired doneness using thermometer reading as your final guide. During last hour of roasting, brush meat every 15 minutes with Mint Glaze (below). Serve any remaining glaze with the finished roast.

Roasts are easier to carve if allowed to rest for 15 minutes after removing from the oven.

MINT GLAZE | Heat 1 (10-ounce) jar mint-flavored jelly, 1 clove crushed garlic, and 1 1/2 tablespoons water, stirring constantly, until jelly is melted.

Herbed Venison and Onions

Good cooking requires proper use of spices and herbs. Otherwise all we would do is boil our meat in a pot or settle it upon a grate over coals or the gas grill. Here is a recipe that wisely uses condiments.

INGREDIENTS

1/4 cup butter or margarine
1 large onion, sliced and separated into rings
8 slices of cooked roast venison
1 tablespoon vinegar
2 tablespoons softened butter or margarine
1/4 teaspoon crushed thyme, tarragon or marjoram leaves

Melt 1/4 cup butter or margarine in medium skillet; add onion and cook until tender. Remove onion from skillet and keep warm. Add meat to skillet; brown quickly on both sides and sprinkle with vinegar. Mix 1 tablespoon softened butter and the crushed leaves; arrange meat and onions on your dinner plates; top the meat with the seasoned butter.

MAKES 4 TO 5 SERVINGS

Chinese Venison Suey

Chinese cooking is more popular than ever in America. Because there are hundreds of Chinese recipes available in cookbooks, ours does not include many. However, here is one that works out well.

Melt butter in medium size skillet; cook and stir meat and onion over medium heat until meat is brown and onion is tender. Add remaining ingredients except pea pods and rice or chow mein noodles. Heat to boiling, stirring occasionally. Add pea pods; cover and simmer 5 minutes. Serve over hot rice or noodles.

INGREDIENTS

1/4 cup butter or margarine

3 cups cooked venison strips, 2x1/4x1/4-inch

1 large onion, sliced and separated into rings

1 (8-ounce) can sliced water chestnuts

1 can beef broth

1 tablespoon soy sauce

2 tablespoons cornstarch

1 (10-ounce) package frozen pea pods

Hot cooked rice or chow mein noodles

Small Game Recipes

Sam's Fried Rabbit

After initial parboiling (pressure cooker style), rabbit pieces can be set aside for later cooking—or delivered directly to the hot skillet.

INGREDIENTS

2 cottontail rabbits cut in five
    serving sections
Sprinkle garlic powder
Sprinkle sweet basil
Sprinkle pepper
6 ounces Mr. Yashida's Original
    Gourmet Sauce (may substitute
    teriyaki glaze)
4 beef bouillon cubes
1 can chicken broth

Lightly brown rabbit pieces with olive or canola oil in skillet. Transfer to pressure cooker. Just cover with water. Pressure cook 10 minutes. Remove, drain, dry meat on paper towel. Place tenderized pieces in lightly oiled skillet. Brown both sides over medium heat. Sprinkle with garlic powder, sweet basil and pepper. Add half can chicken broth plus bouillon cubes. Add gourmet sauce; simmer 10 minutes on low turning pieces. Add remainder chicken broth. Simmer 5 minutes. Remove pieces, strain liquid (sauce) into bowl. Serve with sauce over rice, glazed carrots. This is finger food. Consider finger bowls and generous-size napkins.

Twice-Fried Old-Time Turtle Soup

Another recipe from old-time literature slightly modified here. It lends a slightly more familiar flavor to turtle meat than some other recipes. This recipe requires a full two pounds of boned turtle meat.

Soak turtle chunks in cold water and baking soda overnight in refrigerator. Transfer meat to pressure cooker and cover with water. Add teriyaki and Worcestershire Sauce. Secure lid and set regulator. Pressure cook for 15 minutes. Let pressure drop normally. When cooker is safe, remove meat and coat each piece with flour. Fry in skillet over medium heat. Remove meat and drain on paper towel. In large bowl combine flour, baking powder, eggs, milk and salt. Use enough milk to create a dough-like batter. Coat each piece of meat with batter and fry again until golden brown. In large kettle combine meat with stock or broth. Add garlic powder, pepper, onion, paprika and Virginia Olson's Savory Seasonings Fish Blend. Bring to a boil and then reduce heat. Simmer soup 1/2 hour. Have potatoes and celery precooked in pressure cooker and add to the soup.

INGREDIENTS

2 pounds boned turtle meat
1 tablespoon teriyaki
1 tablespoon Worcestershire Sauce
2 cups flour
Milk
1/4 teaspoon salt
2 quarts chicken stock or broth
Dash of garlic powder
Dash of ground pepper
1/2 onion, diced
Sprinkle of paprika
1/8 teaspoon Virginia Olson's Savory Seasonings Fish Blend
2 large potatoes, peeled and diced
4 celery stalks, diced

Appalachian Possum

There are many fine recipes from wise cooks from the Appalachian belt. Many come from days long ago when self-sufficiency was a high premium among these fine people. This recipe is an old one, slightly modified here.

Preheat oven to 375 degrees. Soak possum in cold saltwater for 8 to 10 hours. Rinse meat in cold water. Refrigerate on clean towel for 2 to four 4 hours. Stuff possum cavity with fruit and vegetables from ingredients list. Close cavity with string or skewer. In roasting pan, submerse meat halfway in water and add bouillon cubes, bay leaves, celery and onion. Roast for 2 hours; turn meat over to expose other side to liquid. Reduce heat to 300 degrees and roast an additional hour. Meat should be tender at this point. Test with fork and if not done, reduce heat to 250 degrees and roast 1 more hour. Remove bay leaves before serving.

INGREDIENTS

1 possum, whole
2 quarts cold water
1/8 cup of salt
6 beef bouillon cubes
4 bay leaves
2 apples, halved
2 oranges, peeled and halved
8 to 10 grapes
2 celery stalks, chopped
1 medium onion, chopped

Turtle Soup

Old-timers knew the food value of large turtles. A Louisiana friend is keeping his grandfather's recipe alive. Here it is slightly modified with dressing instructions included.

INGREDIENTS

1 snapping or other edible turtle
1 pound pork meat, diced
2 quarts strong chicken stock
4 ounces Mr. Yoshida's Original
    Gourmet Sauce (or teriyaki
    sauce)
8 carrots peeled and cut into
    sections
1/4 cup medium sherry
3 cups cooked barley

Remove head of turtle and allow fluids to evacuate briefly. Boil whole turtle in pot of salted water for about 3 minutes. Remove. Cool down a little and then remove top shell and outer skin. Cross-split the lower shell. Remove entrails and claws. Soak in salt water for 1 to 2 hours. Boil in pot again with lower shell intact. When flesh cooks free from shell, cut shell away. Dice boneless meat. Brown pork meat in skillet with canola oil (not olive oil). Pressure cook boneless turtle meat with pork in stock and gourmet sauce (about 20 minutes). Add carrots and sherry. Pressure cook again for 2 or 3 minutes (or time required to cook carrots through). Remove lid. Add cooked barley. Simmer uncovered for 20 minutes.

Fried Frog Legs

Considered a delicacy by those who appreciate tasty food, frog legs are easy to make. Personal taste and food prejudice, however, dictates whether to serve them to dinner guests. In some areas the large bullfrog is in abundance, but check local laws before frogging. Bullfrogs are rightly considered game food by management agencies.

INGREDIENTS

Bullfrog legs – any quantity
Eggs
Breadcrumbs
Salt
Pepper
Paprika
Worcestershire Sauce
Butter

Skin legs (easily done). Soak in saltwater/vinegar solution for 30 minutes. Drain and dry meat. Sprinkle meat with salt, pepper and paprika. Bread with egg and breadcrumbs. Fry until golden brown in olive or canola oil with dash of Worcestershire sauce and 1 or 2 pats of butter toward end of cooking cycle.

Crayfish Boil

Another edible delicacy that may be in abundance near a hunting camp. Eating crayfish requires a certain patience and talent in getting to the meat. But crayfish lovers believe it's worth the trouble.

Clean crayfish by tearing off the end of the tail, which automatically releases inner matter. Boil in crab boil, which is found at grocery stores, usually near the fresh fish counter. Boil until red in color. Salt and pepper to taste—easy on the pepper. Prepare sauce of melted butter and lemon juice. Peel crayfish and eat with sauce.

INGREDIENTS

Crayfish – any amount
Crab boil
Melted butter
Lemon juice
Salt
Pepper

Squirrel Stew

Squirrel stew was a standby of pioneers and homesteaders in early America. It simmered on the hearth until the meat was cooked tender. Today we have the pressure cooker and Crock-Pot for squirrel stew. Both are used in this recipe.

Braise squirrel meat with olive oil in medium skillet. Increase heat to medium-high and add Worcestershire and teriyaki sauces while stirring meat. Raise to high heat and add wine. Blend with continuous stirring to cook off alcohol, leaving the flavor behind. Lower heat to medium and add stock or chicken broth. Bring to a boil. Pour entire contents of pan into pressure cooker. Just cover with water. Pressure cook for 20 minutes. Let steam off. Check for tenderness. If not tender, pressure cook 10 more minutes. Place contents of pressure cooker in Crock-Pot. Add carrots, tomatoes and potatoes. Set Crock-Pot on low and cook until carrots and potatoes are done.

INGREDIENTS

4 squirrels sectioned (see
    Chapter 12)
Olive oil
1 tablespoon Worcestershire Sauce
2 tablespoons teriyaki sauce
1 cup burgundy wine
2 cups stock or equal amount of
    chicken broth
1 garlic clove, pressed or crushed
1/8 teaspoon pepper
1/2 white onion left intact
8 carrots, peeled and diced
1 large can of tomatoes
4 potatoes, peeled and cubed

Brandied Squirrel with Vermouth

The heart of this squirrel recipe is the brandy and vermouth. For those who do not care for these flavors, this recipe is best left alone.

Parboil squirrel with Worcestershire Sauce in pressure cooker 15 minutes. Remove from cooker. Discard liquid. Heat olive oil in skillet; brown meat in skillet. Lower heat. Add garlic and onion. Cook for 5 minutes. Add brandy and vermouth. Be aware of possible flame-up. Simmer for 30 minutes. In separate skillet cook mushrooms with butter and port. Add to meat and simmer 5 minutes. Put heavy cream in saucepan and warm. Beat egg yolks in a bowl. Place squirrel pieces on a serving platter and keep warm. Stir warm cream into juices remaining in the skillet (wine sauce). Remove 1/2 cup of mixture in the skillet and blend with beaten egg yolks. Return this to the skillet along with the port wine. Simmer on low for 5 minutes. Pour all contents of pan (sauce) over meat.

INGREDIENTS

4 squirrels sectioned (See Chapter 12)

2 teaspoons Worcestershire Sauce

Olive oil

1/2 bunch green onions

2 cloves garlic, crushed

1 cup brandy

1/2 cup dry vermouth

1/4 cup port wine

2 pounds mushrooms, sliced

2 tablespoons butter

1 1/2 cups heavy cream

3 egg yolks

Fried Bushytail

Parboiling to tenderize helps this recipe. Use pressure cooker to save time.

Parboil squirrel meat, parsley, bay leaf and sweet basil in enough water to just cover meat in pressure cooker. Remove tenderized meat and discard juices from pressure cooker. Sprinkle meat with lemon pepper, black pepper, paprika and garlic powder. Heat canola or peanut oil to medium-low in skillet. Fry squirrel meat for about 10 minutes with frequent stirring. Add soy sauce, bouillon cubes and stock or broth to skillet. Cover skillet and simmer until all ingredients are blended, especially bouillon cubes. Serve with rice or potatoes, green vegetable, salad—cook's choice.

INGREDIENTS

4 squirrels sectioned (See Chapter 12)

1/2 bunch parsley, cut not chopped

4 bay leaves

1/4 teaspoon sweet basil

Lemon pepper

Black pepper

Paprika

Garlic powder

Canola or peanut oil

6 tablespoons soy sauce

1/2 cup broth or stock

8 chicken bouillon cubes

Colonial Rabbit

This recipe was located in a draft on colonial cooking. As with so many recipes from the distant past, this one becomes a fine dish on the table. I've modernized the recipe with canned broth and tomato puree.

Do the usual 20-minute parboiling of rabbit pieces with a dash of Worcestershire Sauce in pressure cooker. Heat olive oil in skillet. Flour meat and brown in skillet. Remove meat from pan. Add chicken broth. Bring to a boil. Stir in onions, carrots, bay leaves and garlic. Simmer for 20 to 30 minutes. Add tomato puree and continue to simmer. Remove 1/4 cup juice from skillet and combine with ice water and flour, mixing until smooth. Return this mixture to skillet and continue simmering. Add sherry and currant jelly. Return rabbit pieces to skillet. When rabbit is cooked through, remove from skillet. Strain to catch any bones. Sauté mushrooms in butter and add to dish. Side dishes—cook's choice.

INGREDIENTS

2 rabbits sectioned (See Chapter 12)
Worcestershire Sauce
Flour
Olive oil
1 can chicken broth
1/2 onion, diced
3 carrots, peeled and sliced
3 bay leaves
1 garlic clove, pressed
1 small can of tomato puree
1/4 cup ice water
2 tablespoons flour
1/2 cup medium sherry, optional
4 tablespoons currant jelly
1 pound mushrooms, sliced

Hasenpfeffer

Kenn Oberrecht, hero of Chapter 28 on caring for the catch, reveals his German background in this borrowed recipe for cottontail rabbit. This recipe can also work for young snowshoe hares, but it is recommended for cottontails. Once again the pressure cooker does the work.

Place rabbit pieces in bowl and cover with vinegar and water. If not enough liquid to cover, add a little more water. Add bay leaves, pepper, salt and onion. Set aside to marinate for at least 48 hours and up to 72 hours in the refrigerator. Remove rabbit pieces prior to cooking but do not discard marinade. Dry pieces with paper towel. Flour heavily. Brown all sides of floured meat. Strain two cups of marinade into pressure cooker. Add two cups broth or stock. Pressure cook for 12 to 15 minutes depending upon cooker. Overcooking can break meat down, while undercooking does not produce the desired tenderizing results. Allow cooker to rest 3 to 5 minutes and then carefully release pressure under running water. Remove rabbit pieces. Keep them warm. Add the sour cream and gingersnap cookie pieces to the liquid in the pressure cooker. Heat, stirring constantly, until the mixture gains a sauce like consistency. Serve rabbit pieces with sauce.

INGREDIENTS

3 rabbits in serving pieces (see Chapter 12)
4 cups white vinegar
4 cups water
6 bay leaves
1 teaspoon pepper
1 1/2 teaspoons salt
3 onions sliced
3 cups sour cream
16 ginger cookies, broken into small parts
Canola or olive oil
Flour
2 cups broth or stock

INGREDIENTS
〰〰〰〰〰〰〰

2 hares, hind legs and backstrap
   only
2 tablespoons flour
2 tablespoons pure lard
2 tablespoons butter or margarine
1/2 teaspoon salt
4 tablespoons wine vinegar
3 teaspoons brown sugar
1/4 teaspoon pepper
3 cups chicken broth
1 small onion, chopped

INGREDIENTS
〰〰〰〰〰〰〰

2 rabbits, cut into serving pieces
2 egg yolks, beaten
3 cups milk
1 1/4 cups flour
1 teaspoon salt
1/2 cup canola oil
4 teaspoons currant jelly
2 tablespoons chopped parsley

Sweet and Sour Hare

The hare (snowshoe hare where I hunt) is a dark-meat small game animal. While it may be different in various areas, the hare can become tough with maturity, and the flavor seams to grow stronger. A young hare only is called for in this dish.

The meat is soaked overnight in vinegar/salt solution, using enough water to cover the meat, four tablespoons salt and two tablespoons white vinegar. Brown the flour in the lard with butter or margarine. Add meat and all the rest of the ingredients. Cover and simmer very slowly for about two hours (must be cooked through and tender). Good with rice and vegetables.

A Different Fried Rabbit

This recipe is for cottontails, not hares. It varies just enough from our other fried rabbit recipes to deserve a place in the book. As always, the rabbit is sectioned with the tough skin over the backstrap removed. Soak for 2 to 4 hours in saltwater with a little white vinegar. Parboil pieces for 10 to 15 minutes before frying. (Use a pressure cooker for par boiling).

Combine the beaten egg yolks with one cup of milk. Add 1 cup flour gradually to mix in smoothly. Add salt. Mix well. Dip rabbit pieces into this batter and fry on medium heat for 10 minutes. Reduce heat to low and cook pieces through (turn frequently). To make gravy add the remaining flour to the contents in the skillet after straining contents to ensure that all bones are removed. Add remaining milk to pan slowly, stirring constantly. Heat to thickening point. Allow individuals to add salt and pepper to their taste. Gravy is good over rice. You can also shred meat from the bones, mix with cooked rice and pour gravy over meat/rice.

Roast Rabbit

This is a very simple dish, but tasty. Even though the rabbits will be roasted, cut them into serving pieces and parboil for about 20 minutes in pressure cooker with a dash of Worcestershire sauce.

Dry rabbit pieces on paper towel. Salt and pepper the pieces. Prepare stuffing per directions on package. Spread half the stuffing on a large piece of aluminum foil in the bottom of a roasting pan. Press pieces of rabbit meat into the stuffing. Cover pieces of meat with remainder of stuffing. Cover with aluminum foil. Roast at 275 to 300 degrees (depending upon oven) for about 1-1/2 to 2 hours (must be cooked tender, but parboiling already helped that). Do not allow to dry out. Check from time to time. Sprinkle with chicken stock or chicken broth if necessary to prevent drying out. Good with a green salad and any vegetable.

INGREDIENTS

2 cottontail rabbits
salt
pepper
garlic powder
paprika
prepared stuffing
2 tablespoons pure lard
2 tablespoons butter or margarine

Roast Squirrel

Squirrels are all dark meat. A little parboiling is in order with a couple tablespoons of Worcester sauce in the pressure cooker water. It's very important that the pieces of meat receive a good soaking on salt water with vinegar for at least four hours before parboiling.

Dry squirrel meat on paper towel after parboiling and dress with oil and lemon juice. Allow meat to stand in this mixture of oil and lemon juice for 1-1/2 hours. Moisten breadcrumbs with milk. Sauté mushrooms and chopped onion and add to moist breadcrumbs. Add rest of ingredients to breadcrumbs. Lightly oil a large sheet of aluminum foil in the bottom of a roasting pot with olive oil. Place half the breadcrumbs on this sheet. Press in meat pieces. Cover with remaining breadcrumbs. Cover with aluminum foil. Put lid on roasting pan and roast at 300 to 325 degrees until meat is tender; about 2 hours. Don't allow drying out. Check from time to time and add beef broth if necessary.

INGREDIENTS

3 to 4 tree squirrels (medium size)
1 cup canola oil
1/4 cup lemon juice
2 cups bread crumbs
1/2 cup half and half
2 cups sliced mushrooms
1/2 teaspoon salt
1/8 teaspoon pepper
1/2 medium white onion, chopped
olive oil

Stewed Squirrel

This is another simple, but good, recipe. Parboiling the squirrel pieces before stewing especially enhances it. Squirrel meat can be rich and delicious, but may also be tougher than cottontail rabbit. Soak squirrel pieces first in saltwater and vinegar for about four hours before stewing.

Add squirrel to stock in pressure cooker. Add bouillon cubes, onion, bacon, and bay leaves. Cook for 20 to 30 minutes (check in between to see if meat is tender). Let steam off for last time. Add cooked barley and carrots. Bring pressure up for 3 to 4 minutes to cook carrots. Serve with Italian or French bread.

INGREDIENTS

3 medium squirrels, sectioned

1 minced onion

2 bay leaves

1/2 pound bacon, cut into squares and cooked

2 quarts chicken stock

2 chicken bouillon cubes

3 cups cooked pearl barley

1 pound carrots diced large (more if desired)

Roast Opossum

Backcountry folks learned to disregard food prejudice with possum, making up a variety of dishes with the meat. Individual taste puts the possum lower on the list of edibles than either rabbit or squirrel. However, for those who wish to try this "different" meat, here is one way to prepare the singular and different opossum. But before cooking the head and tail must be removed, the carcass must be thoroughly cleaned and soaked in a strong brine (about a cup of salt to two gallons of water) overnight. Next day, rinse with boiling water.

Place prepared stuffing mix in the roasting pan. Add all ingredients. Mix well to distribute lemon juice. Section opossum. Braise meat well in a little canola oil. Stick braised pieces of meat down into stuffing mix in roasting pot. Roast on low heat (about 275 degrees) until meat is tender.

INGREDIENTS

1 large opossum

Prepared stuffing mix

1/2 bunch parsley, chopped well

One small onion, chopped

1 teaspoon lemon juice

1 clove garlic, minced

Canola oil

Rabbit Stew South of the Border

This is a zesty dish, but need not be overly hot, but that depends, in part, upon the chilies.

Pressure cook rabbit pieces until meat can be shredded from the bone. Discard the liquid that the rabbit was cooked in. In a cooking pot combine tomatoes, chilies, onion, dash each salt, pepper, paprika. Add mushrooms. Add cream of chicken soup and one-half soup can of broth. Cook on low heat until well blended. Add sour cream to taste. Simmer for five minutes and serve.

INGREDIENTS

3 rabbits
1 can tomatoes
1 small can green chilies, chopped
1 medium onion, chopped
Salt
Pepper
Paprika
1 pound mushrooms, cut
1 can cream of chicken soup
Broth
Sour cream

Bird Recipes

INGREDIENTS

2 cups plain white rice cooked

1 1/2 pounds gameburger

1 bunch parsley

1/4 teaspoon oregano

1/4 teaspoon sweet basil

1/2 bunch green onion, chopped

1 garlic clove, minced or chopped
   fine

1/8 teaspoon pepper

3 tablespoons Parmesan cheese
   grated

1/8 teaspoon sage

4 hard-boiled eggs

Optional: half cup peeled and
   diced celery

Chef Sam's Turkey Stuffing

This is the stuffing Chef Sam prepared for Christmas and Thanksgiving turkey. It's a meal in itself.

Microwave rice in large covered bowl until done. Leave in bowl. Cook gameburger. Place cooked gameburger on dish with paper towel, microwave for one minute to reduce grease and/or moisture. Add gameburger to rice. Mix thoroughly. Add the rest of the ingredients; mix well. Stuff turkey, adding one-half hard-boiled egg in layers. Put leftover stuffing in covered Pyrex or other oven-safe cooking dish. Toward end of cooking cycle for turkey, bake leftover stuffing for 30 minutes in 300-degree oven. Mix stuffing cooked in bird with leftover stuffing cooked on its own. Serve hot. Also excellent cold later with turkey sandwiches and cranberry sauce.

Quail and Honey Butter

Quail of all kinds are gourmet simply fried in the pan with a few condiments. This little dress-up is simply a way to present these fine gamebirds with a little different flare.

Prepare honey butter first by blending the last three ingredients well; set aside in refrigerator for at least two hours. When ready to cook birds, dust with garlic powder, paprika and very lightly with onion powder. Fry in light oil until just done. Put birds on cookie sheet covered with aluminum foil and coat each with the honey butter. Place in oven at 200 to 225 degrees for 20 minutes, less if the oven cooks on the hot side. Serve with cook's choice of green vegetable and salad or any other side dish.

INGREDIENTS

2 quail or many more
Garlic powder
Paprika
Onion powder
Butter or margarine

1 cup honey
1/2 cup mustard
4 cups mayonnaise

Hawaiian Pineapple Game Bird

This recipe is workable with upland birds of darker meat as well as light. Its ingredients impart a friendly familiar flavor.

Place boned meat in a 12x8x2-1/2-inch baking dish. Combine all other ingredients except the rice in a medium saucepan and heat until bubbly. Pour sauce over boned meat and bake at 350 degrees for 1 hour. Lay cooked meat on a bed of hot rice. Spoon sauce on generously.

INGREDIENTS

1 large game bird boned (such as pheasant)
1 can cream of chicken soup
1 1/2 cups crushed pineapple
1 tablespoon soy sauce
1/2 teaspoon dried minced onion
1/4 teaspoon ginger
1/2 teaspoon dried parsley flakes
4 cups hot cooked rice

Game Bird Florentine Style

This is a rather common recipe found in many cookbooks. The only difference here is game meat in place of domestic.

2 1/2 pounds boned game bird
    pieces
1 (10-ounce) package fresh
    spinach
6 tablespoons butter or margarine
3 cloves garlic, peeled and minced
1/4 cup fine dry bread crumbs
1/4 cup grated Parmesan cheese

Bring 1 quart of lightly salted water to a boil in a 12- to 14-inch skillet. Add the bird pieces and simmer, covered, for 20 minutes. Preheat the broiler. Trim the coarse stems from spinach and wash the leaves. Pat them dry on paper towel. Melt 3 tablespoons of the butter in a 4-quart saucepan; add garlic and cook uncovered over moderately low heat for 1 or 2 minutes or until golden colored, but not fully browned. Add spinach and cook, stirring, until the leaves are limp – 4 to 5 minutes. Transfer spinach to a buttered 9x9x2-inch baking dish. Remove the game pieces from the water; pat dry with paper toweling; and place the meat on top of the spinach. Melt the remaining butter. Mix in the breadcrumbs and cheese. Sprinkle the mixture over the meat. Place about 4 inches from oven broiler; heat for 3 or 4 minutes.

Lemon Baked Game Bird

This recipe is useful for game bird with fuller flavor, and though sage grouse are best treated to Universal Marinade, younger birds can be prepared using this method of cooking.

1/2 cup flour
1 teaspoon dried tarragon,
    crumbled
1 1/4 teaspoons salt
2 1/2 to 3 pounds of boned game
    bird meat into serving pieces
4 tablespoons butter or margarine
1/3 cup lemon juice
1 tablespoon grated yellow onion
1 clove garlic, peeled and minced
1/8 teaspoon black pepper

Preheat the oven to 400 degrees. Combine flour, tarragon and 1 teaspoon of the salt in a paper bag. Add boned bird pieces a few at a time. Shake the bag to coat each piece well with the flour mixture. Remove the pieces from the bag and shake off excess flour mixture. Melt butter or margarine in the oven in a 13x9x2-inch baking dish. Coat floured meat pieces on all sides with this warm butter. In a small bowl, mix the lemon juice, onion, garlic, pepper and remaining 1/4 teaspoon salt. Drizzle this mixture evenly over the boned bird pieces and bake uncovered for 40 minutes.

Judy's Sour Cream Enchiladas

This is another big hit from south of the border. It's not overly complicated to prepare; however, it does require a little time. The meat from just about any game bird works, although young (only) sage hens are best thoroughly marinated in Universal Marinade first.

Preheat oven to 350 degrees. Spray a 2-quart casserole pan with cooking spray. Heat oil in medium skillet; cook onion until clear. Add soup, milk, meat, chili and sour cream; heat until bubbly. Quickly dip tortillas in hot mixture; place in casserole pan making layers of dipped tortillas, soup mixture and cheese. Top with cheese. Bake uncovered for 25 to 30 minutes until cheese is melted and the mixture is bubbly.

INGREDIENTS

1 dozen corn tortillas
1 small onion, chopped
1 tablespoon cooking oil
1 (10-ounce) can cream of chicken soup
3/4 cup milk
1 1/2 cups cooked boned game bird, cubed
1/4 cup diced green chili
1/2 cup sour cream
1/2 pound grated Monterey Jack or Colby cheese

Judy's Roast Duck

This is one more way to fix a duck. It does not mask duck flavor, but it does enhance it.

Preheat oven to 300 degrees. In a large bowl submerse the skinned ducks in water and baking soda and soak for 2 hours. Rinse and dry meat. Rub well with lard. Mix diced apples, onion and parsley. Stuff this mixture into ducks' cavities. Place ducks in a roasting pan half-filled with water; add bouillon cubes and garlic to water. Sprinkle ducks with paprika. Cover the birds and roast for 1 hour. Turn birds over and add chicken broth or stock. Roast covered for an additional hour. Turn birds breast-side up; add apple juice and re-cover. Reduce heat to 250 degrees and roast until meat is tender. Discard contents of cavities before serving.

INGREDIENTS

3 large ducks, skinned
1 to 2 quarts water
1/8 cup baking soda per quart of water
Lard
3 apples, diced
1 large onion, sliced
3/4 bunch fresh parsley
6 beef bouillon cubes
3 cloves garlic, crushed
Sprinkle of paprika
1 can chicken broth or 2 cups stock
1/2 cup apple juice

Chef Sam's Quail European

This is another simple recipe designed with table appeal and good flavor. It's the basting sauce that makes the difference. Multiply the recipe sensibly for additional birds.

INGREDIENTS

8 quail
1/4 cup butter
1/4 cup dry sherry
1 clove garlic, crushed
Paprika
Canola oil
Teriyaki sauce
2 cups stock or chicken broth for
    steaming
1 cup stock or chicken broth for
    basting sauce

Rub each quail with canola oil; dust with paprika; add a teaspoon of teriyaki sauce inside each bird's cavity. Place birds in roasting pan with two cups stock or chicken broth for steaming. Cover pan and roast birds in slow oven (225 to 250 degrees), basting with the following combination: butter, sherry, crushed garlic and stock or chicken broth. Serve with side dishes of choice. Consider white rice and broccoli with hollandaise sauce.

Game Chef's Salad

This is a good recipe for using a small amount of leftover upland gamebird meat. For example, a quail or two might be left over from last night's supper. Or pheasant. Just about any gamebird works here.

INGREDIENTS

2 to 3 cups gamebird meat, boned
    and cubed
1/2 cup Swiss cheese, cut into nar-
    row strips
1/4 cup green onion, chopped
1/4 cup celery, diced
Lettuce
1/3 cup real mayonnaise
1/3 cup prepared chili sauce
2 hard-boiled eggs, cut into 6
    pieces each
Pitted olives, optional

The lettuce is the body of this chef's salad and as such is varied in amount. A half head of iceberg lettuce makes a good-sized bowl of salad. Mix together all other ingredients except hard-boiled egg pieces, which must be carefully folded in afterward or the pieces will break up into bits of hard-boiled egg. Pitted olives, amount to suit cook, can be placed on top of finished salad as a garnish.

Simply Baked Pheasant

There's not much preparation time with this dish, only some oven time. In order to maintain tenderness, roasting pan must be covered. A piece of aluminum foil between pan and lid helps hold steam in. To cook two pheasants instead of one add extra ingredients as required; however, be careful with tarragon leaves, which can overpower the dish.

Lightly fry breasted pheasant in a little olive or canola oil. Does not have to be cooked through. Place breasted pheasant in roasting pan. Cook green onion and halved mushroom. Mix mushroom/onion, with liquid and all other ingredients. Pour over pheasant meat. Cook at 300 degrees until meat is done through.

INGREDIENTS

1 large breasted pheasant
2 cans mushroom soup
1 pound fresh mushrooms
Butter
1/2 bunch green onions
1 cup broth or stock
1/4 cup medium sherry, optional
1/4 teaspoon tarragon
2 garlic cloves, crushed
1 teaspoon Worcestershire Sauce
Canola or olive oil for browning

Upland Bird Cacciatore

This dish dresses up just about any gamebird without masking the inherently good flavor or texture of the meat.

Heat 1/8-inch salad oil in large skillet. Mix flour, salt, pepper and paprika; coat bird pieces with flour mixture. Cook meat in oil over medium heat until light brown. Mix spaghetti sauce, mushrooms, water, garlic, parsley flakes, and olives. Drain fat from skillet. Pour sauce over meat; heat to boiling. Reduce heat; cover tightly and simmer until thickest pieces of meat are tender, about 30 minutes. While bird simmers, cook spaghetti as directed on package. Drain. Serve bird on spaghetti platter.

INGREDIENTS

Salad oil
1/2 cup flour
1 teaspoon salt
1/4 teaspoon pepper
1/4 teaspoon paprika
3 pounds bird pieces
1 (28-ounce) jar meatless
  spaghetti sauce
1/2 pound fresh mushrooms, cut
  in 1/2- or 1/4-inch pieces
1/2 cup water
1/2 teaspoon instant minced garlic
2 teaspoons parsley flakes
1/2 cup sliced pitted ripe olives
8 ounces uncooked spaghetti

MAKES 4 OR 5 SERVINGS

Sage Hen Steaks

Sage hen is dark meat that can have a sage taste. It's considered by many cooks to be one of the hardest upland birds to cook successfully. This recipe reduces the sage flavor significantly and turns the breasted meat into a good meal.

INGREDIENTS

2 sage hen breasts, boned and cut into steaks (two to four steaks per side depending on size of bird)
Universal Marinade – see Chapter 25
Flour/cracker mix
Canola oil
Margarine

Marinate breasted sage hen steaks in Universal Marinade for no less than 6 hours and up to 24 hours. Remove from marinade but do not dry off. Coat heavily with 50/50 mixture of cracker meal and flour (prepare soda crackers with rolling pin). Fry meat until done but not hard in a mixture of 2/3 canola oil and 1/3 margarine. Serve very hot from the skillet with buttered mashed potatoes. Do not save marinade. Do not make pan gravy from leftover marinade.

Upland Bird Italian Style

This dish works well with dark or light meat birds, although sage hen may be a little too strong.

INGREDIENTS

2 pounds breasted upland bird meat, cut in squares
Canola oil
1/4 cup flour
1/2 teaspoon salt
1/4 teaspoon paprika
1/8 teaspoon pepper
1 jar (approximately 16 ounces) spaghetti sauce (plain)(or same amount homemade sauce)
1 pound fresh mushrooms
1/2 bunch green onions
Butter
1/4 teaspoon garlic
1/4 bunch freshly parsley, chopped
Spaghetti pasta (angel hair)

In bowl, mix flour, salt, paprika and pepper. Coat boned pieces of meat with mixture. Fry pieces until just done in oil. Do not overcook. Remove from pan. Cook mushrooms with butter and diced green onion in large skillet. Mix mushrooms/onion with spaghetti sauce. Add garlic and parsley to sauce. Put sauce in skillet with mushrooms and onion. Add meat to pan and simmer. While meat in sauce simmers, cook spaghetti. Angel hair pasta cooks faster than regular when time is a consideration. Drain pasta. Place on plate. Cover with sauce and meat. Good with green salad.

Chef Sam's Camp Cooked Grouse

This is another way of making grouse that does not take a lot of the cook's time but results in a tasty dish. It works with any grouse, except sage grouse. It's intended for camp, but can be prepared at home as well.

Rub grouse with olive oil. Cut potatoes as if making French fries. Place potatoes on large double pieces of aluminum foil. Sprinkle with salt. Place four pats of butter on top of potatoes. Layer sliced zucchini on potato slices. Salt lightly. Layer boned grouse on zucchini slices. Pour sauce over all. Sprinkle lightly with garlic powder and oregano. Seal foil package. Use extra foil if necessary. Lay foil package on medium coals at camp. Cover with coals. Very hot coals can ruin this dish. Allow coals to die down. Normally, in the time it takes coals to die down the grouse meat is cooked. Coals from pine or other softwoods do not work well. Use charcoal briquettes or hardwood coals.

ALTERNATE METHODS | Can also be cooked on a grate over coals or at home over coals on the gas grill or in the oven. Serve with pasta.

FOR PASTA | Boil to done, remove, drain; combine butter, sweet basil and Parmesan cheese.

INGREDIENTS

2 large grouse or 4 small grouse, boned
Olive oil
Salt
Garlic powder
2 peeled potatoes, sliced as fries
2 peeled zucchini, sliced
1 cup primavera sauce
1/2 teaspoon oregano
4 pats butter

Chef Sam's Pheasant

The heart of this recipe is the sauce that cooks up with the pheasant during baking. Although Chef Sam made his own sauces entirely from scratch this recipe has been modified in the interest of time with the use of canned chicken soup in place of the original sauce.

Combine all ingredients except paprika in a covered baking dish (such as Pyrex). Dust with paprika. Bake on low heat (250 to 300 degrees) until pheasant is tender. Serve with wild or white rice.

INGREDIENTS

2 boned pheasants
1 can cream of chicken soup
1 cup stock or broth
2 ounces cream
1/2 cup apple cider
3 teaspoons Worcestershire sauce
2 tablespoons Mr. Yoshida's Original Gourmet Sauce
1 chopped onion
1 pound mushrooms
1 bunch green peppers
Paprika

Cornbread Pot Pie Crust

1 cup flour
1 tablespoon baking powder
2 tablespoons sugar
1 cup milk
1 cup yellow cornmeal
1 teaspoon salt
1 egg, lightly beaten
1/4 cup vegetable shortening

This recipe goes with Leftover Wild Turkey Crock-Pot Pie, but is placed separately because it works perfectly with leftover stews and even roasts, the latter with meat and vegetables diced before covering with a cornbread crust.

Combine cornmeal, flour, baking powder, salt and sugar in mixing bowl. Blend in egg, milk and shortening. This mixture is poured over the top of the ingredients in the stoneware of the Crock-Pot for the Turkey Pot Pie recipe, or it can be poured over leftover stew or cubed roast meat and vegetables. For the first, remove the interior stoneware part of the Crock-Pot. Place in oven pre-heated to 325 degrees. Bake for 15 minutes or until the crust is golden brown. Allow to rest for 10 to 15 minutes before serving.

Camp Soup

Meat/various species
Soup base*
Canned broth, amount to suit
    amount of meat
Canned corn
Canned new potatoes
Sweet basil
Chicken bouillon cubes

This soup was designed on a turkey hunt where the breast meat was set aside for home cooking, leaving the legs. There was also a cottontail rabbit drawn, washed, cooled and ready for cooking. In a different camp there were two quail ready for the pot along with boned meat from a deer carcass skinned, bagged and cooling in the draw. The imaginative cook will think of other meats to use. The reason I rely on a pressure cooker in camp is speedy cooking when hungry hunters come in from the field. This soup can be ready to eat in well under an hour including prep and cooking time.

Exact amounts of ingredients are impossible to give without knowing the amount of meat for the soup. With 2 pounds of meat use 1 package of soup base, 2 cans of broth along with 1 bouillon cube and sweet basil to provide sufficient body for the soup. Don't overdo the bouillon because soup base is often composed in part of bouillon. Place meats into pressure cooker (or pot). Mix soup base per directions. Pressure cook until meat is done. Drop in can of corn and can of new potatoes; bring to boil; simmer until soup is very hot. Serve with bread or crackers.

*Packaged soup base is available in the grocery store in several brands, including Knorr.

Wild Turkey Breast Crock-Pot

This is another good recipe from the Rival company for their excellent Crock-Pot. It is somewhat modified here with regard to wild turkey instead of a domestic bird. Only the breast is used in this recipe. The legs of the wild turkey can be used to make soup. This recipe is simple and time saving.

Combine all ingredients except turkey breast. Place turkey breast in the stoneware section of the Crock-Pot. Ladle remaining ingredients over top. Cook on low for about 10 hours.

INGREDIENTS

1 wild turkey breast

1/4 cup garden vegetable flavored whipped cream cheese (if not available use regular cream cheese whipped)

1 tablespoon soy sauce

1/4 cup stock or chicken broth

1/4 teaspoon Worcestershire Sauce

1/4 teaspoon crushed garlic

1/2 teaspoon fresh (diced) or dried sweet basil

1/4 teaspoon fresh (diced) or dried thyme

2 tablespoon butter or margarine

1 tablespoon parsley flakes or fresh chopped

1/4 teaspoon sage

1/4 teaspoon pepper

Northern Italian Gamebird

Best with lighter meat gamebirds such as blue grouse. Sage grouse or waterfowl not recommended.

Cook boneless meat until done in a little canola or olive oil over medium heat.. Place cooked meat in glass baking dish with cover (such as Pyrex). Sauté garlic clove in a little butter. If wine is chosen, add to pan with garlic and bring to a boil. Set aside. Sauté mushrooms and green onion in a little butter. Combine garlic, onion, mushrooms and wine with cooked meat. Combine soup and sour cream. Sprinkle with paprika. Mix soup mixture with meat and bake in 300-degree oven for 45 minutes. Ladle total contents of baking dish over cooked noodles. Top with parsley and Parmesan cheese. Serve with salad on the side.

INGREDIENTS

1 1/2 pounds breasted bird meat, no bones

1 can mushroom soup

1 pound mushrooms, buttons halved or larger mushrooms quartered

2 cups sour cream

1/4 teaspoon paprika

2 tablespoons parsley, chopped

1 garlic clove, chopped

1 bunch green onion, chopped

Butter

1/2 cup medium sherry, optional

Parmesan cheese, grated

1 pound noodles

Ordinary Wild Turkey

This is the everyday way to roast a wild turkey. The most important part of the recipe is the liquid for steaming the bird tender. Wild turkeys are more lean than domestic and can turn out tough if cooked the same as a Butterball®. Cooking a wild turkey underground is another way of ensuring tenderness and moisture.

INGREDIENTS

1 wild turkey
Lard
Garlic powder
Onion salt
Pepper (fresh ground if possible)
Paprika
4 cans chicken broth
1 cup Mr. Yoshida's Original Gourmet Sauce
4 chicken bouillon cubes
Chef Sam's stuffing (see page 280)

Wash and dry turkey. Rub all over with lard. Stuff the cavity with Chef Sam's Wild Turkey Stuffing (made with rice). Follow recipe for remaining stuffing as well as stuffing that goes into the turkey. Place stuffed bird in roasting pan with broth and bouillon cubes. Sprinkle garlic powder, onion salt, pepper and paprika over bird as it rests in the roasting pan. Cover bird with aluminum foil. Then add the lid to the roasting pan. The idea is to lock in steam. Set oven for 250 degrees. Start bird early. It may take six hours or more to steam the turkey tender. Serve with standard turkey dinner side dishes.

Grouse Italian in Foil

Another good recipe for cooks in a hurry who don't want the meal to turn out like something that was prepared in a hurry.

INGREDIENTS

Salad oil
6 meaty pieces of grouse
Salt to taste
3 medium potatoes, pared
2 medium zucchini
1/3 cup catsup
1 teaspoon oregano leaves
1/4 cup melted butter or margarine
3 (18x12-inch) pieces of heavy-duty aluminum foil
Parmesan cheese

Heat oven to 400 degrees. Brush oil on grouse pieces; lightly sprinkle with salt. Cut potato lengthwise into 1/8-inch slices. Place 1/3 of the potato slices on each piece of foil; lightly sprinkle with salt. Cut zucchini into 1/4 inch slices. Place equal amounts of zucchini on potato; lightly sprinkle with salt. Place grouse pieces on zucchini. Mix catsup, oregano and melted butter or margarine; spread evenly top each piece of grouse. Wrap securely in foil (may need to double wrap the foil). Bake until grouse and vegetables are tender, about 1 hour. Sprinkle with Parmesan cheese when serving.

Wild Turkey in the Pit

This is just one of many different pit cooking methods. Wild turkeys are leaner than their domestic cousins. They can cook up tough with ordinary turkey recipes. This recipe ensures tenderness and moisture. Stuffing a pit-cooked turkey can be done, but the bird cooks through and through best with an empty body cavity. Chef Sam's Turkey Stuffing can be baked outside the bird and offered on the serving table as a side dish.

INGREDIENTS

1 wild turkey
Lard
Butter or margarine
2 cans broth
Paprika
Pepper
Garlic powder
2 oranges, peeled but not sectioned

Wash bird one last time and dry thoroughly. Place bird on extra large sheet of aluminum foil. Massage with lard. Place 1 stick of butter or margarine, oranges and 1 can of chicken broth inside bird. Sprinkle garlic powder, pepper and paprika over bird. Fold foil over top and seal carefully. Seal bird in a second layer of foil. Place on third layer of foil. Pour a half can of broth over bird. Place bird on fourth piece of foil and pour rest of broth over the top. Seal with a final layer of heavy foil. Dig a pit large enough to hold the bird and a body of coals. Load pit with hardwood, if available, and burn wood down to coals—or use charcoal briquettes. Coals must be hot because they may be snuffed out when the bird is covered in the pit. Remove half the coals from the pit. Lay down an old cookie sheet. Place foiled bird on sheet. Cover with one more extra large piece of foil. Cover bird with removed coals. Replace soil over top of foil. Come back in four to six hours and exhume bird. It should be fully cooked, tender and moist. Experimentation is vital with this recipe because of varying bird sizes as well as coal strength.

Roasted Green Chili Quail

This recipe makes an excellent dish for those who like the flavor of green chilies because this flavor dominates the quail. Bacon also adds its own specific flavor. The roasted chilies can be fresh or canned (whole).

INGREDIENTS

Quail
Roasted green chilies
Bacon
Olive or canola oil

Rub each quail inside and out with oil. Wrap piece of roasted green chili around each bird. Wrap one piece of bacon around the green chili. Hold in place with metal pins or toothpicks. Broil to just done in middle of oven. Too close to heat source tends to overcook bacon before quail is finished.

Upland Bird and Dumplings with Gravy

INGREDIENTS

2 pounds boned upland bird meat

3 tablespoons soy sauce

1 cup flour

1/4 teaspoon paprika

1/8 cup canola or peanut oil

Pepper

Onion salt

1/8 teaspoon sweet basil

1/4 teaspoon prepared or fresh
    crushed garlic

1 can chicken broth or equal stock

I learned to make dumplings from an old friend who often put together a chicken and dumpling supper in camp. Glenn was a cowboy working on a ranch in southern Arizona at the time, One day we decided to try quail and dumplings instead of chicken. The recipe worked. But this one is better yet. See individual recipes for Upland Bird Gravy and for dumplings. Any gamebird will do with the exception of sage hens, which cook up best after thorough marination. See Universal Marinade in Chapter 25.

Place bird in pressure cooker. Add soy sauce and just enough water to cover. Parboil about 10 minutes. Coat meat well with flour/paprika mixture. Heat Dutch oven with canola or peanut oil. Brown floured bird meat in hot oil. Lower heat. While meat is still cooking in the Dutch oven dust with pepper and onion salt. Add sweet basil and crushed garlic while rotating pieces of meat constantly. Add broth or stock. If 1 can is not sufficient to fully cover meat, add more. Cover and simmer until tender. Remove meat and set aside. Make dumplings. Place meat and dumplings on serving dish and ladle gravy over all. (See Special Gravy for Gamebirds recipe.)

Special Gravy for Upland Birds and Dumplings

INGREDIENTS

2 cans broth or equal stock

1/2 stick butter or margarine

2 tablespoons cornstarch

1/8 cup milk

Pepper

Salt

2 chicken bouillon cubes, reduced
    in hot water

This simple white gravy goes well with most game birds. It can be made in camp as well as in the home kitchen.

Bring 2/3 of broth or stock to boil in saucepan. Add reduced bouillon cubes; stir to mix well. Add butter or margarine, dash of pepper and dash of salt. Add cornstarch to remainder of broth, mixing to milk-like consistency. Add milk. While liquid gently boils in saucepan, slowly add cornstarch to thicken. As soon as the gravy thickens, stop adding cornstarch. Or if after using the cornstarch mixture the gravy is still thin, add more cornstarch mixed either with milk or broth, but not water.

Dove in the Skillet

This recipe is ultra-simple but good. It's especially easy in camp with fresh birds. Just about any cooking oil will work, but canola, olive and peanut do especially well because the oil becomes part of the sauce. Try this little recipe with quail or partridge.

Heat skillet to medium hot with just enough oil to cook birds through. Too much oil ruins this recipe because the oil is used as a base for the resulting sauce. Wash and dry dove breasts. Place in skillet with bone side down in the hot oil. Sprinkle with garlic salt. Add rosemary only if that flavor is desired. Cover skillet and lower heat. Let birds cook up to about 10 minutes, then turn to brown meat side. When birds are just cooked through (test with a sharp pointed knife) raise heat or move skillet to hotter part of coal bed. Pour teriyaki sauce or glaze directly into pan and stir. Add butter or margarine, stirring constantly. When liquid in pan reaches a light sauce-like consistency, pour birds and liquid into a serving dish.

INGREDIENTS

10 to 20 doves
Oil – canola, olive, peanut
Garlic salt
Soy or teriyaki sauce
1/2 stick butter or margarine
1/8 teaspoon rosemary, optional

Marinated Quail

Quail need no special treatment to make them taste good; however, the marinade in this recipe does impart a nice flavor. This recipe works well with partridges and doves as well as quail.

Parboil quail with soy sauce no more than 10 minutes in pressure cooker or 20 minutes in a covered pot. Rinse parboiled birds in plain water and dry each one with paper toweling. Place in bowl and completely cover with Universal Marinade or use Zip-Lock type freezer bag to conserve marinade. Marinate for 2 to 4 hours only. Remove birds from marinade, sprinkle with pepper and flour immediately. Skillet-fry in canola or olive oil over medium-low heat, turning frequently to avoid burning flour coating. Do not cover when frying as this tends to steam the flour coating instead of browning it.

INGREDIENTS

8 quail
1/4 cup soy sauce
Universal Marinade (See
   Chapter 25)
Flour
Pepper
Canola oil

Jimmy Levy Smoked Quail

My long-time friend Jimmy Levy inspired this recipe. Oftentimes he drew from his pack several smoked quail for our lunch as we hunted together in the Southwest with a mutual partner, the late John Doyle.

INGREDIENTS

8 quail
1/8 cup salt
2 quarts water
Lawry's Mesquite Marinade
Lard
Pepper
Garlic powder

Soak quail in water with salt for 1 hour. Remove. Rinse. Dry birds thoroughly. Marinate birds for 1 to 2 hours. Remove and dust with pepper (white is preferred but not necessary) and garlic powder. Smoke over coals with hickory chips. Maintain low heat and plenty of smoke. Birds must be cooked entirely through, not rare. This can take time. Use a sharp knifepoint to cut a little slit down to the keel of a bird to test doneness.

Gamebird Soup

This recipe is excellent in camp. The ingredients are neither difficult to transport to camp, nor to keep in camp. It can be made with just about any boned gamebird meat except sage hen. The pressure cooker is perfect for this recipe but it can also be prepared in a covered pot. This recipe uses the pressure cooker.

INGREDIENTS

2 pounds boned gamebird meat
    (see Chapter 13)
Any chicken-flavored prepared
    soup mix or base
2 cans chicken broth
2 chicken bouillon cubes
1/8 teaspoon garlic salt
1 onion, sliced
Parsley flakes
4 cups cooked rice

Place boned gamebird meat in pressure cooker or pot. Add a quart of water and two cans of chicken broth. Add bouillon cubes, garlic salt, onion and parsley flakes. Cook all together until done, about 20 to 30 minutes in pressure cooker depending upon specific cooker. When meat is cooked and soup is blended, add rice. Minute Rice cooks up easily in camp and works well in this recipe.

Upland Bird Orange

This recipe is good with almost any gamebird, the exception, as usual, being sage hens. Pheasants, partridges (including chukars) and grouse work well.

Mix apricot jam, marmalade and orange jam in shallow baking dish, such as Corning Ware. Stir to blend. Place boned gamebird meat in blended mixture. Sprinkle salt, pepper and sweet basil. Cover dish Bake at 300 degrees until meat is cooked through.

INGREDIENTS

2 pounds boned gamebird meat

1 1/2 cups apricot jam

1 cup orange marmalade

1/3 cup concentrated orange juice

Salt

Pepper

Sweet basil

Ordinary Roast Goose

I altered this recipe from an old one that included a number of additional spices and herbs that did not help but rather hindered the final flavor of the goose. And so the recipe becomes ordinary.

Season goose with garlic, seasoned salt, paprika and pepper inside and out. Burst fresh parsley under hot tap water, ring out, dry with paper towel. Place in cavity. Add oranges to cavity. Pour teriyaki marinade, wine, chicken broth and water into roasting pan. Add bouillon cubes. Cover goose with aluminum foil followed by roaster cover. Bake for 1 hour at 300 degrees. Open pan. Add 2 cups water. Bake again for 1 hour at 300 degrees. Open pan. Check moisture level. If necessary, add 1 cup stock or broth plus one cup water. Recover and bake again at 300 degrees until cooked through. When cooked, remove goose from oven. Discard cooking liquids, parsley, and oranges. Goose may be served with stuffing on the side.

OPTIONAL | Goose may be stuffed toward end of cooking cycle with commercial stuffing following directions on container. Remove oranges and parsley first.

INGREDIENTS

1 wild goose

2 cloves garlic, crushed

Seasoned salt

Paprika

Pepper

1/2 bunch fresh parsley

2 peeled oranges whole

1/4 cup teriyaki marinade

1/4 cup medium sherry or port, optional

2 cups chicken broth

2 cups water plus water and/or stock or broth as needed

6 chicken bouillon cubes

Baked Pheasant with Mushroom Sauce

This dish does not take as long as the cook may think. It turns out, however, to taste like a long-labored-over dish.

2 pounds ready-to-serve pheasant pieces
2 tablespoons cooking oil
2 (10.5-ounce) cans of condensed cream of chicken soup
1 pound fresh mushrooms, halved
1 cup chicken broth
1/4 teaspoon tarragon leaves
1/4 teaspoon garlic powder
1/2 teaspoon Worcestershire sauce

Heat oven to 400 degrees. Heat 2 tablespoons cooking oil in a large skillet; cook pheasant pieces until done (about 10 minutes). Place cooked pheasant in ungreased 13x9x2-inch baking pan. Drain oil and wipe skillet. Mix soup, mushroom pieces, broth and seasonings in skillet. Stir until heated; pour over pheasant. Bake until pheasant is hot and sauce is bubbly, about 20 minutes.

Deluxe Baked Pheasant

There is very little work or preparation time involved in this good recipe.

2 tablespoons cooking oil
1/2 cup flour
1 teaspoon salt
1/2 teaspoon paprika
1/4 teaspoon pepper
3 pounds pheasant pieces
1/2 cup chicken broth
1/4 cup apple juice
1 small clove garlic, crushed

MAKES 4 OR 5 SERVINGS

Heat oil in large skillet. Measure flour, salt, paprika and pepper into plastic or paper bag. Shake meat, 2 or 3 pieces at a time, to coat with flour mixture. Brown pheasant pieces in oil over medium heat.

Heat oven to 350 degrees. Place browned pheasant on ungreased 13x9x2-inch baking pan. Mix broth, apple juice and garlic. Pour 1/3 of the broth mixture on the meat. Cover with aluminum foil and bake until tender, 45 to 50 minutes, basting occasionally with remaining broth mixture. Uncover the meat the last 5 minutes of baking time to crisp the pieces.

Side Dish Recipes

Mrs. Kane's Ranch Beans

Mrs. Kane, Arizona lady rancher, always had a big batch of beans cooking on the stove. Passersby were treated to a bowl with fresh bread or flour tortillas.

Mrs. Kane cooked her beans all day at a slow simmer. A pressure cooker, however, is faster. Cube meat, braise in pan with a little oil, drop into pressure cooker with one can of beef broth or equal stock. Add garlic, oregano, basil and pepper. Pressure cook for 20 minutes. Strain juice to any container. Add cubed meat to strained juice; set aside. Pressure cook beans, onion and bay leaves with just enough water to cover beans for 10 minutes. Let steam off. Check. Add liquid as needed, either water or stock. Pressure cook again. Check again. When beans are cooked, drain off part of juice. Add meat and juice that was set aside. Simmer for 10 minutes and serve with buttered bread or flour tortillas.

INGREDIENTS

2 pounds venison
1 can beef broth
1 clove garlic, sliced
1 small onion, sliced
1/4 teaspoon oregano
1/4 teaspoon sweet basil
1/8 teaspoon pepper
4 cups pinto beans
6 bay leaves
1 large can stewed tomatoes

Judy's Homemade Salsa

This salsa is used in many ways. It can be added to boned meat pieces in a skillet during the cooking process, or served with just about any Mexican dish. It is also a major ingredient in Erika's Guacamole recipe (found elsewhere in this book) as well as a dip with corn chips, to flavor tacos or refried beans.

INGREDIENTS

4 to 6 ripe tomatoes
1 medium white onion
2 tablespoons chopped green chilies
1 tablespoon sliced jalapeno
   pepper, optional
1/4 bunch cilantro, chopped
1 teaspoon garlic salt

Chop tomatoes. Can use food processor, but do not puree. Add all the rest of the ingredients and stir to blend.

Indian Pan Bread

It seems that almost every culture on earth has some kind of pan bread, be it a scone, bannock, East Indian fry bread, Native American fry bread, tortilla or other flour-based dough product prepared on a griddle, metal sheet or skillet. This is one more.

INGREDIENTS

4 cups all purpose flour
1 teaspoon salt
3 tablespoons lard
3 cups warm water
1 to 2 tablespoons canola or
   peanut oil

In a large bowl combine flour and salt. Cut in lard. Add water and mix by hand to form stiff dough. On lightly floured board roll dough to 1/2-inch thickness and slice into 3-inch squares. Poke a hole in the center of each square to promote even cooking (same principle as doughnuts or bagels). Heat oil in skillet over medium to medium-high heat. Place squares in oil and fry until brown. Drain on paper towels and serve topped off with powdered sugar, cinnamon and butter.

Mashed Sweet Potato

This easy side dish is a compliment to many recipes. The microwave cooks the sweet potatoes (or yams) fully in no time.

Cook sweet potatoes in microwave on full power in short bursts, checking with a fork for doneness. Cook until soft. Remove skin and place the meat of the sweet potatoes in a flat baking dish. Use a potato masher or fork to mash the sweet potato thoroughly. Stir in brown sugar, cinnamon, butter and salt. Cover with wax paper and microwave for 2 minutes or until hot all the way through. (May need to add extra brown sugar or cinnamon to suit your taste.)

INGREDIENTS

2 cooked sweet potatoes, peeled
1/2 cup brown sugar
1 teaspoon cinnamon (to taste)
1/4 cup butter or margarine
1/2 teaspoon salt

Bannock I

I began making this pan bread not because I was stuck on the trail leading to Nome, but because I read about it in a tale by an Alaskan big game hunter. It turns out, however, that it is a good camp bread with some meals and can be eaten on its own. With a little fruit it's a dessert.

In a medium bowl combine flour, sugar, baking powder and salt. Slowly add margarine until this mixture is a crumbly dough. Add water slowly until dough becomes stiff. Form half-inch thick cakes. Cook in a skillet with margarine over medium heat. Shake pan to move bannock around in the skillet for even doneness.

INGREDIENTS

1 cup flour
1 tablespoon sugar
1 teaspoon baking powder
1/2 teaspoon salt
Margarine

Bannock II

The Bannock I recipe is well suited to the trail or camp. This recipe works in both places as well, but it's a sort of deluxe version.

4 cups flour
1 3/4 tablespoons baking powder
1 teaspoon salt
2 cups sugar
1/2 cup shortening
2 cups milk
2 eggs, beaten
Margarine for cooking

In a medium bowl combine flour, baking powder, salt and sugar. Slowly add shortening, mixing in with a fork. Add milk and eggs. Work into a stiff dough that can be formed into cakes. Make bannock cakes about 1/2-inch thick. Melt margarine in skillet. Add the cakes and cook, shaking the pan to keep the bannock moving for even doneness. Cook over medium heat. High heat can burn the bannock.

Mexican Refried Beans

Making refried beans from canned is fine, but this recipe from scratch is easy and it results in a good product. The little bit of lard that goes into it should not be a problem for weight watchers; however, peanut oil can be substituted.

4 cups dry pinto beans
4 bay leaves
1/2 teaspoon oregano
Pinch of cumin
1/8 teaspoon crushed garlic
3 tablespoons lard
1/4 pound yellow or white cheese
1/2 cup milk

Put dry beans in a colander, rinse with hot water, transfer to pressure cooker. Cover with water two to three inches over top of beans. Add bay leaves and oregano. Pressure cook for 10 minutes; let steam off naturally. Open cooker. Add water as needed. Pressure cook again for 10 minutes. Let steam off naturally. Open cooker. Add water, cumin and crushed garlic. Pressure cook long enough to make beans very soft for mashing. Drain off no more than half of the liquid in the pressure cooker. Transfer cooked beans with liquid to a large frying pan with smoking hot lard. (Be careful not to splash hot lard from pan.) Mash beans smooth right away with long-handled wooden spoon. Add cheese. Stir in. Add milk. Stir in. Results should be smooth refried beans ready to accompany any Mexican style dish.

ALTERNATE | After draining about half of the water from the well-cooked beans, add lard, cheese and milk and mash with a potato masher right in the pressure cooker.

Speedy All-Day Cooked Baked Beans

This is another recipe that looks like it took all day but in fact claimed only minutes of the cook's time. It serves well with a great variety of game dishes, especially Leg O' Lope and other grilled red meats. While the more expensive varieties of canned beans are all the better in this recipe, bargain brand beans also work well.

Cut bacon into squares and cook to done (somewhat crisp). Remove bacon from pan and set aside. Spoon out half of the bacon fat. Cook onions in remaining bacon fat. As soon as onions are done, drop in the full can of beans and return bacon to pan. Stir cooked bacon squares into the beans. Bring pan to very hot briefly. Immediately add one squirt (no more) mustard, brown sugar and barbecue sauce. Stir gently. Cook on low heat for a few minutes. Remove hot beans from skillet to microwave-safe dish. Top off with cheese slices. Microwave until cheese is melted. Serve.

INGREDIENTS

1 large can baked beans
1/2 pound bacon
1/2 onion diced
Mustard
1/4 cup brown sugar
4 slices yellow cheese
1/4 cup prepared barbecue sauce

Boiled Zucchini

This quick side dish is just right with a number of game suppers.

Bring slightly salted water to a boil. Add zucchini pieces. Cover pot and boil squash for about 10 minutes or until tender. (Check with fork after 6 minutes or so.) Drain off all water and place zucchini in a microwave-safe dish. Mix in butter or margarine to taste. Add Parmesan cheese to taste, stirring lightly. To blend cheese, place in microwave for 30 to 60 seconds depending on microwave power.

INGREDIENTS

Zucchini squash, peeled and cut
    in sections
Salt
Grated Parmesan cheese
Butter or margarine

Buttered Cauliflower

Cauliflower should broken into florets by cutting base off and separating by hand. The pieces should be cooked through but not overly soft. They should retain body. Amounts are not given because these vary with the meal. A full head of cauliflower is easily prepared and buttered. Boil salted water in covered saucepan. Add cauliflower. Pour olive oil directly on cauliflower in the saucepan. Amount to taste. Experiment with less at first, perhaps 1 teaspoon olive oil for full head of cauliflower.

Wild Rice

Wild rice was a mainstay of certain Indian tribes. Today it's considered a delicacy and usually commands a price to match. Wild rice does not take the place of white rice directly and it should not be substituted across the board for white rice in recipes. However, as a side dish it fits many different game meals. Here is one way to prepare wild rice.

Melt butter in skillet. Add wild rice and slivered nuts. Stir constantly over low-medium heat until both rice and nuts are golden in color. Place rice and nuts with enough broth to cover both in microwave-safe dish. Have more broth or stock ready. Cover bowl with plastic food wrap and place in microwave. Microwave on full power for 4 or 5 minutes, being cautious about rice using up all of the moisture in the bowl. Microwave cautiously in short intervals, checking frequently for doneness and adding broth or stock as needed. Continue microwaving until rice is tender.

Glazed Carrots

These carrots are tasty and no trouble to make with the pressure cooker.

Cook carrots in pressure cooker until soft—usually 2 to 3 minutes depending upon specific cooker. Remove. Drain all water. Place carrots on a cookie sheet. Coat with brown sugar. Sprinkle with garlic powder. Lace well with butter. Place cookie sheet under broiler. Turn carrots frequently, being careful not to burn them. When the glaze is on the carrots, they're done. Place in serving dish coated with any juices left on the cookie sheet.

INGREDIENTS

(1-pound) bag of carrots, peeled, halved
Garlic powder
Brown sugar
Butter

Mushroom Small Game Sauce

This is good with rabbit or squirrel that has been cooked in a pressure cooker until the meat can be shredded from the bone. Be sure to check carefully for leftover bone slivers in the meat. The shredded meat is mixed into the sauce, after which the meat/sauce combination can be ladled over toast or rice.

Sauté mushroom pieces in butter over low to low-medium heat. Blend in flour slowly, mixing constantly. Add stock or broth to create a cream-like blend in the skillet. Salt and pepper to taste.

INGREDIENTS

3 cups mushrooms, diced medium
6 tablespoons butter
6 tablespoons flour
3 cups whole milk
3 cups stock or broth
Salt
Pepper

Good Green Beans

Another quick and easy recipe that turns out better than just heating green beans out of the can. Good with many different main courses, especially chicken-fried game steaks.

INGREDIENTS

Canned green beans—amount to match main course
Garlic powder
Sweet basil
Butter
Cooked bacon bits

Cook bacon first. Section into small squares. Fry to fairly crisp or remove early from frying pan and finish in microwave on paper towels with short time intervals to ensure crispness while avoiding burning. Place green beans in microwave-safe bowl. Add one teaspoon bacon fat for every 303 size can of beans. Add 1/4 teaspoon sweet basil for each can of green beans. Add bacon bits; sprinkle with garlic powder; add two pats butter per can of green beans; cook in microwave until very hot.

Old Family Sourdough Pancake Starter

Whenever I serve sourdough pancakes to friends in my home or in camp for the first time, I tell the story of how the starter came down from great, great, ever-so-great grandfather and finally to me. Then I let the cat out of the bag, sharing the recipe with everyone. Truth is, this sourdough is ready from start to finish in only 24 hours.

INGREDIENTS

2 cups milk
2 cups flour
1 tablespoon dry yeast
1 1/2 teaspoons baking soda
2 eggs

To make what is known as the sponge, mix all ingredients together in a very large plastic bowl with a snap-on lid. There's going to be considerable expansion here and if the dough does not have enough room to rise, it will overflow the bowl. Snap on lid and place bowl in a warm place to allow yeast to work. Check from time to time, stirring the dough back down as it rises. No need to do this very often. About 24 hours later, the dough is ready to make sourdough pancake batter.

Sam's Tomato Soup

I came up with this recipe some time ago in an attempt to make ordinary canned tomato soup a little bit special. Mix a few things together in one pan and heat up. Of course it goes over great in camp as an accompaniment to game meat taken on the trail—hot soup before grouse or cottontail!

Break up chunks of tomato in stewed tomatoes. Mix all ingredients in saucepan and bring to a strong boil. Immediately lower heat and simmer for about 5 minutes.

INGREDIENTS

2 cans condensed tomato soup

1 can stewed tomatoes

1/8 teaspoon garlic powder or
    crushed garlic

2 bay leaves

1 beef bouillon cube

1/4 teaspoon sweet basil

1 soup can water

Dumplings for Game Dishes

Dumplings are simply dough that is cooked in boiling stock or broth. However, they can add a very special touch to an ordinary dish. The dumplings described here go well with the Upland Birds and Dumpling with Gravy recipe.

Sift together flour, baking powder, salt and sugar in a large bowl. Make a fairly stiff dough by adding lukewarm water a little at a time while working the flour mixture. Bring a pan of stock or broth to a full boil. Reduce to a gentle boil. Drop tablespoon-size balls of dough into hot liquid. Roll dumplings over in hot liquid to ensure full cooking. Finished dumplings will retain white color, but they will be cooked through. Test to be sure by cutting one in half. These dumplings can also be cooked in soup. When prepared that way, the dough is ladled on top of gently boiling soup and cooked through. The entire pot is presented in the center of the table with a large spoon to dip out dumplings and soup simultaneously.

INGREDIENTS

1 1/2 cups flour

3 tablespoons baking powder

1/4 teaspoon salt

1 teaspoon sugar

Lukewarm water to make fairly
    stiff dough

Mexican Hot Chocolate Drink

Fresh cinnamon stick
6 cups milk
1 teaspoon vanilla extract
6 squares unsweetened chocolate, well grated
1 egg yolk
Whites of 2 eggs, beaten stiff
Sugar
1 ounce kahlua, optional

This drink is especially enjoyable in camp on a cool night as hunters rest around the campfire.

Place fresh cinnamon stick into a saucepan with milk and heat but never bring to a boil. Just simmer. Add unsweetened chocolate to simmering milk. Blend chocolate into milk by stirring patiently. Use an eggbeater to blend egg yolk into milk mixture. Quickly beat in egg whites. Stir in sugar to taste—usually 2 or more teaspoons. Add kahlua if desired.

Cache Lake Buckwheat Griddlecakes

2 cups buckwheat flour
2 rounded cups of white cornmeal
1 cup boiling water
3/4 cup milk
1 teaspoon salt
1/2 yeast cake
1/4 cup milk slightly warmed
1/2 teaspoon baking soda
1 teaspoon molasses

Every year I find myself re-reading two books, THE WITCHERY OF ARCHERY about the brothers who promoted bowhunting after the Civil War and CACHE LAKE COUNTRY, John Rowlands' account of living in the North Woods. Rowlands offers several good recipes. This is one of them. He got it from one of his aunts. Buckwheat griddlecakes go especially well on those morning rest days in camp when hunting is set aside to simply enjoy the outdoor world.

The night before, dissolve yeast in 1/4 cup lukewarm milk. Do not overheat milk. Too much heat will kill the yeast. Mix 3/4 cup milk with 1 cup boiling water. Mix buckwheat and cornmeal together. Add salt to the milk and hot water mixture. Add dissolved yeast and beat mixture for about 10 minutes. Place batter in a warm spot for the night. In the morning add the baking soda and molasses to the batter and make the cakes on a stick-free surface with a little butter or margarine on a paper towel as a mop. Great with venison loin.

Cache Lake Indian Pudding

This is another Cache Lake recipe. See remarks for Cache Lake Buckwheat Griddlecakes for details. This recipe works fine in camp with condensed canned milk. The suet can be from venison or it can be the white fat often found on the ribs.

Heat evaporated milk to scalding. Remove from heat. Combine and add all other ingredients, including the suet or fat, to the milk. Return saucepan to stove and cook over low heat for about 30 minutes or until thickened. Place thickened mixture into baking pan. Pour 1 cup cold milk on top of mixture, but do not stir in. Bake in 300-degree oven for 2 to 3 hours. Serve hot topped with brown sugar and cream.

INGREDIENTS

4 cups evaporated milk, heated to
    scalding point
1/2 cup corn meal
2 tablespoons flour
2/3 cup molasses
1/2 cup suet or fat, cut fine
1/2 teaspoon ginger
1/2 teaspoon cinnamon
1 teaspoon salt

Another Dumpling Dinner

Use the Dumplings for Game Recipe provided elsewhere to make the dumpling mix for this dish. Once again, the pressure cooker comes to the fore as a time-saver but this good-tasting treat can be prepared in a pot. Recommended meats: venison, antelope, bear, elk, moose, caribou.

Salt and pepper cubed meat. Flour and brown cubed meat in cooking oil. Place browned meat in pressure cooker or pot. Add broth or stock and gourmet sauce with sufficient water (if needed) to cover meat Add onion, garlic, bay leaves, Worcestershire Sauce. Pressure cook 12 minutes. Check for meat doneness by poking a fork into a large piece. Juices in meat should be fully brown, not red. Let steam off safely under small stream of cool water. Add potatoes. Pressure cook for 2 minutes. Let steam off. Add celery and carrots. Add dumpling dough on top of hot liquid in pressure cooker, using a tablespoon to measure out individual dumplings. Pressure cook for 2 more minutes. Let steam off and simmer for 10 minutes.

INGREDIENTS

3 pounds boned red game meat,
    cubed
Cooking oil
8 potatoes, quartered
10 carrots, peeled and sliced
4 onions, peeled and sliced
4 stalks celery, peeled and sliced
3 bay leaves
2 teaspoons Worcestershire Sauce
1/2 cup Mr. Yoshida's Original
    Gourmet Sauce
2 garlic cloves, finely chopped
3 cups broth or stock
Pepper
Salt
Flour

Mexican Refried Beans

INGREDIENTS

4 cups dry pinto beans
6 bay leaves
1/4 teaspoon crushed garlic
1/4 teaspoon oregano
Yellow cheese, white cheese, or
    mixed white and yellow
1/8 cup milk
Lard

In a hurry? Canned refried beans work all right in this recipe, but dry pinto beans are recommended. Beans can be cooked long and slow in a regular pot or much quicker in a pressure cooker. Ingredients vary in this recipe. Some cooks prefer a lot of cheese. Others less cheese. Some like more or less milk.

Check beans for rocks a small handful at a time. Place beans in colander or large strainer. Wash beans under hot running water. Use a stove ring between electric stove burner and bottom of pressure cooker to prevent burning beans on bottom of cooker. Place beans into pressure cooker and cover with water. Add bay leaves, garlic and oregano. Pressure cook for 15 minutes. Let steam off carefully. Check for water level. Add water as needed. Pressure cook again for 15 minutes. Check for both water level and doneness. Beans must be cooked soft in order to refry (mash) them. When beans are soft, strain out some, but not all, of the liquid. Mash beans with a potato masher, incorporating the liquid left in the cooker. Melt lard in large frying pan, amount according to taste (start with 3 rounded tablespoons). When lard is hot, ladle in beans stirring constantly. This is the refried part of refried beans. Cook for few minutes. Grate or slice cheese. Add cheese—amount to taste—try 1-1/2 cups to begin with. Blend cheese completely. Add milk and blend in.

Sourdough Pancakes

INGREDIENTS

2 cups sourdough batter
2 eggs
1 teaspoon baking soda
1 tablespoon canola oil

This recipe uses the sourdough sponge that's made overnight. After the mixture rests for 24 hours it becomes sourdough batter. This recipe is simple in camp—and good.

Combine batter and eggs; stir in baking soda (vital to recipe) and canola oil. Mix well. Cook on griddle or pan over medium heat.

Erika's Guacamole

The base of this recipe is Judy's Homemade Salsa, which appears elsewhere in the recipe section. The body of the recipe is mashed avocado. This is the way my daughter-in-law Erika Judd makes it.

Cut avocado lengthwise and remove pit. Scoop out avocado meat. Place in mixing bowl. Add rest of ingredients, blending well. Serve with tortilla or other chips.

INGREDIENTS

3 to 4 avocados
1 cup Judy's Homemade Salsa
1/8 teaspoon garlic powder
Sprinkle seasoned salt
1/8 teaspoon lime juice

Fruit Salad

This fruit salad can be prepared in camp as well as at home provided all contents are kept fresh. Great with a big breakfast of fried venison steaks. Fresh pineapple is excellent in this recipe.

Cut banana to bite-size pieces. Peel apples; cut to bite-size pieces. Place both in bowl. Add the rest of ingredients and mix gently. Prepare before beginning rest of meal and allow to rest until the meal is ready to serve. This blends the sugar into a light sauce.

INGREDIENTS

2 bananas
2 apples
2 kiwi, peeled and sliced into bits
2 oranges, sliced into bits
1 cup blueberries
2 cups pineapple bits (fresh if at
    all possible)
2 cups seedless grapes
2 teaspoons sugar

Creamy Scalloped Potatoes

This is just one of several good side dishes included in the book to help the reader with relatively easy-to-make recipes to dress up a game meal.

1/4 cup butter or margarine

1/4 cup flour

Salt and pepper to taste

3 cups milk

7 medium potatoes, pared and
    thinly sliced

1 medium onion, thinly sliced

1 tablespoon butter or margarine

MAKES 6 SERVINGS

Heat oven to 350 degrees. Melt 1/4 cup butter in saucepan over low heat. Blend in flour and seasonings. Cook over low heat, stirring until mixture is smooth and bubbly. Stir in milk until mixture is well blended. Heat to boiling, stirring constantly. Spray a 2 1/2-quart casserole dish with cooking spray. Divide potatoes into thirds. Arrange potatoes in dish in 2 layers, topping each with half the onion and 1/3 of the white sauce. Top with remaining potatoes and sauce. Dot the top with 1 tablespoon of butter or margarine. Cover and bake for 30 minutes. Uncover and bake until potatoes are tender, about 40 minutes. Let stand 5 or 10 minutes before serving.

Pan Gravy

This pan gravy is easy to make and adds greatly to many dishes, including chicken-fried (breaded) antelope or venison steaks. A little extra broth or stock can be added to stretch the amount of gravy.

INGREDIENTS

1 tablespoon drippings (fat and
    juices from fried meat)

1 tablespoon flour

1/2 to 3/4 cup liquid (broth,
    milk, vegetable liquid or water)

Salt and pepper to taste

Remove meat to warm platter; keep warm while preparing gravy. Drain off excess drippings, leaving browned meat particles in pan. Mix in flour. Cook over low heat, stirring until mixture is smooth and bubbly. Continue stirring while you add the liquid. Heat until boiling, stirring constantly. Boil and stir for 1 minute. If desired, stir in a few drops of bottled brown bouquet sauce for color. Season with salt and pepper.

Zucchini Parmesan

This is another good side dish to dress up a game meat meal. It goes with any number of recipes.

Cut 2 medium zucchini into 2x1/2-inch strips. Heat 1 inch salted water (1/2 teaspoon salt to 1 cup water) to boiling. Add zucchini. Cover and heat to boiling; cook until tender, 7 to 9 minutes. Drain. Add 1 tablespoon butter or margarine and toss. Sprinkle 2 tablespoons grated Parmesan cheese on zucchini.

INGREDIENTS

2 medium zucchini
1 tablespoon butter or margarine
2 tablespoons parmesan cheese, grated

MAKES 4 OR 5 SERVINGS

Cauliflower with Nutmeg Butter

Recipes like this one go a long way in making a full game meat dinner. And it's ultra simple to make.

Heat 1 inch of salted water (1/2 teaspoon salt to 1 cup water) to boiling. Add cauliflower. Cover; heat to boiling. Cook until tender, 12 to 15 minutes. Drain, turn into serving dish. Dot with butter and sprinkle lightly with nutmeg.

INGREDIENTS

1 small head of cauliflower
Butter
Nutmeg

Small Game Stuffing

INGREDIENTS

2 medium onions, chopped fine
4 cups bread crumbs
1/4 bunch parsley, chopped fine
1 chopped red pepper
1/4 teaspoon soy sauce
1 mild Italian sausage
Stock or broth

This is a universal stuffing for just about any small game and a number of different birds, such as grouse. While called a stuffing it's actually a mix into which sectioned small game or bird pieces are buried in a roasting pan, after which the meat and the stuffing is cooked together on low heat until the meat is well cooked and tender.

The ingredients are settled into a container into which is added sufficient broth to create a stuffing texture (sticky). Sausage is cooked as hamburger and then mixed in (not left whole).

OPTIONAL | Add well-cooked giblets, sliced fine.

Big O Pancakes

My friends Herb and Norla Meland have a standing joke about Saturday night supper. "Let's have something different," they say, and "something different" always turns out to be pancakes instead of a main course supper. To elevate the meal to memorable goodness, serve with breaded venison steaks as described in the beginning of Chapter 25. This pancake recipe is a favorite of fishing author Kenn Oberrecht, AKA Big O. The good news is that this from-scratch pancake recipe is little more trouble than using a mix.

Place flour, baking soda and sugar in a mixing bowl. Separate eggs. Whip egg whites until stiff and set aside. (A common eggbeater works well.) Add egg yokes to buttermilk and blend, stirring with spoon. Add buttermilk/egg yolk blend to flour mix. Blend into creamy batter. Add 1 tablespoon peanut oil. Blend egg whites into batter with spoon. Cook pancakes on griddle or stick-free skillet with light base of butter or margarine. First pancake may not turn out perfectly. So try a second pancake before adding second tablespoon of peanut oil to batter. Experiment. If second pancake sticks, add the oil.

TIP | Melt butter or margarine on skillet or in pan. Wipe out excess with paper towel. Use butter/margarine soaked paper towel to prepare griddle or skillet before making next pancake(s).

INGREDIENTS

2 cups flour, regular or Wondra
2 teaspoons baking soda
1 tablespoon sugar
3 cups plus buttermilk
2 large eggs
1 to 2 tablespoons peanut oil

Index

More Books for Outdoor Enthusiasts

301 Venison Recipes
The Ultimate
Deer Hunter's Cookbook
by *Deer & Deer Hunting* Staff
Mouth-watering recipes have made this cookbook a hunter's classic. Look no further for delicious meals that will feed a hungry bunch at deer camp, or serve special guests at home.
Comb-bound • 6 x 9 • 128 pages
Item# VR01 • $10.95

Hunting North American Big Game
by Durwood Hollis
North America offers a wealth of big game hunting opportunities and this volume provides an overview of the most popular big game species, where to hunt for them, and the equipment, guns, and strategies for success.
Softcover • 8½ x 11
320 pages
300 b&w photos
16-page color section
Item# NABG • $24.95

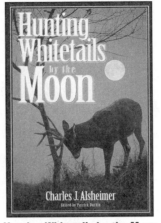

Hunting Whitetails by the Moon
by Charles J. Alsheimer
Teaches deer hunters how to use autumn moon cycles to predict peak times to hunt rutting white-tailed bucks. Insightful text is supplemented with more than 100 photos and illustrations to teach hunters how to succeed.
Softcover • 6 x 9 • 256 pages
100 b&w photos
Item# LUNAR • $19.95

Quality Deer Management
The Basics and Beyond
by Charles J. Alsheimer
This full-color book thoroughly explores the tenets of QDM, including land development, proper animal harvest, obtaining good adult-doe to antlered-buck ratios, and developing nutritious food sources.
Hardcover • 8¼ x 10⅞
208 pages
200+ color photos
Item# QDMGT • $39.95

Fishing Digest
Edited by Dennis Thornton
Offers complete coverage of new fishing gear, tackle, and equipment, a directory of more than 1,400 leading fishing guides and charters, and state license fees and regulations. Lists top fishing resorts, state and national parks, and tourism resources by state.
Softcover • 8½ x 11 • 320 pages
200 b&w photos
Item# FSH1 • $24.95

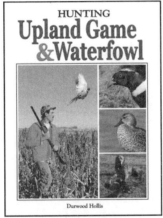

Hunting Upland Game & Waterfowl
by Durwood Hollis
With information on preferred habitat, how to hunt, and what gear is required for each species, this essential reference provides everything needed for successful upland game and waterfowl hunting.
Softcover • 8½ x 11 • 256 pages
325 b&w photos
16-page color section
Item# HUWG • $24.99

Modern Whitetail Hunting
by Michael Hanback
With advice from one of the foremost hunting writers in the world today, learn where mature bucks live and what triggers their movements, best early and late-season strategies, up-to-date tree stand, rattling, calling, and scent tricks, how to hunt huge deer on small lands, and much more. Get the advice of Mossy Oak's top big-buck hunters.
Softcover • 6 x 9 • 224 pages
100 b&w photos
8-page color section
Item# MWH • $19.99

Benoit Bucks
Whitetail Tactics for a New Generation
by Bryce Towsley
This highly anticipated follow-up volume details the "second generation" of the Benoit family, brothers Shane, Lanny, and Lane, established trophy deer hunters who are every bit as successful as their legendary father. Adventure stories recount the excitement of the chase, sharing the secret strategies that led to success-or sometimes failure-and most importantly, what was learned from those hunting experiences.
Hardcover • 8¼ x 10⅞
224 pages
150 b&w photos
16-page color section
Item# HBB2 • $29.99

Big Bucks the Benoit Way
Secrets from America's First Family of Whitetail Hunting
by Bryce Towsley
This book presents the tried-and-true hunting strategies of the legendary Benoit family. Readers learn the secrets and strategies for bagging the big bucks.
Hardcover • 8½ x 11
208 pages
150 b&w photos
16-page color section
Item# HBB • $24.95

Mapping Trophy Bucks
Using Topographic Maps to Find Deer
by Brad Herndon
From inside corners and double inside corners to the perfect funnel and mastering the wind, get a better concept of using the wind and understanding topographical maps. Illustrations show details of how deer move, where to place your stand, and how to use the wind to ensure a successful whitetail hunt.
Softcover • 8¼ x 10⅞
192 pages
150 color photos
Item# TRTT • $24.99

Successful Small Game Hunting
Rediscovering Our Hunting Heritage
by M. D. Johnson
Photos by Julia Johnson
Improve your skills as a hunter with this new guide offering instruction, education, advice, suggestions, and humor. This book goes beyond the basics-rabbit and squirrel-to include snipe, rails, and band-tailed pigeons. You'll be presented with the latest in technology, wisdom, strategies, and tactics of hunting small species. Eat what you bag with the featured recipe section.
Softcover • 8¼ x 10⅞
144 pages
150+ color images
Item# SSGH • $24.99

Whitetail Rites of Autumn
by Charles J. Alsheimer
Discover what a typical day is like for a rutting buck during November! This exquisite pictorial of the whitetail species provides new insight into understanding the rut: the seeking, chasing, and breeding, beyond the rehashed information any serious deer hunter already knows-or should know.
Hardcover • 9 x 11½
208 pages
175 color photos
Item# RTSAU • $34.99

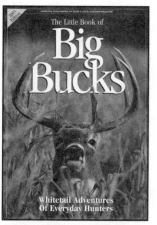

The Little Book of Big Bucks
From the Publisher of *Deer & Deer Hunting* Magazine
Arranged in eight easy-to-digest chapters, this comprehensive guide provides insight into all of the important elements of deer hunting, including possible second chances at mature bucks and chasing whitetails across America. Complete coverage includes references with state-by-state agency information, Web sites for hunting gear manufacturers and hunting organizations, and tips for airline travel.
Softcover • 5¼ x 8
208 pages
130 b&w photos
Item# LBBB • $12.99

Camping Digest
The Complete Guide to Successful Camping
by Janet Groene
Designed to outfit campers with everything they need to know for an enjoyable outdoors experience, this reference lists camping gear, national and state parks, leading campgrounds, and U.S. travel organizations. Feature articles offer advice on equipment, campgrounds, setting up, and enjoying the great outdoors.
Softcover • 8½ x 11
320 pages
200 b&w photos
Item# CRV1 • $24.95

The Complete Venison Cookbook
From Field to Table
by Jim & Ann Casada
Whip up delicious recipes and complete menus for a great venison meal. Jim and Ann Casada cover the proper care of meat and field dressing, health benefits of eating venison, and helpful hints for easy, inexpensive dining.
Comb-bound • 6 x 9
208 pages
Item# CVC • $12.95

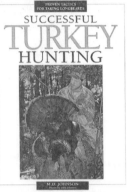

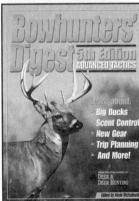